Ratings Analysis

The Theory and Practice of Audience Research

LEA's COMMUNICATION SERIES
Jennings Bryant/Dolf Zillmann, General Editors

Selected Titles in the Communication Series include:

Butler•Television: Critical Methods and Applications, Second Edition

Eastman•Research in Media Promotion

Keirstead•Computers in Broadcast and Cable Newsrooms: Using Technology in Television News Production

MacFarland•Future Radio Programming Strategies: Cultivating Listenership in the Digital Age, Second Edition

Metallinos•Television Aesthetics: Perceptual, Cognitive, and Compositional Bases

Orlik•Electronic Media Criticism: Applied Perspectives, Second Edition

Plum•Underwriting 101: Selling College Radio

Sterling/Kittross•Stay Tuned: A Concise History of American Broadcasting, Third Edition

For a complete list of titles in LEA's Communication Series, please contact Lawrence Erlbaum Associates, Publishers, at www.erlbaum.com

Ratings Analysis

The Theory and Practice of Audience Research

Third Edition

James G. Webster
Northwestern University

Patricia F. Phalen
The George Washington University

Lawrence W. Lichty
Northwestern University

LAWRENCE ERLBAUM ASSOCIATES, PUBLISHERS
2006   Mahwah, New Jersey   London

Lawrence Erlbaum Associates, Inc., Publishers
10 Industrial Avenue
Mahwah, New Jersey 07430
www.erlbaum.com

Cover design by Tomai Maridou

Library of Congress Cataloging-in-Publication Data

Webster, James G.
Ratings analysis : the theory and practice of audience re-
   search /James G. Webster, Patricia F. Phalen, Lawrence W.
   Lichty. — 3rd ed.
      p.   cm. — (LEA's communication series)
   Includes bibliographical references and index.
ISBN 0-8058-5409-6 (cloth) — ISBN 0-8058-5410-X (pbk)
1. Television programs—Ratings—Methodology. 2. Televi-
   sion viewers.   3. Radio programs—Ratings—Methodol-
   ogy. 4. Radio audiences. I. Title. II. Series. III. Phalen,
   Patricia F. IV. Lichty, Lawrence Wilson.
HE8700.65 W42 2005
384.54'3—dc22   2005040071
                                                      CIP

Books published by Lawrence Erlbaum Associates are printed
on acid-free paper, and their bindings are chosen for strength
and durability.

Printed in the United States of America
10 9 8 7 6 5 4 3 2 1

To

Debra Webster
John and Betty Phalen
Sandra Lichty

Contents in Brief

Contents

Preface

As we noted in the preface to the first edition, this book was written with two groups of people in mind. First, it is intended for anyone who needs more than a superficial understanding of audience research. This would certainly include many people who work in advertising, the electronic media, and related industries. For them, audience data are a fact of life. Whether they have been specifically trained to deal with research or not, their jobs typically require them to make use of "the numbers" when they buy and sell audiences, or make marketing, programming, and investment decisions. The second group includes those who are not compelled to use audience data, but who nevertheless should know something about it. In this group we would include academics, critics, policymakers, students of mass media, and even interested members of the general public. For both groups of readers, we have tried to make the book as plainspoken as our subject matter allows.

None of that has changed in the third edition. But the world of audience research has changed since the last edition of this volume was published. Global demand for audience ratings has increased as more and more media systems are being driven by advertising revenues. At the same time, a host of newer technologies, like DVRs, interactive media, digital cable, and direct broadcast satellites, have presented advertisers and programmers with new challenges and opportunities. In the United States, Arbitron acquired RADAR, making Arbitron the sole supplier of radio ratings. It has also pushed the development of portable peoplemeters, which could revolutionize audience measurement for radio, television, and perhaps other media. Nielsen Media Research, which is now under the same corporate umbrella as AC Nielsen, has begun deploying peoplemeters into local markets, and is moving aggressively into other areas of audience measurement. All of these changes are, of course, reflected in the new edition.

The book is divided into three major parts. The first begins with an overview of audience research in its different forms, from academic studies to commercial audience measurement. In subsequent chapters we illustrate the major applications of audience research in advertising, programming, financial analysis, and social policy. The second part describes the nature of audience research data. It summarizes the history of the audience measurement business, the research methods most commonly used, and the kinds of ratings research products that are currently available. Part III discusses the analysis of audience data. It begins by offering a framework within which to understand mass audience behavior, and it concludes with two chapters devoted specifically to the analysis of ratings data.

ACKNOWLEDGMENTS

We are indebted to many people for making this book a reality. First are those individuals identified in earlier editions. Their contributions live on in the new work. In the third edition, we are particularly indebted to the following people for their support, guidance, and insights: Roger Baron, George Bailey, Pierre Bouvard, Elizabeth Bruen, Ed Cohen, Pete Cold, Ellen Crawley, Michael Dowling, Anne Elliot, Kathleen Fox, David Giovannoni, Karen Gyimessi, David Gunzerath, Davina Lynn Kent, Stacey Lynn Koerner, David LeRoy, Roberta McConiche, Aaron Meacham, Rachel Mueller-Lust, Steve McGowan, Bruce Rosenblum, Robert Verbanac, Jack Wakshlag, Ned Waugaman, and Justin Wyatt. We are also indebted to countless others at different media and measurement companies for providing data and examples of how research is used. These include Arbitron, comScore Media Metrix, Nielsen Media Research, Nielsen//NetRatings, TiVo, Veronis, Suhler Stevenson, and the several major trade associations. Much of what is good about this book is a credit to them. Anything that is bad, we managed to introduce in spite of their help.

Open letter to students using *Ratings Analysis*

If a tree falls in the forest and no one is there to hear it, does it make a sound? Or, if a medium has no audience, does it deliver its message? The answer almost certainly is that it does not. Does it matter? It absolutely matters, because the business of media relies on its ability to deliver an audience for its messages, both commercial and content. In 2005 marketers will spend more than $60 billion on television advertising alone, so having reliable audience measurement is vital.

Ratings Analysis could well have as its subtitle "How to Succeed in the Media Business," for there is little doubt that wherever your career goals in media lead, understanding the role of audience research will be essential. You will need to develop a practical knowledge of ratings research as well as a theoretical understanding of the ways audiences take shape.

As the world of media changes with new technologies and an ever-expanding array of options for viewing, listening, and reading, research is essential to understanding the ability of each medium to reach and retain audiences. Every business model in media has a research component. In advertising sales the importance of audience is clear. The value of the medium is typically based on the audience delivered. Ratings are at the heart of effective media planning and can provide compelling evidence for demonstrating unique market position based on geography, demographics, loyalty, and other factors. In television, ratings analysis is used to support decisions about retaining or canceling shows, as well as determining which new programs will be made. For content gatekeepers the question is not only who is in the audience, but whether or not they stay for succeeding programs, editions, or pages. Before any new vehicle is launched there must be a reasonable assurance that the audience to support its goals will be there.

So, the need for measuring and understanding audiences has never been greater, or more challenging. Conducting survey research, for example, requires more creativity in today's diverse, mobile, and time-challenged society. Our clients are demanding more detailed data, in multiple varieties, even as they themselves recognize how difficult it is to make sense of it all.

As you learn how *Ratings Analysis* fits into the fascinating and complex world of media, I am confident that you will appreciate that knowledge truly is power, and that understanding the audience will help you to unlock the power of media, and strengthen your own role within the industry.

Welcome to the world of research.

Susan D. Whiting
President and Chief Executive Officer,
Nielsen Media Research

I

APPLICATIONS

Chapter 1

An Introduction to Audience Research

Audiences are essential to the operation of mass media. They fund the industry by purchasing tickets, paying for subscriptions, and renting videos. They are sold to advertisers for billions of dollars. They are the source of the media's economic and social power. Yet, electronic media audiences are elusive. Dispersed over vast geographical areas, tucked away in homes, businesses, and automobiles, they remain unseen by those who try to know and manage them. Only through audience research do they become visible. This research, especially ratings research, is crucial to electronic media and is the central focus of this book. Here, we explore the development of audience ratings and the ways these data can be analyzed and applied.

TYPES OF AUDIENCE RESEARCH

We begin by considering several broad categories of audience research. These categories neither exhaust the possibilities, nor are they mutually exclusive. In fact, they include many forms of research not discussed in subsequent chapters. We identify them here to help the reader distinguish the various goals, assumptions, and methodologies of researchers, and to acquire the basic vocabulary of audience research.

Applied Versus Theoretical

Applied research, often called *action research*, provides practical information that can guide decision making by describing some phenomenon of interest or illuminating the consequences of a particular course of action. Applied research is typically concerned with an immediate problem or need, and rarely makes any pretense of offering enduring explanations of how the world works. Nevertheless, this research sometimes yields useful insights for grander attempts at theorizing.

In the media industries, applied research dominates audience analysis. Examples from print media include recall studies to determine if people remember seeing an advertisement, copy testing to assess the effectiveness of messages, and studies that describe the characteristics of people who read various publications. Examples from electronic media

1

include survey research to assess the appeal of celebrities and popular music, auditorium testing to evaluate programming, and ratings research to measure the size and composition of audiences. As you can see, all of these studies have practical applications.

Another type of applied research, sometimes treated as its own category, is *methodological research*. This is, essentially, research on research. As explained in the chapters that follow, many audience research companies (e.g., Arbitron and Nielsen) rose to prominence by developing new research methods. They are in the business of selling a research product and, like any self-interested company, they engage in product testing and development. Methodological audience research might include questions like: "Can we measure TV viewing more accurately?" or "How can we improve the response rate to our surveys?" or "Can we design a better questionnaire?" Many of these issues and practices are addressed in the section on audience data.

Theoretical research tests more generalized explanations of how the world operates. If those explanations, or theories, are broad and well supported by evidence, they are useful in many different settings. Although theoretical research is sometimes done in industrial settings, it is more common in the academic world. Examples include experiments designed to identify the effects of watching violence on television, or investigations of how and why people use media. Studies such as these typically go beyond the specific problems of individual organizations.

Neither applied nor theoretical research is reliably defined by the type of research method used by the investigator. Surveys, experiments, in-depth interviews, content analyses and the like can all serve applied or theoretical purposes. To make matters even more complicated, a specific piece of research could conceivably serve either purpose depending on who is reading the study and the lessons they learn. This flexibility is probably a good thing, but it does mean that the boundary between applied and theoretical research is sometimes difficult to determine.

Another distinction made in audience studies overlaps with our discussion of applied versus theoretical work. In the early 1940s Paul Lazarsfeld, whom most regard as a founder of communication research, suggested that we distinguish between *administrative* and *critical studies* research (Lazarfeld & Stanton, 1941). Administrative research generally takes the status quo as given, and focuses on improving existing operations and institutions. Obviously, all applied research has an administrative purpose. But administrative research can also be theoretical. Kurt Lewin, yet another founder of communication research, was fond of saying, "Nothing is as practical as a good theory" (Rogers, 1994, p. 321). For the first half of the 20th century, much of what passed as communication theory was, in fact, administrative in character.

Critical studies are a bit harder to define. This research makes no pretense of administrative usefulness, and many critical scholars would strenuously reject any practical application of their work. Researchers in this tradition tend to stand apart from the status quo and ask questions like, "In whose interest is all this going on?" or "What do media mean to people?" Critical studies can certainly be based on empirical data, but they are generally more self-consciously ideological than most administrative audience research. Whether they are "theoretical" in the way social scientists use the term is an interesting question, but one that goes beyond the scope of this book.

Quantitative Versus Qualitative

Industry researchers and academics alike often make a distinction between quantitative and qualitative research. Unfortunately, these terms are ambiguous, even among media industry professionals. A proper academic definition would say that *quantitative research* reduces the object of study to numbers, which facilitates the study of large numbers of people and the use of statistical analysis. *Qualitative research* produces non-numeric summaries such as field notes or transcribed comments from an interview. While qualitative methods allow an investigator to delve deeply into a given topic, results are usually not generalizable to large groups of people.

Unlike the differences between theoretical and applied research, qualitative and quantitative categories tend to be associated with particular research methods. Quantitative studies rely heavily on surveys, experiments, and content analyses, which lend themselves to the easy quantification of data. For example, the results of a telephone survey that required respondents to agree or disagree with a long list of statements could be expressed in numbers, for example, "1" for agree and "2" for disagree. Similarly, an experimenter might quantify physiological responses like heart rates or eye movements to identify response patterns. And a political communication researcher might assign a number to each politician quoted in news reports during a presidential campaign in order to identify reporting biases.

Qualitative methods such as group interviews or some form of observation, usually produce non-numeric results. However, this is where some of the confusion in terminology begins. Investigators sometimes take data gathered with "qualitative" methods and assign numbers to them in order to track the prevalence of ideas or phrases. Thus the rich text of respondent interviews or field notes, characteristic of qualitative methods, ends up looking a great deal like quantitative research.

A further inconsistency occurs because most media professionals equate the term quantitative research with "audience ratings." These estimates of audience size and composition are limited to the relatively small number of characteristics that most interest advertisers (e.g., age and gender). As we will see in the chapters that follow, ratings form a kind of "currency" that drives media industry revenues. They are of such overwhelming importance to the media that some textbook writers simply draw a distinction between ratings and nonratings research (e.g., Wimmer & Dominick, 2002).

In industry, the term qualitative generally means any research that isn't focused exclusively on measures of audience size and composition. Included are studies that address less routine audience characteristics such as lifestyles, values, attitudes, and product purchases, or work that centers on the causes and consequences of exposure. While these data never replace ratings as the currency used to buy and sell media, they are, by our stricter academic definition, "quantitative" because they reduce the characteristics of interest to statistical summaries. Evidently, professionals in the real world of mass media ignore our "proper" academic definitions.

Of course, there are examples of true qualitative work in industry. *Focus groups*, for example, involve gathering a small group of people to talk at length about some topic of interest. Krueger and Casey (2000) define this type of study as "a carefully planned discussion designed to obtain perceptions on a defined area of interest in a permissive, non-threatening environment" (p. 5). A common way to conduct a focus group is to show participants programs or commercials and ask them to discuss their reactions with the group, led by a trained interviewer. Based on this discussion, researchers report a summary and analysis of respondent comments. Focus groups are a popular way to assess radio station formats, local news, program concepts, and a host of new products.

Another approach to studying audiences that has gained popularity in the last two decades is called audience *ethnography*, an umbrella term that describes several related techniques. Some ethnographies are very much like focus groups; others involve studying what people, like the fans of a particular program, post on Internet chat rooms or fan Web sites. Still other ethnographies introduce observers into places of interest like schools or households. The ABC television network, for example, recently conducted an ethnographic study of how people use DVRs by placing field researchers in homes in the New York City area. At the extreme end of the spectrum, ethnographers immerse themselves in the site of study for months or even years. This might require the researcher to actually live among the people being studied, and involves a commitment more typical of academic ethnographies. The best ethnographies produce a depth of understanding that is hard to match with quantitative methods.

Syndicated Versus Custom

The final distinction we will draw is between syndicated and custom research. *Syndicated research* is a standardized product that is sold to multiple subscribers. Audience ratings reports, for instance, serve all users in a particular market. Table 1.1 lists the major suppliers of syndicated audience research and the kinds of products they sell.

This list is representative rather than comprehensive. As commercial mass media have spread around the globe, many countries have developed their own domestic audience research services. Additionally, several companies provide comparative media reports that track both advertising placement and the cost to reach listeners or viewers in various markets. Some organizations audit the reporting methods and circulation claims of the media; and trade associations publish reports and newsletters that offer data to a wide number of readers. All in all, the media industries are awash in numbers. Moreover, as the media environment becomes more complex, the ability to assess and use these numbers has become increasingly important.

Syndicated research has several advantages relative to other kinds of research. Because the cost of a syndicated study is shared by many subscribers, each user pays just a fraction of the entire bill. Additionally, because the same reports serve clients who have competing interests, research syndicators are motivated to be objective. The semi-public nature of the documents makes it harder for any one entity to misrepresent the research, while the standardization of report formats facilitates routine uses of the data. Though they are imperfect, syndicated data, like audience ratings, often become the official numbers used to transact business.

Custom research, which is tailored to meet the needs of a particular sponsor, is seldom available to outsiders. These studies may be commissioned from specialists, like news and programming consultants, or they may be conducted by an in-house research department. Many major market radio stations, for example, track public tastes in music through a survey-type telephone study called *call-out research*. Researchers call a sample of potential audience members and ask them to listen to the "hook," or most memorable phrase, of several popular songs. Stations often adjust their *playlists* based on the results.

Another way to test the audience appeal of new programs is to use a *program analyzer*, a device that CBS developed in the late 1930s. Researchers bring respondents into an auditorium and ask them to listen to programs and vote at regular intervals on what they like and dislike. At present, this device is used for *pilot testing* in television to assess the potential of new program concepts, and for *maintenance research* on established programs to test factors like story-line appeal and the strength of characters. Political consultants use the program analyzer to measure audience response to candidate speeches, televised debates, and news segments during an election campaign.

Custom research may be valuable to a single user, but it has limited value otherwise. The sponsors of call-out or program analyzer research would be loath to share the results with anyone outside their organizations, and if they did, the information would be regarded with a good deal of suspicion. Methods are difficult to verify, and it is assumed that the sponsor has some self-serving motive for promoting the results.

TABLE 1.1
Suppliers of Syndicated Audience Research

AGB Group www.agb.com/	Provides TV audience measurement using peoplemeters. In joint venture with Nielsen Media Research it will serve 30 countries.
Arbitron www.arbitron.com	The preeminent supplier of radio audience ratings in some 290 markets in the US and a proponent of portable people meters.
Claritas www.claritas.com/	Operates a system called PRIZM that provides zip code level data on demographics & lifestyles. Sometimes combined with information on media use. Owned by VNU.
comScore Media Metrix, Inc. www.comscore.com/metrix/	Operates large panels providing data on Internet usage in the US and dozens of countries.
erinMedia www.erinmedia.net	Uses data from digital cable set-top boxes married with zip code level data in selected markets to provide analysis of very large samples.
IAG Research www.iagr.net/default.jsp	Measures effectiveness of product placements with nightly surveys of viewer recall of programming and brands.
ITVX http://www.itvx.com	Measures product placement performance; provides consulting services to marketers using product placement.
Information Resources, Inc. (IRI) http://www.infores.com/public/ us/default.htm	Conducts BehaviorScan which matches consumer purchases to exposure to TV ads. Has partnered with TiVo to study the impact of DVRs.
International Demographics Inc. www.themediaaudit.com	Produces the Media Audit, a telephone survey of 84 local markets featuring media use and consumer information.
Knowledge Networks, Inc. www.knowledgenetworks.com/	Conducts both custom and syndicated reports including MultiMedia Mentor, and is developing a ratings-like measure of Yellow Pages usage.

Marketing Evaluations Inc.www.qscores.com/	Publishes scores, called "Q Scores," that measure the public's familiarity with and liking of TV programs, brands, and celebrities.
Mediamark Research Inc (MRI) www.mediamark.com/	Publishes a national survey with product usage and demographics, with general measures of print and electronic media use
Mendelsohn Media Research (MMR) www.mmrsurveys.com	Does a national mail questionnaire of affluent respondents measuring consumer behaviors and use of print and electronic media
MobilTrak www.mobiltrak.com/index.cfm	In selected markets, uses geographically dispersed detection units that monitor which radio stations are being used in passing cars.
Nielsen Entertainment www.nielsen.com/ nielsen_entertainment.html	Provides measurement of movie audiences, music, video, book sales and interactive media. Owned by VNU
Nielsen Media Research www.nielsenmedia.com/	The preeminent supplier of TV audience ratings in the United States and provider of related services in over 40 countries. Owned by VNU
Nielsen//NetRatings www.netratings.com/	Specializes in Internet audience measurement and related services. In partnership with Nielsen Media Research and AC Nielsen provides services in 13 countries.
Scarborough Research www.scarborough.com/	Provides local market reports on demographic, shopping, lifestyle, and media usage data. Owned by Arbitron and VNU.
Simmons Market Research Bureau (SMRB) www.smrb.com/	Publishes a national survey with demographics, product usage, and general measures of print and electronic media use.
Taylor Nelson Sofres (TNS) www.tsn-global.com/	A large international marketing research group providing audience measurement in 25 countries.

Although much research conducted in colleges and universities is customized, it is generally referred to as *original* or *primary research*. When academic studies are published in scholarly journals they are reviewed by other experts in the field. This process provides some assurance that the authors used defensible research procedures. Occasionally, academics or university research centers are commissioned by industry to do customized studies that may have greater public credibility.

The attributes of both syndicated and customized research are sometimes combined in *hybrid studies*. Once research syndicators produce their reports, they have vast stores of raw data. In an age of computers it is a simple enough matter to tap into those databases to produce specialized reports. Because they are based on existing data, these studies are called *secondary analyses*.

An example of a hybrid analysis is the *audience flow study* that can be produced from the Nielsen Media Research database. With original data, it is quite possible to track how viewers move from one channel or program to the next. As we will see in chapter 3, this information can be useful to programmers when they make scheduling decisions. And researchers can use these data to develop mathematical models of audience behavior. The Claritas company, for example, links census data to existing estimates of media use and can thereby describe audiences by income levels and a host of lifestyle variables.

Hybrid studies have a number of advantages. They are certainly in the syndicator's interest since they can generate additional revenues while requiring very little additional expenditure. Clients may also find that they are cheaper than trying to conduct original custom research to answer the same questions. Moreover, since the results are based on syndicated data, they have the air of official, objective numbers.

For all these reasons, secondary analyses of existing data can be enormously valuable. But they must also be done with caution and an understanding of what is sound research practice. Quite often, when data are sliced up in ways that were not intended at the time of collection, the slices become too small to be statistically reliable. We will have much more to say about the problems of sampling and sample sizes in chapter 7.

COMMERCIAL AUDIENCE RESEARCH

The type of audience research that is at the heart of our book is *commercial audience research*. The definition of commercial research might seem simple: studies conducted to support commercial enterprise, usually for a price. But, as critical scholars point out, even academic research that appears to have the purest of motives is typically undertaken in service of institutional interests. Someone, whether a university or a foundation or a media company, is buying the research product by paying the bill. Does this make all research somehow "commercial?" For the purposes of this book, we offer a more specific description of commercial audience research.

The Characteristics of Commercial Research

The first attribute of commercial audience research is its administrative purpose, which may be applied or theoretical. Another is the quantitative methodology used in these studies. They are quite often based on survey research, though as we saw earlier, independent consultants are sometimes hired to conduct focus groups. The term certainly includes syndicated research, although large sums of money are sometimes paid for customized studies. Commercial research is usually focused on exposure to media and the business of audience measurement, and it is almost always concerned with aggregates and not any individual audience member.

Most of these distinctions have been thoroughly reviewed in the preceding section, but the last point deserves special comment. Audience analysts usually study the behavior of large numbers of people. They probably don't care whether Bob Smith sees an early evening newscast, but they do care how many men ages 35 to 64 will watch. This interest in mass behavior, which is typical of much social scientific research, is actually a blessing. Trying to explain or predict how any one person behaves, moment-to-moment, day-to-day, can be an exercise in frustration. After all, human beings are complex creatures with different moods, impulses, and motivations. However, when you aggregate individual activities, the behavior of the mass is often quite predictable—and the business of selling audiences to advertisers is built on predictions.

This science of predicting mass behavior and audience characteristics has been called *statistical thinking*. It was developed in the 18th century by, among others, insurance underwriters. Consider, for example, the problem of life insurance. Predicting when any one person will die is almost impossible, but if you aggregate large numbers, you can estimate how many people are likely to expire in the coming year. You need not predict the outcome of each individual case to predict an outcome across the entire population. In the same sense, we do not need to know what Bob Smith will do on a given evening to predict how many men his age will be using television.

One important consequence of focusing on the mass rather than individuals is that audience behavior becomes much more tractable. We can identify stable patterns of audience size and flow. We can develop mathematical equations, or models, that allow us to predict audience behavior. Some have even gone so far as to posit "laws" of viewing behavior. These laws, of course, do not bind each person to a code of conduct. Rather, they are statements that mass behavior is so predictable that it exhibits law-like tendencies. This kind of reasoning is typical of commercial audience research and underlies many of the analytical techniques we discuss in the last chapters.

Whether this is the best way to study audiences is debatable, but for the most part, that's the way commercial audience research operates. Leo Bogart, a well-known advertising executive and author of several books on the media, made the point rather directly: "The bulk of communication research is commercial research and is addressed to the question of measuring audiences, rather than to study of the process through which audiences reject or inject the information presented to them" (Bogart, 1996, p. 138).

Criticisms of Commercial Research

Commercial audience research, as described previously, is the subject of several criticisms. Any thoughtful user of audience research should at least be aware of them. One of the more common complaints is that commercial audience research tells us very little about why people use mass media or the consequences of that use. These questions, so the argument goes, ought to be the central concern of communication research. They are certainly important matters, and it is true that audience measurement sheds very little light on these questions. About all that can be said in defense of commercial audience research is that most studies were never designed to answer such questions. Every type of research has certain limitations. It is the job of the user to know what those limitations are and, if need be, how to overcome them.

Critics also claim that commercial audience research fosters undesirable consequences by reducing people to neat numerical summaries. The first problem, pertaining especially to "official" syndicated reports, is that people will regard the numbers as incontrovertible facts. Most published numbers are estimates, not nearly as "hard" as an inexperienced user might imagine. Here again, the user must know where the numbers come from and what they mean. This is why we pay considerable attention to critiquing the methods used to generate audience research reports.

A related problem derives from the fact that commercial audience research is a product in the media marketplace. According to critics, sellers skew their research products in favor of clients' needs. In the words of an old proverb, "He who pays the piper calls the tune." While this criticism might seem reasonable, an analysis of economic motivations suggests a weakness in the argument. Because companies selling audience measurement serve diverse clients in the market, they would lose their businesses if they drifted too far from fairness and objectivity.

The final concern, voiced mainly by critical scholars, is that commercial audience research is an instrument of repression. The whole business of commodifying audiences by turning people into numbers is, at the very least, dehumanizing. By doing so, commercial audience research participates in the control and colonization of the masses. The validity of this last criticism seems to be in the eye of the beholder. Other academics have argued that audience research actually empowers audiences by giving them a voice (Webster & Phalen, 1997).

RATINGS RESEARCH

Audience ratings are undoubtedly the most visible example of commercial audience research. They hold a unique place in industry practice and public consciousness. Hugh Beville, a former network executive who is often referred to as the "dean" of broadcast audience research, made the following observation:

> Ratings are a powerful force in broadcasting and telecommunications. They determine the price that will be paid for programs and the pay that performers will receive. They govern the rates that advertisers will pay for 60-second or 30-second or smaller commercial units in and around each program. Ratings determine stations' audience and rank order in their market, and to a large degree they dictate the profitability of broadcasting stations and their value when they are put up for sale. The salary and bonus compensation of key network and station officials is also governed by ratings success. Ratings results ultimately determine whether top management and program and news management in television and radio broadcast organizations will retain their jobs, be promoted, or demoted. (Beville, 1988, p. xi)

The preoccupation with audience ratings goes beyond the media industry. Unlike any other form of syndicated research, ratings have worked their way into popular culture. Almost everyone has heard about the "Nielsens," and formed some opinion about them. As Larson (1992) has argued:

> Most viewers know Nielsen only as the maker of the bullets that killed such shows as "Star Trek" and "Twin Peaks," but to think of its ratings exclusively in terms of their show-stopping power is to underestimate the depth of Nielsen's influence over the culture, content, and business of television, and therefore, over the evolution of our consumer culture itself. Nielsen *is* television. (p. 105)

While it's easy to get swept into overstatement, audience ratings are certainly influential. In fact, many people in the electronic media use the terms "ratings" and "audience research" interchangeably, as if to imply nothing else really matters. Because this book deals extensively with the analysis of ratings data, it seems appropriate to consider why ratings are such a visible and pervasive form of audience research.

It should be noted from the outset that we use the term *ratings* as shorthand for a body of data on people's exposure to electronic media. Strictly speaking, ratings are one of many audience summaries that can be derived from that data. As we will see in chapter 6, ratings research came into being in the 1930s because the rapidly growing radio industry wanted to turn broadcasting into a mass advertising medium. At the time, newspapers and magazines had the advantage with advertisers because they could prove readership with subscription data. Radio stations had no comparable measure of listenership, so advertisers had no credible way to determine who was listening to the programs or the commercials they contained. Ratings solved the problem by providing estimates of the unseen audience. To make people aware of this new service, C. E. Hooper, one of the pioneers of ratings research, deliberately publicized what he called *Hooperatings*. To this day, broadcast media are almost totally dependent on advertising revenues, and in turn on ratings as the sole measure of the invisible audience. Ratings are widely reported in the trade press, and they often make their way into more popular media.

The other key to understanding the power of ratings is to appreciate the sheer pervasiveness of broadcasting itself. Radio and television totally dominate the consumption of mass media in the United States and much of the world. Table 1.2 summarizes the number of hours the average American spends with each of several media in the course of a year.

Some caution is in order when reading this table. While the numbers are presented as additive, media use sometimes overlaps leading to the possibility of some double counting. These are also averages, so any one person's profile might look quite different from the overall patterns presented here. Even so, the numbers are staggering. The average person spends roughly 10 hours a day with media. Of this about three fourths of their time is spent with some form of radio or television. Other media pale by comparison. Old competitors for the advertisers' dollars, like

TABLE 1.2
Hours Per Person Per Year Using Media

	1998		2003		2008 Projected	
	Hours	Percent	Hours	Percent	Hours	Percent
Television	1551	46.7%	1745	47.7%	1931	47.6%
Radio	911	27.4%	1002	27.4%	1120	27.6%
Recorded music	275	8.3%	184	5.0%	167	4.1%
Consumer Internet	39	1.2%	176	4.8%	236	5.8%
Daily newspapers	186	5.6%	171	4.7%	164	4.0%
Consumer magazines	134	4.0%	121	3.3%	110	2.7%
Consumer books	118	3.6%	108	3.0%	104	2.6%
Home video	51	1.5%	70	1.9%	110	2.7%
Videogames	45	1.4%	69	1.9%	98	2.4%
Movies in theaters	13	0.4%	13	0.4%	14	0.3%
Interactive TV		0.0%	2	0.1%	5	0.1%
TOTAL	3323	100.0%	3661	100.0%	4059	100.0%

Note. Source: Adapted from the Veronis Suhler Stevenson, 2004, *Communications Industry Forecast & Report*. Reprinted by permission.

newspapers, are losing audience. New competitors, like the Internet, still have a very long way to go. It is small wonder that the electronic mass media figure so heavily in the public consciousness.

By extension, it is clear why audience ratings loom so large for virtually everyone connected with the electronic media. They are the tools used by advertisers and broadcasters to buy and sell audiences. They are the report cards that lead programmers to cancel some shows and to clone others. Ratings are road maps to our patterns of media consumption, and as such, might be of interest to anyone from a Wall Street banker to a social scientist. They are the object of considerable fear and loathing, and they are certainly the subject of much confusion. We hope this book can end some of that confusion, and lead to an improved understanding of audience research and the ways in which it can be used.

The book is divided into three major parts. The first examines the many users of audience research and how they tend to look at the numbers. The second part considers the audience data itself, reviewing the history, methods, and reporting formats of commercial research. The final part provides a way to understand and analyze audience data, including a general framework for explaining audience behavior and rather specific analytical techniques.

RELATED READINGS

Ang, I. (1991). *Desperately seeking the audience*. London: Routledge.

Beville, H. (1988). *Audience ratings: Radio, television, cable* (Rev. ed.). Hillsdale, NJ: Lawrence Erlbaum Associates.

Ettema, J., & Whitney, C. (Eds.). (1994). *Audiencemaking: How the media create the audience*. Thousand Oaks, CA: Sage.

Krueger, R. A., & Casey, M. A. (2000). *Focus groups: A practical guide for applied research* (3rd ed.). Thousand Oaks, CA: Sage.

Lindlof, T. R., & Taylor, B. C. (2002). *Qualitative communication research methods* (2nd ed). Thousand Oaks, CA: Sage.

Moores, S. (1993). *Interpreting audiences: The ethnography of media consumption*. London: Sage.

Napoli, P. M. (2003). *Audience economics: Media institutions and the audience marketplace*. New York: Columbia University Press.

Webster, J., & Phalen, P. (1997). *The mass audience: Rediscovering the dominant model*. Mahwah, NJ: Lawrence Erlbaum Associates..

Wimmer, R., & Dominick, J. (2002). *Mass media research: An introduction* (7th ed.). Belmont, CA: Wadsworth.

Chapter 2

Audience Research in Advertising

Broadcasters sell audiences. Despite some appearances to the contrary, that's the heart of their business. Virtually all other actions support that function. But traditional broadcasters aren't the only businesses that sell audiences. Newer media like cable, Direct Broadcast Satellite (DBS), the World Wide Web, and interactive media offer ways to reach them as well.

The people who buy these audiences are advertisers. They are interested in capturing the attention of the viewer or listener to convey some message. The message might be as simple as introducing people to a new brand or reminding them of an old one, or it might involve trying to change their attitudes toward a person or product. Often advertisers attempt to influence their behavior in some way. Whatever the purpose, advertisers need access to audiences, if only for a moment. They pay the media for this opportunity.

The challenge for media and advertisers alike is that audience are invisible. Unlike print media, which can approximate readership by tracking the number of issues they sell, broadcasters have to rely on statistical estimates of listenership. We discuss these estimates in the next section of the book. Suffice it to say that advertisers' need to buy audiences, and broadcasters' eagerness to sell, brought the ratings services into being. As a consequence, advertisers have an enormous stake in the audience measurement business and wield considerable influence in shaping the form of ratings data. Without advertiser support, electronic media ratings as we know them would not exist.

The buying and selling of audiences takes place at many levels. A large national marketplace is dominated by a few broadcast and cable networks, syndicators, and major corporate advertisers. In local markets, individual stations sell to area merchants. And national spot and regional markets provide access to specific geographical areas. This trade in audiences is commonly organized by medium into radio, broadcast television, cable, and, increasingly, Internet. Table 2.1 summarizes total ad revenues for each medium, illustrating patterns of market growth. In the United States alone, advertising is a multi-billion-dollar business.

Each marketplace has developed its own institutions and practices, which affect how audience data are analyzed and interpreted. The following section describes the major markets for electronic media audiences. In chapter 8 we describe the ratings information available in each one.

TABLE 2.1

Advertising Revenues of Electronic Media[a]

Year	Radio[b]			Television[c]				Cable[d]		Internet	Total
	Network	Spot	Local	Network	Spot	Local	Synd	Network	Spot/Local		
1950	$132	$119	$203	$85	$31	$55	$—	$—	$—		$625
1960	45	208	402	820	527	280	—	—	—		$2,282
1970	49	355	853	1,658	1,234	704	—	—	—		$4,853
1980	158	746	2,643	5,130	3,269	2,967	50	50	50		$15,063
1985	329	1,320	4,915	8,285	6,004	5,714	540	612	139		$27,858
1990	433	1,626	6,780	9,863	7,788	7,856	1,109	1,802	737		$37,994
1995	426	1,920	9,124	11,600	9,119	9,985	2,016	3,993	1,634		$49,817
2000	1,029	3,596	15,223	15,888	12,264	13,542	3,108	10,673	4,124	8,087	$79,447
2001	919	2,898	14,552	14,300	9,223	12,256	3,102	10,494	4,122	7,134	$51,866
2002	1000	3,275	15,134	15,000	10,920	13,114	3,034	10,881	4,355	6,010	$76,713
2003	1033	3,470	15,100	15,030	9,948	13,520	3,434	12,085	5,110	7,267	$78,730

Note. Fox was counted as syndication prior to 1990, and as network after 1990. UPN, WB, and PAX were counted as syndication after 1990. Reprinted by permission of Interactive Advertisers Association.

[a]Revenue in millions.

[b]Radio Advertising Bureau.

[c]Television Bureau of Advertising.

[d]Cabletelevision Advertising Bureau. Spot/Local includes regional sports.

[e]Interactive Advertising Bureau/PricewaterhouseCoopers.

15

NATIONAL MARKETS

Broadcast and Cable Networks

For advertisers who need to reach vast national markets, network television has much to offer. Overall, the major television broadcast networks still draw the largest audiences, although radio and cable networks also compete in the national marketplace.

As a practical matter, the network television market is divided into smaller markets called *dayparts*, which are defined by time of day and program content. Because each designation is associated with specific audience characteristics, the various dayparts appeal to different advertisers and generate different amounts of sales revenue.

Prime time, the most important of the network dayparts, includes all regularly scheduled programs from 8 p.m. to 11 p.m. EST, Monday through Saturday, and 7 p.m. to 11 p.m. on Sunday. Networks generate their highest revenues during prime time because they attract the largest audiences. Advertisers like this daypart because they can simultaneously reach a wide variety of people across the entire nation, including people who work during the day. Access to this mass market, however, is not cheap; the most popular prime time programs are the most expensive.

Daytime is the second most lucrative daypart. For the networks, daytime extends from 7 a.m. to 4:30 p.m. EST, Monday through Friday. This audience is much smaller and, with the exception of early news programs, disproportionately female. As a result, it appeals most to advertisers who want to reach women, especially full-time homemakers. Companies selling household products like soap and food frequently buy spots in this time period, paying far less than prime time advertisers.

The *sports* daypart is defined strictly by program content. Among the most important network sports programs are major-league games like those of the NFL or NBA. These events attract men to the audience and, as might be expected, advertisers who buy most heavily in this daypart include breweries, car and truck manufacturers, and companies that sell automotive products. The cost of advertising in sports varies widely—mostly as a function of audience size—all the way up to the Super Bowl, which can cost over $2 million per 30-second spot.

The *news* daypart is defined more by program content than by simple time periods, although there is a correlation between news and time of day. This daypart includes the network's evening news programs, weekend news programming, and news specials and documentaries. Excluded from this daypart are the morning news programs (considered daytime) and regularly scheduled prime time programs like *60 Minutes*, even though these programs might be produced by network news divisions. The news daypart tends to attract an older audience, so it is especially appealing to companies that sell products like pharmaceuticals, healthful foods and luxury items.

Late night begins at 11:30 p.m. EST Monday through Friday. Its best-known programs are *The Tonight Show With Jay Leno*, and *Late Show With David Letterman*, which have dominated the time period for years. Not surprisingly, the audience during this daypart is small and almost entirely adult in composition.

Many public interest groups and regulators view the *children's daypart* as one of the most important electronic media markets. This market includes the Saturday and Sunday morning children's programs, a time period that critics once dubbed the "children's ghetto," as well as weekday programming aimed at children. Although children watch a great deal of television at other times, the children's daypart offers advertisers the most efficient way to reach this audience through broadcast television. Among the largest advertisers in this daypart are cereal and candy makers and toy manufacturers. The cost of a 30-second spot varies as the demand changes by season. An advertising spot at Christmastime, for example, might cost three times as much as it would in the months that follow.

Markets can also be defined by when the actual buying takes place. Transactions occur in different stages throughout the year, with some advertisers purchasing time well in advance of airdate and others purchasing time just a few months or weeks before broadcast. These different rounds in the buying process are called the *upfront* market, the *scatter* market, and the *opportunistic* market.

The upfront market is the first round of buying. Each spring and early summer, major advertisers tell the media what kind of audiences they want to buy in the upcoming television season. Network salespeople respond with proposals, called *avails*, that detail program audiences and the cost to reach them. Obviously, networks want to charge as much money as possible for their audiences, while advertisers want to maximize the number of viewers they get for their money. The process is complicated by uncertainty—no one knows exactly which audiences will watch programs in the fall line-up, especially the new ones. Consequently, the upfront market is the occasion for much high stakes gamesmanship. When the market closes, major advertisers have committed several billion dollars to the networks for time throughout the coming year.

Although this method of buying ties up advertisers' budgets for months to come, the upfront gives them access to the best network programs. Because these companies make long-term commitments to the network, they generally get more favorable rates than will be available later in the year. In fact, to lessen the advertiser's risk, networks often give *audience guarantees* to ensure that the total audience estimates will be delivered, even if the networks have to run additional commercials, called *make-goods*, for free.

The *scatter market* operates within a shorter time frame. Each television season is divided into quarters. In advance of each quarter, advertisers may wish to buy time for specific purposes such as advertising seasonal products or running some limited campaign, not envisioned during the upfront buying. Because advertisers are usually less flexible in the scatter market, and networks buyers are generally at a disadvantage, prices in the scatter market are usually higher than they were in the upfront. At times, however, market conditions could favor the buyer. Programs that were high risks in the upfront market will have track records when scatter buying occurs—this means a less risky investment for the advertiser. Additionally, if the networks have a slow season, rates could actually be lower in scatter than in the upfront.

The *opportunistic market* occurs as the television season progresses. Although most of the networks' inventory is purchased during the upfront and scatter markets, some time might become available closer to airdate. Perhaps deals negotiated early in the season fell through as a result of cuts in an advertiser's budget or the implementation of new marketing strategies. Or perhaps changes in network lineups, such as the cancellation or rescheduling of a program or the addition of a special event, resulted in extra inventory. These changes would relieve advertisers of their commitments, and create opportunities for the last-minute purchase of airtime. The circumstances might favor the network, or they might give the advantage to an advertiser. Buyers and sellers often use such opportunities to settle debts from past business deals. For example, a salesperson with extra inventory might offer a low-cost spot to a particular buyer who has been an excellent customer. Or a buyer may purchase a spot to help the seller out because the salesperson has given him preferential treatment in the past.

Despite their long domination of the national television marketplace, the broadcast networks are facing increased competition. Cable television, which once served as a glorified antenna by bringing broadcast signals to areas with poor over-the-air reception, now offers viewers many additional networks. About two thirds of all television households currently subscribe to cable. More recently, direct broadcast satellites have extended the reach of these newer networks to over 80% of all homes with television. Today the average television household receives over 100 channels of programming. Most of these national networks would like nothing better than to steal away some of the broadcast network's audience and revenues.

Table 2.2 lists the top 40 national cable television networks ranked by the number of television households (TVHH) capable of receiving their signal. All of these services depend, at least in part, on advertising revenues to make money. Note, however, that even the oldest and most popular cable networks reach about 80% of all American homes—less than the major broadcast networks. The near universal coverage of broadcast networks gives them an edge over cable in building the largest television audiences. Cable networks have, however, developed other strategies for selling their audiences.

The most obvious competitive strategy is to target a particular kind of viewer. Note the number of networks in Table 2.2 that offer programming for just a part of the audience. MTV, for example, is designed for teens and young adults. Nickelodeon and the Cartoon Network appeal to children. Lifetime is a network for women; Spike TV is for men. BET targets African Americans. To the extent that cable networks offer media buyers these specific audiences, they may be a more efficient buy for an advertiser. Further, cable networks are often more willing to work with advertisers to develop special programming or promotional efforts to enhance the impact of commercials.

Not only do cable networks offer the prospect of fewer "wasted" exposures, they often sell access to their audiences for less than the networks charge. Broadcast networks, perhaps because of their greater reach or the prestige associated with hit programs, command a premium in the marketplace. So, while a broadcast network might charge $25 for access to a thousand adults age 18 to 49 during prime time, cable networks might charge only $10 for the same number of viewers. Obviously, cable networks would like to charge broadcast network rates, but the laws of supply and demand in the current marketplace mean cable has to sell audiences at bargain prices.

Like cable, Direct Broadcast Satellite (DBS) services can sell national advertising. And, like all its media competitors, DBS needs credible audience estimates to attract advertisers. In 2003, Nielsen agreed to develop a measurement system for rating satellite delivered programming; DirecTV became its first client for the new service. Until then, commercial time on DirecTV was sold based on viewer estimates extrapolated from similar programming and distribution channels. True satellite ratings were a significant boost to the sales effort.

Although television networks, whether broadcast, cable, or satellite, command much of our attention these days, we should recall that the first networks were radio. Permanently established by the late 1920s, these radio networks set in place many practices and traditions that are evident in network television today. And even though television has moved to center stage in our lives, now commanding the lion's share of the advertising revenues, radio networks have been an important social and cultural force in American life. In fact, radio still offers advertisers an alternative to reach a national audience.

The national radio networks in operation today are controlled by only a handful of companies. The business is dominated by the original networks, now more than 70 years old, and by radio program *syndicators*. Among the most important networks are ABC, Premiere, and Westwood One, each of which offers multiple services including news, music, and political and sports talk programming. Syndicators, although not "networks" per se, provide specialized radio formats via satellite to a large number of stations all over the country. These formats include all types of popular music, call-in sports and political conversation. Some feature well-known personalities like Rush Limbaugh and Don Imus, and are carried by hundreds of radio stations simultaneously. Stations can receive news programs from news-gathering or-

TABLE 2.2
Top 40 Cable Networks 2004 by Television Household Coverage

Network	TVHH (000)	% of all TVHH
Discovery	88,566	82%
ESPN	88,338	81%
USA Network	88,054	81%
CNN	88,047	81%
Turner Network Television (TNT)	88,033	81%
TBS Superstation	88,014	81%
Nickelodeon	87,609	81%
A&E	87,598	81%
Lifetime	87,571	81%
Weather Channel	87,536	81%
Spike TV (TNN)	87,367	81%
ABC Family	87,077	80%
The Learning Channel	87,057	80%
ESPN2	86,976	80%
MTV	86,783	80%
CNN Headline News	86,490	80%
VH1	86,364	80%
CNBC	86,138	79%
History Channel	86,130	79%
Cartoon Network	86,035	79%
American Movie Classics	85,478	79%
Home & Garden TV	85,351	79%
FOX News Channel	85,313	79%
Comedy Central	85,201	79%
Animal Planet	84,929	78%
Entertainment TV (E!)	84,117	78%
Food Network	83,906	77%
FX	83,783	77%
Disney Channel	83,768	77%
TV Land	83,165	77%
SCI-FI Channel	83,058	77%
MSNBC	81,610	75%

Court TV	80,364	74%
Black Entertainment TV (BET)	78,395	72%
Bravo	76,191	70%
Country Music Television (CMT)	75,056	69%
Travel Channel	75,010	69%
TV Guide Channel	67,633	62%
WGN Superstation	61,127	56%
Hallmark Channel	58,908	54%

Note. Data are from Nielsen Media Research, 2004.

ganizations like Associated Press and United Press International as well as cable services such as CNN, Fox News, and ABC's ESPN. And group owners can distribute programming to their own stations, essentially functioning as ad hoc networks.

Syndication

Stations are in constant need of programming. Even network affiliates must fill large blocks of time not programmed by the networks. To do this, broadcasters rely on a variety of program sources, including one that is particularly relevant to a discussion of advertising—*barter syndication*.

Barter syndication has fairly straightforward origins. Basically, advertisers found they could use a station's need for programming to get their message across to an audience. They could produce a program, place their ads in it, and offer it to stations without charging a license fee. Stations found this attractive because they acquired new programs without having to pay cash for them; they could even sell spots in the programs if the original sponsor did not use them. With the growth of satellite program distribution in the 1980s, this simple idea gave rise to a rapidly growing new advertising marketplace.

In general, the barter syndication market works like this. A distributor either produces programs, owns the rights to existing shows, or works on behalf of another producer to sell programs to local stations. The sales arrangement could be "all barter," meaning that a station gives the syndicator all available commercial time to sell in the national market. Sometimes the agreement is a hybrid, called "cash-plus-barter," which, as the name suggests, requires stations to pay a fee for the program as well as accepting ads placed by the syndicator. Depending on the specific terms of the deal, stations might also sell some local spots in a cash-plus arrangement.

Syndicators determine the terms of a deal before they place a program in the marketplace. Trade publications print lists of these arrangements at the beginning of each calendar year, just before the National

Association of Television Programming Executives (NATPE) conference. At NATPE syndicated programs are marketed intensely to potential buyers, especially those from medium and small markets. Table 2.3 reproduces part of this list for the 2004 NATPE convention. Although barter terms may change to meet market demand, this list gives a good indication of the type of deals syndicators are seeking. Individual barter contracts may require stations to broadcast programs in a specific daypart, such as early fringe. Requirements like this are typical of popular programs, like *Wheel of Fortune*, that are especially desired by stations. Note that some of the programs listed in Table 2.3 aren't scheduled to be available until a year or two after they are sold.

In addition to the terms of sale, program buyers are interested in the number of markets that have already purchased (or "cleared") the programs. The more stations that acquire a program, the larger is the potential audience. If one station in every market agrees to air a program, the distributor would, hypothetically, have the same reach as a major television network. As a practical matter, once a program is carried on enough stations to reach 70% of U.S. households, it is sold to advertisers in much the same way as network time.

Just like their network counterparts, the barter syndication firms approach national advertisers and their ad agencies to sell commercial time. They sell in the upfront, scatter, and opportunistic markets, and may even guarantee audiences like the networks. In fact, advertisers may use barter syndication as a supplement to their purchases of network time or as a substitute for it. Sometimes program environments are available through barter that are not offered by traditional broadcast networks. For example, game shows and talk shows are available mostly through syndication. Still, the major benefit of advertising on a barter program is reaching an audience at a somewhat lower cost than other national or regional alternatives.

Despite some similarities, buying time in barter syndication is not quite comparable to network advertising. Many programs, especially those produced for first-run syndication, are sent to all stations in the country at the same time, and at least run on the same day. But other types of programming, off-network syndication for example, may air at different times in different markets. Weekly syndicated programs might even air on different days, which complicates the process of predicting audiences.

Barter syndication and related ways to package advertising for national or regional audiences are almost certain to grow. Satellite communications have made the rapid, cost-efficient delivery of programs feasible. Stations pick up these syndicated program feeds if they perceive this to be in their best interests, perhaps even preempting more traditional networks. Assuming an effective way to buy and evaluate audiences, advertisers are likely to use these alternative routes for reaching the public. Such ever-changing syndicated networks are also likely to pose some of the most interesting challenges for audience analysts.

TABLE 2.3

NATPE Clearances, 2004

Program	Distributor	Type	Terms	Launch
On Air With Ryan Seacrest	Twentieth	hour strip	cash+barter	Jan. 2004
The Tony Danza Show	Buena Vista	hour strip	cash+barter	Fall 2004
The Insider	Paramount	half-hour strip	cash+barter	Fall 2004
The Jane Pauley Show	NBC Enterprise	hour strip	cash+barter	Fall 2004
Pat Croce: Moving In	Sony	half-hour strip	barter	Fall 2004
Life & Style	Sony	hour strip	cash+barter	Fall 2004
Untitled Lopez Show	Universal	hour strip	cash+barter	Fall 2004
Untitled Lifestyle Show	Universal	strip	cash+barter	Fall 2004
According to Jim	Buena Vista	half-hour sitcom	cash+barter	Fall 2006
Alias	Buena Vista	weekend hour	barter only	Fall 2005
Bernie Mac	Twentieth	half-hour sitcom	cash+barter	Fall 2005
Fear Factor	NBC Enterprise	hour strip	TBA	Fall 2004
George Lopez	Warner Bros.	half-hour sitcom	cash+barter	Fall 2005
Girlfriends	Paramount	half-hour strip	cash+barter	Fall 2004
Grounded for Life	Carsey-Werner	half-hour sitcom	cash+barter	Fall 2005
Malcolm	Twentieth	half-hour strip	cash+barter	Fall 2004
My Wife and Kids	Buena Vista	half-hour sitcom	cash+barter	Fall 2005
One on One	Paramount	half-hour sitcom	cash+barter	Fall 2005
Reba	Twentieth	half-hour sitcom	TBA	Fall 05 or 06
Sex and the City	HBO	half-hour sitcom	cash+barter	Fall 2005
24	Twentieth	weekend hour	TBA	Fall 2005
Twilight Zone	New Line	half-hour strip	barter only	Fall 2004
Yes, Dear	Twentieth	half-hour strip	cash+barter	Fall 2004

Note. Data are from "Sizing Up the Market," *Broadcasting & Cable,* January 12, 2004, p. 21.

23

LOCAL MARKETS

Broadcast networks reach national markets by combining the audiences of local affiliated stations. Similarly, national cable networks aggregate the viewers of local cable systems. But an individual station or cable system can sell its own audiences to advertisers who want to reach their local customers. These audiences are attractive to businesses that trade in a concentrated geographical area, and to national or regional marketers who want to advertise in specific markets. The former create a market for *local sales*; the latter take part in the *national spot market*.

Broadcast Stations

The physics of broadcasting are such that a station's signal has geographic limits. In light of this, the Federal Government decided to license radio and television stations to specific cities and towns across the country. Larger population centers have more stations. Naturally enough, people spend most of their time listening to nearby stations because the signal is clearest and the programs are of local interest. In television, the major ratings service uses this geographically determined audience behavior to define the boundaries of a local media market area. Nielsen calls these markets *designated market areas* (DMAs).

Appendix A lists the 210 U.S. television markets designated by Nielsen. There are even more radio markets. In both cases, market size varies considerably. New York, for instance, has over 7 million TV households, whereas Glendive barely has 5,000. Indeed, buying time on a major station in New York might deliver more viewers to an advertiser than a buy on national cable network. Conversely, many small market radio stations might have audiences too small for a ratings company to measure economically. This point is best illustrated by the fact that regular radio ratings are available to less than half of the stations in the country. Of course, measured stations account for the overwhelming majority of all radio listening.

These vast differences in audience size have a marked effect on the rates that local broadcasters can charge for a commercial spot. The price of a 30-second spot in prime time might be $400 in Des Moines and $4,000 in Detroit. Other factors can affect the cost of time, too. Is the market growing, or has it fallen on hard times? Is the population relatively affluent or poor? How competitive are other local media, like newspapers? Even factors like a market's time zone can affect the rates of local electronic media.

Other characteristics that vary with market size are the volume and sophistication of the ratings users who analyze audience information. As we will discuss in chapter 8, many radio markets are measured just twice each year. Audiences in major TV markets, on the other hand, are measured continuously. Because of this, and the greater number of advertising dollars available in major markets, the buyers and sellers of media in those markets tend to be more experienced with and adept at analyzing ratings information.

In most markets, the largest buyers of local advertising include fast food restaurants, supermarkets, department stores, banks, and car dealers. Like network advertisers, these companies often employ an advertising agency to represent them. The agency can perform a number of functions for its client, from developing a creative strategy, to writing copy and producing the ads. Most important in this context, the agency's media department projects the audience for various programs, plans when the ads are to run, buys the time, and evaluates whether the desired audience was delivered. Smaller advertisers, or those in smaller markets, may deal directly with local stations.

Because of the different types of people and organizations involved, local time-buying decisions vary from intuitive judgments made by a merchant who thinks a certain number of ads on a local station will generate extra business, to choices based on complex analyses of ratings information. Indeed, many small radio stations and cable systems sell without using any ratings information at all. Increasingly, though, the process of buying and selling time depends on the use of ratings.

Although specific terminology may differ from organization to organization, the purchase of local time generally works like this. The advertiser or its agency issues a request for avails. In effect, the buyer is asking what spots are available for sale on the local stations. Avail requests typically specify the buyer's target audience, preferred dayparts, and estimated budget. Station salespeople respond by proposing a schedule of spots to deliver some or all of the requested audience. At this point, the buyer and seller negotiate differences over the projected rating and the cost of a spot. Assuming the parties reach an agreement, buyers place an order and the spots air. After the campaign, the next available ratings information is analyzed to determine whether the expected audience was actually delivered. As in network buying, this last stage in the process is called *post-buy analysis*.

As noted earlier, national and regional advertisers participate in the national spot market when they buy spots on local stations. For example, a snow tire manufacturer might want to advertise only in northern markets. Similarly, a maker of agricultural products might wish to buy time in markets with large farm populations. In fact, such national spot buys constitute the largest single source of revenues for many TV stations. The question is, how can so many local stations deal effectively with all these potential time buyers? It would be impractical for thousands of stations to have their own personnel trying to contact each and every national advertiser.

To solve this problem, an intermediary called a *station representative* (or *rep firm*) serves as the link between local stations and national advertisers. Rep firms for both television and radio stations are located in major media markets like New York and Chicago. Television reps usually represent only one client per market, in order to avoid any conflict of interest. Radio reps may serve more than one station in a market, as long as their formats don't compete for the same audience. Rep firms vary according to the number of stations they represent, and the types of services they offer to clients. Some firms provide stations with research services or advice on programming. Most importantly, though, rep firms monitor the media buys that national advertisers are planning, and they try to secure some portion of that business for their stations.

The station sales force and the salespeople at the rep firm under contract with the station are essentially selling the same commercial time. This can cause some conflicts. Local advertisers could be shut out of a daypart because national advertisers secure the inventory, or vice versa. In Las Vegas, for example, local businesses pay a premium to advertise in early news programs in order to reach visitors who are deciding where to go for the evening. This means that national advertisers cannot purchase time in local broadcast news without paying very high rates. Instead, they may turn to cable television to reach those audiences.

Cable Systems

Cable systems are now capable of offering local advertising opportunities. Usually, this involves inserting a local ad in a cable network, but it could also mean sponsorship of locally produced programs. There are two limitations to this process. First, just like cable networks, cable systems simply can't reach every member of the available television audience. Second, as is the case with small market radio stations, the audience for most local cable systems is too small to measure economically. In this case, advertisers must guess at audience size and composition. However, Nielsen is in the process of introducing peoplemeters into local market areas, which should do a better job of capturing cable viewing. Further, as more cable systems begin to provide programming via digital set-top boxes, they'll be able to count the number of households using each channel. While these improvements will help level the playing field in the local ad market, local cable is likely to be at a disadvantage for some time.

Eventually though, cable systems might enjoy an advertising advantage because they are not just local, they are "ultra-local." In many TV markets, programming is fed to different neighborhoods by different headends. Each headend is capable of inserting ads for its own coverage area, so an advertiser can create a patchwork of small coverage areas to suit its needs. A local merchant could run a spot across a group of interconnected headends, reaching only those viewers who live in a certain part of town. Or a chain restaurant might run one commercial across the entire market, but vary the address of the closest local outlet. Similarly, since cable franchise areas, almost by definition, conform to governmental boundaries within the market, cable seems a likely venue for political advertising. These potentials are being exploited more and more as cable rep firms develop.

INTERNET

Newer modes of communication don't necessarily conform to the "local versus national" distinction that has defined traditional media markets. In the last decade, advertisers began to exploit a new way to reach audiences: the World Wide Web. In the latter half of the 1990s advertising dollars started pouring into the Web. While a recession slowed ad expenditures in 2001 and 2002, the industry has now largely recovered (see Table 2.1). Just like radio and television, however, the viability of Internet advertising requires that there be independent audience measurement firms verifying the number and characteristics of Web users.

Perhaps unsurprisingly, the Internet audience research business has developed along the same lines as broadcast audience measurement. Concepts like "impressions," "reach," "frequency," and "audience duplication" are used to summarize and evaluate the Web users. Just as their broadcast counterparts, Web sites are represented in the advertising market by rep firms. These firms provide a variety of services for the sites they represent, but foremost among them is soliciting advertising revenue for their clients.

There are some major differences between broadcasting and the Internet that affect the ways that audiences can be tracked. The most important difference is that everyone who visits a Web site is being sent content directly from a server. This computer can keep track of everyone who accesses content. The server can, in effect, produce a census of all Web site users, eliminating the need for sampling altogether. In fact, one of the first ways to measure Internet audiences was to count the number of "hits" that the server received. But hits are very imprecise measurements—100 hits might indicate that 100 different people visited the server, or that one person visited 100 times. Additionally, this statistic can be affected by *click fraud*, which the industry defines as any attempt to artificially inflate the number of hits by repeatedly accessing the site. Servers attempt to solve this problem by placing a *cookie* on the hard drive of each user that views a page. The cookies identify those who make return visits. Servers can also track the IP addresses of visitors to gather information about their audiences. These approaches are called "server-centric" measurement. Each approach has certain flaws, but even if they worked perfectly they would still leave gaps in the Web site's knowledge of its audience.

Server-centric measures have two major liabilities from an advertiser's perspective. First, even if Web site operators are honest in reporting server activity, advertisers never know for sure. Ever since the beginning of the 20th century, advertisers have required objective, independent auditors to verify the circulation claims of media, first print and now the Internet. Second, server-centric measurements provide, at best, very limited information about who is visiting the Web site. The information that advertisers value most (e.g., demographics, etc.) must typically be provided by a panel of users who agree to participate in a study. This "user-centric" measurement is very similar in concept to what ratings companies have been doing since the 1930s.

Two major audience measurement companies vie for supremacy in the field of Internet measurement: Nielsen//NetRatings and comScore Media Metrix. We will talk more about each in the chapters that follow. For now, it's important to note that both maintain very large samples of Internet users, at home and at work, who have agreed to report information about themselves and to have their Web surfing behavior recorded. These data are aggregated into various reports, which are available to clients willing to pay for independent estimates of the size and composition of Web site audiences.

Another major difference between Internet and other electronic media is the definition of exposure. Historically, broadcast and cable have counted the opportunity to see or hear an ad as exposure to that message. Based on this measure, traditional media make claims about reach, or the number of impressions they delivered. Stakes are higher on the Internet. Advertisers want more information about Web pages than a number of ad impressions based on broad opportunities to view. Because Internet content, including ads, is served by a computer, some advertisers want to know how many people actually clicked on the ad to get more information. This alternative head-counting technology, unique to the Internet, offers a second type of currency called *click-throughs*. Critics of this alternative, however, argue that it is too restrictive because it fails to account for impressions that might do useful things like build brand awareness. DoubleClick, a major ad-serving company on the Internet, has suggested an intermediate measure called *view-through*, that would account for any action taken by a user within a certain time (e.g., 30 days) after seeing an ad. The industry is still trying to sort this out.

Advertising on the Internet is still so new that many decisions remain to be made. Issues as seemingly straightforward as standardizing the size and characteristics of Internet ads are proving difficult. While *banner ads* are still the norm, they are giving way to *leaderboards* that run across the tops of pages and *skyscrapers* that rise up alongside page content. As more and more people access the Internet via fast connections like broadband, so-called *rich media* advertising has grown. These ads feature dynamic content and adopt many of the attention-grabbing techniques of television. The most rapidly growing category of advertising is *keyword search*, in which advertisers bid to have their sites come up first in response to a user's search request (e.g., "find this prescription drug"). This development helps account for the fact that the top 10 Web sites, typically search engines, account for over 70% of all ad spending on the Internet.

Another powerful, but as yet unrealized, potential of the Internet is *addressable advertising*. Because Internet ads can be served independently of Web page content, advertisers can target individual users with specific advertising appeals, regardless of which content they choose. At present most targeting occurs by linking the content of Web pages to a complementary ad (e.g., a travel Web site carries an ad for an airline). But more precise targeting is, in theory, possible. At some point in the future, ads are likely to reach the right consumer at the right time, no matter what content the consumer has chosen to view. When this scenario becomes a reality, the rules for programming advertiser-supported media will have to be rewritten.

RECENT DEVELOPMENTS IN ADVERTISING

Like the electronic media themselves, the advertising marketplace is constantly evolving. There are two broad categories of developments that deserve comment: the growth of advertising worldwide, and the challenges and opportunities posed by newer communication technologies.

Advertising Worldwide

We have looked in considerable detail at advertising in the United States. It is, today, a relatively large and stable marketplace with a dollar volume of activity closely tied to the overall health of the economy. The same is true of other mature industrialized nations, especially those of Western Europe. But in the last few years, more countries have adopted advertising as a means to support and profit from electronic media. While the United States is by far the biggest advertising marketplace, accounting for some $150 billion, or almost half of all advertising expenditures worldwide, other parts of the world are developing rapidly. China, for example, has just overtaken Germany as the third largest advertising market (see Table 2.4). In fact, some project that Asia will overtake Western Europe as the second largest advertising region in the world. Similarly, advertising expenditures in Brazil, India, Russia, South Africa and Indonesia are growing at a much more rapid rate than those of Europe and North America.

Across all 44 markets summarized in Table 2.4, television is the single biggest advertising medium, accounting for over 45% of expenditures. Print media account for the second largest share (38%), but that market is shrinking. Worldwide, the fastest growing medium is the Internet. Of course, with more and more money riding on electronic media, efforts to accurately measure audiences have grown as well.

New Communication Technologies

At a time when more people seek access to media audiences, a range of newer communication technologies present new challenges. As we noted previously, the average U.S. television household receives over 100 chan-

TABLE 2.4
Global Advertising Expenditures

Country	Advertising Expenditures* (in Millions of U.S. Dollars)		
	2000	2002	2004 est
USA	$149,954	$141,325	$154,610
Japan	37,207	34,759	36,889
China	11,837	17,194	22,715
Germany	20,133	18,429	19,160
United Kingdom	13,819	13,390	14,262
44 Market Total**	307,185	298,846	331,437

Note. Data are from Spheres of Influence: Advertising Expenditure Trends Report (January, 2004) Initiative Futures Worldwide.

*Includes expenditures on TV, Radio, Newspapers, Magazines, Cinema, Outdoor and Internet.

**Markets include; Arabia, Argentina, Australia, Austria, Belgium, Brazil, Canada, Chile, China, Colombia, Czech Republic, Denmark, Estonia, Finland, France, Germany, Greece, Hungary, India, Indonesia, Ireland, Israel, Italy, Japan, Latvia, Lebanon, Lithuania, Mexico, Netherlands, New Zealand, Peru, Poland, Portugal, Russia, Singapore, South Africa, Spain, Sweden, Switzerland, Taiwan, Thailand, UK, Uruguay and USA.

nels of programming. With remote control devices, viewers can skip commercials by changing channels, perhaps even choosing noncommercial pay services. More disconcerting from the advertiser's perspective are digital video recorder (DVRs), like TiVo, that allow viewers to pre-record programs with advertising, then skip the commercials altogether. Of course, some segments of the audience may avoid the clutter of ads on radio and television by opting for interactive media like video games. Taken together, these technologies empower viewers in a way that seems to threaten the entire system of advertiser-supported media.

As a result, advertisers are exploring alternate strategies to bring their messages to the public's attention. One tried-and-true technique that has received renewed interest is *product placement*, a strategy that has been used for some time in the film industry. If people won't watch a commercial for some product, then place the product in the program itself. You may remember the movie *E.T.: The Extraterrestrial*, in which E.T. was lured by Reese's Pieces. More recently, the judges on *American Idol* could be seen sipping cups of Coca-Cola. Hundreds of millions of dollars are now spent on product placement in television, and it's expected the practice will soon exceed $1 billion in the United States alone.

In a similar vein, advertisers are being more deliberate about placing logos and slogans in sporting events. Billboards in a baseball outfield, or surrounding a soccer pitch, can produce valuable exposures. In fact, chroma-key technology can create "virtual billboards" that only exist in the televised images of a game. NASCAR seems to have sold every available square inch on drivers' cars and uniforms. Messages woven into the fabric of a program or event are difficult for viewers to miss. And ratings companies, like Nielsen Media Research, now offer services that estimate the size and composition of the audience that is actually exposed to those images.

Marketers are also exploring less traditional advertising options. Although European movie theaters have shown ads for some time, this practice has met resistance in the United States. But the captive movie audience is proving hard for advertisers to resist, and cinema advertising is one of the most rapidly growing ad venues in North America. Advertisers can buy spots in the short program before a feature film, and show either the same commercials they use for television, or new ones produced specifically for the film-going audience. A newly formed trade association, the Cinema Advertising Council (CAC), performs the same kind of promotion and lobbying tasks as its electronic media counterparts: the Television Bureau of Advertising (TvB), the Cable Advertising Bureau (CAB), the Radio Advertising Bureau (RAB), the Interactive Advertising Bureau (IAB), and the Syndicated Network Television Association (SNTA). Nielsen Media Research, partnering with cinema advertising sales organizations, has launched a new service to measure theater audiences. This service provides the viewing data that allows cinema sales reps to compete with broadcasting and the World Wide Web for a share of the advertising market.

Advertisers are also testing the effectiveness of commercials in video games. This gives them better access to young men, who are a desirable, and often hard to reach, segment of the market. Initial research indicates that gamers actually like the presence of ads and identifiable products in their games, because they enhance the realism of the gaming environment. As you might expect, Nielsen has recently announced its plans to measure the audiences for this new advertising venue.

RESEARCH QUESTIONS

Obviously, the buying and selling of audiences happens in a number of different places and involves people with different motivations and levels of sophistication. There are, nonetheless, a handful of recurring research questions that transcend these differences. By distilling these from the previous discussion we can see more clearly how ratings data are used in the context of advertising. The four basic questions users ask of the ratings data concern the size and composition of the audience and the cost to reach potential customers.

How Many People Are in the Audience?

More than any single factor, the size of the media audience determines its value to advertisers and, in turn, its value to the media. There are a number of different ways to express audience size. We'll discuss the most common of these now, and leave more technical definitions until the last part of the book.

Ratings are the most frequently used descriptors of audience size. Indeed, this term is so widely recognized that we chose to use the term in the title of this book. A rating is the percentage of households or people tuned to a particular station. Figure 2.1 shows the simplest version of a ratings calculation and other standard expressions of audience size.

Two characteristics of a rating should be noted. First, the population figure on which the rating is based is the total *potential audience* for the program or station. For local stations, that is usually the market's population equipped with radios or television sets. For all intents and purposes, that's the entire population. It does not matter whether those sets are in use or not; the population estimate is the same for all ratings calculations. In this context, it means that the denominator of the ratings term does not vary from station to station, or program to program, or time period to time period. To say a TV program had a rating of 20, then, means that 20% of the entire population in the market tuned to the show. Second, populations can be composed of different building blocks, or *units of analysis*. Television households, for example, form a common

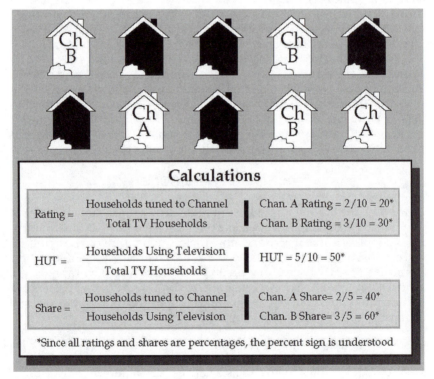

FIG. 2.1. Simple rating and share calculations.

population of interest. In this case, one rating point means one percent of the homes equipped with television in the given market area. In radio, television, and the Internet, we also describe populations of people. Here, we might talk about a station's ratings among men or women of a certain age. As you could tell from our discussion of network dayparts, a program could have a relatively high rating among women and a small rating among men (e.g., daytime).

Another way to describe the size of the audience is to express it in absolute terms, the projected total size of the audience. Local radio audiences are usually counted in the hundreds of people. Television audiences are numbered in the thousands at the local level, and in the tens of thousands or millions at the network level. In some ways, absolute estimates of audience size are more interpretable. To know that a local station had a rating of 25, for example, gives you little idea how many human beings were actually in the audience unless you know the size of the market. It's quite possible, therefore, that a 25 rating in one market means a smaller audience than a 15 rating in a larger market.

Ratings and absolute numbers are just different expressions of the same measurement—audience size. They are derived from the same data. Further, they are only estimates, not values we know to be perfectly accurate. In fact, much time and effort goes into collecting data on which reliable estimates can be based.

In addition to ratings, it is frequently useful to summarize the total number of people using the medium at any point in time. When households are the units of analysis, this summary is called *households using television*, or *HUT level* for short. Figure 2.1 illustrates how this measure is calculated. As you will note, HUT levels are typically expressed as a percentage of the population. As with ratings, though, it's possible to express them in absolute terms. If individuals are being counted, *persons using television*, or PUT, is the appropriate term. In radio, the analogous term is *persons using radio* (PUR).

Not everyone uses television or listens to radio at the same time, so HUT levels vary throughout the day. In fact, they change in a very predictable way, hour to hour, and week to week. Because of this, many audience analysts prefer to see the audience expressed as a percentage of the HUT level, rather than the total population. It's as if they were saying, "I can't affect the size of the total audience in any given time period, so just tell me how I did relative to the competition." The measure that expresses this is called an audience *share*. Figure 2.1 summarizes the share of audience calculation. It is quite possible for a program to have a large share and a small rating. This happens when popular programs air at times when few people are watching television. In fact, unless everyone is using the medium at the same time, a program's share will always be larger than its rating. It should also be apparent that shares, by themselves, give you no indication of the absolute size of an audience. As explained in chapter 10, buyers and sellers use shares and HUTs (or PUTs) to estimate predicted ratings.

Advertisers typically run a series of ads over a period of days or weeks. In some ways, then, the audience for a single commercial is less important than total audience exposure over the entire campaign. To provide some assessment of total exposure, ratings for each individual commercial can be summed across the campaign. This grand total is referred to as *gross ratings points*, or GRPs. The term is used quite commonly in advertising, and almost nowhere else.

GRPs provide a crude measure of audience exposure to commercials over the course of a media campaign. Advertisers use them before a buy to estimate the total audience they want to reach, and they calculate actual GRPs after the campaign to determine whether it was successful. The avail request described earlier usually features a statement about the number of GRPs the buyer wants to accumulate.

As useful as GRPs can be for planning and evaluating advertising efforts, the statistic masks some every important features of audience behavior. Rather like counting hits on a Web site, 100 GRPs could mean that 100% of the audience has seen a commercial just one time. However, it could also mean that one percent of the audience has seen the ad 100 times. Without further analysis, it is difficult to know what's happening.

How Often Do the Same People Show up in the Audience?

To determine the audience behavior underlying GRPs, we need information on how each individual uses a medium over time. For example, we might want to know whether two programs with equal ratings were seen by the same or two entirely different groups of people. This is a question of *audience duplication*. Fortunately, the same data that allow us to estimate gross measures of audience size like ratings, shares, and GRPs, also allow us to assess cumulative measures like audience duplication.

Advertisers are, understandably, interested in how many different people see their message, and how often they see it. These concerns are addressed by measures of reach and frequency, respectively. The *reach* of a commercial is defined by the total number of unduplicated individuals who are exposed to the ad—everyone who saw it at least once. It is often expressed as a percentage of the total possible audience, just like a rating. In fact, there is a special kind of rating called a *cumulative rating*, or *cume*, that measures the unduplicated audience for a station. In either case, the statistic represents the total number of different individuals who appear in the audience over some specified period of time. Internet measurement services report a similar number called *unique visitors* to various Web sites.

Certain media are better at achieving large cumulative audiences than others. Prime time network television, for example, produces considerable reach for a commercial message, since its audiences tend to be quite large. Further, many people only watch TV during prime time and, therefore, are reachable only in that daypart. As a result, advertisers are often willing to pay a premium for prime time spots. Cable networks, on the other hand, are limited by the penetration of cable systems, and so cannot hope to achieve penetration levels much in excess of 80%.

The second factor of interest is the *frequency* of exposure. The question here is how many times on average did an audience actually see or hear the message? Measures of frequency provide the answer. Usually, information on the frequency of exposure is expressed as an average (e.g., "The average frequency was 2.8"). Of course, no one actually sees an ad 2.8 times, so it may be more useful for the advertiser to consider the full distribution on which the average is based. For example, if the advertiser believes that a person must see an ad three times before it's effective, then he or she might want to know how many people saw the ad three or more times.

As with reach, different media are better or worse at achieving a desired frequency. If, for example, you wanted to market a product to Spanish-speaking audiences, buying time on a Hispanic station might produce relatively low reach, but relatively high frequency. Similarly, radio can be an effective medium for achieving a high frequency of exposure, since the audiences for many stations tend to be loyal to station formats.

Reach and frequency bear a strict arithmetic relationship to GRPs. Specifically, reach multiplied by average frequency will equal gross rating points. If you know any two elements in this simple equation, you can derive the third. Unfortunately, advertisers usually know only GRPs, since only ratings are easily obtained from published reports. However, a number of agencies and audience researchers have developed mathematical models that estimate reach and frequency given GRPs alone. These and other techniques of modeling audience behavior are discussed in the last chapter.

Who Are the Audience Members?

Throughout this section we have referenced the need for different advertisers to reach different kinds of audiences. If the size of the audience is the most important determinant of its value, the composition of the audience is not far behind. In fact, advertisers are increasingly interested in presenting their messages to specific subsets of the mass audience, a strategy called *market segmentation*. This strategy plays a very important role in advertising and, in turn, has a major impact on the form that ratings data take.

Audiences are segmented according to the traits of viewers or listeners. Researchers call these characteristics *variables*. Almost any attribute can become a variable, as long as it's reasonably well defined. In practice, viewer or listener attributes are usually grouped into one of four categories.

Demographic variables are the most commonly reported in ratings data. By convention, we include in this category such attributes as race, age, gender, income, education, marital status, and occupation. Of these, age and gender are the most frequently reported audience characteristics, and the standard reporting categories featured in ratings books. So, for example, advertisers and broadcasters will often buy and sell "women 18 to 49," "men 18 to 34," and so on. Most buying and selling of audiences is done on the basis of demographic variables.

Demographics have much to recommend them as segmentation variables. For one thing, everyone in the industry is used to working with them. When you talk about an audience of women or 18- to 34-year-olds, everybody knows exactly what you're talking about. On the other hand, there may be important differences between two women of the same age, differences that are potentially important to an advertiser. Therefore, additional methods of segmentation are used.

Geographic variables offer another common way to describe the audience. We have already encountered one of the most important, designated market areas or DMAs. Just as people differ from one another with respect to their age and gender, so too, they differ in terms of where they live. Every TV viewer or radio listener in the country can be assigned to one particular market area. Obviously, such distinctions would be important to an advertiser whose goods or services have distinct regional appeal.

Other geographic variables that are commonly used in ratings research are county and state of residence (including breakouts by county size), and region of the country. Tracking a person's zip code is one popular tool of geographic segmentation. With such finely drawn areas, it is often possible to make inferences about a person's income, lifestyle, and station in life. These zip-code-based techniques of segmentation are commonly referred to as *geo-demographics*.

Behavioral variables draw distinctions among people on the basis of their behaviors. The most obvious kind of behavior to track is media use. We need to know who watched a particular program before we can estimate the size of its audience. With this kind of information, it is possible to describe an audience not only in terms of age and gender, but also in terms of what else they watched or listened to. Such audience breakouts, however, are only occasionally provided by the ratings service.

The other behavioral variables that weigh heavily in an advertiser's mind are product purchase variables. Because most advertisers want to reach the audience that is most likely to buy their product, what better way to describe an audience than by purchase behaviors? For example, we could characterize an audience by percentage of heavy beer drinkers, or the average amount of laundry soap purchased. One ratings company has called such segmentation variables *buyer-graphics*. As you might imagine, advertisers like this approach to audience segmentation.

Several research companies combine media usage data with other types of variables. Simmons, MRI, Scarborough, and International Demographics offer data on socioeconomic status and lifestyles. This information is particularly useful to marketers targeting potential customers who fit narrower definitions than specific age and gender. Figure 2.2 is an example of the kind of data that can be generated from these studies. The data, from August and September of 2004, show that Houston listeners who planned to buy a new vehicle were more likely to tune to late news on KTRK and KPRC. While this kind of information can be extremely valuable to advertisers, access to it comes at a price. Only those organizations that pay subscription fees can use this data in their sales or buying efforts.

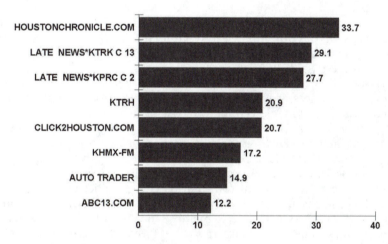

The Media Audit Ranker Report
ADULTS

Report Market:	HOUSTON, TX	CUME RATINGS
Report Period:	AUG-SEP 2004	
TARGET:	PLAN BUY--NEW CAR/VAN/TRUCK/SPORT UTILITY	

TOTAL AUDIENCE: 3,676,100   % IN TARGET AUDIENCE: 9.1%   TARGET AUDIENCE: 335,100

HOUSTONCHRONICLE.COM	33.7
LATE NEWS*KTRK C 13	29.1
LATE NEWS*KPRC C 2	27.7
KTRH	20.9
CLICK2HOUSTON.COM	20.7
KHMX-FM	17.2
AUTO TRADER	14.9
ABC13.COM	12.2

RANK	MEDIA	CUME PERSONS	CUME RATING
1	HOUSTONCHRONICLE.COM	112,900	33.7
2	LATE NEWS*KTRK C 13	97,400	29.1
3	LATE NEWS*KPRC C 2	92,900	27.7
4	KTRH	69,900	20.9
5	CLICK2HOUSTON.COM	69,400	20.7
6	KHMX-FM	57,700	17.2
7	AUTO TRADER	50,000	14.9
8	ABC13.COM	41,000	12.2

[RADIO = 7-DAY CUME] [DAILY NEWSPAPER = 5-DAY CUME] [OTHER PRINT MEDIA = 4-EDITION CUME] [TV NEWS = 7-DAY CUME] [WEB SITE = PAST 30 DAYS]

BASED ON 95 TOTAL RESPONDENTS OUT OF THE TOTAL SAMPLE OF 1,040 ADULTS AGE 18+

Information is Subject to All Limitations and Restrictions as Stated in the original Survey.
THE MEDIA AUDIT PROGRAM & REPORT COPYRIGHT 2004 BY INTERNATIONAL DEMOGRAPHICS INC.
10333 RICHMOND AVE. SUITE 200 - HOUSTON, TX 77042 713/626-0333 [2.12]
HOU204IN

FIG. 2.2. The media audit ranker report. Reprinted by permission of International Demographics, Inc.

Psychographics draw distinctions among people on the basis of their psychological characteristics. While definitions of what belongs in this broad and amorphous category vary, they typically include things like people's values, attitudes, opinions, motivations, and preferences. One type of psychographic variable that has attracted attention recently is variously labeled *viewer loyalty, involvement,* and/or *engagement.* The idea here is that, as new technologies empower audience members with ever more choices, it's increasingly important for advertisers to know which people are particularly committed to which media products. Some evidence suggests that those who are very engaged with a program (e.g., its fans) are more attentive to the ads contained within. Although such traits can, in principle, be very valuable in describing an audience, psychographic variables are often difficult to define and measure precisely.

How Much Does it Cost to Reach the Audience?

Advertisers and the media, as well as middlemen like ad agencies and station reps, all have an interest in what it costs to reach the audience. Those on the selling side of the business try to maximize their revenues, whereas buyers try to minimize their expenses.

Although it is true that broadcasters and other forms of electronic media sell audiences, it would be an oversimplification to suggest that audience factors alone determine the cost of a commercial spot. Certainly, audience size and composition are the principal determinants, but several factors have an impact. Advertisers pay a premium, for example, to have their message placed first in a set of advertisements (a *commercial pod*). We have already pointed out that advertisers who buy network time early in the upfront market can get a better price. Similarly, advertisers who agree to buy large blocks of time can usually get some sort of quantity discount. Remember that these transactions happen in a marketplace environment. The relative strengths and weaknesses of each party, their negotiating skills, and, ultimately, the laws of supply and demand all affect the final cost of time.

These factors are represented in the rates that the media charge for commercial spots. It is common practice for an individual station to summarize these in a *rate card,* which is usually a table or chart that states the price of spots in different dayparts or programs. The rate card is a planning guide, but the actual rates are subject to negotiation. Although the estimated cost of a commercial spot is important to know, from the buyer's perspective, it is largely uninterpretable without associated audience information. The question the buyer must answer is, "What am I getting for the money?" This cannot be answered without comparing audience ratings to the rates that are being charged.

There are two common ways to make such comparisons. One technique is to calculate the *cost per thousand* (CPM) for a given spot (the "M" in this expression is the Roman numeral for 1,000). To determine CPM, you take the cost of commercial time and divide it by the size of the commercial audience, expressed in thousands. CPMs can be produced for households, for women ages 18 to 49, or for whatever kind of audience is most relevant to the advertiser. The calculation provides a yardstick with which to measure the efficiency of buying time on different stations or networks. The second method of comparison is to calculate a *cost per point* (CPP). Like CPM, this calculation requires dividing the cost of time by a measurement of the audience—in this case, rating points. Because ratings are not based on the same audience sizes across markets, the cost of a point will vary from market to market. A rating point in New York will be more expensive than a rating point in Indianapolis because it represents more people. CPPs are useful, however, because they are easy to relate to GRPs. If, for example, an ad campaign is to produce 200 GRPs, and the CPP is $1,000, then the campaign will cost $200,000.

This sort of arithmetic reveals the economics that drive the industry. It is also a common form of ratings analysis among the buyers and sellers of time. But the media are complex organizations that can and do use audience information in a variety of ways. Similarly, those who want to study or regulate mass communication have found that the data gathered for the benefit of advertisers can offer many insights into the power and potential of the electronic media. In the chapters that follow, we discuss many of these applications. First we turn to the use of audience data in programming.

RELATED READINGS

Albarran, A. (2001). *Management of electronic media* (2nd ed.). Belmont, CA: Wadsworth.

Albarran, A. (2004, January 12). Sizing up the market. *Broadcasting and Cable, 21.*

Bogart, L. (1996). *Strategy in advertising: Matching media and messages to markets and motivations* (3rd ed.). Lincolnwood, IL: NTC Business Books.

Poltrack, D. F. (1983). *Television marketing: Network, local, cable.* New York: McGraw-Hill.

Sissors, J. Z., & Baron, R. B. (2002). *Advertising media planning* (6th ed.). Chicago: McGraw-Hill.

Turow, J. (1997). *Breaking up America: Advertisers and the new media world.* Chicago: University of Chicago Press.

Warner, C. (2003). *Selling media: Broadcast, cable, print and interactive* (3rd ed.). Ames, IA: Iowa State Press.

Chapter 3

Audience Research
in Programming

To give value to commercial time, the electronic media must attract audiences. Broadly speaking, that's the job of a programmer, who may be anyone from the president of a huge media conglomerate to someone working for a radio station in a small rural community. In the world of advertiser-supported media, the programmer effectively sets the "bait" that lures the audience. In order to do this, he or she must know a great deal about audiences. After sales and advertising, the most important application of audience data is in programming.

Programming involves a range of activities. A programmer must determine where to obtain the programming itself. Sometimes that means playing an active role in developing new program concepts and commissioning the production of pilots. For most TV stations it means securing the rights to syndicated programs, some of which have already been produced. In this capacity the programmer must be skillful in negotiating contracts and in predicting the kinds of material that will appeal to prospective audiences. Programmers are also responsible for deciding how and when that material will actually air on the station or network. Successful scheduling requires that a programmer know when different kinds of audiences are likely to be available, and how those audiences might decide among the options offered by competing media. Finally, a programmer must be adept at promoting the programs in a schedule. Sometimes that involves placing ads and promotional spots to alert the audience to a particular program or personality. It can also involve packaging an entire schedule of programs in order to create a special station or network "image." In all of these activities, ratings play an important role.

The way in which these programming functions take shape, and the priorities facing individual programmers, differ from one setting to the next. Occasionally, in small stations, the entire job of programming falls on the shoulders of one person. In larger operations, however, programming involves many people. Often the job of promoting programs and developing a certain image is turned over to specialized promotions departments, especially in an increasingly competitive media marketplace.

The most significant differences in how programmers function depend on the medium in which they work. In the early 1950s, television forced radio to adapt to a new marketplace. No longer would individual radio programs dominate the medium. Instead, radio stations began to specialize in certain kinds of music or in continuous program formats. The job of a radio programmer became one of crafting an entire program service. Further, the vast supply of music from the record industry meant that stations could be less reliant on networks to define that service. In contrast, television built audiences by attracting them to individual programs. Although some cable networks now emulate radio by offering a steady schedule of one program type (e.g., news, music, weather, financial and business information, or comedy), most television programmers still devote more attention to the acquisition, scheduling, and promotion of relatively distinct units of content.

In the case of broadcast network affiliates, most program development and acquisition is done at the network level. However, affiliated stations do program certain dayparts, such as news, early fringe, and late night. There are also some independent television stations that program the entire broadcast day. In order to explain how audience research is used in programming, we consider the specific programming practices of each form of electronic media.

RADIO PROGRAMMING

There are more than 10,000 commercial radio stations in the United States and another 2,000 noncommercial educational ones, each offering different—sometimes only slightly different—programming and each reaching unique audiences. Most radio stations, from the smallest to the largest markets, have a *format*. A format is an identifiable set of program presentations or style of programming. Some stations, particularly those in smaller markets with fewer competitors, may have wider ranging formats that try to include a little something for everyone. Most stations, however, zero in on a fairly specific brand of talk or music.

Radio formats are an important characteristic of this medium for two related reasons. First, radio tends to be very competitive. In any given market, there are far more radio stations than TV stations, daily newspapers, or almost any other local advertising medium. To avoid being lost in the shuffle, programmers use formats to make their station seem unique or special so it will stand out in the minds of listeners and induce them to tune in. This strategy is called *positioning* the station. Second, different formats are known to appeal to different kinds of listeners. Because most advertisers want to reach particular kinds of audiences, the ability to deliver on a certain demographic is important in selling the station's time.

Radio formats run the gamut from classical to country to contemporary hits, and stations choose names like "Smooth Jazz," "Big Band," "Classic Rock," and "Adult Contemporary" to identify their programming. Radio programmers, consultants, and analysts have fairly specific names for nearly 40 different formats. However, most of these are usually grouped in about 20 categories. The most common labels, along with their share of the total U.S. audience, are reported in Table 3.1. The remaining columns are index values indicating the strength of each format in various regions of the country. A value of 100 means the format is attracting the same share as the national average. An index of greater than 100 means this region spends more time than average with a particular format. For example, the South Central states have an index of 156 in the country music category, meaning that this format has a 56% greater appeal to listeners in the South Central states than it does nationwide.

There are different ways to program a radio station. Some stations do all of their own programming. They identify the specific songs they will play, and how often they will play them. They may also hire highly visible—and highly paid—disc jockeys, who can dominate the

TABLE 3.1

Radio Station Formats by Regions of the U.S.

	U.S.	NE	MA	ENC	WNC	SA	SC	Mt	Pac
News/Talk	16%	133	110	109	118	80	67	94	119
Adult Contemp	13	152	113	104	101	96	72	104	95
Country	13	67	55	107	153	116	156	112	62
Contemp Hit	10	119	122	79	79	97	107	94	97
Rock	9	116	101	109	146	85	97	124	83
Urban	7	25	112	121	58	161	146	7	27
Oldies Hits	7	99	97	116	115	98	80	107	103
Spanish	6	26	86	43	8	59	132	128	225
Religious	5	19	54	103	109	161	151	72	63
Alternative	4	148	101	92	95	83	76	169	110
Standards	3	177	110	99	83	100	69	126	91
New Age/Jazz	2	22	107	112	75	96	62	116	146
Classical	2	120	116	92	92	101	81	95	104

Note. Source: Arbitron Radio Today based on national database which includes about 13,900 stations for Spring 2003. First column is total U.S. by share of audience. It totals less than 100 because of stations with different formats. The remaining columns index for the regions of New England, North East, Mid-Atlantic, East North Central, West North Central, South Atlantic, South Central, Mountain, and Pacific. Reprinted by permission of Arbitron.

personality of the station during certain dayparts. This kind of customized programming is particularly common in major markets, and it is often accompanied by customized research. Not only do these stations buy and analyze published ratings reports, but they are also likely to make use of computerized access to a ratings database, and to engage in a variety of nonratings research projects. We discuss customized analyses of ratings data in chapter 8. The most typical nonratings research includes *focus groups*, which feature intensive discussions with small groups of listeners, and *call-out* research that involves playing a short excerpt of a song over the telephone to gauge listener reactions. Consultants also conduct customized research to investigate how radio audiences react to potentially offensive materials, to assess listener awareness of particular program services, to measure the impact of advertising (for example on bus cards, billboards, or TV spots), and to judge the popularity of particular personalities or features (news, traffic, weather, contests, etc.) on the station.

Many stations, however, depend on a syndicated program service or network to define their format. Sometimes, large group owners like Clear Channel, which owns more than 1,200 stations, provide programming to their stations on a regional or format basis. Some stations rely on prepackaged material for virtually everything they broadcast, except local advertising and announcements. To do this they subscribe to a program service, usually provided to the station by a satellite feed. Other stations do some of their own original programming during the most listened-to morning hours and use syndicated services during the remaining hours of the day.

Most radio stations don't worry about ratings research because the majority are located in small to very small communities. Arbitron defines and measures radio listening in more than 280 market areas, the smallest with a population of less than 80,000. Even at that, the company publishes audience estimates for only about one third of the nation's more than 12,000 radio stations. Of course, measured stations account for the vast majority of the industry's listening and probably 90% of its revenues.

We discuss the specific kinds of research questions that can be addressed with ratings data in the pages that follow. Other things being equal, programmers with access to ratings data are in a better position to know their audiences than those who have no ratings. They know, for example, that many of the popular ideas about radio use are untrue. Ratings show that the 6 a.m. to 10 a.m. daypart, long known as *morning drive* time, is when radio audiences are largest. However, the greatest percent of listeners in automobiles is during *afternoon drive*, from 4 p.m. to 6 p.m. And while midday, from 10 a.m. to 3 p.m., is often considered the best time to reach women working in the home, ratings indicate that in most markets just about as many men are listening to the radio as women. Further, there are often almost as many car listeners during midday as either morning or afternoon drive time. The average adult spends about 20 hours a week, nearly 3 hours per day, listening to radio. Contrary to popular belief, teens are not the heaviest users of radio—they listen less than any other demographic group. But teens do comprise the largest part of the audience after 7 p.m. All of these audience profiles may vary from market to market, but the only way to know is by consulting a ratings report.

Noncommercial radio outlets also use quantitative audience estimates. National Public Radio (NPR) stations, for example, receive ratings, even though they are not listed in the ratings book alongside their commercial counterparts. In some markets they are even among the highest rated local stations. While audience data are not used in quite the same way, they may be important for fund-raising. Many of the larger stations have the functional equivalent of a sales department that regularly uses audience estimates to attract underwriting. Ratings are also used by programmers to make many of the same decisions a commercial station does about program popularity, scheduling, and promotion.

Completed Arbitron diaries can be an important source of information for radio programmers. Each page of a diary is scanned into a computer and can be sorted by various categories. This makes it possible for a programmer or a consultant hired by the station to check, for example, whether people are remembering call letters or station slogans correctly. They can also read comments respondents write on the diary that are not part of the regular reporting process.

With the addition of satellite radio, the measurement and analysis of radio audiences became more complicated. Although XM and Sirius do not yet provide appreciable competition in any single radio market, some industry experts think satellite radio will impact the industry the way FM affected AM or the way cable affected broadcast television. Carmakers are beginning to install satellite receivers as standard or optional equipment, and the recent acquisition of several important radio personalities, including Howard Stern and NPR's Bob Edwards, along with the ability to provide local market traffic and weather information, could lead to large subscription increases over the next few years. While the service is still relatively small—less than 4 million subscribers in early 2005 compared to nearly 20 million weekly Internet radio listeners and 280 million who sample broadcast radio each week—analysts expect the patterns to change dramatically.

TELEVISION PROGRAMMING

Broadcast

At the other end of the spectrum is the business of programming a major television network. Although television programmers share some of the same concerns as radio programmers, they are confronted with a number of different tasks. One important difference is the extent to which a network programmer is involved in the creation of new programs. Ratings data are certainly valuable for this task, but program development relies especially on talents for anticipating popular trends and tastes, and setting in motion productions that will cater to those tastes. Network programmers who have that talent, like Fred Silverman, the late Brandon Tartikoff, or more recently Jeffery Zucker and Kevin Reilly of NBC, Les Moonves and Nina Tassler of CBS, Stephen McPherson of ABC or Gail Berman of Fox are as well known in the business as any on-screen celebrity.

Programmers at local television stations spend less time on the actual production of new programs, and more time on purchasing them in the syndication market. There are several different kinds of syndicated products available, and more enter the pipeline every season. *Off-network* syndicated programs are those that originally aired on a broadcast network and are now available to individual stations. In general, they are among the most desirable of all syndicated programming from the standpoint of ratings potential. In 2004, for example, the highest rated syndicated programs included *Everybody Loves Raymond*, *Seinfeld*, and *Friends*.

Off-network programs work well in syndication for a number of reasons. They typically have high production values—something that viewers brought up on network fare have come to expect. They also have a track record of drawing audiences, which can be reassuring for the prospective buyer. In fact, only network series that have been on-air for at least 4 or 5 years usually make it to syndication. One reason for this is that local programmers schedule reruns as strips, airing different episodes Monday through Friday at the same time of day. To sustain stripped programming over several months, they must own a good number of programs. In general, this means that there must be 100 episodes before a series is viable in syndication; only the most popular network shows stay on the air that long.

Once they reach syndication, however, off-network programs can continue to attract new audiences for decades. *M*A*S*H*, for example, was enormously successful on CBS, and while there have been no new episodes in more than a quarter of a century, the program is still successful in syndication—not only on broadcast stations, but on network cable as well. Newer off-network programs, some available even before their original run ends, get the most desirable time slots, while older series get displaced to less desirable times. Nevertheless, with so many stations and so many hours to fill, even the older programs, especially those that were very popular or have semi-cult status, still seem to find an audience. The durability of off-network series means they have an extensive ratings history, which is especially useful in programming. Prospective buyers can compile detailed information from many different markets, analyzing the relative success of one program versus another, or the flow of audience from one program to and from another.

During the late 1990s and early 2000s, networks started to rely on *reality programs* like *Survivor* and *Fear Factor* to draw mass audiences. These unscripted shows affected the syndication market by decreasing the number of off-network series that could draw audiences in syndication. Unlike scripted comedies and dramas, reality programs do not attract large audiences when they are repeated. After all, the fun of reality programs is to find out who "wins." Once that is known, audiences lose interest in viewing the series.

Syndication has also been affected by the trend toward vertical and horizontal integration in the media industries. A single owner can now have substantial financial interest in the production of programs, their distribution through syndication, and the stations or cable networks to which they can be sold. In the case of broadcast syndication, this means that first priority will usually be given to the co-owned stations. In turn, these stations will usually comply with the seller's scheduling requirements. This situation presents a challenge for stations that have to find new sources of programming, and for independent syndicators who have to fight for fewer available time slots.

In recent years, cable has become a significant player in the syndication market. Some cable networks, such as TVLand, depend almost exclusively on reruns of old programs. Others complement their schedule of new programs and films with vintage series that are likely to appeal to specific target audiences. Mystery fans can watch *Perry Mason* on the Hallmark Channel or *Murder, She Wrote* on A&E. *Saturday Night Live* fans can watch reruns on Comedy Central, and science fiction fans can watch the earliest episodes of *The Twilight Zone* on the Sci Fi channel. An *off-cable* syndication market has also emerged, most recently with *Sex and the City* finding a place on TBS.

The demand for quality off-network product has exceeded the supply. One result, aside from rising prices, is an increase in the number of programs being produced specifically for the syndication marketplace—or *first-run* syndication. Traditionally, first-run syndication has included both game shows and talk shows—program types that cost relatively little to produce. Inexpensive or not, shows like *Wheel of Fortune* and the *Oprah Winfrey Show* have been highly successful in the ratings. The market for first-run programming has been greatly aided in the past few years by instantaneous and relatively inexpensive satellite distribution. This allows syndicators to insert advertising spots and function like mini-networks. The technology has also led to the production of new made-for-syndication programs with "newsier" formats like *Entertainment Tonight, Inside Story*, and *Access Hollywood*.

There are other sources of programming, like movie packages or regional networks, but whatever their origin, the acquisition of syndicated programming is one of the toughest challenges a TV programmer has to face. Usually the deal involves making a long-term contractual agreement with the distributor, or whoever holds the copyright to the material. For a popular program, that can mean a major commitment of resources. A mistake can cost an organization millions of dollars, and the programmer a job.

Buying and selling syndicated programming is often accompanied by an extensive use of ratings data. Distributors use the ratings to promote their product, demonstrating how well it has done in different markets. These data are often prominently featured in trade magazine advertisements. Buyers use the same sort of data to determine how well a show might do in their market, comparing the cost of acquisition to potential revenues. This is discussed in greater detail in chapter 4.

Once a network or a station commits to program production or acquisition, television programmers at all levels have more or less the same responsibility. Their programs must be placed in the schedule so as to achieve their greatest economic return. Usually that means trying to maximize each program's audience, taking into consideration the competition each show faces in the market. For affiliates, the job of program scheduling is less extensive than for others, simply because their network assumes the burden for much of the broadcast day. Even affiliates, though, devote considerable attention to programming before, during, and just after the early local news. The prime access daypart, just before network prime time, is usually the most lucrative for an affiliate. Audience levels rise through the evening and the station need not share the available commercial spots with its network.

In television, as in radio, program production companies, network executives, and stations use a variety of nonratings research to sharpen their programming decisions. This may include the use of one or more measures of program or personality popularity. Marketing Evaluations, for example, produces a syndicated research service called TVQ that provides reports on the extent to which the public recognizes and likes different personalities and programs. Scores like these can be used by programmers when they make scheduling decisions. Knowing the appeal of particular personalities might tell them, for example, whether a talk show host would fare well against the competition in a fringe daypart.

Other program-related research includes theater testing, which involves showing a large group a pilot and recording their professed enjoyment with voting devices of some sort. All networks and most program producers use some type of testing research in the program production process. The largest program testing facility is in Las Vegas. Strange as it may seem, researchers recruit audiences—between the swimming pool and the lobby—of a large hotel. Pilots, commercials, and other program material are shown while respondents, seated at a computer, record data about themselves and give periodic reactions to the material being shown. This method, which identifies individual and cumulative responses to program elements, traces its origins back to the original Stanton–Lazarsfeld Program Analyzer of the late 1930s. Program executives can see this information almost instantly on their office computers in Los Angeles, New York, or anywhere. Ultimately, however, ratings are a programmer's most important evaluative tool. As one network executive said, "Strictly from the network's point of view a good soap opera is one that has a high rating and share, a bad one is one that doesn't" (Converse, 1974).

Cable

As we implied previously, programming for some cable networks is similar to radio, and for others it is more like over-the-air television. Cable networks like WGN and TBS, for example, began as local stations and became national *super stations* by distributing their service via satellite. These and others like them often include a variety of programs in their lineups, much like television stations. The major difference between cable and local television though is that cable programmers seek more narrowly targeted audiences than do television broadcasters. Lifetime and Oxygen are programmed for women; ESPN and Spike for men; and the Cartoon Network and Nickelodeon for children. Some cable services concentrate on one type of content, such as news, talk, travel, cooking, and weather. You'll often find, however, that even specialized services use some variety of formats to broaden their audience. For example, virtually all have tried different forms of documentary programming as part of their schedule. Even the Westerns Channel offers documentaries about Western stars and directors, and The Weather Channel presents *Storm Stories* nightly.

Although heuristic devices can oversimplify complex processes, they can be useful in identifying underlying concepts. Programming strategies, for example, can be visualized on a continuum from traditional broadcast scheduling to newer forms of cable or narrowcasting. While programming patterns for each service have remained relatively distinct throughout most of television's history, some programmers are now testing alternative approaches. Broadcasters, for example, are using programming models that originated on public television or cable, such as repeating popular programs within the same week. Some original network programs are repeated on cable channels, usually co-owned networks, soon after their first run. To further complicate the situation, the growing ability of viewers to build their own schedules with various recording and on-demand technologies is likely to change the role of the programmer altogether.

Although services like HBO and Showtime do not need audience estimates to sell advertising, pay cable ratings are still a valuable commodity. High ratings generate interest from media critics, analysts of pop culture, journalists and potential subscribers. When pay cable series like *The Sopranos* earn higher ratings than broadcast competitors, they attract the attention of Hollywood and Wall Street. Successful production efforts generate revenue for re-investment into new programming, such as HBO's $100 million production of *Band of Brothers* and the company's $60 million investment in *Angels in America*. As these channels gain popularity and take ratings away from commercial networks, broadcasters complain that the playing field is uneven. Due to differences in regulation and societal expectations, cable is able to address themes that are banned from over-the-air television.

Pay cable's business model depends on recruiting at least one subscriber in a household and convincing them to renew their subscription year after year. About 5% of premium subscribers cancel in any given year, so the cable sales department must continually replace lost revenue at the same time they sign on new subscribers. Programmers maintain the quality of the schedule by offering theatrical movies, often before anyone else has the rights. They are able to secure this early *window* by making long-term deals with various studios. They also use promotional campaigns to create demand for, and buzz about, the channel's original programming. HBO's recent dominance of the Emmy Awards certainly proves how well they have succeeded on this front.

THE INTERNET

As we saw in the previous chapter, the World Wide Web is creating opportunities for advertisers to reach audiences. This means that the content of Web pages is becoming increasingly important. "Programming" on the Web can mean anything from the simplest personal Web page to the most sophisticated corporate sites, to actual multimedia programs that viewers watch on their computer screens. For many radio stations it simply means making the station available to a much wider audience. For some networks and producers it means offering complete programs in streaming video. Many PBS documentaries, for example, are now online for anyone who missed them at the time they were first broadcast. Just like the more traditional electronic media, content must be planned to attract Internet audiences in the first place and to hold their attention. The industry has even developed a kind of syndication market for Web content. Research suggests that Internet users build a set of favorite Web resources, just as radio listeners and cable television viewers develop a set of favorite channels that they watch repeatedly.

There are a few major differences, though. Content on the Web can be personalized in a way that was never before possible. If users allow cookies to be stored on their computers, a programmer could theoretically serve very individualized messages—a capability that interests Web advertisers. There is also an immediate feedback mechanism with the Internet that doesn't exist in radio and television. Through e-mail, Internet users can communicate directly with the programmer.

The relationship between the more traditional electronic media and the World Wide Web is still in its earliest stages of development. Broadcast networks and stations maintain Web sites that offer additional services to the viewers they already reach over the air, and to new "viewers" who

make initial contact via the Web. They often provide advertising availabilities on these sites to enhance the value of broadcast advertising. Networks have experimented with showing trailers for films on their Web
sites, an option that media buyers for the studios find attractive.

Established media seem increasingly interested in partnering with
Web sites and search engines to exploit cross-promotional opportunities. But they are also facing competition from Web sites for advertising
revenue. In late 2004, Arbitron and comScore Media Metrix joined
forces to launch a ratings service for online radio, one of the fastest
growing programming options on the Internet. Borrell Associates pre-
dicts that advertising on online radio sites will reach 300 million by
2009, and that the growth in audience is likely to come from traditional
over-the-air broadcasters.

In whatever way the Internet evolves, and whatever connections
form between old media and new, the need for audience information is
certain. Programmers need ratings-type data to track the most popular
sites and determine the services most valued by particular audiences.

RESEARCH QUESTIONS

Many of the research questions that a programmer tries to answer with
ratings data are, at least superficially, no different than those asked by a
person in sales and advertising: How many people are in the audience?
Who are they? How often do the same people show up in the audience?
This convergence of research questions is hardly surprising because the
purpose of programming commercial media is, with some exceptions,
to attract audiences that will be sold to advertisers. The programmer's
intent in asking these questions, however, is often very different. Programmers are less likely to see the audience as some abstract commodity, and more likely to view ratings as a window on what "their"
audiences are doing. They need to understand not only the absolute size
of a program audience, but why they are attracting particular audiences and what could be done to improve program performance.

Did I Attract the Intended Audience?

Because drawing an audience is the objective of a programmer, the most
obvious use of ratings is to determine whether the objective has been
achieved. In doing so, it is important to have a clear concept of the intended, or target, audience. Although any programmer would prefer an
audience that is larger to one that is smaller, the often quoted goal of
"maximizing the audience" is usually an inadequate expression of a
programmer's objectives. More realistically, the goal is maximizing the
size of the audience within certain constraints or parameters. The most
important constraint has to do with the size of the available audience.
That is one reason why programmers are particularly alert to audience

shares. Increasingly, however, it is not the programmer's intention to draw even a majority of the available audience. In other words, the programmer's success or failure is best judged against the programming strategy being employed.

Radio programmers, and increasingly those at cable networks, are largely concerned with cultivating well-defined target audiences. An experienced radio programmer can fine-tune a station's demographics with remarkable accuracy. Much of this has to do with the predictable appeal that a certain kind of music, and talk, has for listeners of different ages and gender. Table 3.2 lists some of the more common station formats and percent of their total audiences in different age categories. Obviously, you cannot expect to attract many young people with Oldies music, or many older listeners with Alternative music. In chapter 10 we discuss how to depict these sorts of audience characteristics on a *demographic map* of stations that some programmers find quite useful.

TV programmers, like their counterparts in radio, may devote their entire program service to attracting a particular demographic. But they would usually also like to broaden their appeal and reach without driving away their loyal viewers. This is most evident in some of the newer, and most specialized, cable networks that have emerged in the last 15 years. As noted, many cable services, like MTV or Nickelodeon, have been programmed to draw certain age groups that their owners believe will be attractive to advertisers. These services are not catering to everyone.

Even those conventional television stations that offer a variety of program types must gauge the size and composition of program audiences against the programming strategies they employ. One common programming strategy is called *counter-programming*. This occurs when a station or network schedules a program that has a markedly different appeal than the programs offered by its major competitors. For example, independents tend to show light entertainment (e.g., situation comedies) when the affiliates in the market are broadcasting their local news. The independents are not trying to appeal to the typical, often older, news viewer, and their ratings should be evaluated accordingly. Programmers may try counter-programming stunts to attract viewers who are not interested in the special events covered by other stations in the market. One station in Chicago, for example, broadcast a lineup of romantic dramas that it called "The Marriage Bowl" to compete with the college football games on New Year's day. Remember that counter-programming does not necessarily mean using weaker programming opposite the popular programs. It means offering a different combination of appeals. In 2004–05, for example, CBS finally toppled NBC from 17 years of winning Thursday night by putting its most popular programming—*Survivor* and *CSI*—opposite a *Friends* spin-off and the aging *ER*.

One way to increase the likelihood of attracting the intended audience is through the use of promotional spots. Ratings data can be very useful in identifying programs with similar demographic profiles so that pro-

TABLE 3.2
Radio Station Formats by Age and Gender

	12–17	18–24	25–34	35–44	45–49	50–54	55–64	65+	Men	Women
CHR	27%	27%	24%	14%	4%	2%	2%	1%	43%	57%
Alt	13	22	29	21	8	4	2	1	64	36
Urban	14	18	21	21	8	7	7	4	44	56
Rock	6	15	25	32	12	6	3	1	72	28
AC	5	10	20	25	12	10	11	8	36	64
Country	5	9	15	20	10	9	16	16	47	53
Oldies	3	6	11	21	16	16	19	9	50	50
NA/Jazz	2	3	10	21	14	15	19	17	48	52
Class	1	2	7	11	8	11	22	38	47	52
Stand	1	3	5	8	6	7	18	52	46	54
Span	6	17	29	22	7	6	7	7	51	49
Relig	5	6	14	21	12	10	15	18	35	65
Nws/Tlk	1	3	11	18	10	11	18	29	60	40

Note. Source: Arbitron Radio Today based on national database which includes about 13,900 stations for Spring 2003. Rows for age may not add to 100% because of rounding. Men and Women include only listeners 18+ years old. Reprinted by permission of Arbitron.

motional announcements appealing to a particular audience can be scheduled when members of that target group are watching. As we discuss more fully in chapter 10, though, most programmers are limited by budgets and time to using the gross audience measurements provided in the ratings books to approximate audience overlap. These are, at most, a rough guide.

Noncommercial media also care about attracting an audience. Public broadcasters in the United States, or public service broadcasters around the world for that matter, must ultimately justify their existence by serving an audience. This can only be done if an audience is identified and measured. Therefore, many public stations use ratings as well. National Public Radio (NPR), with the Corporation for Public Broadcasting (CPB), has provided audience estimates to NPR stations since 1979. The Public Broadcasting Service (PBS), which distributes much of the programming to noncommercial stations, subscribes to national ratings for several months of each year to judge the attractiveness of its programming. And many individual stations subscribe directly to Nielsen or indirectly through research consultants who analyze the data for them.

Although they do not have sponsors in the traditional sense, public broadcasters care very much about reaching, even maximizing, their audiences. For one thing, many organizations that put up the money for programming are interested in who sees both their programs and the underwriting announcement. The more viewers there are, the happier is the funding agency. Further, public stations are heavily dependent on donations from the audience. Only those who are in the audience will hear the solicitation. Thus, many public TV broadcasters pay considerable attention to their cumes and ratings.

Even if one has no funding concerns in mind, programmers in a public station well might ask a question like "How can I get maximum exposure for my documentary?" Often documentaries and "how-to" programs can earn the same or a higher rating when repeated during weekend daytime or late night than they do during the first run in prime time. A careful analysis of audience ratings data could reveal when the largest number of those in the target audience are available to view, or whether the intended audience really saw the program.

How Loyal Is My Audience?

Audience loyalty is difficult to define precisely because it means different things to different people. Typically, *channel loyalty* is the extent to which audience members stick with, or return to, a particular station, network, program or Web site. Loyalty is something that manifests itself over time. Despite all the positive images the word connotes, we should point out that audience loyalty is quite different from audience size—the attribute most valued by time buyers. Programmers are interested in audience loyalty for a number of reasons. First, in the most general sense, it can give them a better feel for their audience and how they use the programming that is offered to them. This knowledge can guide other scheduling decisions. Second, audience loyalty is closely related to advertising concepts like reach and frequency, so it may affect the way an audience is sold. Finally, it can provide an important clue about how to build and maintain the audience you do have, often through a more effective use of promotions.

Radio programmers use a number of simple manipulations of ratings data to assess audience loyalty. Although the heaviest radio listening is in the morning when people wake up and prepare for the day, listeners are turning their radios on and off several times during the day. They also listen in their cars or at work. To maintain ratings levels, a radio station must get people to tune in as often as possible and to listen for as long as possible. Radio programmers employ two related measures, *time spent listening* (TSL) and *turnover*, to monitor this behavior. Using a simple formula based on the average ratings and cume ratings that are in the radio book, one can compute TSL for any station in any daypart. Turnover is the ratio of cume audience to average audience, which is basically the reciprocal of TSL.

If you listen to just about any radio station you can hear how they try to keep you tuned in—naming the songs or other items coming up, running contests, and playing a certain number of songs without commercial interruption. To programmers, these tricks of the trade are for *quarter-hour maintenance*—that is, trying to keep listeners tuned in from one quarter hour to the next. The 15-minute period is important, because it is the basic unit of time used to compute and report all ratings. By tracking TSL and audience turnover measures, the programmer can see how well the audience is being retained.

The importance of TSL varies according to the specific format of a station. All would like to keep their listeners tuned as long as possible—but that is more likely for stations with narrower, more specialized formats such as country, urban, Spanish, or religious. But even these may share audience if there are several similar stations in the market. One particularly troubling change for broadcasters is the loss of younger listeners. Figure 3.1 shows that the largest losses in TSL between 1998 and 2004 came from the younger, 18–24 and 25–34 demographics.

Another measure of loyalty that is common in radio programming is called *recycling*. Because ratings books routinely report station audiences for morning and afternoon drive time combined, it is possible to determine how many people listened at both times. This can be a useful insight. If the number is relatively small, for example, stations may offer similar programming, or they may do more promotion. The precise calculations of time spent listening, turnover, and recycling are presented in chapter 11.

The same basic research question is relevant in television programming as well. Do the people who watch the early evening news on a particular station return to watch the late news? If the answer is no,

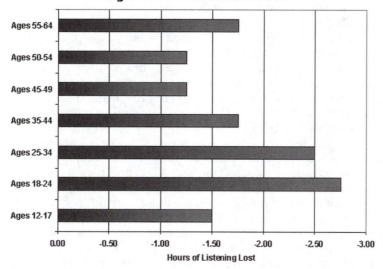

FIG. 3.1.   Ages 18–34 have dealt radio largest TSL losses since 1998. Reprinted by permission of Arbitron and Borrell Associates.

especially if the early news is successful, it would make sense to promote the later newscast with the early news audience. Unfortunately, because of the way TV ratings are published, it is not possible to deduce this from information on the printed page. Customized breakouts of the ratings data will, however, answer that question, and many more. In chapter 11 we illustrate how to analyze TV network audience flows throughout the evening.

What Other Stations or Programs Does My Audience Use?

In some ways, this is just the opposite of the preceding question. Although there are some people who will listen to one, and only one, station, it is more common for audience members to change from one station to another. In radio, we noted that no two stations are programmed precisely alike or reach exactly the same audience, but several stations in a large market may have very similar, or complementary, formats. For example, listeners who are interested in news and information in the morning might prefer a more relaxing dose of "lite rock" on the drive home, and so use two different stations almost equally. Or, listeners might not like a so-called "shock jock" on the station in the morning but are attracted to another comic talker in the afternoon. Whatever the reasons, many people listen to at least two stations each day. Programmers know that many of their listeners hear four or five other stations in a week. Radio listeners may have favorite times for choosing different formats, for example, news in the morning or jazz at night. It is important for a programmer to be able to assess the use of other stations.

In the largest markets, a station may be one of 60 or more radio signals available to listeners. However, the important competitors for most programmers are the other stations trying to reach a similar target audience. These are likely to be stations with a similar format. In general, advertisers only buy one or two stations deep to reach the specific demographic target they seek most. Knowing as precisely as possible where your listeners spend the rest of their radio time is very important.

The use of ratings information and a few tabulations will enable a programmer to know all the other stations with which he or she shares listeners. Two types of information are most relevant. The first is the *exclusive cume*, or the number of people who listened to just one particular station during specific dayparts. Although this is actually a measure of station loyalty, when it is compared with the total cume, it reveals the proportion of a station's audience that has also used the competition. That does not tell you which stations they are, however. This information is conveyed through a statistic called *cume duplication*, which reveals the extent to which the audience for one station also tunes to each of the other stations in the market. Table 3.3 illustrates levels of audience duplication by stations of different formats.

While many listeners have a favorite station that they attend to most of the time, they may also try other stations with similar formats or try something completely different. That there is so much overlap among stations suggests that people have varied tastes and that they might like other fare during different times of the day or week. It is clear, however, that stations share the most listeners with stations of similar appeal. See in Table 3.3 that there is high cume duplication between two contemporary hit (CHR) stations, and between all-news, sports, and talk stations. Although they are not shown in Table 3.3, in this same market three stations that program mostly "album-oriented rock" overlap with each other an average of 35%. All told, the number of stations in the market, and especially the number with similar formats, makes a considerable difference in the amount of overlap or cume duplication. The least overlap is among stations that appeal to very different age categories, say various types of rock and middle-of-the-road. There is also little sharing of audience for programming of distinctly different tastes—see Table 3.3 to compare classical and rock or country and urban.

Only one in 10 persons listens to only a single station during the week. You can check that for any station or demographic category by looking at the exclusive cume section of the ratings book. Most listen to two or three different stations—younger people use more stations than do older listeners, and more different stations are chosen on average in larger markets where more stations are available. You can compute the average number of stations heard for any demographic category in any daypart by adding the cumes of all stations and dividing the total by the market cume reported at the bottom of the page.

To get a detailed look at how home listeners tune to different stations, programmers can study tuning to their station in great detail using a computer program such as Arbitron's Maximi$er. Researchers can use this program to tabulate persons in the sample who heard any given station—your station—by all the categories of demographics. You can see which other stations your listeners tune in, and when they are likely to do so. It is possible to see whether your cume audience consists of listeners who used it as their primary station, or heard it only occasionally. Further, the program gives demographic information about each reported listener and the zip code in which they live. The zip code data is often used by stations to find "holes" in their signal area or places to do more advertising—billboards, for example. You can customize a presentation to an advertiser showing precisely what type of listener you can offer, based on demographics and other lifestyle and consumption variables.

This kind of information is valuable to television organizations as well as to radio stations. In fact, the average TV viewer undoubtedly watches more channels than the average listener uses stations. Programmers can use promos for the station most effectively by knowing when different kinds of viewers are tuned in. Sometimes that will mean paying attention to the geo-demographics of the audience, just like an advertiser. But it is especially important to know when people who watch a competitor's program are watching your station. That can be the perfect opportunity to entice those viewers with promotional messages.

How Do Structural Factors Like Scheduling Affect Program Audience Formation?

One of the recurring questions a television programmer must grapple with is how to schedule a particular program. Often, scheduling factors are considered at the time a program is acquired. In fact, some programs sold in barter syndication require stations to broadcast them at a particular time. As we saw in chapter 2, that is because the syndicators also sell time to advertisers, and only certain scheduling arrangements will allow them to deliver the desired audience. In any event, how and when a program is scheduled will have a considerable impact on who sees it.

Programmers rely on a number of different "theories"—really just strategies—for guidance on how to schedule their shows. Unfortunately for the student, there are nearly as many of these theories as there are programmers. A few of these notions have been, or could be, systematically investigated through analyses of ratings data. Among the more familiar programming strategies are the following.

A *lead-in* strategy is the most common, and the most thoroughly researched. Basically, this theory of programming stipulates that the pro-

TABLE 3.3
Cume Duplication

Share	Station	CHR1	CHR2	Urb	AOR	Lite	Jazz	Cou	Cls	Old	MOR	Sports	Talk	News1	News2
4.6	CHR 1	—	38	32	27	22	16	19	8	20	6	6	9	12	9
2.9	CHR 2	30	—	8	43	12	9	13	8	17	5	13	9	8	8
7.2	Urban	24	8	—	7	6	22	3	3	4	2	4	3	6	5
2.9	Alb Rock	15	30	5	—	7	5	11	2	14	2	10	7	4	6
4.5	Lite	16	11	11	9	—	19	20	12	19	14	12	12	12	15
4.8	Jazz	11	7	7	7	18	—	6	7	9	11	12	12	15	15
3.5	Country	10	9	9	11	15	5	—	5	19	9	9	13	6	9
1.7	Classical	3	3	3	1	6	10	3	—	5	12	8	6	11	8
3.4	Oldies	14	15	12	18	19	10	26	10	—	12	14	13	12	14

	6.1	2.0	4.3		3.6	2.3
MOR/Talk	4					
Sports	2					
Talk	5					
News 1	10					
News 2	5					

MOR/Talk	Sports	Talk	News 1	News 2
4	4	6	8	6
4	4	6	8	6
2	5	7	6	7
13	5	9	14	11
11	5	10	18	12
12	4	7	10	9
25	6	10	27	14
11	5	9	14	11
—	10	21	28	22
26	—	19	27	22
27	10	—	27	21
23	6	17	—	24
28	11	20	35	—

Note. Source: Computed using Arbitron Maximi$er, Winter 1998. Figures show the Metro Cume Duplication for 14 of 33 stations in a very large market. Stations are listed here by format rather than their call letters. Formats are: Contemporary Hit Radio (also called Top 40; 2 stations), Urban (also called Black), Album Rock, Lite (or Light), Smooth Jazz (includes some New Age), Country, Classical, Oldies Rock, a so-called full-service Middle-of-the-Road music and talk, Sports Talk, Talk, and All-News (2 stations); News2 also does some play-by-play sports. The share of audience for each station is also given in the column at the far left.

Read each column down, so that for all listeners who hear the CHR1 station anytime during the week 30% also listen to CHR2; 24% hear the Urban station. Note, for example, that those who tune in either one of the all-news stations also listened to the other news station more than they heard any other format. While the classical station, shown above, has very little overlap with other formats it does share half of its audience with another station in this market that also programs classical music. Reprinted by permission of Arbitron.

gram that precedes, or leads into, another show will have an important impact on the second show's audience. If the first program has a large rating, the second show will benefit from that. Conversely, if the first show has low ratings, it will handicap the second. This relationship exists because the same viewers tend to stay tuned, allowing the second show to inherit the audience. In fact, this feature of audience behavior is sometimes called an *inheritance effect* (see Webster & Phalen, 1997). The ratings differential between *The Late Show* with David Letterman and *The Tonight Show* with Jay Leno is attributed, in part, to strength of the lead-in audience provided by CBS and NBC affiliates, respectively. There are many other examples.

Another strategy that depends on inheritance effects is *hammocking*. As the title suggests, hammocking is a technique for improving the ratings of a relatively weak, or untried, show by "slinging" it between two strong programs. In principle, the second show enjoys the lead-in of the first, with an additional inducement for viewers to stay tuned for the third program. NBC used this strategy quite effectively during the 1990s with its Thursday night lineup. By scheduling new programs in the hour and a half between *Friends* and *ER*, the network was able to build audiences for programs like *Frasier*, which it later moved (along with its new audience) to another time period.

Block programming is yet another technique for inheriting audiences from one program to the next. In block programming, several programs of the same general type are scheduled in sequence. The theory is that if the viewers like one program of a type, they might stay tuned to watch a second, third, or fourth such program. Public broadcasting stations have used this strategy to build weekend audiences by scheduling blocks of "how-to" programs. In many cases, this block earned some of the highest ratings for stations. A variation on block programming is to gradually change program type as the composition of the available audience changes. For example, a station might begin in mid-afternoon when school lets out by targeting young children with cartoons. As more and more adults enter the audience, programming gradually shifts to shows more likely to appeal to grownups, thereby making a more suitable lead-in to local news. Basic cable channels, like TVLand, sometimes do "stunts" that resemble block programming. For example, they may schedule marathons in which many, or all, of the episodes of a program are aired over a period of days. Mini-marathons may show 6 or more hours from one program.

All of the strategies described here attempt to exploit or fine-tune *audience flow* across programs. Incidentally, many of these programming principles were recognized soon after the first ratings were compiled in the early 1930s. Then, as now, analyses of ratings data allowed the programmer to investigate the success or failure of the strategies. Basically, this means tracking audience members over time. Conceptually, the analytical techniques needed to do that are just the same as those used to study the loyalty, or "disloyalty" of a station's audience. We discuss both the theory and practice of such cumulative analyses in the last section of the book.

When Will a Program's Costs Exceed Its Benefits?

Ultimately, programming decisions must be based on the financial resources of the medium. Although some new stations or networks can be expected to operate at a loss during the start-up phases of operation, in the long run the cost of programming must not exceed the revenues that it generates. This hard economic reality enters into a programmer's thinking when new programming is being acquired or when existing programming must be canceled. Because ratings have a significant impact on determining the revenues a program can earn, they are important tools in working through the costs and benefits of a programming decision.

When stations assess the feasibility of a new television program, whether syndicated or locally produced, it is typical to start with the ratings for the program currently in that time period. Based on current ratings and station rates, analysts calculate the revenue that can be generated in that time period. This can become very complex because many factors, including uncertainty about the size and composition of a new program's audience, affect the revenues a program generates. We discuss the business of predicting program revenues more fully in chapter 4.

If a programmer is not evaluating programs to acquire, he or she may have to worry about when a program should be canceled. Much of the press about television ratings has been over network decisions to cancel specific programs that are well liked by small, often vocal, segments of the audience. Ordinarily, a program will be canceled when its revenue-generating potential is exceeded by costs of acquisition or production. The cost of 1 hour of prime time programming has risen steadily over the years. Today, 1 hour of prime time drama can easily cost over $1 million to produce. The final episodes of *Friends* cost NBC $10 million apiece. At the same time, the cancellation threshold in ratings has fallen over the years. In the mid-1970s, networks routinely canceled programs when their ratings fell into the high teens. By the mid-1990s, programs with ratings in the low teens could remain in the schedule (see Atkin & Litman, 1986; Hwang, 1998). Nowadays, only the top 10 programs have ratings in the double digits and the average prime time rating for ABC, CBS, and NBC ranges between 6.0 and 9.0. In fact, many programs on lesser broadcast networks now survive with ratings in the 2.0 to 4.0 range.

Dwindling ratings, which are the result of increased competition for the viewer's attention, can be tolerated for a number of reasons. First, the total size of the television audience has increased, so one ratings point means more viewers. Second, CPMs have increased. Third, the FCC now allows networks to own the programs they broadcast, which enables them to make money in off-network syndication. And fourth, ratings don't tell the cost/benefit story unless they are evaluated relative to production costs. For example, the highly rated *Friends* cost more than six times as much per episode as its lower rated replacement, *Joey*. Even though the 18- to 49-year-old audience is only about half of what it was when *Friends* was scheduled, Thursday remains NBC's most profitable night. This is an extreme example, but it clearly demonstrates how analysts must balance audiences against program costs.

The job of programming is probably more challenging today than at any time in the past. There is certainly more competition among electronic media than there has ever been, making the task of building and maintaining an audience more difficult. TV programmers, in particular, must contend with more stations, more networks, and newer technologies like the Internet, video on demand, DBS, and the DVR. As they face these challenges, programmers will continue to rely on analysis of ratings data to understand the audience and its use of media.

RELATED READINGS

Carroll, R. L., & Davis, D. M. (1993). *Electronic media programming: Strategies and decision making*. New York: McGraw Hill.

Ettema, J. S., & Whitney, C. D. (Eds.). (1982). *Individuals in mass media organizations: Creativity and constraint*. Beverly Hills, CA: Sage.

Ferguson, D. A., & Eastman, S. T. (2001). *Broadcast/cable programming: Strategies and practices* (6th ed.). Belmont, CA: Wadsworth.

Fletcher, J. E. (Ed.) (1981). *Handbook of radio and TV broadcasting: Research procedures in audience, program and revenues*. New York: Van Nostrand Reinhold.

Fletcher, J. E. (1987). *Music and program research*. Washington, DC: National Association of Broadcasters.

Gitlin, T. (1983). *Inside prime time*. New York: Pantheon Books.

MacFarland, D. T. (1997). *Future radio programming strategies: Cultivating listenership in the digital age* (2nd ed.). Mahwah, NJ: Lawrence Erlbaum Associates.

Newcomb, H., & Alley, R. S. (1983). *The producer's medium*. New York: Oxford University Press.

Chapter 4

Audience Research
in Financial Analysis

While the most obvious uses of audience data are in sales and programming, ratings are also helpful to financial managers and economists who analyze media markets. In effect, media analysts can't estimate future revenues without estimating future audiences.

The value of the audience commodity should be apparent by now. Audiences are a critical component in the media's ability to make money, and they frequently determine whether a particular media operator succeeds or fails. As the principal index of the audience commodity, ratings data are often used in day-to-day financial planning, as well as in more theoretical studies of industry economics. In these applications, audience information is employed to answer questions that are somewhat different from those posed by advertisers or programmers.

Media owners and managers are most immediately concerned with the financial implications of ratings data. Advertiser-supported media are in business to make a profit, and in order to do that they try to minimize their expenses while maximizing their revenues. We have already seen how the profit motive affects programming decisions. But business expenses also include salaries, servicing the firm's debt, and a host of mundane budget items. Reducing these expenses boosts profit, but there is a limit to how much cost cutting can be done. The only other way to improve profitability is to increase revenues.

For commercial media, increasing revenues generally implies increasing income from advertising sales. Broadcast stations generate virtually all of their revenues from time sales. In radio, the majority of this income is generated from local advertisers; in television the split between local and national spot revenue varies. Some stations, especially those in large markets, might get roughly equal amounts of revenue from each source, while others depend more heavily on local advertising than on national spot. Networks also depend heavily on advertising revenues, although cable networks typically derive additional income through direct payments from cable systems. And program syndicators can realize substantial revenues from selling barter time to national advertisers.

The financial analysis of media markets concerns people who work for media companies as well as those not directly involved in buying and selling audiences. Media organizations generally have separate finance departments to conduct ongoing analysis for planning, monitoring, and evaluating business decisions. Wall Street analysts project the financial health of media firms in order to evaluate investments. Trade organizations, such as the National Association of Broadcasters (NAB) and the National Cable & Telecommunications Association (NCTA), conduct financial analyses to assess the economic health of their industries and to lobby on behalf of their clients. Economists from industry and academe study the characteristics of economic transactions in media markets. And policy organizations like the FCC conduct financial analyses to determine the impact of their policies on the marketplace.

We consider first the more applied questions characteristic of corporate financial managers. Our goal is not to explain financial management in detail, as that is done elsewhere (e.g., Albarran, 2001; Sherman, 1995), but rather to show the critical importance of audience ratings in financial planning. Of course, specific processes and procedures vary across firms and even within departments at a given company. We are more concerned with the factors that remain more or less constant across organizations so that the reader can focus on the concepts rather than the formats of particular analyses.

Within media organizations, financial analysis cuts across all functional areas. For example, the sales department projects advertising revenue and sets prices for advertising time, while the programming department analyzes the costs and income potential of programs. Both groups have to work together because decisions made in one department affect decisions in the other. However, each contributes a very different expertise, and often a different set of priorities. A finance department will typically use information from all areas of the organization to generate its own analyses and financial projections. If the organization is part of a group, as is occurring more and more with widespread consolidation in the radio and television industries, a corporate finance department affects the process. We will say more about the effects of consolidation on financial planning later in the chapter.

The quantitative reports from services such as Nielsen and Arbitron offer financial analysts the most important audience data. The reason is straightforward—ratings provide an index to revenues. While the correlation is not perfect, as we explained in chapter 2, the ratings represent an excellent predictor of advertising income. In fact, although financial analysts may use audience data in different ways, they need the same understanding of ratings as do programmers and sales managers.

There are, of course, dozens of questions related to finance that can be asked of ratings data. We concentrate on broad questions that illustrate their use in assessing the ongoing economic activity of the firm, planning expenditures, determining the value of media firms, and specifying the relationship between audiences and revenues.

RESEARCH QUESTIONS

How Effectively Does the Organization Compete for Market Revenues?

Monitoring the financial performance of an organization requires on-going analysis of both the sales effort and market conditions. In its simplest form, this analysis involves comparing revenues earned with the potential revenues available in the marketplace. Because revenues are heavily determined by audience size and composition, a station's share of market revenue should reflect its share of audience. A statistic called the *power ratio* (also called the *conversion ratio*) expresses this relationship. The calculation is very simple:

$$\text{Power ratio} \quad = \quad \frac{\text{Share of market revenue}}{\text{Share of audience}}$$

This calculation estimates the percent of revenue your station earns for every audience share point. Audience share information, which comes from ratings services, is readily available to Nielsen and Arbitron subscribers. The revenue part of the equation is more problematic. A media firm knows its own sales figures, obviously, but would not ordinarily have access to data from competing organizations. There are organizations that routinely collect this information, such as TNS Media Intelligence/CMR or Nielsen Monitor-Plus, but such data are subject to error. Usually these services rely on self-reports of prices based on the word of buyers and salespeople. Both groups have an incentive to give false information. Sellers would want to estimate the highest prices possible so that their clients wouldn't think that they overpaid, and buyers would want to estimate the lowest prices possible so that they wouldn't appear to have made bad deals. Consequently, such data have serious limitations in terms of estimating total market revenues.

This problem has been addressed in some media markets by independent auditing firms that conduct confidential market share analyses. These firms collect sales data directly from media clients and report those figures in monthly, quarterly, or yearly reports. These reports are available only to the clients who take part in the analysis. Usually the organizations that subscribe to the services find out only the overall market revenue and their own share of that revenue, although in some markets they have access to competitors' data as well. Table 4.1 shows the kind of information that typically appears in a broadcast market share report. In the sample city's local market, the total radio advertising revenue in December was $4,577,000. Of that total, $351,000 went to the hypothetical radio station WCPA—a figure representing 7.7% of the market's radio advertising during the month. The next highest share of revenue was 8.0%, and the next lowest was 7.2% (note that the stations garnering those shares are not identified). WCPA can calculate its power ratio with this information. If Arbitron shows an audience share

TABLE 4.1

Radio Revenue Report (in $$ thousands)

December, 2004

Revenue category	Sample city			WCPA					Rank		Nearest shares			
	Revenue			Revenue			Revenue share				Dec-04		Dec-03	
	Dec-04	Dec-03	% chg.	Dec-04	Dec-03	% chg.	Dec-04	Dec-03	2004	2003	above	below	above	below
Local	4,577	4,351	5%	351	264	33%	7.7%	6.1%	6	6	8.0%	7.2%	6.1%	5.9%
National	601	600	0%	53	39	36%	8.8%	6.5%	6	7	10.1%	8.8%	6.8%	4.2%
Network	58	45	29%						8	6	5.2%		6.7%	
Total Cash Sales	5,236	4,996	5%	404	303	33%	7.7%	6.1%	6	7	8.1%	7.6%	6.6%	5.7%
Trade	460	380	21%	31	50	38%	6.7%	13.2%	8	3	8.0%	5.4%	14.7%	12.6%
Total Sales	5,696	5,376	6%	435	353	23%	7.6%	6.6%	6	7	7.8%	7.5%	7.3%	5.8%

Note. Source: Adapted from sample report provided in Hungerford, Aldrin, Nichols, and Carter, *The Hungerford Radio Revenue Report: Users Guide.* Reprinted by permission of Hungerford, Aldrin, Nichols, & Carter, P.C., CPAs and Consultants.

of 7%, for example, then WCPA's power ratio is 1.1. This means that the station earns 1.1% of total advertising revenue for every 1% of audience share. Generally the Arbitron shares are adjusted to reflect share of audience only among those stations that report revenue figures. The value of this system is that it allows the media to evaluate their sales effort without compromising proprietary information.

The power ratio can be calculated on the basis of any demographic. If a radio station format were designed to appeal to men 18 to 49, then the sales department would want to know its share against that group. The statistic can also be calculated on any daypart for which information is provided by the auditing firm. However, the conversion ratio by itself conveys very little information. Analysts also look at trends in the daypart to find out whether the share of revenue is increasing or decreasing and determine whether this is a result of audience share differences or changes in overall sales revenue. Results must also be compared to historical data on the performance of particular formats in a market, because different formats can be expected to garner different shares of sales revenue.

What Is the Value of a Programming Investment?

After its investment in personnel, a broadcast station's largest cost item is generally programming. Each program purchase is evaluated according to its potential to generate revenue for the station. Analysts must determine how much money the programs will earn for the station and how much revenue will be lost by displacing other programs from the schedule. This may involve fairly straightforward analysis of costs and revenues, or it could involve complex analysis of properties such as sports rights.

Several factors determine the balance of costs and benefits in a program purchase decision. In general, these include the license fee that the seller is asking, the amount of time available for local advertising sales, the likely price that spots in a program will command in the advertising marketplace, the opportunity cost of purchasing the program, and the revenue that the program is likely to generate over the life of the contract. Because programs are often purchased 3 or 4 years before stations can air them, analysts need to generate planning estimates for 3 to 5 years into the future. The information needed to conduct this analysis requires input from several departments in the organization.

When a program property becomes available, financial decision makers put together a *pre-buy analysis*. Although the format will differ from organization to organization, the information needed is essentially the same. One of the most important elements in the revenue projection is the estimated audience the program will attract. Predicting an audience is both art and science, involving historical data as well as experienced judgment. The historical data are in the form of ratings.

In the case of an off–network syndicated television program, for example, analysts are interested in how a program performed in its original run on the network. The national ratings indicate its popularity and the composition of its audience. However, a program might have earned poor ratings nationally, but perform well in an individual market. Several factors explain this difference. The show might have a distinct cultural appeal in certain parts of the country, or it might simply have been carried on stronger stations in some markets than in others. The difference could also be attributable to different demographic profiles of potential audiences across DMAs. Whatever the reasons, analysts must take local market characteristics and preferences into account when they project program ratings.

Analysts are able to study the performance of programs in previous syndication runs because some syndicated programs are sold for two or more cycles. If a program is being considered in its second cycle, the ratings earned in its first cycle would be of major importance. Using some of the syndication ratings sources that we describe in chapter 8, analysts could compare how the program did in its original network run with how it performed in syndication. They could use this information to predict how it might do a third time around.

Analysts might also look at ratings for programs that are similar in content to the one being evaluated. This strategy is especially important in cases like first–run syndication, where there are no historical track records to consult. If analysts assume the program will attract audiences similar to others of its type, they can project ratings based on those audiences. The savvy user of audience data will, of course, consider not only program content but also the scheduling patterns of those programs.

Predicted rating also depends on the place in a schedule that the program is likely to occupy. Competition varies by daypart, by season, and by day of the week. Also, as we explain in chapter 9, time periods command different levels of available audience, so ratings vary considerably across dayparts. Programmers consider all of this when they decide on a schedule; financial analysts factor the information into their revenue calculations.

Some large media organizations may have all the resources in–house to make these kinds of predictions, but most firms will rely on information supplied by services such as rep firms. Programmers at rep firms may even be involved in program purchase decisions, helping programmers and general managers evaluate and negotiate deals. More often, they serve a consulting role, providing ratings information that they collect for their clients. They can share not only the ratings data, but the experience gained in various markets. This expertise can be very valuable to financial planners.

Revenue projections also take into consideration the number of spots available for sale in a given program. This availability depends on the program length and on commitments to other uses for those spots. A barter program, for example, will have less time available for local sale than a syndicated program purchased with cash. Stations might also reserve spots for promotional announcements, making this inventory unavailable to the sales staff. These variables affect the number of units sold to advertisers, and thus the revenue generated from time sales.

Just as researchers use historical ratings information and experience to project the likely audience for a program, salespeople use historical data and their firsthand knowledge of market conditions to estimate a *cost per point* (CPP) that the program will earn. The way a program is scheduled will have a significant effect on the prices that the advertising sales staff can charge. Even if a program is projected to earn a very high rating, it cannot be sold at a prime time cost per point if it is scheduled in late fringe.

Table 4.2 illustrates a sample pre-buy analysis for a fictitious program called *Family Time*. Due to space constraints, the table covers only the first 3 years of a 6-year analysis, but it is sufficient to illustrate many of the factors we have discussed. The first columns give information about the season and likely scheduling patterns. Programmers determined that *Family Time* should start in early fringe, probably maintaining that time slot for the first few years. Subsequent columns report estimates that affect quarterly revenue projections.

Working with other departments at the station, financial analysts estimate the ratings that the program will achieve, the likely price it will command in the advertising marketplace, and the predicted sell-out percentage (percent of available advertising time sold). In this case they estimated that the program would get a 6.0 household rating in the first year when it airs at 5:30 p.m. In the second and third years of the contract the rating drops to 5.0, and by the end of the year 2007 the program is projected to earn a 4.0. This drop in projected ratings is based on the assumption that some of the available audience has already seen the series, and that competing stations might offer more recent or otherwise more attractive programming. Although the data are not shown in Table 4.2, programmers plan to move *Family Time* to the early afternoon toward the end of the contract, which brings the estimated audience down to a 3.0.

The cost per point varies by quarter, and the cost per spot (also called *average unit rate*) varies according to the estimated rating and the CPP. These figures represent the value that salespeople think the program has in the marketplace. Sellers offered the program on a cash-plus-barter basis, asking for 1 minute of barter time for the first 2 years of the contract. Note that the station is selling 11 avails through the 3rd quarter of 2006 when it regains the minute of barter time it gave to the syndicator as part of the original contract. The station estimates that 95% of the available spots will be sold during the first 2 years of its run, dropping to 90% in Year 3. The last column, net revenue, is calculated by combining the advertising cost and sell-out information with the total number of times the program is aired.

TABLE 4.2
Prebuy Analysis

KZZZ Family Time prebuy (analysis for first 3 years of contract)

Primary run

Qtr	Year	Time period	HH Rtg	CPP ($$)	Average Unit Rate ($$)	Avails*	SO %	Airings	Net Rev. ($000)
3rd/4th	2004	MF 5:30pm	6.0	110.00	660	11	95%	85	586.2
1st Q	2005	MF 5:30pm	6.0	80.00	480	11	95%	65	326.0
2nd Q	2005	MF 5:30pm	6.0	120.00	720	11	95%	65	489.1
3rdQ	2005	MF 5:30pm	6.0	90.00	540	11	95%	65	366.8
4thQ	2005	MF 5:30pm	5.0	114.40	572	11	95%	65	388.5
1st Q	2006	MF 5:30pm	5.0	83.20	416	11	95%	65	282.6
2nd Q	2006	MF 5:30pm	5.0	124.80	624	11	95%	65	423.9
3rdQ	2006	MF 5:30pm	5.0	93.60	468	11	95%	65	317.9
4thQ	2006	MF 5:00pm	5.0	119.00	595	12	90%	65	417.7
1st Q	2007	MF 5:00pm	5.0	86.50	432	12	90%	65	303.6
2nd Q	2007	MF 5:00pm	5.0	129.80	649	12	90%	65	455.6
3rdQ	2007	MF 5:00pm	5.0	97.30	486	12	90%	65	341.5
4thQ	2007	MF 5:00pm	4.0	123.80	495	12	90%	65	347.6
1st Q	2008	MF 5:00pm	4.0	90.00	360	12	90%	65	252.7

*Avails = Gross avails–barter–promos (one spot is reserved for promotional announcements in this program). This analysis assumes a 4% annual growth rate. This is reflected in the Cost Per Point.

This analysis is completed, quarter by quarter, for the life of the contract. Financial analysts projected that *Family Time* would generate close to $7.1 million in revenue, while costing the station only about $1.6 million in license fees. This means that the program would make a profit of $5.5 million over its 6-year contract—attractive, but highly unlikely in the real world. Most programs are likely to show a much smaller margin of profit.

The revenue that a program will generate is only part of the financial calculation. Analysts also need to consider the alternative uses of airtime, and whether these alternatives would be more profitable for the station. Perhaps a different program scheduled in the same time slot would sell at a higher cost per point. Or a program with more local avails would be more profitable than an all-barter program. The question that has to be answered in each instance is whether the benefits of acquiring a property justify the lost revenue from other options. Another way of phrasing this is that financial planners must consider the *opportunity cost* of scheduling one program instead of another. This consideration affects all levels of the analysis.

Another factor in assessing the costs and benefits of acquiring a program is its effect on the rest of the schedule. High-profile programs, such as *Oprah Winfrey* or major sporting events, might attract new viewers and create promotional opportunities to build audiences for other parts of the schedule. They could provide large lead-in audiences to locally produced programs, such as news. Or the schedule might benefit from a *halo effect* that brings viewers to the channel. Higher ratings for these other programs would translate into higher revenues overall.

There is no standard threshold that determines whether a program is acquired after the pre-buy analysis. Different types of programs have vastly different profit margins. In the off-network syndication market for example, a blockbuster program often earns less for the station in direct advertiser revenue because so much of the advertising time is given up for national barter. But, for the image reasons listed previously, the program could be an excellent asset. Other shows might be projected to attract comparatively small audiences, but with the sale of all local availabilities would generate higher profits. Usually, financial managers and programmers will seek a mix of both kinds of shows.

Sports-rights deals require a more complex analysis than regular programs or series. They also require, in the opinion of some industry professionals, more "instinct." Deal structures vary widely, from a team purchasing a 3-hour block from a station and selling the time themselves to deals that share production costs and leave the media organization to sell the time. Arrangements such as revenue sharing are not uncommon. This means that the same types of questions are asked about ratings predictions and opportunity costs, but there are additional considerations specific to the sports property. One complicating factor is that the times and lengths of games often fluctuate from week to week. This means that the regular schedule will be interrupted in inconsistent ways, which could drive regular viewers from the channel. It also means that advertisers in these regular programs might be bumped if a game goes late, and this has repercussions on the way the time is sold. However, while the analysis will differ based on the proposed terms of the deal, the basic question remains the same: What can I earn with one option compared to another? We have seen that the likely audience each option will attract is a key factor in assessing whether the balance of revenue lost and gained is in the organization's favor.

We noted earlier that group ownership affects financial planning at local media organizations. The corporate culture of a group owner, as well as its long-term image goals, are likely to affect decision making at the station level. Stations that used to function on their own before the consolidation of ownership might be subject to corporate approval in decisions such as program purchases. For example, a station might determine, based on a pre-buy analysis, that a sports programming opportunity is not in the best interests of the local sales effort. This decision would not be in the best interests of a group owner that wanted to create a national image as a "sports broadcaster." The national goals of the company would have to figure into the cost/benefit calculation made by the individual station.

Consolidation of businesses might also mean consolidation of financial expertise. As corporate financial analysts gain experience across many different markets, they can incorporate that knowledge into pre-buy analyses for individual group-owned outlets. Ordinarily, a smaller organization that is unaffiliated with a media group would not have access to this kind of expertise on a regular basis. In any case, group ownership means that program acquisition decisions are no longer made in isolation. Financial analysts at the newly acquired company might be accountable to financial managers at the corporate office. Program purchase decisions may require corporate approval or, in some instances, come from corporate programmers to the local stations as a *fait accompli*.

The results of financial analyses are used by program directors and general managers when they negotiate deals. The information gives them an indication of reasonable program prices and the highest price they should be willing to pay. It also helps them negotiate specific terms, such as the amount of barter time given to the syndicator. Because the value that local television stations attach to a spot could be very different than the value syndicators assess, stations might want to keep more time for local advertising sales. We should note that this example is hypothetical. Buyers in most markets do not have the option to negotiate the amount of barter time, although some of the smaller markets can still do this.

Although all departments have to co-operate in financial analysis, there is frequently tension among them. Agendas and priorities differ significantly. For example, the program director wants to build an audience over the course of a day, while the sales account executive wants inventory to sell potential clients. These programs may or may not fit the program director's strategies. From time to time a programmer may decide to pre-empt regular programming to cover a particularly important news event. This creates problems for the sales staff. If regular programs are continually pre-empted, then advertisers need *make-good* spots to compensate for lost audiences. The finance department is likely to be aware of all these priorities, but has to remain focused on bottom-line considerations that benefit the company as a whole.

We have centered this discussion on the acquisition of syndicated programs, but the same principles apply to program production and distribution decisions. Before producing a 1-hour first-run syndication program, for example, the production company would have to look at audience information for similar 1-hour shows. They would estimate the clearance that they would be able to achieve, and the likely audience shares they would garner. The supply of similar programming would also be a consideration, because supply and demand affects prices in both the program and advertising markets. Syndicators develop detailed projections to estimate the net profit or loss they can expect from a new program. This involves predicting ratings in all markets, the average cost per thousand that advertisers will pay, and the likely revenue from license fees. Analysts also factor in the estimated cost of promotion efforts and publicity as well as agency commissions and other expenses.

This type of analysis also takes place with the introduction or change of locally produced programs. For example, a station might want to add a half hour of local news. Financial analysts would look at other markets or similar stations to determine the profitability of expanding news operations. They would have to predict the audience for a new schedule, and determine whether the benefits justify a potential loss of viewers.

In order to assess the accuracy of the financial planning process, financial analysts may conduct a *post-buy analysis* after a program runs. The process is similar to the one described in chapter 2 for advertising post-buys. Basically, the planning procedure is repeated after the "real" data are collected, and the results are compared to the predictions prior to investment. If any significant discrepancies are found, further analysis identifies whether the error was due to faulty audience projections, unforeseen changes in viewing patterns or market conditions, or lower than expected advertising rates.

What Is the Value of a Media Property?

Many media companies are publicly traded, meaning that individual or institutional investors can go to a stock exchange and buy shares in the company. Just as investors would study the prospects of any potential acquisition, a thorough financial analysis is critical for decisions involving media concerns. This is likely to include an inspection of a company's ratings performance—past, present, and future. Even if shares in a media company are not traded on exchanges, investors can buy properties directly. Stations are brokered much like houses. Here again, investors must determine whether the property to be acquired will generate sufficient revenues to make the acquisition worthwhile. Projecting audience ratings is a critical element in making those judgments.

Financial analysts also recognize that, although audiences are an important determinant of media revenues, there may well be some discrepancy between a media property's share of the audience and its share of market revenues. They must consider many other factors. This can have practical implications for evaluating the desirability of different acquisitions. Table 4.3 illustrates how a financial analyst might go about evaluating the long-term revenue potential of a television station. The top line across the table represents the net market revenue for all television stations in the market. This number is likely to be a function of the overall market economy, especially the annual volume of retail sales. It is estimated by looking at historical trends in the market, and making some carefully considered judgments about the economic outlook for those sectors of the economy that are especially important. The second line represents the station's current and estimated share of the television audience. Here again, the analyst would consider recent trends and the chances that the station's overall ratings performance will improve or decline. As we will see in chapter 9, there are many factors that affect a station's ability to attract an audience. In this particular example, the analyst estimated that the station would eventually be able to attract and hold 25% of the audience.

But this does not necessarily mean that the station can expect to capture 25% of total market revenues. In fact, this station has regularly commanded a smaller share of market revenues than its share of the audience. In other words, it undersells its audience share. That factor is recognized in the third line across the table. The analyst believed that the

TABLE 4.3

Station Revenues Based on Audience Share Projections

	2004	*2005*	*2006*	*Maturity*
Net market revenue	$70 million	$74 million	$80 million	X
Station audience share	21%	22%	23%	25%
Over/under sell factor	0.80	0.83	0.86	0.90
Station revenue share	16.80%	18.30%	19.80%	22.50%
Station Revenue	$11,760 million	$13,540 million	$15,840 million	X(.225)

undersell factor could be improved, but to be conservative, projected that share of revenue would always fall short of audience share.

Once these factors have been estimated, it is possible to make a reasonable projection of station revenues. When these revenue estimates are compared with projected operating expenses, the analyst can determine whether this property would have sufficient cash flow to cover its debt, and provide the owners with an acceptable return on their investments.

What Determines the Value of an Audience?

While the station's salespeople and financial analysts are very good at reading market signals, they may not be as concerned with quantifying the more abstract determinants of economic value. We have noted that, under a system of advertiser-supported media, audiences are really a commodity. They are bought and sold just like other commodities. They are "perishable," and their supply is unpredictable—but that hardly distinguishes them from other goods in the marketplace. Analysts have tried to figure out what determines their value, just like they do with other commodities. Knowing the determinants of a commodity's price is certainly of practical value to those who do the buying and selling, but it can also help us understand the operation of media industries.

The economic value of an audience is largely determined by supply and demand. Corporations and other organizations demand advertising time, and the media supply it. Generally speaking, when the U.S. economy is strong, and corporate profits are high, demand increases and advertising expenditures rise. While such macroeconomic variables establish an overall framework for prices, a number of factors operate within that framework to determine the value of specific audiences.

On the demand side, some companies cannot curtail their advertising expenditures as easily as others. For instance, the makers of many non-durable goods, like soft drinks, cosmetics, and fast foods, fear significant losses in market share if they stop advertising. Consequently, they may continue to advertise heavily, even if times are hard. Local merchants, on the other hand, will quite often cut advertising budgets to reduce expenses. For these reasons, during an economic downturn, local advertising markets may "soften" more readily than national markets, driving down the price of local audiences.

We have already noted that different advertisers demand different sorts of audiences, and that this interest in market segmentation has had a marked effect on the ratings. Audiences are routinely categorized by their demographic and geographic attributes. Increasingly, they are segmented by psychographics and product-purchasing behavior. Not all audience segments, however, are as easily supplied as others. Some kinds of people spend more time in the audience, and are therefore more readily available to advertisers. Other kinds of people constitute a tiny part of the population (e.g., executives earning more than $500,000) and are, therefore, rare. This tends to make them a more valuable commodity.

All these aspects of supply and demand come into play when determining the value of an audience. Ultimately, such factors are represented in cost calculations (e.g., CPMs) for the electronic media. In fact, advertisers will sometimes make trade-offs between print and electronic media based on the relative cost of audiences. Table 4.4 summarizes recent CPMs for the major advertiser-supported media. Although such contrasts can be an apples and oranges comparison, the price of competing media is another factor that determines the market value of a television or radio audience. This is especially true in local advertising where newspapers can provide stiff competition for the electronic media.

TABLE 4.4

Cost-per-1000 Projections for Five Media

2003–2004

		Cost-per-1000	
	Ad unit	*Men*	*Women*
TV			
Prime (Major Nets)	:30	$28.25	$21.90
Prime (Cable)[1]	:30	10.15	9.75
Early AM (Major Nets)	:30	17.90	11.25
Daytime (Major Nets)	:30		5.60
Early News (Major Nets)	:30	13.35	10.50
Late Fringe (Major Nets)	:30	28.10	24.00
Radio			
Network	:30	10.15	8.50
Spot	:30	11.15	10.70
Magazines			
Business	P4C	25.00	
Women's Fashion	P4C		10.15
Newspapers[2]			
Dailies	1/3 P B&W	23.75	22.65
Out-of-Home	30 sheet	4.90	5.15

Note. Source: © 2004, TV Dimensions 2004, Media Dynamics, Inc., New York, NY. Reprinted by permission.

[1]General Audience Cable Channels.

[2]Top 100 Markets.

What Contribution Do Ratings Make to Revenues?

The preceding discussion runs the risk of suggesting that audiences have some inherent value that translates directly into revenues. A number of factors can account for the fact that there is not a lock-step relationship between audience size and revenues. These may be of considerable importance to both economic and financial analysts.

The first thing to remember is that audiences of the electronic media are, themselves, invisible. The only index of this commodity is ratings data—an estimate of who is probably out there. In a very real sense, rating points, not audiences are bought and sold. As long as such audience estimates are the only way to know the size and shape of the audience, they effectively become that commodity. Although ratings companies are under considerable pressure to produce accurate audience measurements, certain biases and limitations do exist. Some may be inherent in research methods, others reflect the way ratings businesses have responded to marketplace demands. In any event, the media must generally operate within the constraints imposed by the ratings, and that may be a hindrance to selling certain audiences. In effect, the ratings data themselves can distort the link between audience size and audience revenues.

For example, we have noted that cable has gradually eroded the audience for broadcast television. The cable industry, however, has had some difficulty marketing that audience because historically the ratings business has been geared to estimating broadcast audiences. With the introduction of the peoplemeter, and the expansion of passive meters into additional local markets, Nielsen is now in a better position to provide cable ratings. The shifts in share of revenue illustrate how that change has affected the placement of advertising. Table 4.5 shows how advertising expenditures have changed over the years. While radio's share of revenue has remained fairly steady since the early 1980s, cable has claimed an increasing share at the expense of broadcast television.

The second thing to remember is that audiences are made available to advertisers in the form of spot announcements, and these spots are limited in number. A broadcaster could exhaust the inventory of available spots before meeting the demand for audiences. If demand is high early in the buying season, and broadcasters sell out, then even those advertisers who would pay a premium to reach the intended audiences will be unable to purchase spots. The result is that some audience revenues would go unrealized.

The amount of advertising time sold by electronic media is affected by several factors. By tradition, certain dayparts have more commercials than other dayparts. Prime time, for instance, has fewer spot announcements than late night or daytime television. The type of station also affects the amount of commercial inventory. Network affiliates have less time to sell to local advertisers than independents, because network programming reduces the size of their inventories. Inventories can be in-

TABLE 4.5
Share of Total TV/Radio Advertising Revenue[a]

Year	Radio	Television	Cable
1950	73%	27%	0%
1960	29%	51%	0%
1970	26%	74%	0%
1980	24%	75%	1%
1985	23%	74%	3%
1990	23%	70%	7%
1995	23%	66%	11%
2000	25%	56%	19%
2001	26%	54%	20%
2002	25%	55%	20%
2003	25%	53%	22%

Note. Percentages represent share of total for the 3-media advertising revenues only. Reprinted by permission of the Radio Advertising Bureau.

[a]Based on revenue estimates provided by RAB, TVB, and CAB.

creased by adding commercial time to a program or reducing the duration of spots (e.g., from 30 to 15 seconds), but like cost cutting, there is a practical limit to how much can be done without being counterproductive. Indeed, broadcasters sometimes argue about how much commercial time can be sold within each hour before listeners might be driven away to another station. Stations frequently try to lure listeners to a new, or revised, format by presenting very few commercials or guaranteeing X commercial-free minutes.

Even if ratings data were completely accurate and inventories more flexible, audiences are not the only factor in determining revenues. A sales force must take audience data into the marketplace and persuade advertisers to buy the commodity. Selling is a very human, and often imperfect, process. Some sales managers are more aggressive than others in their approach to time buyers. Some salespeople are more effective than others in dealing with clients. In addition, no two advertisers are alike. Some, for example, may purchase heavy schedules early in the season and routinely receive quantity discounts. The net result is that two audiences that seem to be identical may sell for different amounts of money.

Economists have devoted a good deal of attention to the relationship between audience ratings and audience revenues. In addition to the factors we have already described, there are other, less benign, explanations for a discrepancy between an audience's size and its market value. If, for instance, there are relatively few competitors in a market, they may be tempted to collude and set prices above competitive levels. Although we know of no cases of such collusion, the potential exists. What is clear, however, is that demand does affect price. Advertiser demand for TV has been, and will probably remain, high. This has meant higher rates (proportional to the audience delivered) in markets with fewer stations. In less concentrated markets, the cost of audiences tends to be lower, but studies of this sort have not been conclusive.

RELATED READINGS

Albarran, A. (2001). *Management of electronic media* (2nd ed.). Belmont, CA: Wadsworth.

Alexander, A., Owers, J., Carveth, R., Hollifield, C. A., & Greco, A. (Eds.). (2004). *Media economics: Theory and practice* (3rd ed.). Mahwah, NJ: Lawrence Erlbaum Associates.

McKnight, L. W., & Bailey, J. P. (Eds.). (1997). *Internet economics*. Boston: MIT Press.

Napoli, P. M. (2003). *Audience economics: Media institutions and the audience marketplace*. New York: Columbia University Press.

Owen, B. M., & Wildman, S. S. (1992). *Video economics*. Cambridge, MA: Harvard University Press.

Sherman, B. L. (1995). *Telecommunications management: Broadcasting/cable and the new technologies* (2nd ed.). New York: McGraw-Hill.

Turow, J. (1997). *Media systems in society: Understanding industries, strategies and power* (2nd ed.). New York: Longman.

Veronis Suhler Stevenson. (current edition). *Communications industry forecast & report*. New York: Author.

Vogel, H. L. (2004). *Entertainment industry economics: A guide for financial analysis* (6th ed.). Cambridge: Cambridge University Press.

Chapter 5

Audience Research in Social Policy

Electronic media play a central role in modern economic and social life. They facilitate the exchange of goods and services, help elect political candidates, and open or close the *marketplace of ideas* that is so essential to democracies. They may even shape our perceptions of reality. Given the powers commonly attributed to media, it is no surprise that they've been studied by social scientists from a wide variety of disciplines.

Since the earliest days of radio broadcasting in the 1920s, proponents and critics wondered how the medium would affect society. By the 1930s, a high-powered government committee on social trends appointed by President Hoover listed more than 150 effects of radio, from homogenizing regional cultures to encouraging morning exercise (Ogburn, 1933). Newly formed networks also began assessments of the radio audience, and academics, especially from psychology, sociology, marketing, and education, became interested in researching the new medium.

Frank Stanton, a pioneer in communications research who later became president of CBS, published one of the first scholarly studies of the radio audience in 1935. Academics took an immediate interest, especially in the use of media for political purposes in the U.S. and Germany. They began to examine the use of radio by Franklin Roosevelt, as well as various religious and political demagogues. And they studied the manipulation of motion pictures by Adolf Hitler. In 1935 Hadley Cantril and Gordon Allport of Harvard University published *The Psychology of Radio*, reporting many of their early findings on topics such as these.

Cantril and Stanton eventually secured a grant from the Rockefeller Foundation to study radio audiences. By the time funds were available, however, Stanton was unable to head the project because he had become director of research at CBS. Instead, they asked social psychologist Paul Lazarsfeld to serve as director. The resulting *Princeton Radio Research Project* lasted 2 years before moving to Columbia University and becoming the *Bureau of Applied Social Research*.

The Bureau, often in collaboration with industry, conducted a string of studies that many regard as the real foundation of communications research in the United States. This new field of radio research, especially audience measurement, established Lazarsfeld as one of the founders of the scientific study of communications. In fact, the emergence of ratings research prior to World War II was intertwined with broader developments in the new field of mass communications and the growth of social/behavioral research in general. But electronic media audiences eventually emerged as appropriate subjects for communications research in their own right.

Today audience data play an important, if underappreciated, role in social policy. They often figure in the work of policymakers, social advocacy groups, and academics, who use them to justify policy positions in the most contentious debates about mass media and society. Ratings data are a particularly appealing tool because they are the heart of the media's power. Ask yourself: Why do electronic media have economic value? Because they attract an audience. Why do news and entertainment programs have any social impact? Because they attract an audience. Why do political ads influence elections? Because they attract an audience. Even though ratings information alone cannot reveal the effects of media on society, they can frequently index the potential. Ratings are the currency with which media operate, and because of their wide and continuous availability they are useful for analyzing communications law and social policy.

Among the individuals and institutions most likely to use audience data are (a) the federal government, (b) industry, and (c) the public. The dynamic interactions among these interested parties can determine the course of public policy.

GOVERNMENT

By the mid-1920s it became apparent that broadcasting could not be left to operate as an unregulated marketplace. Demand for broadcast frequencies far exceeded the supply. The U.S. Congress addressed the problem by creating the Federal Radio Commission (FRC), which was replaced by the Federal Communication Commission (FCC) in 1934. The Commission was tasked with licensing stations to ensure that broadcasters operated in the public interest. Although definitions of "public interest" have changed over the years, three interrelated objectives have endured. First, commissioners have tried to limit certain undesirable social effects, especially among children. Second, they've tried to promote greater diversity in media content by taking steps like structuring markets in a way that makes them more responsive to audience demand. And third, like many other regulators, they have passed rules to ensure the overall economic health of the industry they regulate.

The FCC, however, does not have a free hand to implement whatever policies it chooses. Other institutions within the federal government are often involved. The president, the courts, and especially the Congress can and do make their wills known from time to time. In 1996, for example, Congress passed what many call the most sweeping legislation covering communications services since the original Communications

Act of 1934. The *Telecommunications Act of 1996* affected many areas of the business, from ownership to content. It required the FCC to review long-standing rules and revise anything that had become outdated.

Other independent agencies, like the Federal Trade Commission (FTC), or the Copyright Arbitration Royalty Panel (CARP), also deal with matters of communications policy. Some executive branch offices, such as the Department of Commerce or the Department of Health and Human Services, may also enter the picture. In the early 1970s, for example, the Surgeon General oversaw a massive study of the impact of television violence. Studies like this often influence legislators to vote for (or against) particular bills. But many nongovernmental interests also weigh heavily in the policymaking process.

INDUSTRY

The organizations with the most direct interest in communications policy are the media themselves. To advance their interests, some companies, such as large media conglomerates, might act as their own representatives in Washington. Often, however, D.C.-based trade associations do this for them. The most significant trade association for broadcasters has been the National Association of Broadcasters (NAB). The NAB serves commercial broadcasters by lobbying Congress and the FCC, testifying before congressional committees, filing briefs in the relevant judicial proceedings, and participating in rulemakings and inquiries at government agencies. In many of these activities, the NAB submits research that bears on the issue at hand. In fact, the association has a special department of research and information that performs policy studies using ratings data. Another trade group, the National Cable & Telecommunications Association (NCTA), represents the cable industry. The NCTA engages in the same sorts of activities as the NAB, including policy research. Other trade associations, like the Motion Picture Association of America (MPAA), will occasionally use ratings data as well.

THE PUBLIC

Although government and industry have a major influence on the formation of public policy, they don't completely control it. The public itself enters the process in a number ways. Most directly, we elect government representatives. Occasionally, one of these officials takes the lead on a matter of communications policy, inviting us to either support or reject that position. More highly organized public participation comes in the form of public interest groups. Some, like Action for Children's Television (ACT), were formed specifically to affect policymaking. Until its closing in the mid-1990s, ACT drew the attention of Congress and the FCC to problems of consumerism in children's television. Other organizations, like the Parent/Teacher Association (PTA) or the American Medical Association (AMA), express occasional interest in the social control of media even though regulation is not their central focus.

We should also note that the academic community contributes to policymaking. Professors with an interest in broadcasting and the electronic media have been attracted to policy questions dealing with the media's social and economic impact. They can affect policy in several ways. Most notably, they publish research relevant to questions of public policy. Because they are often viewed as experts, and relatively objective, university-based researchers may carry some special influence with the government. Academics may also work as consultants for other participants in the policymaking process, exercising direct influence in a less public, and usually less objective, manner. Finally, of course, they can indirectly affect policy through their students. Many professionals who are involved in determining communications policy today would credit certain professors with influencing their views on matters of law, regulation, and social responsibility.

RESEARCH QUESTIONS

The range of applications for audience ratings in the formation of social policy is reasonably broad. Ratings stand apart from other types of social scientific data because they can be interpreted, or "read," in so many different ways. Nevertheless, ratings are generally used in policymaking to answer one of three broad questions. The questions correspond to the long-term concerns of the FCC that we mentioned earlier: (a) limiting the undesirable effects of media, (b) promoting more diverse and responsive programming, and (c) tending to the economic condition of its client industries.

What Do the Media Do to People?

Policymakers must answer this "effects question" if they hope to limit undesirable effects. As a policy concern, the question certainly predates broadcasting. In the early 1930s, sociologists tried to determine the impact that movies had on young people. Later in the decade psychologists studied the effects of wartime propaganda, and marketing researchers questioned the effect of press coverage on voter behavior. More recent studies focus on issues such as television's ability to distort perceptions of social reality and the role video games play in promoting violence.

Central to these, and all other effects questions, is the cause-and-effect relationship. In its general form, the question is, "Does exposure to the media (cause), make other things happen (effect)?" This is an extremely difficult question for social scientists to answer. An important starting place, however, is knowledge of what people listen to or watch. This is because, by definition, any direct media effect must begin with audience exposure to media messages.

Although an encounter with the media may not determine a particular outcome (again, the effect), hearing or seeing a message does define a certain potential. If many people use a medium, or see an item of content, the potential for effects is great. Advertisers have long realized this fact, and so have paid dearly for access to audiences. The value of this potential is also obvious in the frequently recurring debate over free airtime for political candidates. The opportunity to reach the electronic media audience is perceived by many as a kind of "right" that candidates should enjoy. They assume that citizens' voting behavior will be influenced by exposure to campaign messages. Conversely, if no one is exposed to a message, its impact is never felt.

Academics, too, have recognized that exposure is the wellspring of media effects (e.g., Bryant & Zillmann, 2002). One of the most outspoken scholars has been George Gerbner, a proponent of *cultivation analysis*. Gerbner argued that television content is so uniform, and people are so unselective, that researchers need only compare heavy and light television viewers to determine the medium's social impact. Usually, these arguments are buttressed with data on the sheer amounts of time Americans spend watching (Gerbner, Gross, Morgan, Signorielli, & Shanahan, 2002).

Other academic researchers posit a greater degree of audience selectivity. In fact, studies of *selective exposure*, which we review in chapter 9, have an important place in the history of media research. Although varied in their origins, these studies assume that audience members are capable of discernment and use it in their consumption of media content. Effects depend on the kinds of content they choose. In the Surgeon General's report on TV violence, for example, Israel and Robinson (1972) used viewing diaries to assess how much violence was consumed by various segments of the population. They assumed that heavy viewers of violence-laden programming would be more likely to show its ill effects. Whether one considers specific content or, like Gerbner, TV viewing in general, exposure clearly sets the stage for subsequent media effects.

Government regulators have also used audience information to assess the media's potential to create socially undesirable effects. The FCC uses them, for example, to guide its effort to limit indecent language in broadcasting. Although the Commission might tolerate certain excesses when adults are listening, the presence of young children creates a problem. Some policymakers have tried to channel offensive language away from time periods when children are likely to be in the audience. They use ratings to identify those time periods. Hence, the detrimental effects that might result from exposure to indecent content are, at least, limited by the size of the child audience.

Based on its long history of encouraging *localism* in broadcasting, the FCC has also expressed concern about the audience for local news and public affairs programming. Their effort has been motivated, at least in part, by a desire to keep people informed about issues of public importance. They were convinced, for example, that cable television would

pose a threat to localism by diverting audiences from broadcast stations. In a 1979 report on the relationship between cable and broadcasting, the Commission noted:

> Television may have an important effect in shaping the attitudes and values
> of citizens, in making the electorate more informed and responsible, and in
> contributing to greater understanding and respect among different racial
> and ethnic groups.... Historically, the FCC has encouraged particular
> types of programming—local news, public affairs, instructional pro-
> grams—on these grounds. To the extent that a change in broadcast-cable
> policy would dramatically change the amount by which these programs
> are not only broadcast but also viewed, these issues could be an important
> component of a policy debate. (Federal Communications Commission,
> 1979, p. 639)

In some ways, this line of reasoning is a complement to the logic sup-
porting the indecency rules. Instead of people being harmed by exposure
to something that's bad for them, the FCC expressed concern that undesirable social consequences might flow from people *not* watching something that's good for them.

Today, with the expansion of media options, understanding what
people consume or manage to avoid is increasingly important. In 1980,
the average household could view nine TV stations. Twenty-five years
later a typical household could get over 100 channels of television, not
to mention everything available on DVDs, satellite radio, and the
Internet. This abundance has caused some social critics to worry that
people will choose to hear only like-minded speech and retreat into the
media equivalent of "gated communities" (Sunstein, 2001; Turow,
1997). If people do, in fact, hear only what is agreeable and never encounter dissident voices, it could have undesirable social consequences.
Tracking audience behavior offers a useful way to monitor these
developments (e.g., Webster, 2005).

What Do People Want?

Another important goal of communications policy has been to provide
the public with diverse media content. This objective seems very much
in keeping with our First Amendment ideals, and the benefits that are
thought to result from a free marketplace of ideas. But how does one
achieve diversity? Although policymakers have different opinions on
that subject, the most popular solution has been to structure media industries so that a large number of firms can compete for the attention of
the audience. In theory, competitors respond to audience demand by catering to likes and dislikes as expressed in program choices. The more
competitors, the more likely that various niches will be served. Under
this system, ratings can be thought of as a kind of feedback mechanism.
Arthur Nielsen, Jr. (1988) has described the link between ratings and
preferences as follows:

> Since what the broadcaster has to sell is an audience to advertisers, it fol-
> lows that in order to attract viewers, the broadcaster must cater to the pub-
> lic tastes and preferences. Ratings reveal these preferences. (Nielsen,
> 1988, p. 62)

Many commentators find the industry's argument that they only give the people what they want to be self-serving and deceptive. Most media, they point out, respond to the demands of advertisers, not audience members. Consequently, audiences that are less valuable to advertisers are underserved. Additionally, the advertiser-supported media system requires no measure of the extent to which viewers actually like a particular program, only that they have elected to use it. We review a number of other factors that complicate the link between preference and choice in chapter 9. Nevertheless, a considerable body of theory in both psychology and economics assumes that choice is a function of preference, and this provides adequate justification for the use of ratings in policymaking.

The most relevant of these theories has been developed in the study of *welfare economics*, a branch of the discipline that is concerned with how we can maximize the welfare, or overall well-being, of society. Like other branches of economics, it assumes that people are rational beings who will attempt to satisfy their preferences when choosing goods and services—at least insofar as their pocketbooks allow. Economists refer to this notion as the "theory of revealed preference." Indeed, they make a case that deducing preferences from behavior may be superior to direct questions about a person's likes and dislikes. Because advertiser support imposes no direct costs on viewers (i.e., they do not pay a per program fee), viewer preferences can be freely expressed in program choices. These concepts, and their consequences for how public policy might maximize viewer satisfaction, are fully discussed in Owen and Wildman (1992).

Welfare economists, therefore, have used ratings data to address questions of communications policy. One category of FCC rules that has received intense scrutiny is media ownership. The commission has historically sought to limit certain classes of media (e.g., local newspapers and radio) from owning local television stations, based on the assumption that different owners will contribute different viewpoints to the marketplace of ideas. Unfortunately, existing media may be more adept than newcomers at offering local programming that appeals to viewers. Parkman has, consequently, argued the following:

> If these classes of owners produce more popular programming than
> other classes of owners, the reduction in popular programming should
> be taken into consideration as cost of the diversification policy. To de-
> termine if certain news gathering organizations are more successful
> than others in attracting viewers, we can look at the end result that these
> organizations produce as judged by the viewers, i.e., the ratings. (1982,
> pp. 289–290)

After analyzing the ratings of local television news programs, Parkman concluded that the commission's policy imposed "costs on individual viewers by forcing them to choose programs considered by them as less desirable" (p. 295).

The FCC itself has relied on ratings as a kind of "revealed preference." One notable example is the commission's designation of stations as *significantly viewed*. This concept was introduced into FCC rules in the early 1970s, and was used to determine the popularity of a signal in a given geographical area. Its definition has affected many areas of regulation, such as must-carry, syndicated exclusivity, effective competition, and compulsory copyright. Although the definition changed somewhat over the years, a station was deemed significantly viewed in a market if it achieved a weekly 2% share of audience, and 5% weekly circulation in noncable homes. Estimates like these are made from diary data in most markets, which means they are subject to the kinds of errors we describe in chapter 7. Problems occur when regulators ignore the error estimates and treat these numbers as reliable.

What Are the Economic Implications of Various Policies?

A number of government laws and regulations affect the financial condition of the media and related industries. Because these policies have an impact on the "bread and butter"—or in some cases the Mercedes and BMWs—of those businesses, they attract the attention of many participants in the policymaking process. Even the FCC, which in recent years has favored increased competition in the media, must remain alert to the economic consequences of various policies. After all, the commission is responsible for seeing to it that broadcasting serves the public interest. If broadcasters are driven out of business by some ill-conceived government policy, the commission's mandate might be compromised.

Financial statements that describe the media's revenues, expenses, and profitability are one obvious source of information on the economic condition of the industry. But, for a number of reasons, these data are not always used. For one thing, the commission stopped collecting financial statements from broadcasters many years ago, so the data are not readily available. For another, the harm might be too far advanced to correct economic injury by the time it shows up on company ledgers. A common alternative to a dollars-and-cents measure of economic impact is to use audience ratings. Because ratings measure the commodity that the media sell, policies that adversely affect a station's audience will damage its economic health. Even though ratings and revenues are not perfectly correlated, evidence of lost audiences is often taken as an indication of lost revenues.

Ratings information has been used in several studies to demonstrate audience diversion from established media. Such analyses are frequently used in skirmishes between broadcasters and the cable industry.

Early on in the development of cable, broadcasters claimed economic injury to encourage policies that would restrict cable's growth. They argued that allowing cable to enter a market would threaten the survival of stations by siphoning off valuable audiences. In 1970, Rolla Park at the Rand Corporation assessed this threat through an analysis of local market ratings data. The results of this study helped shape the FCC's 1972 rules on cable television. Again in the late 1970s the commission considered the economic relationship between cable and broadcasting. And again, Park (1979) and a number of interested parties assessed the state of audience diversion through rather sophisticated analyses of audience ratings information. The FCC made extensive references to these studies in its final report.

The Commission also encountered claims of audience diversion in the context of its rules on *syndicated exclusivity*. First adopted in the early 1970s, syndex rules insured that broadcasters who bought exclusive rights to syndicated programming would not have to compete with cable systems that imported the same program on a distant signal. The imported signal, it was argued, would divert audiences that rightly belonged to the local station. In subsequent debates over the rule, the parties at interest (e.g., NAB, NCTA) submitted analyses of ratings data to show that audience losses did or did not occur in the absence of the rule. Although the rule was dropped for some time, the FCC reimposed it, reasoning that "the ability to limit diversion means broadcasters will be able to attract larger audiences, making them more attractive to advertisers, thereby enabling them to obtain more and better programming for their viewers" (Broadcasting, 1988, p. 58).

More recently, ratings data have been used in policy research to analyze television ownership restrictions. The Telecommunications Act of 1996 granted owners of UHF stations special consideration with regard to total audience reach. As stipulated in the Act, the combined audience reach of all stations owned by a single person or entity cannot exceed 35% of the total United States. However, because UHF stations have traditionally operated at a disadvantage compared to VHF stations, lawmakers allowed UHF owners to "discount" their reach estimates. They can count just half of the total station coverage towards the 35% total. Thus, a group owner of all UHF stations might have potential coverage of more than 50% of all TV households, but under the FCC rules that would count as only 25%. To counter a challenge to this arrangement, the NAB prepared a report showing that UHF stations consistently drew smaller audiences because they operate on the UHF band. After accounting for other factors that could cause lower ratings, the NAB found that channel assignment was related to lower ratings. For example, UHF stations affiliated with Fox earned an average of 1 ratings point lower than their VHF counterparts, and NBC affiliates demonstrated a difference of 3.6 ratings points between UHF and VHF stations (Everett, 1998).

Ratings data have also had a substantial impact on the distribution of fees from the *compulsory license*. These fees are paid by cable systems for the right to carry broadcast signals, and they create an annual pool of money close to $200 million. The CARP is responsible for determining how that money should be distributed among various claimants. Those with a claim are copyright holders including program suppliers, commercial broadcasters, public broadcasters, and Canadian broadcasters. It is logical that audience shares would figure in the computation of awards. After all, the economic value of a program or program service rests largely on its ability to attract an audience.

The uses of audience information in legal or regulatory proceedings are considerable. Despite these, and many other applications of the data, it appears to us that social scientists have only scratched the surface of the analytical possibilities. For the most part, these uses of the ratings have dealt with gross measures of audience size. Perhaps that should not be surprising, because such estimates are the most readily available. Indeed, that is what the ratings are. Using ratings to track individuals over time, engaging in what we call cumulative analyses, would seem a logical next step for social scientific inquiry.

Take, for example, the question of media effects. Although the size of the audience exposed to a message may suggest something about its potential effect, so too does the regularity of exposure. Advertisers recognize this concept as frequency—the average number of times audience members see or hear a message. Effects researchers might similarly ask how often people see or hear a particular kind of programming. For example, do all children see about the same amount of violence on television, or do some consume more? Is some segment of the child audience violence junkies? If so, who are those children? Do they come from poor or affluent families? Do they watch alone or with others? The answer to such questions, all of which can be gleaned from audience data, might contribute much to our understanding of the impact of televised violence. Similar questions could be asked about the audience for news and information.

Studies of audience duplication might reveal more about people's preferences for programming as well. Does a particular program have a small-but-loyal following, or is it just small? Programmers and marketing researchers have long recognized a certain feature of audience duplication called channel loyalty. Religious, Spanish language, and at least some news channels are among the kinds of programming that seem to attract small-but-loyal audiences. Does this intensity of use suggest something about how the audience values a service above and beyond the number who use it at any point in time?

Factors other than size and composition also affect the economic value of an audience. Advertisers may specify reach and frequency objectives in their media plans. Those who seek a high frequency of exposure might be willing to pay a premium for that small-but-loyal audience. In a similar vein, channel loyalty and inheritance effects undoubtedly contribute to the audience of a syndicated program. If a station adds value to the program by delivering an audience predisposed to watch, then perhaps the station should have a greater share of credit for a program's success.

Even media critics who distrust social scientific methods might learn more about audience experience with media through inventive uses of ratings data. For instance, analysts of popular culture have become increasingly interested in how people make sense of television programming. One insight from this line of research is that the viewers experience the medium not as discrete programs, but as strips of textual material called *flow texts*. The emergence of flow texts could be studied through analogous research on audience flow.

All of these analyses, and many more, could be realized through the application of commercial audience data. Unfortunately, the effective use of such data in the social sciences and related disciplines has been uneven. In part, that is because the proprietary nature of syndicated research makes it too expensive for strictly academic analyses. We have more to say about buying data in chapter 8. Some academics, however, may fail to exploit the data that are available, simply because they do not recognize the analytical possibilities. We hope the remainder of this book helps remedy the latter problem. Subsequent chapters acquaint the reader with audience measurement services, the data they collect, the products they offer, and the theory and techniques of ratings analysis.

RELATED READINGS

Baker, C. E. (2002). *Media, markets, and democracy*. Cambridge: Cambridge University Press.

Bryant, J., & Zillmann, D. (Eds.). (2002). *Media effects: Advances in theory and research* (2nd ed.). Mahwah, NJ: Lawrence Erlbaum Associates.

Comstock, G., & Scharrer, E. (1999). *Television: What's on, who's watching, and what it means*. San Diego: Academic Press.

Lowery, S., & DeFleur, M. L. (1994). *Milestones in mass communication research* (3rd ed.). New York: Addison-Wesley.

Napoli, P. M. (2001). *Foundations of communications policy: Principles and process in the regulation of electronic media*. Cresskill, NJ: Hampton Press.

Noll, R. G., & Price, M. E. (Eds.). (1998). *A communications cornucopia: Markle Foundation essays on information policy*. Washington: Brookings Institution Press.

Owen, B., & Wildman, S. (1992). *Video economics*. Cambridge, MA: Harvard University Press.

Sunstein, C. (2001). *Republic.com*. Princeton, NJ: Princeton University Press.

Turow, J. (1997). *Breaking up America: Advertisers and the new media world*. Chicago: University of Chicago Press.

II
RESEARCH DATA

Chapter 6

The Audience Measurement Business

Since the beginning of radio, the broadcaster has been interested in how the owner of a receiver reacts to the programs presented over the air. Some of the questions to which the broadcaster, whether he is an educator or advertiser, is anxious to secure the answers are as follows:

1. When does the listener use his receiver?
2. For how long a period does he use it?
3. To what station or stations does he listen?
4. Who listens (sex, age, economic and educational level)?
5. What does he do while the receiver is in operation?
6. What does he do as a result of the program?
7. What are his program preferences?

—*Frank N. Stanton* (1935)

Stanton, who was later to become president of CBS, wrote those words in his doctoral dissertation. Surprisingly little has changed since that time. The electronic media themselves have undergone great transformations, but the basic research question—Who is the audience?—has been one of the most enduring features of the industry. In this chapter we trace the evolution of the audience measurement business. Our purpose is not to offer a comprehensive history of audience measurement, but to help readers better understand the industry's present condition and to better anticipate its future.

Even the first "broadcaster" wanted to know who was listening. After more than 5 years of research, experimentation, and building on the work of many others, an electrical engineer named Reginald A. Fessenden broadcast the sound of human voices on Christmas Eve in 1906. He played the violin, sang, recited poetry, and played a phonograph record. Fessenden promised his listeners he'd be back on the air again for New Year's Eve, and he asked anyone who had heard the broadcast to write him a letter. Apparently, he got a number of letters from radio operators, many of them on ships at sea, who were astonished to hear more than Morse code on their headphones. Other early station operators asked for letters from listeners as well. Frank Conrad, who in 1920 developed KDKA in Pittsburgh for Westinghouse, even played specific records requested by his correspondents.

A need to know the audience quickly became more than just a question of satisfying an operator's curiosity about unseen listeners. By the early 1920s, AT&T had demonstrated that charging clients a toll to make announcements over its station was an effective way to fund the medium. "Toll broadcasting," as the practice was called, soon led to the idea of selling commercial time to advertisers.

By 1928, broadcasting was sufficiently advanced to provide listeners with consistent and quality reception. Many people had developed the habit of listening to radio, and broadcasters in cooperation with advertisers were developing program formats "suitable for sponsorship" (Spaulding, 1963). Although there was some public controversy over whether radio should be used for advertising, the Great Depression that began in 1929 caused radio station owners to turn increasingly to advertisers for support.

For radio to succeed as an advertising medium, however, time buyers had to know who was in the radio audience. Newspapers already provided authenticated figures on circulation through the Audit Bureau of Circulation (ABC). Theater and movie audiences could be measured by ticket sales. Music popularity could be measured by record sales and, later, jukebox plays. But broadcasters and their advertisers were left with irregular, and frequently inadequate, assessments of the size and composition of the audience.

Many radio advertisers, for example, offered coupons or prizes in an attempt to measure response. In 1933 about two thirds of all NBC advertisers made some sort of offer that listeners could send for—mostly novelty items, booklets with information, or a chance to win a contest. Responses were sometimes overwhelming. In answer to a single announcement on a children's program, WLW in Cincinnati received more than 20,000 letters. The program's sponsor, Hires Root Beer, used these responses to select specific stations on which to advertise in the future. But soliciting listener response had risks. The makers of Ovaltine, a drink for children, and the sponsors of Little Orphan Annie, asked fans to send in labels in order to free Annie from kidnappers. As you might imagine, this provoked an uproar from parents.

Early stations used equally primitive techniques to estimate the size of their audience. Some counted fan mail, others simply reported the population or number of receivers sold in their market. Each of these methods was unreliable and invited exaggeration. The networks were somewhat more deliberate about audience measurement. In 1927, NBC commissioned a study to determine not only the size of its audience, but hours and days of listening. The company also sought information on the economic status of listeners, foreshadowing the use of "demographics" now so much a part of audience research. In 1930, CBS conducted an on-the-air mail survey, offering a free map to all listeners who would write to their local stations. CBS compared the response to the population of each county, and developed its first coverage maps. But none of these attempts offered the kind of regular, independent measurement of the audience that the medium would need to sustain itself.

THE DEVELOPMENT OF AUDIENCE MEASUREMENT

The history of ratings research is a story of individual researchers and entrepreneurs, of struggles for industry acceptance, as well as an account of the broadcasting business itself. It is also a story of research methods. Every major ratings research company rose to prominence by perfecting and promoting its own brand of research. Most major changes in the structure and services of the industry have also been tied to research methods. For this reason, we have chosen to organize our discussion of the industry's history around the research methods these firms used.

Telephone Interviews

From 1930 to 1935, the revenues and profits of the network companies nearly doubled, all at a time when the country and most other businesses were in a deep economic depression. Because many American families did not have money to spend on other diversions—and because radio was indeed entertaining—the audience grew rapidly. An important stimulant to that growth was the emergence of a system for providing audience estimates that advertisers could believe. The first such system depended on another technological marvel—the telephone.

Then, as now, advertisers were the driving force behind ratings research; they helped create the first ratings company to conduct regular surveys. In 1927, a baking powder company hired the Crossley Business Research Company to survey the effectiveness of its radio advertising. Two years later, Crossley did a similar survey for Eastman Kodak, using telephone interviews to ask people if they had heard a specific program. At the time, the telephone was an unconventional tool for conducting survey research, but it seemed well suited for measuring something as far-flung and rapidly changing as the radio audience.

Archibald Crossley, the company president and well-known public opinion pollster, suggested to the Association of National Advertisers (ANA) that a new industry association might use the telephone to measure radio listening. His report, entitled "The Advertiser Looks at Radio," was widely distributed and ANA members quickly agreed to pay a monthly fee to support regular and continuous surveys of radio listening. The American Association of Advertising Agencies (AAAA) also agreed on the need for regular radio audience measurements.

This new service, officially called the Cooperative Analysis of Broadcasting, or CAB, began in March of 1930. CAB reports were generally referred to in the trade press simply as "the Crossley ratings." Even the popular press began to note the rise or fall of specific programs or personalities in the ratings. Initially, only advertisers paid CAB for its service, but before long advertising agencies began to subscribe. The networks accessed the reports as well, using them to sell time and to make programming decisions, but their use was "unofficial." Not until 1937 were NBC and CBS allowed to become subscribers, thus sharing the cost and the data.

In the early years, Crossley revised his methods and expanded the amount of information he provided a number of times. By the 1935-1936 season, surveys were conducted in the 33 cities that had stations carrying CBS and the two NBC networks. Calls were placed four different times during the day and respondents were asked to "recall" the radio listening during the last 3 to 6 hours. Hence, Crossley's method of measurement was known as *telephone recall*. Monthly, and later bi-weekly, reports were published that gave audience estimates for all national network programs. Further, three times a year more detailed summaries provided information about station audiences hour by hour, with breakdowns for geographic and financial categories.

However, CAB's methods were flawed. Telephone recall surveys could not reach radio listeners who didn't have telephones. This limitation was less serious in the early years of the service, because the first families to purchase radios were higher income households likely to have telephones. By the end of the 1930s, when the growth of radio homes began to out-pace those with telephones, CAB had to alter its sampling procedures to include more low-income households to compensate.

The most serious limitation to the CAB method was that it required listeners to remember what they had heard. Despite the method's efficiency—it could collect information on listening to several hours of programs—another technique that featured a simultaneous or "coincidental" telephone survey was soon to challenge Crossley's early dominance of the ratings business.

As early as 1929, another soon-to-be famous pollster, George Gallup, measured radio audience size by conducting personal interviews. He then went to work for major advertising agency Young and Rubicam, where he conducted a nationwide *telephone coincidental*. Rather than relying on memory, the coincidental asked people what they were listening to at the time of the call. Gallup was one of a small group of research pioneers who developed this new survey method. Contributions were also made by Pauline Arnold, Percival White, and John Karol, who later became director of research for CBS.

In 1933, Pauline Arnold specifically compared the telephone recall and coincidental methods, as summarized in Lumley (1934):

> The results showed that some programs, which were listened to by many listeners, were reported the next day by only a few. In general, dramatic programs were better remembered than musical programs. However, the rank correlation between the percentage of listeners hearing 25 (half-hour)

programs and the percentage reporting having heard them was about .78. This is a measure of the adequacy of the Crossley survey as compared with the simultaneous telephone survey. (pp. 29–30)

The telephone coincidental provided a methodological advantage that opened the door for CAB's first ratings competitor. This happened when Claude Hooper and Montgomery Clark quit the market research organization of Daniel Starch in 1934 to start Clark-Hooper. George Gallup assisted them in arranging for their first survey. Hooper later wrote that "Even the coincidental method which we have developed into radio's basic source of audience size measurement was originally presented to us by Dr. George Gallup" (Chappell & Hooper, 1944, p. vii). In the fall of that year, Clark-Hooper launched a syndicated ratings service in 16 cities.

Ironically, Clark-Hooper was first supported by a group of magazine publishers who were unhappy with the fact that radio was claiming an ever-larger share of advertiser dollars. They believed that Crossley's recall technique overstated the audience for radio. Although it could be expected that coincidental ratings would capture certain unremembered listening, the publishers hoped that Clark-Hooper would show that many people were either not home or doing something else besides listening to the radio. In fact, the first Clark-Hooper results did show lower listening levels than those of CAB.

In 1938, Clark and Hooper split, the former taking the company's print research business. With great faith in the future of radio, Hooper went into business for himself. His research method was simple. Those answering the phone were asked:

- Were you listening to the radio just now?
- To what program were you listening?
- Over what station is that program coming?
- What advertiser puts on that program?

Then they were asked to report the number of men, women, and children who were listening when the telephone rang.

Hooperatings, as his audience estimates came to be called, were lower than CAB's for some programs but higher for others. As Hooper would argue later, people were better able to remember programs that were longer, more popular, and had been on the air for a longer period of time. Respondents were also much more likely to recall variety programs; they were most likely to forget listening to the news (Chappell & Hooper, 1944, pp. 140–150). Over time, the industry began to regard C. E. Hooper's coincidentals as more accurate than CAB's recall techniques.

But methodological superiority was not enough. As the creature of the ANA and AAAA, CAB was well entrenched with the advertising industry. Recognizing that CAB served the buyers of radio time, Hooper decided to pursue the broadcast media, and he established a service to supply both the buyer and the seller. CAB might see fit to ignore networks and stations, but Hooper would seek them out as clients and provide them with the kinds of audience research they needed. This strategy was perceptive, for today the media account for the overwhelming majority of ratings service revenues.

Hooper also worked hard for the popular acceptance of Hooperatings. To achieve as much press coverage as possible, each month he released information about the highest rated evening programs. This went not only to the trade press, but to popular columnists as well. In this way, C.E. Hooper, Inc. became the most visible and talked about supplier of audience information for the industry. Radio comedians even began to joke about their, or the competition's, Hooperatings.

In addition to promoting popular consciousness of program ratings, Hooper was also responsible for establishing many of the traditions and practices of contemporary audience research. He instituted the "pocketpiece" format for ratings reports, now the hallmark of the national Nielsen ratings, as well as concepts like the "available audience" and "sets in use." He also began to report audience shares, which he called "percent of listeners," and the composition of the audience in terms of age and gender. Thus, by the end of the 1930s the basic pattern of commercial audience research for broadcasting was set.

Hooper and his company were efficient and aggressive. He regularly did research to try to make his methods more accurate or to add new services, especially to help the networks and stations. He was also relentlessly critical of the CAB method that still depended on recall. As a part of this battle, in 1941, Hooper hired Columbia University psychology professor Matthew Chappell to study recall and memory. Two years later they wrote a book trumpeting the advantage of telephone coincidental.

Hooper's aggressiveness paid off. Just after World War II he bought out CAB, which was on the verge of collapse. C. E. Hooper was now the unquestioned leader in ratings research. But even as Hooper reached his zenith, the broadcast industry was changing. The number of radio stations expanded rapidly, and the new medium of television was about to alter the way people used their leisure time. A new methodology and company were ascendant as well. Although he continued to offer local measurement of radio and television, in 1950, Hooper sold his national ratings service to A. C. Nielsen.

Today, telephone interviews are a common data-gathering technique for marketing researchers and public opinion pollsters. Simmons' massive National Consumer Study, which collects data on media use and product purchases from over 25,000 adults, relies on an initial wave of telephone interviews to help place their lengthy questionnaires. Most ratings companies also use telephones in one capacity or another to identify respondents or secure their cooperation. However, since the late 1990s, telephones have fallen out of favor as the principal means to measure day-to-day media usage.

Personal Interviews

In-person, formal interviews were often used in early radio surveys, especially by academics with a background in sociology or marketing. Today, this method is no longer a mainstay of the ratings industry, although personal interviews conducted at home or during the course of focus groups are still widely used to obtain other types of information from audiences. Most notably, Mediamark Research (MRI) conducts over 25,000 hour-long personal interviews each year to gather data on media usage that it later pairs with information on product purchases. While these data do not function like the "currency" of audience ratings, knowing something about personal interviews is relevant to understanding current research practices as well as how the nature of audience measurement can shape the very industry it is intended to serve.

Most of the early Daniel Starch studies for NBC, beginning in Spring 1928, were done by personal interview. And even though the first ratings services had come into existence, CBS commissioned Starch to do a series of reports in the 1930s. CBS argued that this provided more accurate information because Hooper's "telephone calls obviously miss all non-telephone homes—which becomes an increasing distortion as one gets into the smaller communities." Because CBS had fewer and, often, less-powerful affiliated stations than NBC, the network felt it could only benefit from this sort of audience research (CBS, 1937).

In the late 1930s, while Crossley and Hooper argued over different methods of telephone data collection and Nielsen worked to perfect his metering device, the personal interview was still the most accepted method of collecting socio-psychological behavioral information. One man in particular, Dr. Sydney Roslow, who had a doctorate in psychology, became intrigued with the technique while interviewing visitors at the New York World's Fair. With the encouragement of Paul Lazarsfeld, he started to adapt these techniques to the measurement of radio listening.

In the fall of 1941, he began providing audience estimates, called The Pulse of New York, based on a personal interview *roster recall* method that he developed. When respondents were contacted they were given a roster of programs to aid in their recall of listening for the past few hours. Because Hooper, and later Nielsen, concentrated on network ratings, his local service expanded rapidly—especially with the tremendous expansion of stations after World War II. By the early 1960s Pulse was publishing reports in 250 radio markets around the country and was the dominant source for local radio measurement.

The roster recall method had some significant advantages over its competitors. It could include out-of-home listening (e.g., automobile and work), and measure radio use during hours not covered by the telephone coincidental—Hooper was limited to calls from 8 a.m. to 10:30 p.m. Further, it provided demographic details and information on many minority and foreign-language stations popular with those less likely to have phones.

The widespread availability of local radio ratings that captured information on listeners who were hard to reach with other methods had a significant impact on the shape of local radio itself. Pulse's emphasis on measuring audiences in the metro area, versus Nielsen's nationwide measurement of network programs, contributed to the rise of "Top 40" and popular music format stations. Local advertisers were only interested in the number of listeners in their marketing area. These rock music stations were usually lower in power but had very high shares within their smaller coverage area. Thus, Pulse was a boon to the growth of rock formats, just as more and more local stations were coming on the air, and more and more network programs and personalities were transferred to TV or oblivion.

However, by the 1970s still another ratings company, featuring another method, took control of local radio ratings. The American Research Bureau (ARB), which we describe in the sections that follow, used its success with television diary techniques to move into radio. As a subsidiary of a large computer company, ARB had superior computing power that aided in the timely production of market reports. It also appears that the rock and ethnic stations favored by the interview method were not as aggressive in selling to advertising agencies, so agencies came increasingly to accept the diary technique being promoted by news and "easy listening" stations. In 1978, Pulse went out of business.

Meters

As early as the 1920s, broadcasters and advertisers recognized the potential advantages of making a simultaneous, permanent, and continuous record of what people actually listened to on the radio. Technical problems involved in developing such a system were solved in the 1930s, and they were finally in common use by the late 1940s. When these meters finally arrived, however, they had a profound and lasting impact on the ratings business.

While a student at Columbia University in 1929, Claude Robinson—later a partner with George Gallup in public opinion research—patented a device to "provide for scientifically measuring the broadcast listener response by making a comparative record of ... receiving sets ... tuned over a selected period of time" (Beville, 1988, p. 17). The patent was sold to RCA, parent of NBC, but nothing more is known of the device. Despite the advantages of a meter, none had been perfected, leading Lumley (1934) to report:

> Although the possibilities of measurement using a mechanical or electrical recording device would be unlimited, little development has taken place as yet in this field. Reports have been circulated concerning devices to record the times at which the set is tuned in together with a station identification mark. None of these devices has been used more than experimentally. Stanton, however, has perfected an instrument which will record each time at which a radio set is turned on. (pp. 179–180)

The reference was, of course, to Frank N. Stanton, then Lumley's student. For his dissertation, the first paragraph of which began this chapter, Stanton built and tested 10 devices "designed to record set operation for [a] period as long as six weeks" (Lumley, 1934, p. 180). On wax-coated tape, one stylus marked 15-minute intervals while another marked when the set was turned on. The device did not record station tuning but was used to check against listening as recorded on questionnaires. Stanton, by the way, found that respondents tended to underestimate the time they spent with the set on, a bias of recall techniques that holds true even today.

In 1930 and 1931, Robert Elder of the Massachusetts Institute of Technology conducted radio advertising effectiveness studies that were published by CBS. In 1933–1934, he and Louis F. Woodruff, an electrical engineer, designed and tested a device to record radio tuning. The device scratched a record on paper by causing a stylus to move back and forth as the radio tuner was moved across the dial. Elder called his device an *Audimeter*, and sought a patent. Discovering the previous Robinson—now RCA—patent, he received permission from RCA to proceed. The first field test used about 100 of the recorders in the Boston area. In 1936, Arthur C. Nielsen heard a speech by Elder describing the device and apparently began negotiating to buy the rights to the technique immediately.

An electrical engineering graduate of the University of Wisconsin, Nielsen had first opened a business to test the efficiency of industrial equipment. When he began in 1923, it was a period of great expansion for inventing, manufacturing, and the rapid deployment of new assembly-line techniques. The business survived but did not prosper. Ten years later a pharmaceutical client suggested to a Nielsen employee that what they really needed was information on the distribution and turnover of their products. In response, Nielsen developed a consumer survey based on a panel of stores to check inventory in stock. The business grew rapidly, a food index was added, and the company prospered. The A. C. Nielsen Company was on its way to becoming the largest marketing research firm in the world. But it was the acquisition of the Elder-Woodruff Audimeter that would ultimately serve to imprint the Nielsen name in Americans' consciousness.

With his engineering background, and the profits from his successful indices, Nielsen redesigned the device. There were field tests in 1938 in Chicago and North Carolina to compare urban and rural listening. Despite war shortages, by 1942 the company launched the Nielsen Radio Index (NRI), based on some 800 homes equipped with his device. Nielsen technicians had to visit each home periodically to change the paper tape in the device, which slowed data collection. However, the company also provided information about product purchases, based on an inventory of each household's "pantry." Having already established a good reputation with advertisers, Nielsen began to make progress in overtaking the dominant ratings supplier, C. E. Hooper. Figure 6.1 pictures the earliest paper tape Audimeter.

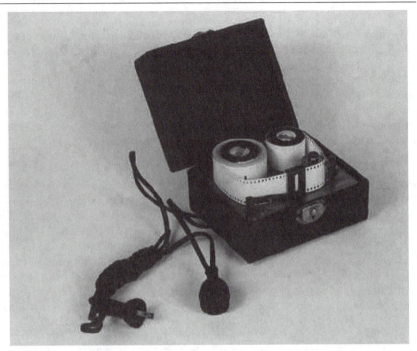

FIG. 6.1. The first Audimeter (1936). Source: Nielsen Media Research. Reprinted by permission.

During the 1950s, Nielsen continued to expand his ratings business and to perfect the technology of audience measurement. As we noted, in 1950 he acquired Hooper's national ratings service. In the same year he initiated the Nielsen Television Index (NTI), the company's first attempt to measure that fledgling medium. By the middle of the decade, he launched the Nielsen Station Index (NSI) to provide local ratings in both radio and television. His engineers perfected a new version of the Audimeter that recorded tuner activity on a 16mm film cartridge. More importantly, the cartridge could be mailed directly to Nielsen sample households and then mailed back to Nielsen headquarters, thereby speeding the rate at which data could be collected. Nielsen had also begun to use diaries for gathering audience demographics. To improve their accuracy, he introduced a special device called a "recordimeter," that monitored hours of set usage, and flashed a light to remind people to fill in their diaries.

The 1960s were more tumultuous, not just for Nielsen but for all ratings companies. In an atmosphere charged by quiz show scandals on television, reports of corruption and "payola" in the music industry, as well as growing social unrest, the U.S. Congress launched a far-reaching investigation of the ratings business. Recognizing the tremendous impact that ratings had on broadcasters, and concerned about reports of shoddy research, Oren Harris, chairman of the House Committee on Interstate and Foreign Commerce, orchestrated a lengthy study of industry practices. In 1966, the Harris Committee issued its report. Although it stopped short of recommending legislation to regulate audience measurement, the investigation had a sobering effect on the ratings business—effects that are still evident today in the scrupulous detail with which methods and the reliability of ratings are reported, and the existence of the Media Rating Council (until 1982 the Broadcast Rating Council; from 1982 to 1998 the Electronic Media Rating Council).

As the premier ratings company, Nielsen was particularly visible in the congressional hearings, especially its radio index. In response, Mr. Nielsen personally developed a new radio index that would be above criticism. Unfortunately, potential customers resisted the change because of the increased costs associated with data collection. Angered by this situation, in 1964 Nielsen withdrew from national radio measurement altogether. In fact, a year earlier Nielsen had discontinued local radio measurement, leaving Pulse unchallenged.

A new company, Statistical Research Inc. (SRI), eventually filled the void left by the demise of Nielsen's radio service. SRI was formed in 1969 by Gerald Glasser, a statistics professor at New York University, and Gale Metzger, former director of research for the Nielsen Media division. Three years later, the company took over operation of a collaborative industry research effort called *Radio's All Dimension Audience Research (RADAR)*, which continued to produce reports on radio network audiences. In 2001, the RADAR brand was acquired by Arbitron, and SRI was sold to Knowledge Networks.

Since the 1950s, Nielsen has been the sole supplier of national TV network ratings. For a time in the 1980s, it appeared it might face a serious challenger. Audits of Great Britain (AGB), a ratings company with operations in Europe and Asia, had developed a new measurement technology called a "peoplemeter." AGB hoped to establish itself in the U.S. market with this innovative device. As we will see in the next chapter, peoplemeters expanded the capabilities of traditional household meters by allowing viewers to enter information about who was watching television. AGB worked hard to get funding from the industry, including advertisers and the media. Within a couple of years it had sufficient support to wire the Boston market with peoplemeters and begin a field test of the system. Nielsen responded by announcing plans to test and implement a national peoplemeter service of its own. In 1987, Nielsen began basing its NTI services on a sample of households equipped with peoplemeters. AGB held on for a time, but with equivocal support from the industry, especially the broadcast networks, its position was untenable. In 1988, it ended its U.S. operations.

The need to measure Internet audiences has introduced some new types of metering to electronic media analysis. Firms like Nielsen and Arbitron have traditionally used survey research techniques and specially installed meters to measure mass media consumption. Newer companies intent on measuring computer usage have simply taken advantage of existing desktop machines. That is, usage is tracked with software products that consumers who agree to be part of the sample download onto their computers. This system of tracking is currently the mainstay of the Internet ratings business.

Diaries

In the 1920s, many radio set builders and listeners were not interested in programs at all. Instead, they were trying to hear as many different and distant stations as possible. In order to keep track of those stations, they kept elaborate logs of the signals they heard and when they heard them. They noted information such as station call letters, city of origin, slogans, and program titles. Despite this early form of diary keeping, and the occasional use of diaries by radio ratings firms, the diary method did not become a mainstay of commercial audience research until the rise of television.

The first systematic research on dairies was done by Garnet Garrison. In 1937 he began to "experiment developing a radio research technique for measurement of listening habits which would be inexpensive and yet fairly reliable" (Garrison, 1939, p. 204). Garrison, for many years a professor at the University of Michigan, noted that at the time the other methods were the telephone survey, either coincidental or unaided recall, personal interviews, mail analysis or surveys, and "the youngster automatic recording." His method, which he called a "listening table," borrowed something from each because it could be sent and retrieved by mail, included a program roster, and was thought to be objective. His form provided a grid from 6 a.m. to midnight divided into 15-minute segments, and asked respondents to list station, programs, and the number of listeners. He concluded that:

> With careful attention to correct sampling, distribution of listening tables, and tabulation of the raw data, the technique of "listening tables" should assist materially in obtaining at small cost quite detailed information about radio listening. (Garrison, 1939, p. 205)

CBS experimented with diaries in the 1940s, but apparently thought of the data as applicable only to programming rather than to sales. Diaries were used to track such things as audience composition, listening to lead-in or lead-out programs, and charting audience flow and turnover. In the late 1940s, Hooper also added diaries to his telephone sample in areas "which cannot be reached practically by telephone." This mixture of diary and coincidental was never completely satisfactory. Indeed, one of the reasons for the slippage of Hooper against Nielsen was that the telephone method was, for the most part, confined to large metropolitan areas where TV first began to erode the radio audience. Hence, Hooper tended to understate radio listenership.

It was not until the late 1940s that diaries were introduced as the principal method of a syndicated research service. As director of research for the NBC-owned station in Washington, DC, James Seiler had proposed using diaries to measure radio for several years. The station finally agreed to try a survey for its new TV station. NBC helped pay for several tests, but Seiler set up his own company to begin a regular ratings service.

He called the company American Research Bureau (ARB), and in Washington, just after the war, its name sounded very official, even patriotic. ARB issued its first local market report in 1949. Based on a week-long diary, which covered May 11–18, it showed the Ed Sullivan's "Toast of the Town" Sunday variety program with a 66.4 rating. "Wrestling," on the ABC affiliate at a different time got a 37.5, and "Meet the Press" on NBC got a 2.5.

By fall, the company was also measuring local TV in Baltimore, Philadelphia, and New York. Chicago and Cleveland were added the next year. The company grew slowly at first—as both television and the diary research methodology gained acceptance. Diaries were placed in TV homes identified by random phone calls. From the beginning, Seiler was careful to list the number of diaries placed, and those "recovered and usable." Further, "breakdowns of numbers of men, women, and children per set for specific programs [could] be furnished by extra tabulation" (American Research Bureau, 1947, p. 1).

Another research company had begun diary-based ratings in Los Angeles in 1947, using the name Tele-Que. The two companies merged in 1951, thus adding reports for Los Angeles, San Diego, and San Francisco and bringing to ARB several young, bright researchers such as Roger Cooper and R. R. "Rip" Ridgeway, who would help lead the company's growth.

Through the 1950s, ARB emerged as the prime contender to Nielsen's local TV audience measurement, especially after 1955 when it took over the local Hooper TV ratings business. The company expanded, and by 1961 it was measuring virtually every TV market twice a year, and larger markets more often. The networks and stations responded by putting on especially attractive programming during these "sweeps" periods. In 1965, after Nielsen quit local radio, ARB began using diaries to provide local radio reports. These, as we have seen, eventually put Pulse out of business.

ARB even tried to one-up Nielsen by developing a meter whose contents could be retrieved over a telephone. In 1957, ARB placed meters in 300 New York City households and began to provide "instantaneous" day-after ratings. Generally speaking, this move met with the approval of advertisers and the media because it meant Nielsen might face more effective competition. Unfortunately for ARB, Arthur Nielsen and his engineers had patented almost every conceivable way of metering a set. ARB's new owner, a firm named CEIR, was forced to pay Nielsen a fee for the rights to the device. Nevertheless, this spurred Nielsen to quickly wire a New York sample with meters, and later, in 1973, to introduce a *Storage Instantaneous Audimeter (SIA)* as the data-collection device for its full national sample.

For many years, ARB was the undisputed provider of local radio ratings. One firm, Birch/Scarborough Research, did, for a time, challenge its dominance in radio measurement. Tom Birch, a radio programmer, began conducting research for his own benefit. Soon, other stations asked him to do *call-out research* for them as well. From this beginning, he gradually started measuring radio use. In 1980, he was providing a service, based on telephone interviews, to 18 markets. This later expanded to more than 250 markets. Once again, the media industry generally welcomed competition in the ratings business, but, in the end, was unwilling to adequately fund a second service. Birch eventually discontinued the ratings business in 1992, and sold its qualitative Scarborough service to its former competitor.

In 1973, ARB changed its name to Arbitron. What had sounded so patriotic after the Second World War evoked a "big brother" image after the turbulent 1960s. Two decades latter, Arbitron finally conceded the field of local TV measurement to Nielsen. As TV stations' budgets tightened in the more competitive media environments of the late 1980s and early 1990s, most could no longer afford to buy two ratings services. The balance tipped in Nielsen's favor, and it became the de facto currency in local TV. In November of 1993 Arbitron left the television audience measurement business to focus exclusively on local radio. To this day, the diary remains the backbone of its ratings service. Arbitron has, however, recently developed an innovative portable peoplemeter capable of measuring both radio and television (discussed in chapter 7). This puts them back into the business of measuring television audiences, though not for the moment, in the United States. The development of major audience ratings research methods is summarized in Table 6.1.

THE AUDIENCE MEASUREMENT BUSINESS TODAY

While many companies collect data on audiences, the ratings business is dominated by a few firms. Nielsen Media Research and Arbitron are currently the principal suppliers of ratings data in television and radio, respectively, while comScore Media Metrix, Inc., and Nielsen//NetRatings vie for preeminence in Internet measurement. In fact, competition is sometimes more apparent than real. VNU, a large Dutch conglomerate, now owns all or part of Nielsen Media Research, A. C. Nielsen, Claritas, and Nielsen//NetRatings. VNU and Arbitron have been involved in a joint venture to develop a "single source" system that collects media use and product purchase information from the same household. These two companies jointly own Scarborough Research. Arbitron and comScore launched a service to measure Internet radio audiences. On the global stage, there are few major players as well. TNS, AGB, and Nielsen Media

TABLE 6.1

Milestones in Ratings Research

Person/Company	Methodology	Notes
Archibald Crossley Cooperative Analysis of Broadcasting (CAB)	Same-day telephone recall	Founded in 1930 Supported by the Association of National Advertisers Measured national network programs
Claude Hooper and Montgomery Clark Clark-Hooper; later Hooper, Inc.	Telephone coincidental	Founded in 1934 First supported by magazine publishers Produced "Hooperatings" Bought out CAB after WWII
Sydney Roslow The Pulse of New York	Interviews— roster-recall	Founded in 1941 Measured local radio stations Went out of business in 1978
Arthur C. Nielsen A. C. Nielsen Company, later Nielsen Media Research	Audimeter (later added diary collection)	Launched "radio index" in 1942 Acquired Hooper's national business in 1950 Ended radio measurement in 1964 to focus on TV Begins use of peoplemeters for national ratings 1987 Begins use of peoplemeters for local ratings 2004
James Seiler American Research Bureau, later Arbitron	Diary (later added meter collection)	First survey in 1949 Merged with Tele-Que in 1951 Took over Hooper's local business in 1955 Begin R&D on portable peoplemeters 1992 Left television business in 1993 to focus on local radio Acquired RADAR 2001
Tom Birch Birch Radio	Telephone recall	Provided competitive service to Arbitron until 1992
Gale Metzger and Gerald Glasser Statistical Research, Inc.	Telephone recall (for RADAR)	Founded RADAR in 1969 to measure network radio Acquired by Knowledge Networks 2001; sold RADAR to Arbitron.
Media Metrix, later comScore Media Metrix	Software to record Internet usage	Parent company developed PC Meter in 1995 Merged with RelevantKnowledge in 1998 Partnered with Arbitron 2004 to measure Internet radio
NetRatings, later Nielsen/NetRatings	Software to record Internet usage	Founded 1997 Partnered with Nielsen 1998

Research all supply audience ratings services to multiple countries, and the latter two agreed to create a new company called AGB Nielsen Media Research. In countries where these firms are not the sole suppliers of audience measurement, they frequently have joint ventures or license their measurement technology to others. In China, for example, TNS has partnered with a local company to create CSM, which provides ratings data. TNS has, in turn, licensed portable peoplemeter technology from Arbitron for use in Belgium and Singapore.

Smaller audience research firms often carve out niches that are unfilled by the larger firms, but they rarely provide the currency that is used to buy and sell audiences. Rather, they serve to complement the established ratings companies. And, like the first ratings companies, they are often the work of inventive entrepreneurs. For example, MobilTrak, founded in 1998 by Jim Christian, monitors passing cars to determine the radio station to which they're tuned. Christian invested $10 million to $15 million of his own money to develop monitors sensitive enough to detect the radiation coming off car antennas, yet small enough to place on utility poles. With enough monitoring stations throughout the market, local media buyers, like car dealers, can identify which stations are most frequently heard in their immediate geographic area. This allows them to discriminate among stations that might have comparable ratings.Why do a few large firms dominate the audience ratings business? The answer has to do with the economics of audience measurement and the politics of media industries. To produce the refined audience estimates that are increasingly demanded by advertisers and their agencies, ratings companies have had to make increasingly large investments. Household meters are more expensive than diaries, and peoplemeters are more expensive still. Further, as the media environment becomes more complex, audiences become more fragmented, and advertisers address more narrowly defined markets, sample sizes need to be much bigger just to keep up. This means that the cost of producing a ratings report is going up.

Not only are expenses increasing, but they must be incurred at the beginning of the process. Before the first report can be produced, samples must be drawn, meters or other data collection technologies must be developed or licensed and then deployed, and the people and machinery needed to crunch the numbers must be in place. This problem is hardy unique to audience measurement. Almost any kind of pre-recorded entertainment or information has the same economic characteristic. Economists sometimes refer to these as "first copy costs." They represent a significant barrier for a new competitor who wants to enter the business.

Once an incumbent has incurred those costs, however, producing and selling additional reports involves little or no additional expense. The data are there, already bought and paid for. In fact, if clients access the data through a password-protected Web site, even the cost of printing additional reports is eliminated. Economists call such products "public goods." One person's consumption of the good does not diminish the quantity available for others. Among other things, this means that an existing ratings company can lower its prices when it faces a competitive threat.

But the staying power of incumbents is not just a matter of pure economics. We have called ratings data a kind of currency in the industry. They are used to value, buy, and sell audiences. In fact, some commentators have noted that since the audiences themselves are unseen, ratings points are literally what are bought and sold. An industry does not go about changing or revaluing its currency lightly. Many institutional practices have grown up around the supply of a particular kind of information, delivered in a particular format at particular times. The users may understand that the data are less than perfect, but at least they've all agreed that it will form the basis for their commerce. Even if a newcomer could offer technically superior audience measurement, changing the currency might not be worth the disruptions (Phalen, 2003). So, despite a genuine desire for better, more accurate data, there is a kind of inertia that grips the people who use the ratings.

Of course, there are other reasons why markets do not always embrace change. Media industry reaction to the introduction of new measurement technologies offers a lesson in the politics of audience research. Consider peoplemeters, which were first used in the United States in the late 1980s. As we have seen, no ratings research method is perfect, and no system of estimating audiences is without bias. These biases work to the advantage of some and the disadvantage of others. When peoplemeters were introduced, cable networks saw an immediate advantage—the new technology produced reliable data on small, demographically targeted audiences. Broadcasters saw cable's gain as their potential loss. After many delays and challenges, the industry finally accepted the new meters—but one wonders how long Nielsen would have waited to make the change if AGB hadn't forced their hand.

In 2004, it was déjà vu all over again. For reasons we discuss in the following chapter, Nielsen decided to introduce peoplemeters into local market measurement. Once again the change worked to the benefit of some and the detriment of others. Even though the industry had over 15 years experience with this technology, even though it is widely understood to be an improvement over diaries, battle lines were drawn. News Corp, the owner of Fox TV stations, went so far as to subsidize a public advocacy group that charged the new system undercounted minority viewers, thus threatening programming aimed at those groups. Politicians were induced to write letters to Nielsen. The Media Ratings Council reviewed implementation plans. Congressional hearings were even held. In the end, Nielsen prevailed. But it illustrates the political minefield that awaits those who would change the ratings system.

More changes are on the horizon. These are being driven by the emergence of new media technologies that simultaneously empower media users, fragment audiences, and sometimes create a record of their use. Cable and satellite television have provided viewers with many more choices than ever before. Major broadcast networks which once garnered audience shares of 30 or 40, are now fortunate to break into double digits. More recently the Internet, satellite radio, video games, DVRs, and video on demand (VOD) have fragmented audiences even further. Moreover, many of these technologies make it easier for users to avoid conventional commercial messages. As we noted in chapter 2, advertisers are adapting as best they can, by placing products in older media and advertising in newer media. But in order for any of these strategies to be fully realized, they will need to develop their own agreed-on currency.

This creates an opening for new forms of audience measurement. DVRs typically create a record of what is watched live, replayed, or skipped altogether. Nielsen is now partnering with TiVo to create a large sample of DVR users to provide solid evidence of how these devices are being used. Cable systems that offer VOD or DVR functions in digital set-top boxes might well do the same thing. Nielsen is beginning to measure interactive media, product placements, and exposure to brand images in televised sporting events. Even older media like billboards, cinemas, and the yellow pages are looking for ways to create "ratings-like" data that will increase their appeal to advertisers. Each field is sufficiently unsettled that either a well-known name like Nielsen or Arbitron, or a new company with a novel approach, might become the preferred scorekeeper.

Advertisers, too, are pushing for measurement systems that will help them assess the return on their investment (ROI) in advertising. Historically, ratings companies have estimated the size of program or average quarter-hour audiences. The number of people exposed to an ad was then inferred from the surrounding program content. However, with more people able to skip ads, there will be increased pressure to estimate the audience for specific commercials. With more and more measurement done by peoplemeters, that should be possible. Often times, the true pay-off of an ad is measured in its impact on product sales. Making that linkage requires measurement systems that track both an individual's exposure to advertising and his or her subsequent purchases. These are called single source systems and, as we noted previously, Arbitron and VNU—with help from Procter & Gamble, the world's biggest advertiser—are working on just such a system.

Predicting the future is always a perilous business. It remains to be seen which of these many new forms of audience measurement will find buyers, and which of those will become the currency for newer media. It seems safe to say, though, that ratings data are likely to remain a powerful presence for many years to come. These numbers have been a central feature of the broadcast industry and the public's perception of that industry for three quarters of a century. Networks, stations, program syndicators, Web sites, advertisers, agencies, and virtually every other related business prosper or suffer by them. One need only glance at the trade press to realize how pervasive ratings data are. In fact, the general public now receives rather detailed ratings reports in publications like

USA Today, The New York Times, Wall Street Journal, and many other daily newspapers. As the electronic media become more competitive, as advertisers increasingly seek both global and highly targeted markets, and as the methods of research and analysis become increasingly sophisticated, it seems certain that ratings will continue to influence the shape and the psyche of media in the United States and around the world.

RELATED READINGS

Beville, H. M. (1988). *Audience ratings: Radio, television, cable* (Rev. ed.). Hillsdale, NJ: Lawrence Erlbaum Associates.

Buzzard, K. S. (1990). *Chains of gold: Marketing the ratings and rating the markets.* Metuchen, NJ: Scarecrow Press.

Chappell, M. N., & Hooper, C. E. (1944). *Radio audience measurement.* New York: Stephen Daye.

Ettema, J. S., & Whitney, D. C. (Eds.). (1994). *Audiencemaking: How the media create the audience.* Thousand Oaks, CA: Sage.

Lumley, F. H. (1934). *Measurement in radio.* Columbus, OH: The Ohio State University Press.

Napoli, P. M. (2003). *Audience economics: Media institutions and the audience marketplace.* New York: Columbia University Press.

Phalen, P. F. (1998). The market for information systems and personalized exchange: Business practices in the market for television audiences. *Journal of Media Economics, 11*(4), 17–34.

Chapter 7

Audience Research Methods

A great many decisions are made on the basis of audience data. We have seen that billions of dollars are spent on the media in accordance with the ratings. Perhaps it is even fair to say that millions of lives are affected by the programming and policy decisions that hinge on this information. Yet no method for producing audience data is without bias or limitations. It is, therefore, important to understand where the data come from and how research techniques affect the final product.

Although the practice of commercial audience research has changed over the years, certain issues have endured. For the most part, these involve questions of research methods. Techniques of audience sampling and measurement are as important today as they were when Archibald Crossley launched the CAB. They will, undoubtedly, define future debates about the quality of ratings data as well, whether for traditional broadcast and cable audience research or for new media like the Internet.

This chapter describes the methods used by audience measurement companies and, in particular, the ratings services. We do not intend to review every technical detail in the production of audience data. For those who wish a timely and detailed description of methodology, the ratings firms can provide the necessary documents. It is our intention to give readers enough grounding in the research methods these companies use so that they can assess the strengths and weaknesses of the numbers, and understand most of the technical jargon they will encounter in ratings reports. We begin with sampling, and then turn to issues of measurement methods. We concentrate on methods used in most commercial audience research as outlined in chapter 1.

SAMPLING

When researchers collect information about electronic media audiences, they are interested in an entire population of radio listeners, Internet users, or television viewers. Because it would be logistically impossible to survey all users of a given medium, research companies estimate audiences from a subset of the population called a *sample*. It would simply take too long and cost too much money to contact everyone. That is certainly the case with a population of some 110 million television households. Virtually all survey research, from marketing studies to public opinion polls, depends on sampling. Indeed, sampling is used in many scientific endeavors. As Arthur Nielsen, Sr. was fond of saying, "If you don't believe in sampling, the next time you have a blood test, ask them to take it all out."

In any survey research, the quality of the sample has a tremendous impact on the accuracy of the information collected. All samples can be divided into one of two classes: probability, and nonprobability samples. They differ in the way researchers identify who will participate. *Probability* samples, sometimes called *random samples*, use a process of random assignment in which everyone in the population has an equal, or known, probability of selection. Probability samples are expensive and time-consuming to construct, but researchers generally have more confidence in them than in *nonprobability* samples, which depend on happenstance or convenience to determine participation.

All the ratings companies described in this book are trying to achieve, or at least to approximate, the benefits of probability sampling. Their technical documents are laced with the language of probability samples. To develop the needed working vocabulary, therefore, one must be familiar with the principles of probability sampling. The following discussion is designed to provide that familiarity, in a way that does not assume a background in quantitative methods on the part of the reader. Those already familiar with sampling may wish to skip to the section on measurement.

Sampling begins with a definition of the population that the researcher wants to study. This requires a decision about what kind of things will be studied—called *elements* or *units of analysis* in the parlance of researchers. In ratings research, units of analysis are either people or households. Because the use of radio is individualistic, radio ratings have long used people as the unit of analysis. It is more appropriate to speak of television households as units of analysis, although the buying and selling of advertising time is done on the basis of populations of people who are defined by demographics (e.g., women 18–34 years old).

Researchers must define the *population* (or *universe*) so they can tell who is a member. For example, if we were attempting to create national television ratings, all households in the United States with one or more sets might be appropriate. Local markets are often more problematic, because households might receive signals from two or more cities. As a practical matter, Nielsen defines *Designated Market Areas (DMAs)* by assigning every county to one and only one market. Assignments are based on which television stations the people in a particular county watch.

Once the population is defined, the researcher obtains a complete list of all elements in a population. From this list, called a *sampling frame*, specific elements are chosen for the sample. For example, if we have a sampling frame of 1 million television households in Baltimore and randomly pick one home, we would know that it had a one-in-a-million chance of selection—just like every other home in the population.

Hence, we would have met the basic requirement of probability sampling. All we would have to do, then, is repeat the process until we have a sample of the desired size.

The procedure we have just described produces a *simple random sample*. Despite its conceptual elegance, this sort of sampling technique is seldom used in audience measurement because the real world is less cooperative than this approach to sampling assumes. It is virtually impossible to compile a list of each and every television home in the United States and draw from it a random sample. Researchers use more efficient and powerful sampling designs. The most common sampling techniques of the ratings companies are described here.

Sample Designs

Systematic Random Sampling. One probability sampling technique that involves only a minor variation on simple random sampling is called *systematic random sampling*. Like a simple random sample, this approach requires the use of a sampling frame. Usually, ratings firms will buy sampling frames from companies whose business it is to maintain and sell such lists. Typically, these frames are lists of telephone households. Homes with unlisted numbers can be included through the use of randomly generated numbers. Frames that have been amended in this way are called *expanded* or *total* sampling frames.

Once an appropriate frame is available, systematic sampling is straightforward. Because you have a list of the entire population, you know how large it is. You also know how large a sample you want from that population. Dividing population size by sample size lets you know how often you have to pull out a name or number as you go down the list. For example, suppose you had a population of 10,000 individuals and you wanted to have a sample of 1,000. If you started at the beginning of the list and selected every 10th name, you would end up with a sample of the desired size. That "nth" interval is called the *sampling interval*. The only further stipulation for systematic sampling—an important one—is that you pick your starting point at random. In that way, everyone has had an equal chance of being selected, again meeting the requirement imposed by probability sampling.

Systematic sampling, as the ratings companies implement it, is not perfect. For one thing, an absolutely complete list of the population is almost impossible to obtain. People living in temporary or group housing may be hard to track down. In many markets, a substantial portion of households are without a telephone. If lists are limited to homes with telephones, some people will be under-represented in the final ratings report. Conversely, households with more than one telephone number may have a greater probability of selection than other homes. Any of these factors can introduce biases into samples.

Multi-Stage Cluster Sampling.   Fortunately, not all probability samples require a complete list of every single element in the population. One sampling procedure that avoids that problem is called *multi-stage cluster sampling.* Cluster sampling repeats two processes: listing the elements and sampling. Each two-step cycle constitutes a stage. Systematic random sampling is a one-stage process. Multi-stage cluster sampling, as the name implies, goes through several stages.

A ratings company might well use multi-stage sampling to identify a national sample. After all, coming up with a list of every single household in the nation would be quite a chore. However, it would be possible to list every single county in the United States. If that were done, the research company could then draw a random sample of counties. In fact, this is essentially what Nielsen does to begin the process of creating a national sample of U.S. households. After that, block groups within those selected counties could be listed and randomly sampled. Third, specific city blocks within selected block groups could be listed and randomly sampled. Finally, with a manageable number of city blocks identified, researchers might be placed in the field, with specific instructions, to find individual households for participation in the sample.

Because the clusters that are listed and sampled at each stage are geographic areas, this type of sampling is sometimes called a *multi-stage area probability sample.* Despite the laborious nature of such sampling techniques, compared to the alternatives, they offer important advantages. Specifically, no sampling frame listing every household is required, and researchers in the field can contact households even if they do not have a telephone.

However, a multi-stage sample is more likely to be biased than a single-stage sample. This is because, through each round of sampling, a certain amount of error accompanies the selection process—the more stages, the higher the possibility of error. For example, suppose that during the sampling of counties described earlier, areas from the Northwestern United States were over-represented. That could happen just by chance, and it would be a problem carried through subsequent stages. Now suppose that bias is compounded in the next stage by the selection of block groups from a disproportionate number of affluent areas. Again, that is within the realm of chance. Even if random selection is strictly observed, a certain amount of sampling error creeps in. We discuss this more fully later in this chapter when we cover sources of error.

Stratified Sampling.   Using a third kind of sampling procedure, called stratified sampling, can minimize some kinds of error. This is one of the most powerful sampling techniques available to survey researchers. Stratified sampling requires the researcher to group the population being studied into relatively homogeneous subsets, called *strata.* Suppose we have a sampling frame that indicates the gender of everyone in the population. We could then group the population into males and females, and randomly sample the appropriate number from each strata. By combining these subsamples into one large group, we would have created a probability sample that has exactly the right proportions of men and women. Without stratification, that factor would have been left to chance. Hence, we have improved the representativeness of the sample. That added precision could be important if we are studying behaviors that might correlate with gender, such as watching sports on TV, or making certain product purchases like cosmetics and tires.

Stratified sampling obviously requires that the researcher have some relevant information about the elements in a sampling frame (e.g., the gender of everyone in the population). In single-stage sampling that is sometimes not possible. In multi-stage sampling, there is often an abundance of information because we tend to know more about the large clusters we begin with. Consider, again, the process that began by sampling counties. Not only could we list all U.S. counties, but we could group them by the state or region of the country they are in, the size of their populations, and so forth. Other sorts of groupings, such as the concentration of people with certain demographic characteristics, could be used at subsequent stages in the process. By combining stratification with multi-stage cluster sampling, therefore, we could increase the representativeness of the final sample. That is just what most ratings services do.

Cross-Sectional Surveys. All of the sample design issues we have discussed thus far have dealt with how the elements in the sample are identified. Another aspect of sample design deals with how long the researcher actually studies the population or sample. *Cross-sectional* surveys occur at a single point in time. In effect, these studies take a snapshot of the population. Much of what is reported in a single ratings book could be labeled cross-sectional. Such studies may use any of the sampling techniques just described. They are alike insofar as they tell you what the population looks like now, but not how it has changed over time. Information about those changes can be quite important. For instance, suppose the ratings book indicates that your station has an average rating of 10. Is that cause for celebration or dismay? The answer depends on whether that represents an increase or decrease in the size of your audience, and true cross-sectional studies will not tell you that.

Longitudinal Studies. These studies are designed to provide you with information about changes over time. In ratings research, there are two kinds of longitudinal designs in common use: *trend studies* and *panel studies*. A trend study is one in which a series of cross-sectional surveys, based on independent samples, is conducted on a population over some period of time. The definition of the population remains the same throughout the study, but individuals may move in and out of the population. In the context of ratings research, trend studies can be created simply by considering a number of market reports done in succession. For example, tracing a station's performance across a year's worth of ratings books constitutes a trend study. People may have moved to or from the market in that time, but the definition of the market (i.e., the counties assigned to it) has not changed. Most market reports, in fact, provide some trend information from past reports. Panel studies draw a single sample from a population, and continue to study that sample over time. The best example of a panel study in ratings research involves the metering of people's homes. This way of gathering ratings information, which we describe later in the chapter, may keep a household in the sample for years.

The way that individuals are targeted for inclusion in a sample affects the end result of audience research. We've seen that techniques like random digit dialing can bias a sample by systematically eliminating nontelephone households from the frame. It is often difficult to develop a sampling frame that includes the entire population. In the case of Internet users, for example, there is no readily available list of everyone with access to the Web. One reason is that the universe changes daily. Some measurement companies have tried to circumvent this problem by asking potential respondents to sign up online. But this creates other problems by making the sample nonrandom. The cost of various methods of recruitment has to be balanced with the limitations that these methods impose. The consumer of audience research data should understand how respondents were solicited to assess how this might affect the end result.

Sources of Error

One of the principal concerns of both users and producers of audience research is error in the data. The concept of "error" is not just a matter of mistakes being made. Rather, it addresses the extent to which ratings information based on samples fails to report what is actually happening in the population. Error is the difference between what the ratings estimate to be true, and what is true. An understanding of where error comes from, and how audience research companies do or do not deal with it, is one characteristic of a sophisticated user.

There are four sources of error in ratings data: *sampling error, nonresponse error, response error,* and *processing error.* The first two involve sampling, and so, are dealt with here. The last two involve measurement and the production process, respectively, and are covered in the sections that follow.

Sampling Error. This is the most abstract of the different kinds of error we discuss. It is a statistical concept that is common to all survey research. Basically, it means recognizing that as long as we try to estimate what is true for a population by studying something less than the entire population, there is a chance that we will miss the mark. Even if we use very large, perfectly executed random samples, it is possible that they will fail to accurately represent the populations from which they were drawn. This is inherent in the process of sampling. Fortunately, if we employ random samples, we can, at least, use the laws of probability to make statements about the amount of sampling error we are likely to encounter. In other words, the laws of probability will tell us how likely we are to get accurate results.

The best way to explain sampling error, and a host of terms that accompany the concept, is to work our way through a hypothetical study. Suppose that the Super Bowl were played yesterday and we wanted to estimate what percent of households actually watched the game (i.e., the game's rating). Let us also suppose that the "truth" of the matter is that exactly 50% of U.S. homes watched the game. Of course, ordinarily we would not know that, but we need to assume this knowledge to make our point. The true population value is represented in the top half of Fig. 7.1.

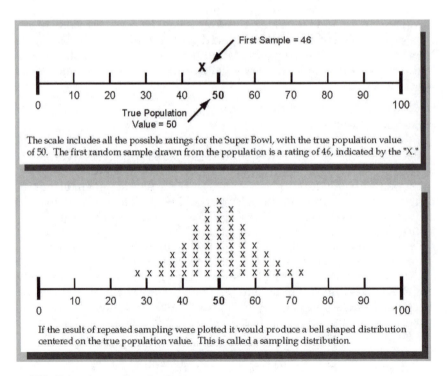

FIG. 7.1.   A sampling distribution.

In order to estimate the game's rating, we decide to draw a random sample of 100 households from a list of all the television households in the country. Because we have a complete sampling frame (unlikely, but convenient!), every home has had an equal chance to be selected. Next, we call each home and ask if they watched the game. Because they all have telephones, perfect memories, and are completely truthful (again, convenient), we can assume we have accurately recorded what happened in these sample homes. After a few quick calculations, we discover that only 46% of those we interviewed saw the game. This result is also plotted in the top half of Fig. 7.1.

Clearly, we have a problem. Our single best guess of how many homes saw the game is 4 percentage points lower than what was, in fact, true. In the world of media buying, 4 ratings points can mean a lot of money. It should, nevertheless, be intuitively obvious that even with our convenient assumptions and strict adherence to sampling procedures, such a disparity is entirely possible. It would have been surprising to hit the nail on the head the first time out. That difference of 4 ratings points does not mean we did anything wrong, it is just sampling error.

Because we have the luxury of a hypothetical case here, let's assume that we repeat the sampling process. This time, 52% of the sample say they watched the game. Better, but still in error, and still a plausible kind of occurrence. Finally, suppose that we draw 1,000 samples, just like the first two. Each time we plot the result of that sample. If we did this, the result would look something like the lower half of Fig. 7.1.

The shape of this figure reveals a lot, and is worth considering for a moment. It is a special kind of frequency distribution that a statistician calls a *sampling distribution*. In our case it forms a symmetrical, bell-shaped curve indicating that, when all was said and done, more of our sample estimates hit the true population value (i.e., 50%) than any other single value. It also indicates that although most of the sample estimates clustered close to 50%, a few were way off. In essence, this means that, if you use probability sampling, reality has a way of anchoring your estimates and keeping most of them fairly close to what is true. It also means that sooner or later, you are bound to hit one that's way off the mark.

What is equally important about this sampling distribution is that it will assume a known size and shape. The most frequently used measure of that size and shape is called the *standard error* (SE). In essence, this is the average "wrong guess" we are likely to make in predicting the ratings. For those familiar with introductory statistics, this is essentially a standard deviation. It is best conceptualized as a unit along the baseline of the distribution. Figure 7.2 gives the simplest formula for calculating standard error with ratings data.

What is remarkable about the standard error and what you will have to accept on faith unless you want to delve much more deeply into calculus, is that when it is laid out against its parent sampling distribution,

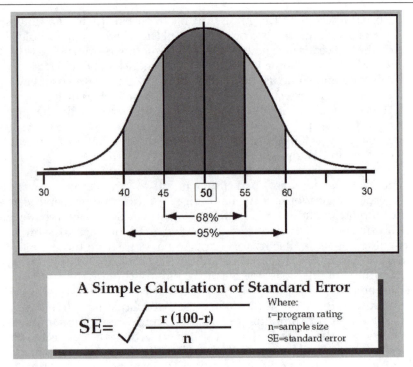

FIG. 7.2.   Relationship of standard error to sampling distribution.

it will bracket a precise number of samples. Specifically, plus or minus one SE will always encompass 68% of the samples in the distribution. Plus or minus 2 SE (technically, that should be 1.96), encompasses 95% of all samples. In our example, the SE works out to be approximately 5 ratings points, which means that 68% of the hypothetical samples will have produced results between 45% and 55% (i.e., 50% plus or minus 5 percentage points). That relationship between SE and the sampling distribution is depicted in Fig. 7.2.

None of this would be of interest to anyone other than a mathematician, were it not for the fact that such reasoning provides us with a way to make statements out the accuracy of audience data. Remember that in our first sample, we found 46% watching the Super Bowl. Ordinarily, that would be our single best guess about what was true for the population. We would recognize, however, that there is a possibility of sampling error, and we would want to know the odds of the true population value being something different than our estimate. We could state those odds by using our estimated rating (i.e., 46) to calculate SE, and placing a bracket around our estimate, just like the one in Fig. 7.2. Because we know that 95% of all sample means would fall between ± 2 SE, we know that 95% of all sample means will fall between ± 10 points in this example. The resulting statement would sound like this, "We estimate that the Super Bowl had a rating of 46, and we are 95% confident that the true rating falls between 36 and 56."

The range of values given in that statement (i.e., 36 to 56) is called the *confidence interval*. Confidence intervals are often set at plus or minus 2 SE, and will therefore have a high probability of encompassing the true population value. When you hear someone qualify the results of a survey by saying something like, "These results are subject to a sampling error of plus or minus 3%," they are giving you a confidence interval. What is equally important, but less often heard, is how much confidence should be placed in that range of values. To say we are "95% confident," is to express a *confidence level*. At the 95% level, we know that 95 times out of 100 the range we report will include the population value. Of course, that means that 5% of the time we will be wrong, because it is always possible our sample was one of those that was not representative. But at least we can state the odds, and satisfy ourselves that an erroneous estimate is a remote possibility.

Such esoteric concepts take on practical significance, because they go to the heart of ratings accuracy. For example, reporting that a program has a rating of 15, plus or minus 10, leaves a lot of room for error. Even fairly small margins of error (e.g., SE = 1) can be important if the estimates they surround are themselves small (e.g., a rating of 3). That is one reason why ratings services will routinely report *relative standard error* (i.e., SE as a percentage of the estimate) rather than the absolute level of error. In any event, it becomes critically important to reduce sampling error to an acceptable level. Three factors affect the size of that error: complexity of the population, sample size, and sample design. One is beyond the control of researchers, two are not.

The source of sampling error that we cannot control has to do with the population itself. Some populations are just more complicated than others. A researcher refers to these complexities as variability or heterogeneity in the population. To take an extreme case, if everyone in the population were exactly alike (i.e., perfect homogeneity), then a sample of one person would suffice. Unfortunately, media audiences are not homogeneous, and to make matters worse, they are getting more heterogeneous all the time. Think about how television has changed over the years. It used to be that people could watch the three networks, maybe an independent or public station, and that was it. Now most homes have cable or VCRs, as well as more stations to choose from. All other things being equal, that makes it more difficult to estimate who is watching what.

The two factors that researchers can control are related to the sample itself. *Sample size* is the most obvious and important of these. Larger samples reduce the magnitude of sampling error. It's just common sense that we should have more confidence in results from a sample of 1,000 than 100. What is counterintuitive is that sample size and error do not have a one-to-one relationship. That means doubling the size of the sample does not cut the SE in half. Instead, you must quadruple the sample size to reduce the SE by half. You can satisfy yourself of this by looking back at the calculation of SE in Fig. 7.2. To reduce the SE from 5 to 2.5, you must increase the sample size from 100 to 400. You should also note that the size of the population you are studying has no direct impact on the error calculations. All other things being equal, small populations require samples just as big as large populations.

These aspects of sampling theory are more than just curiosities. They have a substantial impact on the conduct and economics of the ratings business. Although it is always possible to improve the accuracy of the ratings by increasing the size of the samples on which they are based, you very quickly reach a point of diminishing returns. This was nicely demonstrated in research conducted by CONTAM, an industry group formed in response to the congressional hearing of the 1960s. That study collected viewing records from over 50,000 households around the country. From that pool, eight sets of 100 samples were drawn. Samples in the first set had 25 households each. Sample sizes for the following sets were 50, 100, 250, 500, 1,000, 1,500, and 2,500. The results are shown in Fig. 7.3.

At the smallest sample sizes, individual estimates of the *Flintstones* audience varied widely around the actual rating of 26. Increasing sample sizes from these low levels produced dramatic improvements in the consistency and accuracy of sample estimates, as evidenced in tighter clustering. For example, going from 100 to 1,000 markedly reduced sampling error and only required adding 900 households. Conversely, going from 1,000 to 2,500 resulted in a modest improvement, yet it required an increase of 1,500 households. Such relationships mean the suppliers of syndicated research and their clients have to strike a balance between the cost and accuracy of audience data.

In practice, several other factors determine the sample sizes used by a research provider. As suggested earlier, more complex populations will require larger samples to achieve a certain level of sampling error. This has meant that radio requires bigger samples than television, because there have been more radio stations to fragment the audience. Similarly, if you intend to study relatively small segments of the audience (e.g., men 18 to 21 years old) you will require larger overall samples. And even though larger populations do not, theoretically, need bigger samples, because of their relative complexity, and the volume of media dollars available, larger markets are studied with larger samples.

The only other factor that the researcher can employ to reduce sampling error is to improve the design of the sample. For reasons that we have already discussed, certain kinds of probability samples, like stratified samples, are more accurate than others. This strategy is commonly used, but there is a limit to what can be achieved. We should also note that when these more complex sample designs are used, the calculation of SE becomes a bit more involved than Fig. 7.2 indicates. We address those revised computations later.

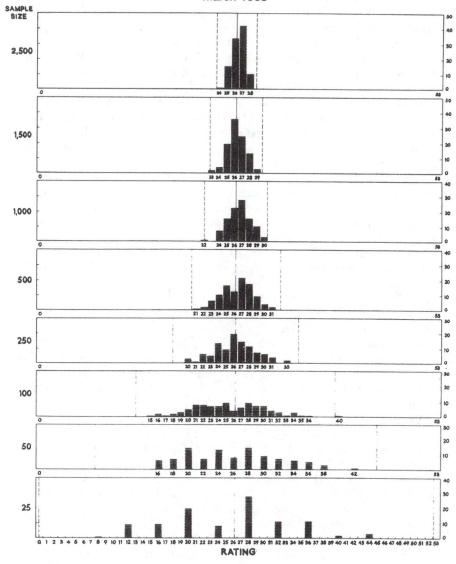

THE FLINTSTONES
U.S. Total Population
March 1963

| True population rating
: Point outside of which 2.6 out of 1,000 sample results should fall according to theory (3σ).
— Represents one sample yielding indicated rating estimate.
Distribution of Sample Ratings Results Based on 100 Diary Samples Each of 8 Different Sizes: 25 to 2500.
Source: CONTAM Study No. 1.

FIG. 7.3.   Effect of sample size on sampling error.

Nonresponse Error.   This is the second major source of error we encounter in the context of sampling. It occurs because not everyone we might wish to study will cooperate or respond. Remember that our entire discussion of sampling error assumed everyone we wanted to include in the sample gave us the information we desired. In the real world that just doesn't happen. To the extent that those who do not respond are different from those who do, there is a possibility that the samples we actually have to work with may be biased. Many of the procedures that the ratings services use represent attempts to correct nonresponse error.

The magnitude of nonresponse error varies from one ratings report to the next. The best way to get a sense of it is to look at the response rates reported by the ratings service. Every ratings company will identify an original sample of people or households that it wishes to use in the preparation of its ratings estimates. This ideal sample is usually called the *initially designated sample*. Some members of the designated sample, however, will refuse to cooperate; others will agree to be in the sample, but then fail to provide complete information. In other words, many will not respond. Obviously, only those who do respond can be used to tabulate the data. The latter group constitutes what is called the *in-tab sample*. The *response rate* is simply the percent of people from the initially designated sample who actually gave the ratings company useful information. Various techniques for gathering ratings data are associated with different response rates. Telephone surveys, for example, tend to have relatively high response rates. The most common measurement techniques, like placing diaries, often produce response rates in the neighborhood of 30%. Furthermore, different measurement techniques work better with some kinds of people than others. The nonresponse errors associated with measurement are discussed in the next section.

Because nonresponse error has the potential to bias the ratings, research companies employ one of two general strategies to minimize or control it. First, you can take action before the fact to improve the representativeness of the in-tab sample. Second, you can make adjustments in the sample after data have been collected. Usually both strategies are employed. Either way, you need to know what the population looks like in order to judge the representativeness of your in-tab sample and to gauge the adjustments that are to be made.

Population or universe estimates, therefore, are essential in correcting for nonresponse error. Determining what the population looks like (i.e., age and gender breakdowns, etc.) is usually done with U.S. Census information. Although the Census is updated only every 10 years, parts are revised, based on sampling, more frequently. Ratings companies often buy more current universe estimates from other research companies. One such company, Claritas, has supplied both Arbitron and Nielsen. Occasionally, certain attributes of the population that have not been measured by the Census Bureau, like cable penetration, must be estimated. To do this, it may be necessary to conduct a special *enumeration study* that establishes important universe estimates.

Once it is known what targets to shoot for, corrections for nonresponse error can be made. Before-the-fact remedies include the use of special recruitment techniques and buffer samples. The most desirable solution is to get as many of those in the originally designated sample as possible to cooperate. Doing so requires a deeper understanding of the reasons for nonresponse, and combating those with counteractive measures. For example, ratings services will often provide sample members with some monetary incentive. Perhaps different types of incentives will work better or worse with different types of people. Following up on initial contacts or making sure that interviewers and research materials are in a respondent's primary language will also improve response rates. The major ratings companies are aware of these alternatives, and on the basis of experience, know where they are likely to encounter nonresponse problems. They sometimes use special recruitment techniques to improve, for example, minority representation in the sample.

If improved recruitment fails to work, additional sampling can increase under-represented groups. *Buffer samples* are simply lists of additional households that have been randomly generated and are held in reserve. If, as sampling progresses, it becomes apparent that responses in one county are lagging behind expectations, the appropriate buffer sample can be enlisted to increase the size of the sample drawn from that area. Field workers might use a similar procedure if they encounter a noncooperating household. In such an event, they would probably have instructions to sample a second household in the same neighborhood, perhaps even matching the noncooperator on key household attributes.

Once the data are collected, another technique can be used to adjust for nonresponders. *Sample weighting*, sometimes called *sample balancing*, is a statistical procedure that gives the responses of certain kinds of people more influence over the ratings estimates than their numbers in the sample would suggest. Basically, the ratings companies compare the in-tab sample and the universe estimates (usually on geographic, ethnic, age and gender breakdowns), and determine where they have too many of one kind of person, and not enough of another. Suppose, for example, that 18- to 24-year-old men accounted for 6% of the population, but only 3% of the in-tab sample. One remedy for this would be to let the responses of each young man in the in-tab count twice. Conversely, the responses of over-represented groups would count less than once. The way to determine the appropriate weight for any particular group is to divide their proportion in the population by their proportion in the sample (e.g., 6% / 3% = 2).

For years, Nielsen used an unweighted sample to project its national ratings. But as it began introducing the same measurement technology in local markets as it used nationally (i.e., peoplemeters), it realized it could greatly increase the size of its national sample, hence reducing sampling error, by folding in the local markets. It order to do that, however, it had to apply weights so the local data didn't swamp the national estimates.

If you think the use of buffer samples or weighting samples is not a completely adequate solution to problems of nonresponse, you are right. Although these procedures may make in-tab samples look like the universe, they do not eliminate nonresponse error. The people who are drawn through buffer samples or whose responses count more than once might still be systematically different from those who did not co-operate. That is why some people question the use of these techniques. The problem is that failing to make these adjustments also distorts re-sults. For example, if you programmed a radio station that catered to 18- to 24-year-old men, you would be unhappy that they tend to be un-der-represented in most in-tab samples, and probably welcome the kind of weighting just described, flaws and all. Today, the accepted industry practice is to weight samples. We return to this topic when we discuss the process of producing the ratings.

The existence of nonresponse error, and certain techniques used to cor-rect for such error, means that samples the ratings services actually use are not perfect probability samples. That fact, in combination with the use of relatively complex sample designs, means that calculations of standard error are a bit more involved than our earlier discussion indi-cated. Without going into detail, error is affected by the weights in the sample, whether you are dealing with households or persons, and whether you are estimating the audience at a single point in time or the average audience over a number of time periods. Further, actual in-tab sample sizes are not used in calculating error. Rather, the ratings services derive what they call *effective sample sizes* for purposes of calculating SE. These take into account the fact that their samples are not simple random samples. Effective sample sizes may be smaller than, equal to, or larger than actual sample sizes. No matter the method for calculating SE, how-ever, the use and interpretation of that number is as described earlier.

MEASUREMENT

Sampling is essential to the audience research business, but methods of measurement are just as important. It is one thing to create a sample by identifying who you want to study; it is quite another to measure audi-ence activity by recording what they see on television, hear on radio, or visit on the Internet. While the sampling procedures used by ratings companies are common to all survey research operations, it's their mea-surement techniques that make them unique.

Technically, *measurement* is defined as a process of assigning numbers to objects, according to some rule of assignment. The "objects" that the audience research companies are usually measuring are people, al-though as we have seen, households can also be the unit of analysis. The "numbers" simply quantify the characteristics or behaviors that we wish to study. This kind of quantification makes it easier to manage the relevant information and to summarize the various attributes of the sample. For example, if a person saw the *CBS Evening News* last night, we might assign him or her a "1." Those who did not see the news might be assigned a "0." By reporting the percentage of 1s we have, we could produce a rating for the CBS news. The numbering scheme that the ratings services actually use is a bit more complicated than that, but in essence, that's what happens.

Researchers who specialize in measurement are very much concerned with the accuracy of the numbering scheme they use. After all, anyone can assign numbers to things, but capturing something meaningful with those numbers is more difficult. Researchers express their concerns about the accuracy of a measurement technique with two concepts: *reliability* and *validity*. Reliability is the extent to which a measurement procedure will produce consistent results in repeated applications. If what you are trying to measure does not change, an accurate measuring device should end up assigning it the same number time after time. If that is the case, the measure is said to be reliable. Just because a measurement procedure is reliable, however, does not mean that it is completely accurate; it must also be valid. Validity is the extent to which a measure actually quantifies the characteristic it is supposed to quantify. For instance, if we wanted to measure a person's program preferences, we might try to do so by recording which shows he or she watches most frequently. This approach might produce a very consistent, or reliable, pattern of results. However, it does not necessarily follow that the program a person sees most often is their favorite. Scheduling, rather than preference, might produce such results. Therefore, measuring preferences by using a person's program choices might be reliable, but not particularly valid.

What Is Being Measured?

One of the first questions that must be addressed in any assessment of measurement techniques is, "What are you trying to measure?" Confusion on this point has led to a good many misunderstandings about ratings data. At first glance the answer seems simple enough. Ratings measure exposure to the electronic media. But even that definition leaves much unsaid. To think this through, two factors need to be more fully considered: (a) What do we mean by "media"? and (b) What constitutes exposure?

Defining the media side of the equation raises a number of possibilities. It might be, for example, that we have no interest in the audience for specific content. As we noted in chapter 5, some effects researchers are only concerned with the how much television people watch overall. Although knowing the amount of exposure to a medium might be useful in some applications, it is not terribly useful to advertisers. Radio station audiences and, to a certain extent, cable network audiences, are reported this way. Here the medium may be no more precisely defined than attendance during a broad daypart, or an average quarter hour.

In television ratings, exposure is usually tied to a specific program. Here, too, however, questions concerning definition can be raised. How much of a program must people see before they are included in that program's audience? If a few minutes are enough, then the total audience for the show will probably be larger than the audience at any one point in time. Some of the measurement techniques we discuss in the following section are too insensitive to make such minute-to-minute determinations, but for other approaches, this consideration is very important.

Advertisers are, of course, most interested in who sees their commercials. So, a case can be made that the most relevant way to define the media for them is not program content, but commercial content. Such "commercial ratings" are not, at present, produced by the major ratings services, but newer measurement technologies raise the possibility that audiences for brief commercial messages could be quantified.

The other aspect of this question is determining what is meant by exposure. Once again, there are a number of possibilities. *Exposure* is usually defined as the choice of a particular station, program, or Web site. Under this definition, the only thing that is relevant is who is present when the set is in use. In fact, some measurement techniques are incapable of recording who is in the room. At best, this represents vaguely defined opportunity to see or hear something. Once it has been determined that audience members have tuned to a particular station, further questions about the quality of exposure are left unanswered.

It is well documented, however, that much of our media use is accompanied by other activities. People may read, talk, eat, play games, or do the dishes while the set is in use. Whatever the case, it is clear that during a large portion of the time that people are in the audience, they are not paying much attention. This leads many researchers to argue that defining exposure as a matter of choice greatly overstates people's real exposure to the media. An alternative, of course, would be to stipulate that exposure must mean that a person is paying attention to the media, or perhaps even understanding what is seen or heard. Interactive technologies that require someone to "click" on a message or icon offer some evidence that they are paying attention, but for most media, measuring a person's level of awareness or perception is extremely difficult to do in an efficient, valid way.

Another shortcoming that critics of the ratings services have raised from time to time is that operational definitions of exposure tell us nothing about the quality of the experience in a more affective sense. For example, do people like what they see, or find it to be informative and enlightening? *Qualitative ratings* such as these have been produced on an irregular basis, not so much as a substitute for existing services, but rather as a supplement. In the early 1980s, the Corporation for Public Broadcasting, in collaboration with Arbitron, conducted field tests of such a system. Another effort was initiated by an independent Boston-based company named Television Audience Assessment, which tried selling qualitative ratings information. That effort failed, and at present, there isn't enough demand in the United States to justify qualitative ratings. As we noted in chapter 2, though, since new technologies are making it harder to reach audiences with commercial spots, it is conceivable that advertisers will want better measures of audience involvement, attentiveness, or receptivity to advertising in the future.

As we discussed in chapter 2, the question of how to define exposure is particularly unsettled when it comes to measuring Internet audiences. Some would argue that the presence of a banner ad on a Web page that has been served to a user is sufficient exposure to warrant counting. Others contend that those "impressions" are insufficient, and that exposure can only be truly recorded when a viewer clicks on the message to receive more information. It remains to be seen what "currency" the industry will ultimately accept.

Obviously, these questions of definition help determine what the data really are and how they are to be interpreted. If different ratings companies used vastly different definitions of exposure to media, their cost structures and research products might be quite different as well. The significance of these issues has not been lost on the affected industries. In 1954, the Advertising Research Foundation (ARF), released a set of recommendations that took up many of these concerns. In addition to advocating the use of probability samples, ARF recommended that tuning behavior be the accepted definition of exposure. That standard has been the most widely accepted, and has effectively guided the development of the measurement techniques we use today.

Measurement Techniques

There are several techniques that the ratings services use to measure people's exposure to electronic media, and each has certain advantages and disadvantages. The biases of these techniques contribute to the third kind of error we mentioned earlier (i.e., response error). *Response error* includes inaccuracies contained in the responses generated by the measurement procedure. To illustrate these biases, we discuss each major approach to audience measurement in general terms. In order to avoid getting too bogged down in details, we may gloss over differences in how each ratings company operationalizes a particular scheme of measurement. Here again, the reader wishing more information should see each company's description of methodology.

Diaries are the most widely used of all measurement techniques. They form the basis of national radio network audience estimates. More importantly, huge numbers of diaries are collected to determine the audiences of local radio and television stations. In one television ratings sweep alone, Nielsen will gather diaries from hundreds of thousands of respondents to produce audience estimates in local markets around the country.

A diary is a small paper booklet in which the diary keeper is supposed to record his or her media use for a 1-week period. To produce television ratings, one diary is kept for each TV set in the household. Figure 7.4 is the first page from a Nielsen television diary. It begins on Tuesday at 5 a.m. and thereafter divides the day into quarter-hour segments ending at 4:59 a.m. Each of the remaining days of the week is similarly divided. During each quarter hour that the set is in use, the diary keeper is supposed to note the relevant call letters, channel number, and program title, as well as which family members and/or visitors are watching. The diary also includes a few additional questions about household composition, and the channels that are received in the home. One major limitation to this method is that the viewing is tied to a set rather than to a person, so out-of home viewing may be significantly under-stated.

Radio audiences are also measured with diaries, but these diaries are supposed to accompany people rather than sets. That way, an individual can record listening that occurs outside the home. Figure 7.5 is the first page of an Arbitron radio diary. It begins at 5 a.m. on Thursday, and divides the day into broader dayparts than the rigid quarter-hour increments of the TV diary. Because a radio diary is a personal record, the diary keeper does not note whether other people were listening. The location of listening, however, is recorded.

Diary placement and retrieval techniques vary, but the usual practice goes something like this. The ratings company calls members of the originally designated sample on the telephone to secure the respondent's cooperation and collect some initial information. Those who are excluded (e.g., people living in group quarters), or those who will receive special treatment (e.g., Spanish-speaking households) are identified at this stage. Follow-up letters may be sent to households that have agreed to cooperate. Diaries are, then, either mailed or delivered to the home in person by field personnel. Incidentally, although respondents are asked to cooperate, diaries can be distributed to those who say they are not interested in cooperating. Quite often, a monetary incentive of $1 or so is provided as a gesture of goodwill, but goodwill is more likely to be used in certain markets with traditionally lower response rates. During the week, another letter or phone call may encourage the diary keeper to note his or her media use. Diaries are designed to be sealed and placed directly in the mail, which is typically how the diary is returned to the ratings company at the end of the week. Occasionally, a second monetary reward follows the return of the diary. In some special cases, homes are called and the diary information is collected over the telephone.

Diaries have some significant advantages that account for their popularity. They offer a relatively inexpensive method of data collection.

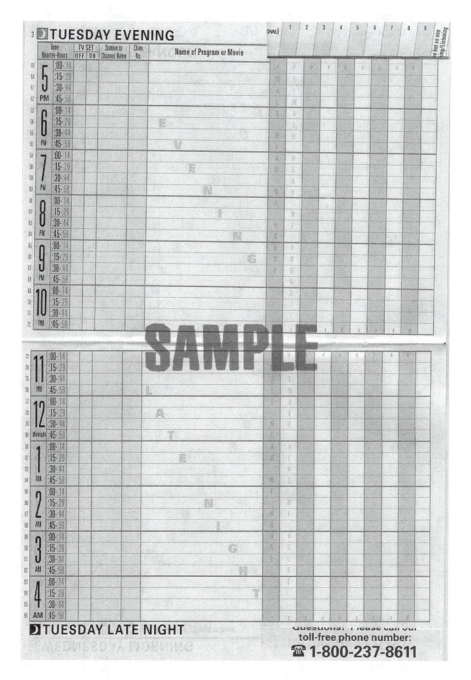

FIG. 7.4.   Sample page from Nielsen television diary. Reprinted by permission of Nielsen Media Research.

THURSDAY

	Time		Station			Place			
	Start	Stop	Call letters or station name. *Don't know? Use program name or dial setting.*	Check (✓) one AM	FM	At Home	In a Car	At Work	Other Place
Early Morning (from 5 AM)									
Midday									
Late Afternoon									
Night (to 5 AM Friday)									

If you didn't hear a radio today, please check here. ☐

1

FIG. 7.5.   Sample of Arbitron diary. Reprinted by permission of Arbitron.

Considering the wealth of information that a properly filled out diary contains, none of the other techniques we discuss here is as cost effective. Most importantly, they report which people were actually in the audience. In fact, until 1987, diaries had to be used in conjunction with more expensive metering techniques to determine the demographic composition of the national television audience. Even now, as peoplemeters are becoming the standard in the larger markets like New

York and Chicago, diaries will undoubtedly continue to be used in most local markets.

Despite their popularity, there are a number of problems associated with the use of diaries, problems of both nonresponse and response error. We have already discussed nonresponse error in the context of sampling. It should be noted, however, that diaries are particularly troublesome in this regard. Response rates on the order of 30% are common, and in some markets will drop below that. Obviously, diary keepers must be literate, but methodological research undertaken by the industry suggests that those who fill out and return diaries are systematically different in other ways. Younger people, especially younger males, are less responsive to the diary technique. African Americans, too, are less likely to complete and return a diary. There is also some evidence that those who return a television diary are heavier users of the medium than nonrespondents.

There are a number of response errors typical of diary data as well. Filling out a diary properly is a good deal of work. There is a fair amount of anecdotal evidence that diary keepers frequently do not note their media use as it occurs, but try to recollect it at the end of the day or the week. To the extent that entries are delayed, errors of memory are more likely. Similarly, it appears that diary keepers are more diligent in the first few days of diary keeping than the last. This "diary fatigue" may artificially depress viewing or listening levels at the end of the week. Viewing during late night, viewing of short duration, viewing of less well-known programming, and viewing of secondary sets (e.g., in bedrooms, etc.) is typically under-reported. Children's use of television is also likely to go unreported if they watch at times when an adult diary keeper is not present.

These are significant, if fairly benign, sources of response error. There is less evidence on the extent to which people deliberately distort reports of their viewing or listening behavior. Most Americans seem to have a sense of what ratings data are, and how they can affect programming decisions. Again, anecdotal evidence suggests that some people view their participation in a ratings sample as an opportunity to "vote" for deserving programs, whether they are actually in the audience or not. While diary data may be more susceptible to such distortions than other methods, instances of deliberate, systematic deception, although real, are probably limited in scope.

A more serious problem with diary-based measurement techniques has emerged in recent years. As we noted earlier, the television viewing environment has become increasingly complex. Most homes now subscribe to cable and have a VCR or DVR attached to their set. In addition, remote control devices are in virtually all households. These technological changes make the job of keeping an accurate diary more burdensome than ever. A viewer who has flipped through 40 channels to find something of interest may not know the channel to which he or she is tuned. Even if they record the channel indicated by the set, they may be in error because cable systems often change the channel designation of an over-the-air station. These changes are difficult to track, although Nielsen gives each home a list of cable systems and channel numbers to improve the accuracy of diary entries. For reasons such as these, it is generally acknowledged that diaries under-report the audience for most cable networks and independent television stations. Other measurement techniques, however, can be used to compensate for many of these shortcomings.

Household meters have been the most important alternative to diary-based audience measurement. The best-known metering device is Nielsen's Audimeter. The original Audimeter recorded radio listening, and required Nielsen field representatives to go to the homes equipped with these devices to retrieve their contents. Later, the record of radio or TV tuning, recorded on motion picture film, was mailed back to the Nielsen office in Chicago. Today, meters are a good deal more sophisticated.

Modern meters are essentially small computers that are attached to all of the television sets in a home. They perform a number of functions, the most important of which is monitoring set activity. The meter records when the set is on and the channel to which it is tuned. This information is typically stored in a separate unit that is hidden in some unobtrusive location. The data it contains can be retrieved through a telephone line and downloaded to a central computer.

For years, that was the scope of metering activity. And as such, it had enormous advantages over diary measurement. It eliminated much of the human error inherent in diary keeping. Viewing was recorded as it occurred. Even exposure of brief duration could be accurately recorded. Members of the sample did not have to be literate. In fact, they did not have to do anything at all, so no fatigue factor entered the picture. Because information was electronically recorded, it could also be collected and processed much more rapidly than paper-and-pencil diaries. Reports on yesterday's program audiences, called the *overnights*, could be delivered.

There were only two major shortcomings to this sort of metering. First, it was expensive. It cost a lot to manufacture, install, and maintain the hardware necessary to make such a system work. That is still true today. As a practical matter, this means that metered measurement is viable only in relatively large media markets (i.e., nationally or in large urban areas). Second, household meters could provide no information on who was watching, save for what could be inferred from general household characteristics. The need to provide precise "people information," which is so essential to advertisers, caused Nielsen to abandon the use of ordinary household meters.

With that, you might imagine that household meters were a thing of the past, but in fact, technological changes in how viewers receive and store TV programming are making the functional equivalent of household meters more ubiquitous than ever. DVRs, like TiVo, have the ability to record exactly what television sets are doing on a moment-to-moment basis. TiVo has worked with Nielsen to turn these data into usable audience information. Similarly, digital cable systems equip homes with set-top boxes that can track set tuning. The combination of these technologies could effectively put a household meter in most homes in the United States. Such broadly based information approaches a census of the audience, and might provide valuable insights. However, since these technologies can only "guestimate" the demographic composition of audiences, it's unlikely that they will be the preferred currency for buying media audiences.

Peoplemeters are the only pieces of hardware that affirmatively measure exactly who within households is viewing the set. They were introduced in the United States in the fall of 1987 to generate national network ratings. In the fall of 2004, Nielsen began using them to generate local ratings in major markets. Peoplemeters operated by Nielsen and others are also in use in dozens of countries around the world. These devices do everything that conventional household meters do, and more. With this technology, every member of the sample household is assigned a number that corresponds to a push button on the metering device. When a person begins viewing, he or she is supposed to press a pre-assigned button on the meter. The button is again pressed when the person leaves the room. When the channel is changed, a light on the meter flashes until viewers reaffirm their presence. All systems have hand-held units, about the size of a remote control device, that allow people to button push from some remote location in the room. Figure 7.6 shows what Nielsen's peoplemeter looks like.

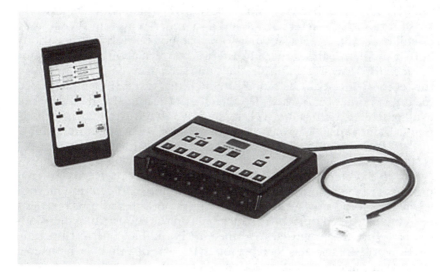

FIG. 7.6.   The Nielsen peoplemeter. Reprinted by permission of Nielsen Media Research.

As with household meters, data are retrieved over telephone lines. At that point, all the button pushing and set-tuning activity can be combined with data stored in a central computer to create "people" ratings. Peoplemeters met with some resistance when they were first introduced in the United States, but that subsided after they were in operation for a few years. More recently, as Nielsen began rolling out local people meters (LPM), another round of controversy erupted. Minority groups, supported by unhappy broadcasters, complained that the technology under-represented African Americans and Hispanics, thereby condemning their preferred shows to cancellation. Though the argument was of dubious merit, it caught the attention of many politicians and resulted in congressional hearings. While this most recent episode serves as an interesting case study in the political economy of audience measurement, the fact is, using peoplemeters is standard operating procedure around the world. They have well-understood biases and limitations. These can, again, be categorized as issues of nonresponse and response error.

As is the case with diaries, a great many people who are sampled refuse to accept a peoplemeter. As always, the question is, "Are those who participate systematically different from those who do not?" Although peoplemeters do not impose a formal literacy requirement, some have speculated that there is a kind of technological literacy required of respondents. Certainly, lapses in button pushing and hardware failures reduce the effective in-tab samples on a day-to-day basis. Moreover, since peoplemeters are tied to TV sets in households, they cannot capture viewing that occurs on small handheld sets, or in bars and other public places.

There are response errors associated with peoplemeters as well. Most notably, the meters are believed to under-represent the viewing of children. Youngsters, it turns out, are not terribly conscientious button pushers. More generally, there is concern about button-pushing fatigue. How, for example, does one interpret instances in which the set is on but no one is reported watching? Household meters used to stay in homes for 5 years. Doubts about the long-term diligence of peoplemetered homes, as well as pressure from the television networks, have caused Nielsen to turnover these households after only 2 years. Even so, some critics still believe that this method of metering is flawed.

Portable peoplemeters (PPM) are an even newer technology that promises to overcome some of the limits of household bound meters, while providing measures of both television and radio usage. This system, developed by Arbitron, depends on the cooperation of broadcasters who are supposed to embed an inaudible code in the audio portion of their signals. Each person in the sample, then, is instructed to wear a pager-sized device that is capable of detecting the code. Whenever the person is within earshot of the broadcast, the meter "hears" it and credits the person with being in the audience. At the end of the day, respondents, whose demographic characteristics are known in advance, place their meters in docking stations where they are recharged and the information they contain is automatically retrieved over telephone lines.

At this writing, portable peoplemeters are licensed for use in Canada, Belgium, and Singapore. They have also been tested in the United States in collaborative efforts between Arbitron and Nielsen. They have a number of advantages over other peoplemeters. They require no button pushing. They can detect any media content that emits the prearranged code. That could include all forms of radio and television, as well as other pre-recorded materials. They even have the potential to record exposure to print media if those publications would insert some sort of radio frequency ID tag *(RFID)*. That means researchers could track cross-media usage with considerable precision. They are also cheaper than household meters since a technician does not need to go into the field to hard-wire them in place. The necessary hardware can simply be mailed to respondents. Even so, it is doubtful that PPMs will be cost-effective in the United States unless they can be deployed as the preferred technology to measure the more lucrative medium of television.

The "holy grail" of measurement technology is what's called a *passive peoplemeter*. Such a device would require no effort on the part of sample participants. The meter would be unobtrusive and capable of, somehow, identifying exactly which people were in the audience. PPMs come close, but people still have to remember to carry them around and dock them at night. Other, household-bound, technologies have been developed as well. One uses a computerized "image recognition" system. Basically, it translates a person's facial image into a set of distinguishing features that it stores in a computerized memory. The meter then scans a predefined visual field and compares the objects it encounters with its memory to identify family members. Pictures of viewers, per se, are not stored or reported, only the incidence of recognized images. Nonetheless, this technology is probably too intrusive for many people's tastes.

Internet measurement software is a data collection methodology used by organizations like comScore Media Metrix to monitor online computer usage. Respondents agree to download software that records Web and other Internet activity. These data are sent back to a central location for processing. The system generates an overwhelming amount of information, which is condensed into a variety of reports for subscribers.

The most obvious disadvantage to this methodology is that users might be reluctant to allow software to run resident on their computers. Privacy is a significant concern when every action is monitored with such precision. It is very likely that people who would allow this technology on their computer will differ from people who do not want it installed. And even if they don't differ in terms of demographic profile, the presence of this monitoring technology might influence their choices when they use the Internet. Another problem is that a great deal of Internet usage occurs in the workplace. If employers are reluctant to allow this software to run on their equipment, then truly random samples of workplace or university users are compromised.

Questionnaires are one of the oldest ways to collect data on audiences or, for that matter, any one of countless social phenomena. There are many books on questionnaire design, so we will not elaborate on their strengths and weakness here. We will, however, conclude with a brief discussion of how question-asking techniques have been used in audience measurement. As we described in chapter 6, phone interviews formed the mainstay of the ratings industry at its inception. While telephone interviews no longer provide the principal means of audience measurement, two techniques have been around long enough to deserve comment: recall and coincidental.

Telephone recall, as the name implies, requires a respondent to remember what they have seen or heard over some period of time. Generally speaking, two things affect the quality of recalled information. One is how far back a person is required to remember. Obviously, the further removed something is from the present, the more it is subject to "memory error." Second is the salience of the behavior in question. Important or regular occurrences are better remembered than trivial or sporadic events. Because most people's radio listening tends to be regular and involve only a few stations, the medium is more amenable than some to measurement with telephone recall techniques.

Like all other methods of data collection, however, telephone recall has certain limitations. If people are only questioned about their previous day's listening, week-long patterns of audience accumulation can only be inferred from mathematical models. We will have more to say about modeling in the last chapter. The use of interviewers can also introduce error. Although interviewers are usually trained and monitored in centralized telephone centers, they can make inappropriate comments or other errors that bias results. Finally, the entire method is no better than a respondent's memory. Even though people are only expected to recall yesterday's listening, there is no guarantee that they can accurately do so.

As C. E. Hooper argued some 50 years ago, *telephone coincidentals* can offer a way to overcome problems of memory. These surveys work very much like telephone recall techniques, except that they ask respondents to report what they are seeing or listening to at the moment of the call. Because respondents can verify exactly who is using what media at the time, errors of memory and reporting fatigue are eliminated. For these reasons, telephone coincidentals were, for some time, regarded as the standard against which other methods of measurement should be evaluated.

Despite these acknowledged virtues, no major ratings company routinely conducts telephone coincidental research. There are two problems with coincidentals that militate against their regular use. First, a coincidental interview only captures a glimpse of a person's media use. In effect, it sacrifices quantity of information for quality. As a result, to describe audiences hour to hour, day to day, and week to week, huge numbers of people would have to be called around the clock. That becomes a very expensive proposition. Second, as with all telephone interviews, there are practical limitations on where and when calls can be made. Much radio listening occurs in cars without cellular phones, and much television viewing occurs late at night when it would be inappropriate to call. These behaviors cannot be captured with strictly coincidental techniques. For these, and other reasons, the coincidental telephone method is no longer used for any regular rating service.

Utterly conventional, paper-and-pencil questionnaires have been the main method of data collection for two major firms: Simmons and MRI. Both companies regularly distribute questionnaires to several thousand respondents. These come in the form of large booklets that can run upwards of 100 pages of primarily fixed response (i.e., check the box) questions. Respondents are asked to report detailed information on lifestyles, opinions, travel, print and electronic media usage, and page after page of very specific information on the products and services they use. This provides a treasure trove of information for advertisers because it allows researchers to relate product purchases to patterns of media use. Unfortunately, the measures of electronic media use are insufficiently precise to be of much use in making programming decisions or executing media buys.

The arrival of inexpensive personal digital assistants *(PDAs)* has occasioned some rather innovative uses of questionnaires. In one effort undertaken by MindShare, a large media services firm, PDAs with pre-loaded questionnaires were distributed to respondents. People would carry the PDAs with them, and, at various times throughout the day, the devices would ring, asking people to fill out a short questionnaire. People would report their mood, where they were, and, depending upon their answers, the PDAs would then take them to specific questions about the media or promotions they might encounter in that location (e.g. at work, in a grocery store, a gas station, etc.). After a couple of days, interviewers reclaimed the devices, and the data they had stored was retrieved and aggregated. This technique is probably too labor-intensive to sustain an ongoing syndicated measurement service, but it produces results that are hard to imagine using more conventional questionnaires.

The principal methods of audience measurement in the electronic media are summarized in Table 7.1. Obviously, the chart does not exhaust the possibilities for data collection. New techniques, or refinements of old ones, are being introduced and tested all the time.

TABLE 7.1

Summary of the Major Methods of Audience Measurement

	Advantages	*Disadvantages*
Telephone recall	Relatively fast turnaround Personal contact with respondent No literacy requirement Generally higher response rates than other methods	Memory problems Deliberate misrepresentation Limited times when researcher can call the home Biased sample—some homes don't have phones Costly method of data collection
Telephone co-incidental	Relatively fast turnaround Personal contact with respondent No literacy requirement No memory problems Generally higher response rates than other methods	Limited times when researcher can call the home Biased sample—some homes don't have phones Costly method of data collection
Diaries	Less costly than other research methods Potential to collect very detailed information including demographics Fairly non-intrusive, completed at respondents' convenience	Time lag to collect and process the data Memory problems Deliberate misrepresentation Literacy requirement Error prone in complex media environments Lower response rates
Household (passive) meters	Fast turnaround Accuracy—records actual set tuning activity No literacy requirement Does not require any effort on the part of respondent Low turnover of sample means that the same households can be studied for several years When built into DVRs or digital cable boxes has potential of very large samples	Cost—very expensive to make, install & maintain as free-standing technology Household level data offers limited demographic information Installation requirements may deter participants and consequently bias the sample May require matching program log information to meter data for program specific information

140

Method	Advantages	Disadvantages
Peoplemeters	Fast turnaround Accuracy—records actual set tuning activity No literacy requirement Continuous measurement allows for analysis of very short time periods Demographic data available	Cost—very expensive to make, install & maintain Requires active participation on the part of respondents (high burn out) Button pushing, especially by children, may be unreliable Intrusiveness of technology may deter participation and bias the sample Sample must be turned over more rapidly than with household meters May require matching program log information to meter data for program specific information
Portable Peoplemeters	Accuracy—records actual exposure to content with electronic codes Can record use of multiple media Fast turnaround No literacy requirement Requires little effort on part of respondent Captures out-of-home media use Continuous measurement allows for analysis of very short time periods Demographic data available	Cost—very expensive to make High sample turnover compared to household-bound meters Requires cooperation of media to embed identifying codes May pick up signals in adjacent locations
PC Meter	Relatively inexpensive since it uses respondent's computers Provides continuous record of Internet (or Web) activity Very large samples are possible	Potential sample bias due to privacy concerns Awareness of metering may alter respondents' behavior

RELATED READINGS

Babbie, E. (2003). *The practice of social research* (10th ed.). Belmont, CA: Wadsworth.

Beville, H. M. (1988). *Audience ratings: Radio, television, cable* (rev. ed.). Hillsdale, NJ: Lawrence Erlbaum Associates.

Churchill, G. A., & Iachobucci, D. (2004). *Marketing research: Methodological foundations* (9th ed.). Belmont, CA: South-Western College Pub.

Gunter, B. (2000). *Media research methods: Measuring audiences, reactions and impact*. London: Sage.

Sissors, J. Z., & Baron, R. B. (2002). *Advertising media planning* (6th ed.). Chicago: McGraw-Hill.

Wimmer, R., & Dominick, J. (2002). *Mass media research: An introduction* (7th ed.) Belmont, CA: Wadsworth.

Chapter 8

Ratings Research Products

Often I read articles that make it clear to me the writer doesn't understand the most basic differences between national ratings, overnight meter ratings and full sweeps ratings.

—Moira Farrell, SVP, Research, King World
(*Electronic Media*, 3/9/98 p. 9)

When it comes to audience research, the old cliché that you can't believe everything you hear applies with a vengeance. Some users of ratings data don't acknowledge that audience information is produced and analyzed in ways that affect its meaning. Whether this is the fault of a journalist who doesn't know the subtleties of audience measurement, or a researcher who spins the data to deliberately mis-state a case, the user of ratings information needs to know where the estimate comes from in order to interpret it correctly. Basic questions about which population is being measured, sample characteristics, and data collection methodologies must be asked before data can be thoroughly understood.

Up to this point we have concentrated on the evolution of audience measurement firms, and how they collect data. However, like any commercial enterprise, research companies must produce goods or services to sell in the marketplace. This means processing an overwhelming amount of data and turning it into information that clients can use for decision making. The result is a vast array of ratings reports and services. In this chapter, we consider some of the products that the ratings companies offer for sale.

The enormous databases that research firms compile allow them to create far more reports than we can possibly review in one short chapter. Moreover, the number of products is on the rise as ratings data are combined with other sources of information, and as computers open up new ways to manipulate, merge, and present the data. Both the data and the formats in which they are presented constantly evolve. In light of this, our description provides only selected examples of the better known and more widely used reports and services. By concentrating on these, we can acquaint the reader with the most common report formats and demonstrate how some of the research concepts we introduced in previous chapters show up in the context of an actual ratings report. We leave it to our readers to explore for themselves the many variations on a theme that the ratings services offer.

The most influential consumers of audience research are those who buy and sell time. Although other users of ratings data are certainly important, this group is critical in terms of product development. For that reason, it makes sense to organize ratings products by the advertising markets they are intended to serve. As described in chapter 2, the local market is comprised of broadcast stations and cable systems, and the national market includes networks, syndicators, and national satellite program providers like DirecTV and EchoStar. We deal with Internet separately, since this nontraditional technology is not limited by the geographic definitions of "market" used by broadcasting and cable. Before discussing the individual research products in each of these markets, we consider the general effects of production procedures on the content of audience research reports.

FROM DATA TO SALEABLE COMMODITY

As we discussed in the previous chapter, issues of sampling and measurement are well known to survey researchers; large bodies of academic literature offer research and theory on these topics. We have, therefore, some well-established criteria by which to judge the work of the ratings services. But sampling and measurement alone do not make a ratings book. The data collected by these methods must undergo a production process, just as other raw materials are turned into products. Here, standards of what is or is not appropriate are harder to come by. Yet, no discussion of ratings methods would be complete without mention of the production process. Every research company processes data a little differently, but they all engage in the same three activities: editing the data, adding information to viewing data, and making projections.

Editing

Audience measurement companies are continually flooded with data that must be summarized and turned into a useful product. One of the most difficult data sources to deal with is the diary. Hundreds of thousands of hand-written diaries arrive at Arbitron and Nielsen each year. They must be checked for accuracy, logical inconsistencies, and omissions. They must also be translated into computer-readable form. The process of getting clean, accurate, complete data ready to be processed is called *editing*. It can be a very laborious activity, and despite serious efforts at quality control, it is here that *processing error* is most likely to occur.

Diary editing involves a number of activities—some can be carried out by computers; others depend on the judgment of editors. First, diaries must be evaluated for inclusion in the tabulations. They are excluded if respondents filled them out during the wrong week, mailed them back too late, or submitted excessively incomplete or inconsistent information. Usable diaries are then checked for logical inconsistencies. In translating diary entries into computer data, operators can use a number of computer aids to check DMA information, such as station call letters, program titles, station slogans and the like. Suppose, for example, that a television diary identifies a specific program as viewed, but associates it with the wrong channel number or call letters. Strict editing procedures usually prescribe a way to resolve these discrepancies.

Suppose, however, that information is just plain missing. Rather than throw out an otherwise usable diary, research companies often "fill in the blanks" through a process called *ascription*. These procedures typically use computer routines to determine an answer with the highest probability of being correct. If, for example, Nielsen receives a diary reporting a 31-year-old male head of household with no age recorded for female head of household, editors consult age and gender tables, and "guess" that her age would be 3 years less than her husband's (i.e., 28). Analogous ascription techniques help determine the identity of stations heard or the duration of media use if such data are missing. While these practices strike some as questionable or improper, ascription is a standard procedure in virtually all survey work, and is typically based on systematic methodological research.

Editing sometimes involves questions of definition. This happens, for example, in the case of data recorded by meters. Should a person who watches less than half a program be included in the program's total audience? The standard practice in television viewing has been to credit one quarter-hour of viewing to a program if at least 5 minutes of use has taken place. Under that definition, of course, a person might show up in more than one program audience in a given quarter-hour. RADAR, Arbitron's network radio audience service, credits radio listening to a commercial or program if a person reports listening to a station at any time during the quarter hour when the commercial or program is cleared.

Often there is no clear right or wrong answer to such questions. It is more a matter of what the industry will agree to accept. As media and measurement technologies change, new questions arise, and the parties at interest must negotiate new solutions. Although the resolution of questions like this might seem arbitrary, solutions are always based on technological or other limiting factors. If some party feels disadvantaged, a particular editing procedure may become the subject of a political struggle within the industry. For example, if a household watches one program, but tapes a second one on the VCR, should that household be credited to the second program's audience? From the late 1970s through the early 2000s, the answer was yes—Nielsen credited viewing to a program when it was taped. However, changes in technology have necessitated changes in the way viewing is counted. TiVo and other forms of DVR can record hours of programming each day, so the assumption that viewers watch all programs they record is no longer tenable. In this new media environment, accurate audience estimates will depend on individual identification codes embedded in each program.

Programs, Schedules, and Other Information

Despite the vast amounts of information collected by diaries, meters, and telephone calls, these data are not, in and of themselves, sufficient to produce audience ratings. Other information must be added to make a complete, usable product. The most important addition to data on people's set-tuning behavior is information about the programming on those sets. At the local level, station schedules are needed to check the accuracy of diary entries. Further, even the most sophisticated of passive household meters are not capable of determining what program was on which channel at what time. These data must be collected and added to the ratings database.

Because radio listening is generally credited to stations, rather than to specific programs, the problem is relatively simple. Arbitron, for example, mails radio stations a "Station Information Packet," in which stations verify their call letters and report their network affiliations, broadcast schedules, and especially current slogans, catch phrases, and station identifications—for example, "96 Rock," "News Radio 88," "All News 67," "Continuous Country," "Z 104," and "98 FM." There are frequent arguments, and occasional lawsuits, over who is entitled to phrases such as "More Music" or "Music Radio." Further, if two stations in nearby markets are at 102.7 and 103.1, there may be confusion if both use "one-o-three" in their phrase. It is useful for station personnel or consultants to look at diaries in order to identify uncredited listeners. As we noted in chapter 3, they also find it useful to read specific comments written by some listeners.

Television viewing, on the other hand, must be associated with very specific programs, so much more detailed information is needed. Historically, ratings companies collected this information directly from the stations, which used program title logs to report programs airing in every quarter hour of every broadcast day across all survey weeks. Handling program schedules like these would be problem enough, but the growth of television technologies expanded the problem immensely. There are nearly 9,000 cable systems in the United States, and the average television household can receive 100 channels. These include dozens of cable networks, access channels, and local stations—the latter sometimes from several different TV market areas. Different cable systems can, and do, carry these services on different channels. Even local TV stations may be reassigned to a new channel number. In any given television market area, there may be several such cable systems—frequently using different channel assignments. Add to this the problem of sports and special events that start and stop at unpredictable times, imagine that situation repeated in various markets around the country, and you will have some idea of what confronts a TV ratings service.

The job of figuring out what is on TV would be easier if every program contained a signature that a machine could simply read. Broadcast networks have cooperated with Nielsen for several years by imposing a special electronic code in the video portion of their broadcast signal. This system, called the *Automated Measurement of Lineups (AMOL)* allows detection devices in each market to determine when affiliates are broadcasting a network program. Beginning in 2005, Nielsen is requiring all national cable and broadcast networks to include audio signatures on their programs to ensure proper crediting of viewership. The new system makes the job of tracking national programming more efficient, but the ratings service will still need to use traditional techniques to identify uncoded programs such as local productions, some network reruns, and some syndication.

In addition to programming information, other data enter into the production of ratings reports as well. For example, stations occasionally have technical difficulties which may affect their audience ratings. These are reported in the ratings book. Stations may also engage in extraordinary activities to boost their ratings during a sweeps period. The ratings services keep an eye out for any special station activities that might bias or distort the ratings, because it is thought to compromise the integrity of the entire process. Depending on the transgression, the ratings companies will either note the offending station's crime in the ratings book, or drop the station's ratings from the book altogether.

Projections

Ultimately, the research services must publish estimates of audience size and composition. They project these estimates from samples. Although the process is complex, we can illustrate the basic logic with a simple example of diary measurement. Suppose we choose a sample of 1,000 individuals from a population of 1 million. Each individual would represent 1,000 people. If 50 people in our sample watch a local news show, we could project the show's actual audience to be 50,000. That is essentially what the ratings services do. They determine the number of people represented by one in-tab diary and assign that diary an appropriate number. If people are the unit of analysis, the number is called *persons per diary value (PPDV)*. If households are the unit of analysis the number is labeled *households per diary value (HPDV)*.

This illustration works quite well if we have perfect probability samples, in which all members of the population are proportionately represented. As we have seen, however, that is never the case. Nonresponse error means that some kinds of people are over-represented, while others are under-represented. Remember, also, that the most common remedy for this problem is to weight the responses of some sample members more heavily than others. Suppose, in the illustration just given, that 18- to 24-year-old males were under-represented in the in-tab sample. Let's say they constitute 4% of the sample, but are believed to be 8% of the population. Males in this group would receive a weight of 2.0 (i.e., 8% / 4% = 2.0). Therefore, to project total audience size for this group, each young man should have a PPDV of 2,000 (i.e., 1,000 × 2.0), instead of 1,000. Conversely, over-represented groups should have PPDVs of less than 1,000.

In practice, the weights that are assigned to different groups are never as extreme as the illustration just given (i.e., they come closer to 1.0). Further, ratings services weight a single respondent on a number of variables besides age and gender to make a final determination. Although this method of audience projection is not without biases, it is generally agreed that it is the best practical remedy for nonresponse errors. When samples change, weights are re-evaluated and adjusted to reflect the new mix of respondents.

Could similar statistical solutions correct for some of the measurement errors we reviewed in the preceding section? After all, we have noted that certain kinds of response errors are associated with certain kinds of measurement. Some work in this area has been done, but there is less consensus on how such statistical corrections should be applied to formal published audience estimates.

The best illustration of this problem occurs in reconciling meter- and diary-based estimates of television audiences. In markets that are measured with passive meters, Nielsen integrates the diary data with the information collected through the household meter to make a single "best guess" as to audience size and composition. Because metered data are assumed to more accurately measure set usage, they are used to fix audience size. Diary data, which often show smaller audiences, are extrapolated to determine the likeliest demographic breakdown. A ratings analyst should know the consequences of these methodological issues when using the services of research companies.

LOCAL RATINGS

Television

The types of ratings data that are available to a TV station differ according to the size of individual markets. Ratings research in larger markets is based on bigger samples, usually offers different measurement options and more services, and is much more expensive. It is no coincidence that larger markets also tend to be much richer in terms of the dollars spent on media. For these reasons, it is important to expand on our earlier discussion of local markets.

Each DMA is a collection of counties in which the preponderance of total viewing can be attributed to local or home-market stations. That is, counties are assigned to markets on the basis of which stations the people in those counties actually view. Figure 8.1 shows a map of all the DMAs in the United States. Notice that DMAs vary substantially in terms of their geographic extension. More importantly for media buyers and sellers, though, these markets differ in terms of population. Appendix A shows a ranking of DMAs by the total number of television households in each. Of course, shifts in the U.S. population cause changes in how mar-

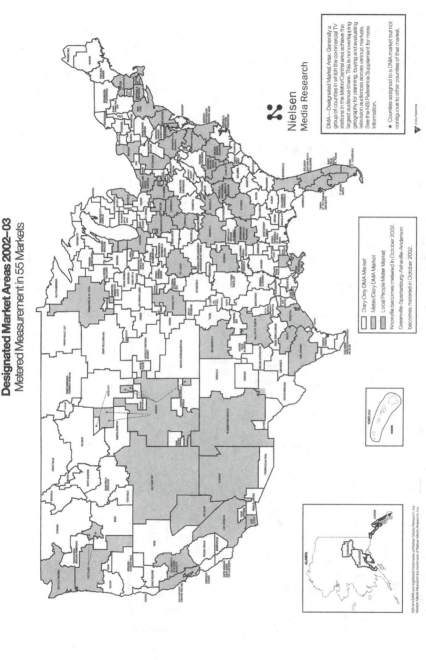

FIG. 8.1. Nielsen Designated Market Areas 2002–2003. Reprinted by permission of Nielsen Media Research.

149

kets are ranked. But because market areas are ultimately defined by viewing behavior, changes in programming, transmitters, cable penetration, and so on can also alter market size and composition.

Every year Nielsen reconsiders how markets should be constituted, and changes do occur. Sometimes, counties on the border between two adjacent markets will be moved from one to the other. Such changes are no small matter. For instance, national spot buys are sometimes made in the "top 20," or "top 50" markets. If the loss of a county causes a market to drop below an important breakpoint, it can have a detrimental impact on every station in the market. However, the new market configuration could also have a differential impact on local stations. Due to factors like geography and transmitter location, some stations cover certain areas of the market better than others. If the county that is moved is one in which a particular station has a clear technical advantage, it could alter the relative standing of stations in the ratings.

The standard local ratings report in television is called a *Viewers in Profile (VIP)*. Figures 8.2 and 8.3, copied from the Denver ratings book, are typical of the first pages you will encounter in any local market report. As you can see, these pages contain a good deal of information about the market. Keep in mind, though, that the printed books have largely been replaced by computer printouts that can be customized. Consequently, individual formats will look quite different, but the underlying concepts remain the same.

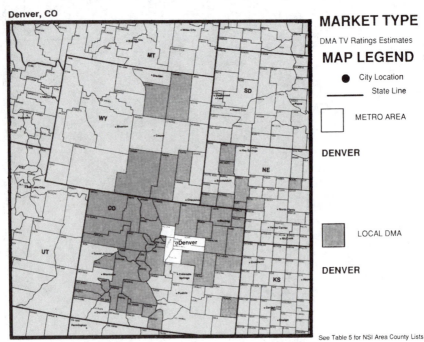

FIG. 8.2.   Sample page from Nielsen Viewers in Profile. Reprinted by permission of Nielsen Media Research.

TABLE 1 - UNIVERSE ESTIMATES - JAN. 2004

AREA	TOTAL HOUSEHOLDS	TV HOUSEHOLDS	TV HOUSEHOLDS BY COUNTY SIZE †			
			A	B	C	D
METRO	1,003,000	981,650				
DMA	1,437,000	1,399,100	1,054,380	103,530	241,190	
%		100	75	7	17	
NSI	2,076,600	2,023,570	1,258,430	349,170	415,970	
%		100	62	17	21	

TOTAL HOUSEHOLDS are estimates produced by Market Statistics, a division of Claritas, Inc., and are copyrighted by them. They are the base against which television penetration estimates have been applied.

TELEVISION OWNERSHIP PERCENTS are Nielsen Media Research estimates based on combining historical projections from the 1960 and 1970 Censuses with estimates from the NSI telephone interviews from a number of all market measurement periods.

HOUSEHOLDS ARE OCCUPIED HOUSING UNITS. The household universe estimates shown in Table 1 are estimates of year-round households, i.e., housing units occupied year round. Seasonal housing units which are occupied only during certain seasons of the year are not included in the Household Universe Estimates. Thus, the number of households during the survey period may differ from the estimate in Table 1.

† See Local Reference Supplement for definition of county size.　　　　LT Less than 1%.

TABLE 2 - PENETRATION ESTIMATES

	PERCENT OF TV HOUSEHOLDS						
AREA	BLACK %	HISPANIC %	MULTI-SET %	VCR %	CABLE TV %	ADS %	CABLE PLUS %
METRO	5.2	13.7			62		
DMA	3.8	13.1	76	91	59	25	84
DENVER	11.3	22.4	NA	NA	NA	NA	NA

Multi-set estimates are based on the metered sample. Multi-set, Cable TV, VCR, ADS and Cable Plus estimates are based on the latest available data. Black and Hispanic estimates are as of January 1, 2004. Cable Plus is defined as the presence of Cable and/or Alternate Delivery System (ADS). See Local Reference Supplement for detail.

TABLE 3 - SAMPLE SIZES: HOUSEHOLDS

		DIARY SAMPLE(1)					
	METER SAMPLE	INITIALLY DESIGNATED HOUSEHOLDS			IN-TAB DIARY HOUSEHOLDS		
AREA	IN-TAB AVG.	LISTED	UNLISTED	TOTAL	LISTED	UNLISTED	TOTAL
METRO	272 (EST'D)	1710	725	2435	666	198	864
DMA(INCL.METRO)	379 (2)	2475	1000	3475	971	284	1255
NON-DMA	---	3976	1219	5195	1676	388	2064 (3)
NSI(INCL. DMA)	379	6451	2219	8670	2647	672	3319

(1) The Non-DMA (Diary) sample is combined with the DMA meter sample for compiling Station Total households; the entire diary sample is used for Audience Composition data.
(2) Yields an approximate equivalent simple random sample size of 740.
(2) + (3) NSI Area Station Total households herein are based on these in-tab samples and yield an approximate equivalent simple random sample size of 1140.
Equivalent simple random sample size is a term sometimes used for the statistical equivalent of the sample size for computing sampling errors or statistical tolerances.
For sample selection procedures in Total Telephone Frame markets, see Local Reference Supplement.

COPYRIGHT 2004 NIELSEN MEDIA RESEARCH - PRINTED IN U.S.A.　　　1

TABLE 4 - TELEVISION STATIONS

CITY OF ORIGIN	STATION	CHANNEL	AFFILIATION
BROOMFIELD	*KBDI	12	PBS
DENVER	*KCEC	50	UNI
DENVER	*KCNC	4	CBS
DENVER	*KDVR+	31	FOX
FORT COLLINS	*KFCT	22	SATELLITE OF KDVR
DENVER	*KMGH	7	ABC
DENVER	*KPXC	59	PAX
DENVER	*KRMA	6	PBS
DENVER	KRMT (L)	41	IND
BOULDER	KTFD (L)	14	TF
DENVER	*KTVD	20	UPN
DENVER	*KUSA	9	NBC
DENVER	*KWGN	2	WB
CASTLE ROCK	KWHD (L)	53	IND
CABLE	AEN (D)		
CABLE	AMC (D)		
CABLE	APL (D)		
CABLE	BRVO (D)		
CABLE	CMD (D)		
CABLE	CNN (D)		
CABLE	CRT (D)		
CABLE	DSC (D)		
CABLE	DSNY (D)		
CABLE	ENCY (D)		
CABLE	ENPN (D)		
CABLE	ESX (D)		
CABLE	FAM (D)		
CABLE	FOOD (D)		
CABLE	FSRM (D)		
CABLE	FX (D)		
CABLE	FXNC (D)		
CABLE	HALL (D)		
CABLE	HBOP (D)		
CABLE	HGTV (D)		
CABLE	HIS (D)		
CABLE	HLN (D)		
CABLE	LIF (D)		
CABLE	MNBC (D)		
CABLE	MTV (D)		
CABLE	NAN (D)		
CABLE	NICK (D)		
CABLE	SFI (D)		
CABLE	SPK (D)		
CABLE	TBSC (D)		
CABLE	TCM (D)		
CABLE	TDSY (D)		
CABLE	TLC (D)		
CABLE	TNT (D)		
CABLE	TOON (D)		
CABLE	TRAV (D)		
CABLE	TVL (D)		
CABLE	USA (D)		
CABLE	VH1 (D)		

(L) THIS LOCAL STATION IS REPORTABLE IN THE DAYPART SECTION ONLY
(D) THIS OUTSIDE STATION IS REPORTABLE IN THE DAYPART SECTION ONLY

IN ADDITION TO THE REPORTABLE STATIONS SHOWN ABOVE, THE FOLLOWING STATIONS ORIGINATE IN OR ARE ASSIGNED FOR REPORTING PURPOSES TO THIS MARKET BUT DID NOT MEET THE MINIMUM REPORTING STANDARDS (SEE REPORTING STANDARDS, INSIDE BACK COVER)

LONGMONT	KDEN	25	IND
STEAMBOAT SPGS	KMAS	24	TEL
GLENWOOD SPRNGS	*KREG	3	CBS
STEAMBOAT SPRGS	KSBS+	63	TEL
STEAMBOAT SPRGS	KSSS	47	TEL
ASPEN	KSZG	20	IND

NOTE: KREG IS A TOTAL SATELLITE OF KREX, GRAND JUNCTION.

KSBS IS LPTV STATION KSBS-LP.
KSGB IS LPTV STATION KMAS-LP.
KSZG IS LPTV STATION KSZG-LP.

Effective with the May 2004 measurement station KSBS changed their channel number from 67 to 47.

* = NSI client

Network affiliation as shown herein is based on information supplied by the networks for use in Nielsen Television Index (NTI). For additional details, see the Local Reference Supplement.

FIG. 8.3.　Sample page from Nielsen Viewers in Profile. Reprinted by permission of Nielsen Media Research.

The first thing to notice on the DMA map is that the television market is divided into several non-overlapping areas. The heavily shaded areas plus the white areas comprise the entire DMA. Note that this particular DMA includes counties from three different states: Colorado, Wyoming, and Nebraska. The reason for this is that Denver stations account for a large share of viewing in those counties through carriage on local cable systems. The area that appears white on this map is what Nielsen calls the *metro area*. This is the market's core retail area, and generally corresponds to the Metropolitan Statistical Areas (MSAs) used by the federal government.

Figure 8.3 contains several tables from the VIP that offer detailed information about the Denver DMA. They are very useful in answering questions about market characteristics and sample size. You can tell from VIP Table 1, for example, that there are 1,399,100 television households in the DMA, and 981,650 television households in the metro area. From VIP Table 2 you can learn that the market is 13.1% Hispanic, and that cable penetration is 59% (much lower than the national average). VIP Table 3 shows that the market is measured with meters and diaries, and that the in-tab sample sizes are 379 and 1,255, respectively. The upper right-hand corner of the page shows the measurement dates: April 29–May 26, 2004. And the list of television stations in VIP Table 4 gives you some idea of the competition in the marketplace.

Markets with Local People Meter technology will have ratings information available all year long, but most television markets will continue being measured with passive meters and/or diaries. Nielsen measures these DMAs at regular intervals throughout the broadcast year. All DMAs are measured at least four times, during November, February, May, and July. These 4-week measurement periods are called ratings *sweeps*. As you may recall, however, the standard diary only records one week's worth of viewing. This means that the diary data collected in a sweep is actually based on four independent samples drawn in consecutive weeks. These data are combined to provide a single month-long estimate of audience size and composition.

A ratings sweep is more that just a random occasion for collecting data. The dates of each sweep are known well in advance, so local stations can and do adapt their programming to attract the largest audiences possible. This may manifest itself in the local television news airing particularly sensational stories, or in the scheduling of the most attractive syndicated programs. Even the networks, which are continuously measured, try to help out their affiliates by running blockbuster movies and heavily promoted mini-series. Sometimes, though, a station will cross the rather ill-defined line between reasonable promotional efforts and illegal practices known as hyping or *hypoing*. These practices artificially inflate the ratings, so that they are not a fair indication of average audiences to the stations. Indeed, such abuses were one of the concerns motivating the Congressional investigations in the 1960s.

Hypoing can involve any one of a number of activities designed to distort or bias ratings results. For example, a station might try to enhance its ratings by directly addressing diary-keepers in its programming, by conducting a survey to learn the identity of actual diary-keepers, or by conducting particularly heavy-handed contests and promotions. If the ratings companies learn of such "special station activities," they may take several different actions from placing a special notice in the ratings book, to deleting the station's audience estimates altogether. A typical warning in a ratings book might be worded as follows:

> Nielsen Media Research has been advised that the following station(s), network program(s), and/or syndicated program(s) conducted a contest, on-air announcement, research survey, or other activity in this market during all or part of the November 2003 measurement period which, in the judgment of Nielsen Media Research, may have affected viewing.

The page would then list any stations or programs that violated the rules against hypoing.

Problems with hypoing during sweeps months have prompted many industry participants to call for continuous measurement of all local markets. This would, in the opinion of many, eliminate the incentive for stations to schedule all their best programming at certain predictable times of the year. And because continuous measurement would give advertisers detailed trend data, it would reduce the ability of stations to strategically inflate ratings levels. While this goal could theoretically be accomplished by installing Local People Meters in all 210 DMAs, the high cost of the technology relative to its benefits for smaller markets will prevent nationwide deployment. Economic benefits are likely to outweigh investment costs only in those markets with the highest advertising revenues.

Assuming that data collection goes according to plan, Nielsen will have about 350,000 diaries to process at the end of a nationwide sweep. Sample sizes vary widely from market to market. The largest markets could have household sample targets of 2,500. The smallest markets, by contrast, have a target of just over 250 households. Response rates also vary, but average around 30%. In any particular market, information on sample placement and response is contained in the local market report.

Local television ratings in the VIP are reported in various ways. Market reports provide audience estimates by daypart, or by narrower time periods. They provide audience trend information for different demographic groups, and they describe audiences for specific television programs. Figure 8.4 is a partial page from the "Time Period Estimates" section of the *Viewers in Profile*, again from the Denver DMA.

Across the top are column headings that describe the contents of the numbers directly below. Down the left-hand side of the page is informa-

DENVER, CO

A full sample page from Nielsen Viewers in Profile showing a detailed ratings grid for DENVER, CO. The leftmost columns list METRO HH (Rating/Share), STATION, and PROGRAM for the FRIDAY 6:00PM – 8:30PM time period. The grid continues with DMA HOUSEHOLD (RATINGS by WEEKS 1–4, MULTI-WEEK AVG, SHARE TREND) and DMA RATINGS (PERSONS, WOMEN, MEN, TNG, CHILD).

Representative station/program rows include:

6:00PM Continued — KCEC AMR OTR VZ-UNI, KCNC NEWS 4 AT 6, KDVR+ SIMPSONS B, KMGH 7 NEWS-6PM, KPXC FAMLY FEUD-PAX, KRMA NEWSHOUR-LEHR, KTVD KING OF QUEENS, KUSA 9NWS-600PM, KWGN FRIENDS, HUT/PUT/TOTALS*

6:30PM — KBDI BBC WORLD NEWS, KCEC AMR OTR VZ-UNI, KCNC HOLLYWD SQUARS, KDVR+ SEINFELD, KMGH WHEEL-FORTNE, KPXC 9 NEWS-PAX-EN, KRMA NEWSHOUR-LEHR, KTVD THAT 70S SHOW, KUSA ENT TONIGHT 30, KWGN EVRYBDY-RAY MF, HUT/PUT/TOTALS*

7:00PM — KBDI ANTO RDSHW-PTV, KCEC MARIAN-NCH-UNI, KCNC JOAN-ARCDA-CBS, KDVR+ FOX MOVIE-FRI, KMGH GEO LOPEZ-ABC, KPXC MGM NT@MOV-PAX, KRMA WASHINGTON WEEK, KTVD AVG. ALL WKS / FRI NITE MOVIE / UPN'S MOV FRI / ROCKIES BSBL, KUSA AVG. ALL WKS / DATELNE FR-NBC / FRASR FNLE5/14, KWGN AVG. ALL WKS / REBA-WB / SPRSTRUSA-5/21, HUT/PUT/TOTALS*

7:30PM — KBDI ANTO RDSHW-PTV, KCEC MARIAN-NCH-UNI, KCNC JOAN-ARCDA-CBS, KDVR+ FOX MOVIE-FRI, KMGH AVG. ALL WKS / BIG HOUSE-ABC / GEO LOPEZ-5/7 / GEO LOPEZ-5/14 / GEO LOPEZ-ABC, KPXC MGM NT@MOV-PAX, KRMA WALL ST-FORTNE, KTVD AVG. ALL WKS / FRI NITE MOVIE / UPN'S MOV FRI / ROCKIES BSBL, KUSA AVG. ALL WKS / DATELNE FR-NBC / FRASR FNLE5/14, KWGN AVG. ALL WKS / WHAT-ABT U-WB / REBA1-5/14-WB / SPRSTRUSA-5/21, HUT/PUT/TOTALS*

FIG. 8.4. Sample page from Nielsen Viewers in Profile. Reprinted by permission of Nielsen Media Research.

154

tion on specific stations and the programs they broadcast. It is organized by day of the week, and within that, by half-hour (and sometimes by quarter-hour) time periods. This particular page reports viewing on Friday from 6 p.m. to 8:00 p.m. At the bottom of each half-hour time period is a line of numbers labeled "HUT/PUT/TOTALS" which provides audience viewing levels by half hour. As we discuss more fully in chapter 10, this gives an indication of the number of people who were available to watch a given program.

After the program title, the first four columns give audience estimates for each of the four weeks that comprise a sweep. This can be useful, because sometimes program variations during a sweep are masked by an "average" rating. For example, note that KTVDs household rating was much higher in Week 3, when the station broadcast a Rockies game, than it was for movies that aired during Weeks 1, 2, and 4.

The remaining columns report average program ratings and shares of one sort or another. For ease of reference, the columns are numbered just below their titles. Columns 7 and 8, for example, contain ratings and share information for television households (TVHH) in the DMA. If you look in the 7:30–8 p.m. time period, you'll see that station KCNC aired *Joan of Arcadia*, and achieved a 5 rating and a 9 share. The following page in this ratings book (not shown) contains projected audience estimates, reported in thousands, for the same programs.

Note also that at the top of the page, below the column headings, are two rows of numbers labeled "R.S.E. Thresholds." This stands for "Relative Standard Error," and it is there to remind users that the numbers reported below are only estimates based on samples, and are therefore subject to sampling error. More specifically, for each column, they indicate the point at which one standard error will constitute either 25% or 50% of an estimate. As you would expect, column estimates based on smaller samples sizes (e.g., women 12–24 versus women 18+) are subject to more error, hence thresholds are relatively high. In the example shown, 1 standard error would be within 25% of the estimate only if the rating among women 12–24 were at least 7.

Nielsen makes ratings data available through a variety of computer programs for buyers and research analysts. Usually, market reports are stored on computer disks, and read by using a desktop computer. Not only can one read the book this way, but more importantly, the audience estimates contained within can be more easily manipulated. This is, essentially, an electronic version of the market report. As computer and audience measurement technology change, these programs are revised and re-issued. The ratings services provide brochures that describe them in detail. Independent vendors such as Audience Analytics, Star Media, and Donnelly also sell software for the analysis of market report data. They obtain a third-party license to download Nielsen data on behalf of their clients, and they provide software with customized applications. The exact capabilities of each package differ, but they can typically locate the relative strengths and weaknesses of each station in the market by ranking on various criteria, identify a package of avails to match an advertiser's request, help manage audience inventories, and project audiences based on historical data. Many of these specific analytical techniques are discussed in the last chapter.

As noted earlier, larger markets like Denver are *metered markets*, which use either Local Peoplemeters or a combination of passive household meters and diaries to generate the ratings. The 56 metered markets (as of 2005) account for about 70% of all U.S. television households, and Nielsen continues to add more each year. Usually there are between 300 and 500 passive meters installed in a given DMA, depending on the size and make-up of the market. The sample size for the five largest LPM markets is 800 households. The installation of Local People Meters will eliminate the need for diary-keeping in those markets.

The availability of metered data affects both the ratings themselves and how those ratings are used. First, as we described in the previous chapter, meter-based data in hybrid markets (passive meter plus diary) are employed to adjust the audience estimates derived from diaries. Second, because data collection is fast, meters, whether passive or LPM, make it possible to deliver overnight ratings. Overnights allow programmers in local markets to respond quickly to audience trends. As was the case with local market reports, Nielsen sells PC-based software to manipulate electronically delivered overnight data. Figure 8.5 shows a sample of overnight data from the Washington, DC market. Each column of numbers represents ratings for a different station, so it is very easy to compare the competition by time period.

Radio

The local radio ratings business is also dominated by one major research provider, Arbitron. This firm measures 286 radio markets yearly—100 markets receive quarterly data; 186 receive data twice per year. Ratings are based on a 12-week survey period rather than the 4-week standard used in local television measurement. Arbitron estimates radio listenership for Metro Survey Areas, which generally correspond to governmentally designated metropolitan areas. In addition, Arbitron routinely reports Total Survey Area (TSA) estimates for the larger geographic area in which radio listening may occur. In the top 100 radio markets, Arbitron reports DMA audiences in the fall and spring, matching its own county designations to Nielsen's television market assignments. The regular Arbitron books contain information for only commercial stations. However, data for public stations is accessible through software products.

Although the 7-day personal diary is the standard way to collect data on radio audiences, other methods are possible. Telephone surveys, for example, seem to favor formats that cater to young listeners. The best single explanation for such differences appears to be response rates.

Washington, DC (Hagrstwn) [8]
NielsenTV DMA Sample: 385 Reporting Households
Daily Grid

Time	HUT	07 WJLA ABC	Rt	Sh	09 WUSA CBS	Rt	Sh	04 WRC NBC	Rt	Sh	05 WTTG FOX	Rt	Sh	20 WDCA UPN	Rt	Sh	50 WBDC WB	Rt	Sh
8:00p	75.3	EXT-HME-8P-ABC	9.4	12	COLD CASE-CB	12.3	16	AMER DRMS-NBC	6.8	9	SIMPSONS-FOX	6.9	9	OUTER LIMITS	1.2	2	CHARMED-WB	3.7	5
	74.5		8.9	12		11.9	16		5.9	8	_7.7_10_74.9	8.4	11		1.4	2		3.6	5
8:30p	75.3		9.8	13		12.2	16		6.1	8	ARRSTD DVL-FOX	7.9	10		1.6	2		3.9	5
	77.3	_9.4_12_75.6	9.5	12	12.2_16_75.6	12.6	16	_6.3_8_75.6	6.6	9	_7.5_10_76.3	7.2	9	_1.3_2_75.6	1.2	1	_3.8_5_75.6	3.9	5
9:00p	76.1	EXT-HM ED-1/30	9.9	13	CBS SUN MOV	13.8	18	LAW&ORD-CI-NBC	11.1	15	FAMILY GUY-FOX	5.1	7	UPN20WK CNMA9	2.1	3	S HRVY BGTM-WI	1.9	3
	77.4		8.6	11	(MAGIC-DAYS)	14.2	18		10.7	14	_4.8_6_76.7	4.5	6	(BABY BOY)	1.7	2		1.2	2
9:30p	77.4		8.8	11		14.5	19		10.6	14	SMPSN-SU930FOX	4.5	6		1.2	2		1.9	2
	76.2	_9.0_12_76.8	8.7	11		14.0	18	10.7_14_76.8	10.5	14	_5.3_7_76.8	6.1	8	_1.6_2_76.8	1.7	2	_2_76.8	1.5	2
10:00p	73.1	DSP HW SPL-ABC	8.8	12		14.1	19	CRSSG JRDN-NBC	7.7	11	FOX5 NWS-TEN	8.6	12	WILL&GRACE WK	1.3	2	WILL&GRACE WK	1.5	2
	71.4		9.4	13		13.8	19		8.9	13		8.2	11	_1.5_2_72.2	0.9	1	_1.5_2_72.2	1.5	2
10:30p	66.6		9.7	15		14.1	21		9.6	14		6.2	9	WILL&GRAC WK [	0.9	1	WILL&GRAC WK [	0.8	1
11:00p	64.8	_9.5_14_69.0	9.9	15	14.1_19_72.9	14.1	22	_8.9_13_69.0	9.4	15	_6.9_10_69.0	4.6	7	_1.8_1_65.7	0.9	1	_1.8_1_65.7	0.8	1
	58.1	ABC7 NWS AT 11	8.8	15	9NEWS AT 11PM	5.2	9	NWS 4 AT 11	9.9	17	SPORTS EXTRA	3.5	6	PAID PROGRAM	2.0	3	PAID PROGRAM	0.5	1
11:30p	50.7	_7.9_15_54.4	7.0	14	_4.3_8_54.4	3.4	7	_8.8_16_54.4	7.8	15	_2.7_5_54.4	1.9	4	_1.4_2_69.2	1.4	3	_0.5_1_54.4	0.5	1
	45.9	WEST WING	5.9	13	SPORTS PLUS	3.4	7	G M SPORTS	4.5	10	SEINFELD SU	1.5	3	MOESHA	0.8	2	JUST SHT-WK B	0.5	1
	42.3	_4.5_10_44.1	3.6	9	_2.4_5_44.1	1.4	3	_4.5_10_44.1	4.5	11	_2.0_4_44.1	2.4	6	_0.8_2_44.1	0.8	2	_0.7_2_44.1	0.9	2

<< - Below Reportable Minimum

Copyright 2005 Nielsen Media Research

FIG. 8.5.   Sample of Nielsen overnight ratings.

Nonresponse among diary keepers is especially acute in younger age groups. These listeners tend to favor formats like rock and urban contemporary. The bias that this creates is the non-response error that we referred to earlier. The under-representation of younger listeners can, in part, be corrected by weighting the data in favor of younger listeners who do return a diary. Unfortunately, those who respond may have different format preferences than their peers who do not respond, and weighting the data by demographic categories cannot compensate for that sort of difference. It is helpful for ratings users to know which groups are under- or over-represented. This information is generally provided in the form of unweighted in-tabs for each demographic compared to population estimates.

Arbitron reports feature a large section called "Listener Estimates" that includes audience trend information. Here, the radio audience is broken out into about 20 demographically defined subsets. Within each demographic category, individual station audiences are reported across several dayparts. Figure 8.6 is an example of part of one page for the Spring, 2004 Arbitron Radio Market Report for Los Angeles.

Each page of the report gives information on five dayparts, noted in the column headings across the top. This page includes station audience estimates among persons 18–49 years old for weekday dayparts. Underneath each daypart heading are four different audience estimates: (a) the projected audience size in an average quarter hour (AQH), (b) the cumulative audience in that same daypart, (c) AQH audience expressed as a rating, and (d) AQH audience expressed as a share. The first two numbers are always reported in hundreds, with the last two zeros understood. Every listener in an AQH will be included in the associated cume audience. Therefore, for any given daypart, the cume will always be equal to or greater than the AQH audience.

Down the left-hand side of the table are the stations reported in the ratings book. Usually these are stations assigned to the home market, but if stations assigned to neighboring markets have significant audiences, they will appear below a dotted line on the same page. Such stations are usually powerful stations from a big city that reach into smaller towns and markets. For each station, listener estimates are provided for the current survey period along with an estimate for the previous four books (markets measured only twice yearly will show a two-book average).

Other data are routinely reported in the Radio Market Report, including AQH and cume audience composition, time spent listening, cume duplication, exclusive cumes, and, because much listening occurs outside the home, "location of listening" estimates. Arbitron can also include selected qualitative information in the regular radio book in about 100 markets where its qualitative services Scarborough or RetailDirect are available.

Arbitron also issues a "County Coverage" report, and uses its national database to generate special reports on individual listener groups and

Target Listener Trends

	Monday-Sunday 6AM-MID				Monday-Friday 6AM-10AM				Monday-Friday 10AM-3PM				Monday-Friday 3PM-7PM				Monday-Friday 7PM-MID			
	AQH (00)	Cume (00)	AQH Rtg	AQH Shr	AQH (00)	Cume (00)	AQH Rtg	AQH Shr	AQH (00)	Cume (00)	AQH Rtg	AQH Shr	AQH (00)	Cume (00)	AQH Rtg	AQH Shr	AQH (00)	Cume (00)	AQH Rtg	AQH Shr
KKLA-FM																				
SP '04	50	1159	.1	.5	87	646	.1	.5	78	587	.1	.5	70	496	.1	.6	18	212		.4
WI '04	36	1203	.1	.3	63	629	.1	.4	54	512	.1	.4	51	568	.1	.4	14	259		.3
FA '03	44	955	.1	.4	97	598	.2	.6	67	414	.1	.5	54	404	.1	.4	10	246		.2
SU '03	35	953	.1	.3	83	552	.1	.6	43	411	.1	.3	44	339	.1	.3	15	183		.3
4-Book	41	1068	.1	.4	83	606	.1	.5	61	481	.1	.4	55	452	.1	.4	14	225		.3
SP '03	37	964	.1	.3	91	626	.1	.6	37	407	.1	.2	62	482	.1	.5	13	168		.3
KLAC-AM																				
SP '04	58	1926	.1	.5	41	245	.1	.3	43	276	.1	.3	76	969	.1	.6	82	1027	.1	1.7
WI '04	33	1099	.1	.3	26	245		.2	38	289	.1	.3	52	594	.1	.4	32	421	.1	.7
FA '03	37	1332	.1	.4	28	257		.2	53	329	.1	.4	60	793	.1	.4	35	586	.1	.7
SU '03	27	581		.3	34	339		.2	16	165		.1	25	254		.2	32	210	.1	.6
4-Book	39	1235	.1	.4	32	272	.1	.2	38	265	.1	.3	53	653	.1	.4	45	561	.1	.9
SP '03	36	1260	.1	.3	32	313	.1	.2	29	248		.2	38	613	.1	.3	48	577	.1	.9
KLAX-FM																				
SP '04	651	7862	1.0	6.1	1445	4913	2.3	8.9	858	5031	1.4	5.7	561	3825	.9	4.4	141	1565	.2	2.8
WI '04	406	6176	.6	3.9	638	3430	1.0	4.1	638	3477	1.0	4.3	417	3015	.7	3.2	126	1456	.2	2.7
FA '03	401	6452	.6	3.8	699	3537	1.1	4.5	545	3279	.9	3.7	397	3162	.6	2.9	144	1530	.2	3.0
SU '03	422	6509	.7	4.0	627	3203	1.0	4.2	635	3724	1.0	4.3	437	3334	.7	3.3	183	1793	.3	3.5
4-Book	470	6750	.7	4.5	852	3771	1.4	5.4	669	3878	1.1	4.5	453	3334	.7	3.5	149	1586	.2	3.0
SP '03	480	6857	.8	4.5	742	3919	1.2	4.8	694	4048	1.1	4.6	466	3203	.7	3.5	193	1832	.3	3.8
KLOS-FM																				
SP '04	283	6685	.5	2.7	460	2813	.7	2.8	441	3111	.7	2.9	368	3363	.6	2.9	92	1579	.1	1.9
WI '04	286	6544	.5	2.7	478	2796	.8	3.1	361	2647	.6	2.4	403	3634	.6	3.1	140	1506	.2	3.0
FA '03	288	6977	.5	2.7	448	3097	.7	2.9	401	3037	.6	2.7	397	3600	.6	2.9	128	1648	.2	3.6
SU '03	327	6969	.5	3.1	520	2958	.8	3.5	425	3180	.7	2.9	408	3572	.7	3.1	189	1740	.3	3.6
4-Book	296	6794	.5	2.8	477	2916	.8	3.1	407	2994	.7	2.7	394	3542	.6	3.0	137	1618	.2	2.8
SP '03	243	6145	.4	2.3	383	2529	.6	2.5	347	2860	.6	2.3	339	3249	.5	2.5	103	1661	.2	2.0
KLSX-FM																				
SP '04	408	5877	.6	3.9	1046	3776	1.7	6.5	600	2973	1.0	4.0	531	2887	.8	4.2	100	1091	.2	2.0
WI '04	364	5400	.6	3.5	910	3293	1.4	5.9	641	2846	1.0	4.3	411	2683	.7	3.1	45	810	.1	1.0
FA '03	284	4728	.5	2.7	684	2718	1.1	4.4	384	2263	.6	2.6	419	2453	.7	3.1	86	920	.1	1.8
SU '03	301	5107	.5	2.9	692	3009	1.1	4.7	369	2338	.6	2.5	508	2710	.8	3.9	66	875	.1	1.2
4-Book	339	5278	.6	3.3	833	3199	1.3	5.4	499	2605	.8	3.4	467	2683	.8	3.6	74	924	.1	1.5
SP '03	338	4929	.5	3.2	815	3061	1.3	5.3	489	2476	.8	3.3	509	2290	.8	3.8	64	793	.1	1.3

FIG. 8.6.   Sample page from Arbitron Radio Market Report for Los Angeles. Reprinted by permission of Arbitron.

formats. One example is the "Radio Today" report issued in 2004. The types of information in this report include demographic profiles for news programming, illustrated in Fig. 8.7. This example shows how news/talk/information listening varies among persons with different levels of education and household income, and among different ethnic and age groups. Arbitron publishes other special reports that give more insight into radio usage within specific demographic populations.

Just like television market data, the information contained in radio market reports is now available on computer. Arbitron markets software products, such as Maximi$er, Media Professional, and Tapscan, that allow media professionals at radio stations, advertising agencies, and marketing organizations to customize ratings analysis.

NATIONAL RATINGS

Network

Network television ratings are certainly the most visible of all the ratings products. Indeed, for most Americans, the Nielsen name has become synonymous with ratings. That identification occurs for good

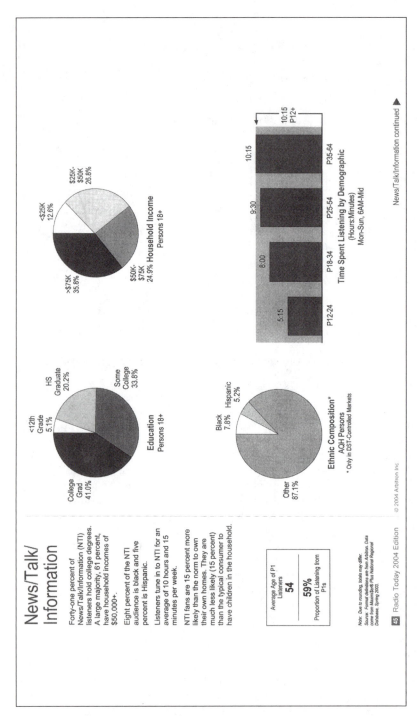

News/Talk/Information

Forty-one percent of News/Talk/Information (NTI) listeners hold college degrees. A large majority, 61 percent, have household incomes of $50,000+.

Eight percent of the NTI audience is black and five percent is Hispanic.

Listeners tune in to NTI for an average of 10 hours and 15 minutes per week.

NTI fans are 15 percent more likely than the norm to own their own homes. They are much less likely (15 percent) than the typical consumer to have children in the household.

Average Age of P1 Listeners
54
59%
Proportion of Listening from P1s

Note: Due to rounding, totals may differ.
Source: Format definitions are from Arbitron. Data come from MaximiSer® Plus National Regional Database, Spring 2003.

45 Radio Today 2004 Edition

© 2004 Arbitron Inc.

Education
Persons 18+

College Grad 41.0%
<12th Grade 5.1%
HS Graduate 20.2%
Some College 33.8%

Household Income
Persons 18+

>$75K 35.8%
$50K-$75K 24.9%
<$25K 12.6%
$25K-$50K 26.8%

Ethnic Composition*
AQH Persons
* Only in DST-Controlled Markets

Other 87.1%
Black 7.8%
Hispanic 5.2%

Time Spent Listening by Demographic
(Hours:Minutes)
Mon-Sun, 6AM-Mid

| P12-24 | P18-34 | P25-54 | P35-64 | P12+ |
| 5:15 | 8:00 | 9:30 | 10:15 | 10:15 |

News/Talk/Information continued ▲

FIG. 8.7. Composition of News/Talk/Information Audience. Reprinted by permission of Arbitron.

reason. For many years, Nielsen has been the dominant supplier of national audience ratings. It is the Nielsens that are often held to account for the cancellation or renewal of network television programs—an explanation that belies the complexity of programming decisions. The Nielsen service that actually provides network ratings is called the *Nielsen Television Index (NTI)*.

As we mentioned in chapter 6, Nielsen used meter/diary methodology for its national television service until 1987 when it switched to the peoplemeter. The initial national peoplemeter sample of 5,000 households has been increasing with the recruitment of additional NTI sample homes and with the addition of LPM samples to the national base. As of December, 2004, the sample consisted of 8,618 households. Each household provides data for approximately 2 years. With an average of about 2.5 people in each home, this sample includes roughly 21,500 individuals. At any given point in time, however, the actual number of respondents providing useful data might be less. Before looking at the reports Nielsen publishes, it is worth reflecting on the enormous amount of data this system generates. Thousands of people using various combinations of broadcast television, cable, satellite services, VCRs, DVDs, and DVRs, being monitored minute by minute over a period of years, creates a vast flow of raw material to be processed into useful reports and services.

The best known, and longest continuously produced, television network ratings report is NTI's National TV Ratings, better known as the *pocketpiece*. So named for its small vest pocket size, the pocketpiece is issued once a week and provides a variety of the most commonly used audience estimates.

Figure 8.8 shows a sample page from a pocketpiece report. In this section of the book, NTI displays the TVHH ratings for prime-time network programs in a way that highlights the scheduling characteristics of those programs. These pages depict the ratings for a Friday night in September. Across the top of the page is a banner indicating the time periods, in quarter-hours, and the HUT level associated with each time period. Note that the HUT level was highest between 9:45 and 10 p.m. During that time, Nielsen estimated that 57.5% of TVHH had a set in use. Because network programs run at different times in different time zones, Nielsen adjusts its audience estimates to Eastern Time.

Down the left-hand side of the page are the various networks, or station categories, that households are likely to watch. On the upper page of the report are—ABC, CBS, NBC, and Fox. On the lower page are estimated audiences for the WB and PAX (not shown).

Audience information is given under each program title by quarter hour, by half hour and by program total. The first number is the average audience for the program, expressed as a rating. To the right of the rating is the projected number of households watching in an average minute. For example, *Joan of Arcadia* on CBS earned a rating of 8.7, which means it was viewed by 9,390,000 households in an average

NATIONAL *NielsenTV* AUDIENCE ESTIMATES — EVE.FRI. SEP.26, 2003

TIME	7:00	7:15	7:30	7:45	8:00	8:15	8:30	8:45	9:00	9:15	9:30	9:45	10:00	10:15	10:30	10:45
HUT	46.1	47.0	48.3	49.9	51.1	52.2	53.7	55.1	55.8	56.4	57.1	57.5	55.6	55.0	54.4	53.8

ABC TV

Programs: ←GEORGE LOPEZ→ · ←HOPE & FAITH→ · ←LIFE WITH BONNIE→ · ←20/20-FRI→

Metric	8:00	8:15	8:45	9:00	9:15	9:30	9:45	10:00	10:15	10:45
HHLD AUDIENCE% & (000)	5.6	6,120	5.9*	7.8	8,420	6.3	6,840	7.2	7,770	6.9*
TA% AVG. AUD. 1/2 HR %	8.6	5.4*		9.6		7.5		11.7	7.5*	
SHARE AUDIENCE %	11	10*	11*	14		11		13	14*	13*
AVG. AUD. BY 1/4 HR %	5.3	5.4	6.0	7.6	8.0	6.4	6.2	7.4	7.5	6.6

CBS TV

Programs: ←JOAN OF ARCADIA→ · ←JAG→ · ←HANDLER, THE→

Metric	8:00	8:15	8:45	9:00	9:15	9:45	10:00	10:15	10:30	10:45
HHLD AUDIENCE% & (000)	8.7	9,390	9.1*	8.7	9,460	8.9*	8.5	9,210	8.5	8.5*
TA% AVG. AUD. 1/2 HR %	11.3	8.2*		11.2	8.6*	15*	11.3	8.5*		
SHARE AUDIENCE %	16	16*	17*	17	15*		16	15*		16*
AVG. AUD. BY 1/4 HR %	8.0	8.4	9.5	8.7	8.5	8.9	8.5	8.4	8.5	8.5

(CBS JAG 9:45 HUT 57.1 column: 8.8)

NBC TV

Programs: ←WANDA AT LARGE→ · ←MISS MATCH→ · ←DATELINE FRI→ · ←BOOMTOWN→

Metric	8:00	8:15	8:45	9:00	9:15	9:45	10:00	10:15	10:30	10:45
HHLD AUDIENCE% & (000)	5.4	5,910	5.7*	5.8	6,310	6.2*	5.3	5,690	5.2	5.3*
TA% AVG. AUD. 1/2 HR %	8.3	5.2*		9.8	5.4*	11*	7.8	5.2*		
SHARE AUDIENCE %	10	10*	10*	10	10*		10	9*		10*
AVG. AUD. BY 1/4 HR %	5.1	5.3	5.7	5.4	5.5	6.5	5.3	5.1	5.2	5.4

(NBC DATELINE 9:45 HUT 57.1 column: 5.9)

FOX TV

Programs: ←LUIS→ · ←BOSTON PUBLIC→

Metric	8:00	8:15	8:30	8:45	9:00	9:15	9:45
HHLD AUDIENCE% & (000)	2.9	3,090	2.2	2,370	3.4	3,720	3.6*
TA% AVG. AUD. 1/2 HR %	3.5		2.6		5.0	3.2*	
SHARE AUDIENCE %	5		4		6	6*	6*
AVG. AUD. BY 1/4 HR %	2.8	2.9	2.2	2.2	3.2	3.3	3.8

(FOX BOSTON PUBLIC 9:30 HUT 57.1 column: 3.5)

Row labels for each network:
HHLD AUDIENCE% & (000)
TA% AVG. AUD. 1/2 HR %
SHARE AUDIENCE %
AVG. AUD. BY 1/4 HR %

FIG. 8.8. Sample page from Nielsen Pocketpiece.

minute. Just beneath the program rating is the program's Total Audience, or cume. In this example, *Joan of Arcadia* had a cume rating of 11.3, which means that more than 1 out of every 10 TVHH tuned in to watch some part of this program. Underneath the Total Audience estimate is the share. In this case, the program had an average share of 16% over the course of the hour. The last row of numbers under the program title is the average audience rating for each specific quarter hour. Note that *Joan of Arcadia*'s audience increased from an 8.0 to a 9.5 rating. Without a separate flow study though, we can't tell whether the extra viewers came from another program's audience or from an increase in the number of households using television. This type of analysis used to require special customized research, but now Nielsen includes simple flow studies as part of its desktop package for subscribers. However, more complex analyses still require custom analysis.

These tables do not tell us anything about the demographic composition of program audiences. The pocketpiece reports that information in a different section of the book. Nielsen arranges network program audience estimates alphabetically and by time period, and reports the estimated viewers per 1,000 viewing households. In these sections, individual program audiences are broken down into age and gender combinations, including categories for "working women" and "LOH 18–49 W/CH < 3" (lady of house age 18–49 with child less than 3). Nielsen also reports the contribution that VCRs make to the total audience, which is usually half a ratings point or less.

With national and local People Meters, Nielsen can provide a potentially overwhelming amount of demographic information within 24 hours of a program's broadcast. As is the case with local metered markets, clients receive national "overnight" ratings every day. To make the data more manageable, clients request certain demographics that they want to see on a regular basis. The immediacy of this data puts pressure on programmers to adjust schedules after only one or two broadcasts.

Another popular Nielsen report is the National Audience Demographics Report, or NAD. Figure 8.9 shows data from one page of this report for November of 2003. The NAD gives us ratings by age and gender for broadcast network prime time programs, and provides information about the duration of the program, its genre, and the number of episodes included in the average. Take, for example, *That '70s Show* on Wednesday night at 8 p.m. The average household rating, for all weeks of November, was 5.4. This translates to 5.83 million homes. The following page (not shown here) reports that the persons 2+ rating for this program was 3.0, which corresponds to 8.24 million people. Notice that ratings in different demographics represent different numbers of people. Three demographic groups show a rating of 3.8: Working Women, Women 25–54, and Teens. However, the numbers of people represented by that 3.8 are 1.96 million, 2.32 million, and .95 million, respectively.

NTI NATIONAL AUDIENCE DEMOGRAPHICS REPORT
NOVEMBER 2003
TABLE 3A – ESTIMATES OF INDIVIDUAL NETWORK PROGRAMS (TOTAL DURATION)
EVENING

PROGRAM NAME / DAY	START TIME	DUR	NTWK	TYPE	WEEKS / MINS	KEY	HOUSE-HOLDS	WORKING WOMEN	15-24	18+	18-24	18-34	18-49	21+	21-49	21-54	25-49	25-54	35-64	55+	TEENS TOTAL 12-17	FEMALE 12-17	TOTAL 12-14	TOTAL 15-17	CHILDREN 6-8	9-11
SUE THOMAS: F.B. EYE SUN	9.00PM	60	PAX	GD	12345 / 300	A B C D	1.0 / 1.07 / / 1	.7 / .38 / 352 / 1	.5 / .09A / .86A / 2A	.8 / .93 / 887 / 2	.4 / .06A / .53A / 1A	.3A / .11A / 103A / 1A	.5 / .31 / 295 / 1	.9 / .91 / 845 / 2	.5 / .29 / 272 / 1	.6 / .69 / 161 / 1	.6 / .26 / 242 / 1	.6 / .39 / 339 / 1	.9 / .53 / 501 / 2	1.4 / .53 / 475 / 2	.3A / .07A / 67A / 1A	.5A / .06A / .52A / 1A	.2 / .03v / 25v / 1v	.4A / .05A / 43A / 1A	.3v / .03v / 28v / 1v	.3v / .04v / 33v / 1v
SURVIVOR: PEARL ISLANDS THU	8.00PM	60	CBS	GV	1234 / 240	A B C D	12.1 / 13.13 / / 19	10.2 / 5.26 / 401 / 23	3.4 / .66 / .50 / 12	9.7 / 10.66 / 912 / 21	3.7 / .49 / 37 / 13	6.5 / 2.09 / 159 / 18	8.8 / 5.68 / 433 / 22	10.1 / 10.52 / 801 / 21	9.4 / 5.53 / 422 / 22	10.0 / 6.88 / 524 / 23	10.1 / 5.19 / 395 / 23	10.7 / 6.54 / 498 / 24	11.5 / 6.63 / 505 / 24	10.3 / 3.64 / 277 / 17	4.5 / 1.10 / 84 / 14	3.9 / .47 / 36 / 13	5.3 / .67 / 51 / 16	3.6 / .44 / 33 / 13	5.3 / .63 / 48 / 18	6.0 / .72 / 55 / 18
SURVIVOR:PEARL ISLAND-W(S) WED	8.00PM	60	CBS	GV	5 / 60	A B C D	11.1 / 12.05 / / 23	8.8 / 4.52 / 375 / 23	3.3 / .64 / 53 / 12	9.0 / 9.88 / 820 / 21	3.6 / .42 / 35 / 12	5.8 / 1.85 / 154 / 18	7.8 / 5.06 / 420 / 22	9.2 / 9.62 / 798 / 21	8.1 / 4.80 / 398 / 23	8.7 / 5.99 / 497 / 23	9.0 / 4.64 / 385 / 23	9.5 / 5.83 / 483 / 24	10.7 / 6.13 / 509 / 25	10.3 / 3.63 / 301 / 19	5.0 / 1.23 / 102 / 17	5.0 / .61 / 51 / 17	6.4 / .81 / 67 / 23	3.4 / .42 / 35 / 12	4.9 / .58 / 49 / 17	6.0 / .72 / 60 / 19
TARZAN - WB SUN	9.01PM	59	WB	GD	1234 / 236	A B C D	1.9 / 2.03 / / 3	1.3 / .69 / 340 / 3	1.6 / .32 / 155 / 5	1.2 / 1.32 / 648 / 19	1.5 / .20 / 96 / 5	1.7 / .53 / 263 / 4	1.5 / .95 / 470 / 11	1.2 / 1.26 / 619 / 7	1.5 / .90 / 441 / 11	1.5 / 1.05 / 514 / 11	1.5 / .76 / 374 / 11	1.5 / .91 / 447 / 11	1.2 / .70 / 343 / 10	.6 / .21 / 104 / 1	1.2 / .29 / 143 / 4	1.7 / .20 / 98 / 5	1.0 / .13A / 63A / 3A	1.3 / .16A / 80A / 4A	1.0A / .11A / 56A / 4A	.9A / .11A / 53A / 2A
THAT '70S SHOW(P-->) WED	8.00PM	30	FOX	CS	12345 / 150	A B C D	5.4 / 5.83 / / 9	3.8 / 1.96 / 336 / 10	4.8 / .95 / 145 / 16	3.8 / 3.39 / 592 / 11	4.7 / .63 / 107 / 17	4.8 / 1.54 / 265 / 14	4.2 / 2.73 / 468 / 11	3.25 / 557 / 7	4.4 / 2.58 / 443 / 12	4.4 / 2.80 / 481 / 10	4.1 / 2.32 / 361 / 10	3.8 / 2.32 / 398 / 7	2.9 / 1.67 / 286 / 7	1.3 / .44 / 76 / 1	3.8 / .95 / 163 / 14	3.4 / .70 / 112 / 12	3.2 / .41 / 70 / 12	4.5 / .54 / 92 / 16	.8 / .10 / 17 / 3A	2.3 / .28 / 48 / 8
THAT '70S SHOW SPEC-TUE(S) TUE	8.30PM	30	FOX	CS	3 / 30	A B C D	4.6 / 5.04 / / 7	3.0 / 1.53 / 304 / 7	2.5 / .49 / 97 / 8	2.4 / 2.65 / 536 / 8	3.1 / .41 / 82 / 11	3.4 / 1.10 / 218 / 10	3.2 / 2.10 / 417 / 8	2.5 / 2.55 / 506 / 5	3.4 / 2.00 / 398 / 8	3.1 / 2.16 / 430 / 7	3.3 / 1.69 / 335 / 8	3.0 / 1.85 / 367 / 7	2.4 / 1.38 / 275 / 5	1.1 / .39 / 77 / 2	3.0 / .75 / 148 / 10	2.2A / .54A / 54A / 7A	2.9A / .41 / 74A / 9A	3.1 / .38 / 75 / 10	.9v / .09v / 19v / 3v	2.8A / .33A / 66A / 8A
THAT '70S SHOW SPECIAL(S) WED	8.30PM	30	FOX	CS	4 / 30	A B C D	6.5 / 7.09 / / 10	4.7 / 2.41 / 340 / 10	6.4 / 1.24 / 123 / 19	3.7 / 4.01 / 566 / 10	6.4 / .85 / 123 / 19	5.9 / 1.87 / 264 / 15	5.3 / 3.43 / 484 / 13	3.6 / 3.76 / 530 / 8	5.4 / 3.48 / 448 / 12	4.9 / 3.35 / 472 / 11	5.0 / 2.58 / 364 / 11	4.5 / 2.75 / 388 / 10	3.5 / 2.01 / 283 / 7	1.2 / .41 / 58 / 2	5.8 / 1.44 / 202 / 18	5.9 / .72 / 101 / 19	4.6 / .58 / 82 / 15	7.1 / .86 / 121 / 22	.7v / .08v / 12v / 3v	2.4A / .29A / 41A / 10A
THAT '70S SHOW-TUE 8P(P-->) TUE	8.00PM	30	FOX	CS	34 / 60	A B C D	4.5 / 4.92 / / 7	3.0 / 1.55 / 321 / 7	3.0 / .59 / 122 / 11	2.4 / 2.62 / 544 / 8	3.3 / .43 / 90 / 12	3.5 / 1.12 / 233 / 11	3.2 / 2.06 / 426 / 9	2.4 / 2.48 / 514 / 5	3.2 / 1.91 / 396 / 8	2.9 / 2.08 / 431 / 8	3.1 / 1.62 / 336 / 11	2.9 / 1.79 / 371 / 8	2.3 / 1.30 / 269 / 5	1.1 / .40 / 83 / 2	2.9 / .69 / 143 / 10	2.4 / .60 / 60 / 8	2.3 / .29 / 59 / 8	3.3 / .40 / 83 / 12	.6v / .07v / 15v / 2v	1.9A / .23A / 48A / 6A

N.B. SEE LEAD PAGE OF THIS SECTION FOR EXPLANATIONS OF SYMBOLS.
Copyright 2003 Nielsen Media Research—Printed in U.S.A.

FIG. 8.9. Sample page from NTI National Audience Demographics Report. Reprinted by permission of Nielsen Media Research.

Nielsen offers a host of other published reports. Among them are a variety of cable network ratings, provided through a division that Nielsen calls *the Nielsen Homevideo Index* (NHI). Special reports on Hispanic audiences are issued through *Nielsen Hispanic Television Index* (NHTI) and *Nielsen Hispanic Station Index* (NHSI). Nielsen Monitor Plus tracks commercials and provides data that helps clients assess their competitive position in various markets. And Nielsen Sports Marketing Service (NSMS) provides special research services for sports marketers and media.

Television, of course, is not the only advertiser-supported medium providing network service to the public. Radio networks still attract millions of advertiser dollars and, although they cannot rival the amounts spent on television, these networks need audience research. As noted in chapter 6, shortly after Nielsen ended its radio network measurement, Statistical Research, Inc. (SRI) initiated a research effort called RADAR to fill the void. This service was based on telephone interviews conducted with a sample of 12,000 respondents. Within each home that was selected through a process of random digit dialing (RDD), SRI randomly selected one individual age 12 or older, and interviewed him or her once a day for the next week.

In July of 2001, Arbitron bought RADAR, and phased out the telephone methodology. The current RADAR service is based on a diary sample that is more than four times as large as the telephone sample used by SRI. While this change allows for measurement of new technologies such as satellite radio, lower response rates relative to telephone methodology caused concern in the radio industry.

Syndication

Nielsen measures audiences for syndicated programming by drawing on both its NTI peoplemeter sample and its NSI diary samples. Because syndication carries national advertising, the industry needs audience estimates that are comparable to broadcast and network ratings. These estimates come from the peoplemeter sample, and are published in the form of pocketpieces and other standard reports similar to the audience information available for networks. In fact, the syndicated pocketpiece looks very much like the network pocketpiece we described earlier, and it is used in the same way by salespeople and media buyers. Additionally, NSI publishes the *Report on Syndicated Programs (ROSP)* after each of the four major sweeps. This report provides program ratings on a market-by-market basis by extracting from local market data the ratings performance of every syndicated program. This information is organized by program so users can see the program's average performance across all markets, as well as how it did in each market that carried the show. This is useful for programmers at local stations and for the syndicators themselves who need to prove success in order to sell the program to more stations.

Figure 8.10 is a page from the Nielsen May 2004 ROSP. It is one of several pages in the report that describe the audience for *Dr. Phil*. Each market that carried the program is listed alphabetically, with the corresponding ratings information displayed across the page. This section provides more than simple audience estimates for the program itself. As we noted in previous chapters, audience size is affected by variables such as competition in the marketplace and rating of the lead-in program. Nielsen's ROSP provides information about both of these variables in every market that carries the program. For example, in Fig. 8.10 we can see that *Dr. Phil* aired in Milwaukee on ABC affiliate WISN at 3 p.m Monday through Friday. Its lead-in was *General Hospital*. In Minneapolis, the program aired at 3 p.m as well, but the lead-in was *Guiding Light* on the CBS affiliate. If station personnel are trying to evaluate the performance of a program in their market, they can look for an appropriate comparison by finding similar market situations. Nielsen produces a similar report for public television called the *Report on Public Television Programs (ROPP)*.

The first page of each program entry (not shown) contains information about the number of markets carrying the show, the percentage of U.S. reached, and the distributor. It also provides time period averages by grouping markets according to when they air the program. Although this report offers an average rating for all broadcasts, this should not be confused with the truly national rating that comes from the national Nielsen sample.

NTI also publishes syndicated reports based on the national sample. Figure 8.11 provides a sample of the November 2003 National Audience Demographics (NAD) report for the *Oprah Winfrey Show*, a first-run syndicated program. The data shown here report Oprah's ratings in various parts of the country and in households with differing demographic characteristics. Overall, the program earned a 7.2 household rating during this measurement period. Reading across the first line of data, we can see that the program gets higher ratings among women than among men. Reading down the first column, we can see that this program gets higher-than-average household ratings in West Central, Southeast, and Southwest regions than it does in other parts of the country. The last line of data tells us that the program earns higher ratings in African American households than it does in the total U.S. (9.6 compared to 7.2). The NAD also includes information (not shown here) about education level, household income, and occupation.

THE INTERNET

For any new media technology to attract the sustained attention of advertisers, a system of audience measurement must be in place. This is as true today of the World Wide Web as it was of radio and television broadcasting 50 years ago. As we explained in chapter 2, in the 1990s

DR. PHIL
60 MIN.

REPORT ON SYNDICATED PROGRAMS
NSI AVERAGE WEEK ESTIMATES
MAY 2004

LINE 1 — REPORTABLE STATIONS / MARKET T.Z. ON AIR / LINE 2 TOTAL DAY STATION CH. NET. DMA SHARE / LINE 3 START NO. OF DAY TIME T/CS. / LINE 4 LEAD-IN-PROGRAM	FOUR WEEK AVERAGE TIME PERIOD AUDIENCES (THIS PROGRAM vs. PRECEDING HALF HOUR) — DESIGNATED MARKET AREA										DMA %		PROGRAM AUDIENCE SECTION (SYNDICATED PROGRAM ONLY) — STATION TOTALS										COMPETING FOUR WEEK AVERAGE TIME PERIOD AUDIENCES — CORRESPONDING TIME PERIOD-3 HIGHEST COMPETING STATIONS		DMA %	
	DMA % HH RTG	SHR	PERSONS SHARE % WOMEN 18+	18-34	25-54	MEN 18+	18-49	25-54	TNS 2-17	CHD 2-11	HH RTG	SHR	(000) vs V/100VH	TOTAL HHLD	TOTAL ADULTS	WOMEN 18+	18-49	25-54	MEN 18+	18-49	TEENS 12-17	CHILD 2-11	STATION	PROGRAM	HH RTG	SHR
1		2	3	4	5	6	7	8	9	10	11	12	13	14	15	16	17	18	19	20	21			22	23

MILWAUKEE CE 10
WISN CH.12 A 12%
M-F 3.00P 20T/C
GENL HOSPITAL

	HH RTG	SHR	W18+	W18-34	W25-54	M18+	M18-49	M25-54	TNS	CHD	DMA%RTG	SHR	(000)/VCVH	HHLD	ADULTS	W18+	W18-49	W25-54	M18+	M18-49	TEENS	CHILD	STATION	PROGRAM
	6	18	33	42	41	14	18	17	15	3	6	18	(000)	58	59	51	27	28	8	3	3	1	WTMJ #	INSD DT/JPRD
	3	11	22	26	23	9	3	4	40	2			V/CVH		102	88	47	47	14	6	5	2	WITI #	JDG JD/JDG JD
																							WMVS #	DRGN TL/SGW CH

MINEAPLS-ST PL CE 10
WCCO+ CH.4 C 16%
M-F 3.00P 20T/C
GUIDING LIGHT

	6	23	43	39	36	22	18	15	12	2	6	23	(000)	115	129	111	45	42	16	8	3	1	KARE	ACCSS H/PRMD
	2	6	12	5	7	7	10	6					V/CVH		112	96	39	37	16	7	3	1	KSTP+	ELLEN
																							KMSP	MONTEL WILLIAM

MINOT-BSMRK-DKN CE 6
KXMC+ CH.13 C 19%
M-F 4.00P 20T/C
FRASIER

	9	36	44	53	52	15	13	15	19	3	9	36	(000)	13	13	12	5	5	1		1		KFYR+	EVRBD-R/JPRD
	1	5	4	2	3	7	1	3					V/CVH		104	93	43	39	12		4		KBMY+	JDG J B/JDG JD
																							KBME+	CBRCHS /ARTHR-

MISSOULA MT 6
KPAX+ CH.8 C 19%
M-F 3.00P 20T/C
HOLLYWD SQUARS

	5	25	34	34	36	15	17	23			5	25	(000)	5.1	5.8	4.9	1.9	2.3	1.0	.4			KECI+#	DAYS-OUR LIVES
	2	13	19	12	22	4	9	9					V/CVH		113	95	38	45	19	9			KTMF+	JDG J B/JDG JD
																							KMMF	JDG HTC/JDG HT

MOBILE-PNS(FWB) CE 6
WALA CH.10 F 10%
M-F 3.00P 20T/C
ELLEN

	5	19	23	23	26	11	11	10	4	1	5	19	(000)	29	30	24	12	13	6	2	1		WKRG	JDG J B/JDG-BR
	1	5	6	8	7	3	6	5					V/CVH		105	85	42	46	20	3	3		WEAR	MAURY POVICH
																							WPMI	ON AIR-RYAN

WBPG CH.55 I 2%
M-F 12.00M 20T/C
5TH WHEEL

	<<		2	2	1	3	3	3		9	<<		(000)	1	1	1							WALA	FRSR BCKR
	<<		1	1	2	2	3	4			<<		V/CVH		116	67							WKRG #	C KLBRN-PD PRG
																							WJTC #	HM MPRV KNG F

MARKET AVG.

											3	14	(000)	15	16	13	6	7	3	1			
													V/CVH		105	84	42	45	21	9			

MONRO-EL DORADO CE 6
KNOE CH.8 C 26%
M-F 3.00P 20T/C
GUIDING LIGHT

	10	31	38	39	39	18	25	23	15	7	10	31	(000)	18	19	16	8	7	3	2	1		KTVE	MONTEL WILLIAM
	11	39	48	50	52	21	27	17	37	32			V/CVH		105	89	44	41	16	9	4	3	KACY	DVRC CR/DVRC C
																							KARD	ON AIR-RYAN

MONTEREY-SALNAS PA 6
KSBW CH.8 N 16%
M-F 3.00P 20T/C
PASSIONS-NBC

	6	29	34	31	36	17	16	15	8	2	6	29	(000)	16	18	15	6	6	3	2	1		KSMS	CLAP M-F-UNI
	2	11	11	14	11	4	4		13	4			V/CVH		116	96	39	38	20	12	4		KION	WAYNE BRADY
																							AABC	5100.00/MTCH G

MONTGOMERY(SEL) CE 7
WAKA CH.8 C 13%
M-F 3.00P 20T/C
GUIDING LIGHT

	3	12	14	9	11	5	5	3	4	2	3	12	(000)	9	9	7	2	2	1	1			WSFA	PPL'S C/JDG JD
	2	8	8	8	10	4	4	4	2	3			V/CVH		97	82	22	28	15	6			WNCF	MAURY POVICH
																							WRJM	AND GRF /JFFRSN

MRTL BCH-FLRNCE EA 5
WBTW CH.13 C 24%
M-F 10.00A 20T/C
MONTEL WILLIAM

	8	35	46	43	42	29	17	20	14		8	35	(000)	25	27	22	8	9	5	1			WFXB	LIVING-ALI&JACK
	7	29	33	27	29	28	28	27	7				V/CVH		107	86	30	34	21	5			WWMB	RIGHT-A WLLMS
																							WPDE	WAYNE BRADY

NASHVILLE CE 8
WSMV CH.4 N 14%
M-F 3.00P 20T/C
#DAYS-OUR LIVES

	8	20	33	36	33	15	22	20	7	3	8	20	(000)	73	73	63	34	31	11	7	1	2	WTVF #	AS WORLD TURN
	5	15	26	29	27	14	20	14	3	3			V/CVH		100	86	46	43	15	10	2		WKRN	JDG JD /JDG JD
																							WUXP	JERRY SPRINGER

NEW ORLEANS CE 12
WVUE CH.8 F 9%
M-F 4.00P 20T/C
JUDGE MATHIS

	7	12	17	18	18	8	8	10	3		7	12	(000)	46	48	39	18	18	9	4	2		WWL	INSD DT/JPRD
	6	13	18	15	16	14	14	23	1	3			V/CVH		105	86	40	39	19	8	4		WDSU	JDG JD /JDG JD
																							WGNO	JERRY SPRINGER

NEW YORK EA 16
WCBS CH.2 C 8%
M-F 3.00P 20T/C
#AS WORLD TURN

	3	10	17	15	17	7	8	8	1	1	3	10	(000)	296	341	284	118	137	57	33	5	7	WABC #	GENRL HOSPITAL
	2	6	11	8	9	5	6	7	1	1			V/CVH		115	96	40	46	19	11	2	3	WNBC #	JUDGE J BROWN
																							WNJU	CRT-FML/CRT-PB

WLNY CH.55 I %
M-F 5.00P 20T/C
ELLEN

	1	1	2	2	3			1			1	1	(000)	38	43	39	23	25	5	3	2	4	WABC	5.00 EYEWT NWS
	<<		1	1	1		1				<<		V/CVH		115	103	60	65	12	6	4		WNBC	LIVE AT FIVE
																							WCBS	CBS2 NWS AT 5P

MARKET AVG.

											2	5	(000)	167	192	161	70	81	31	18	3	4		
													V/CVH		115	97	42	48	19	11	2	2	

NRFLK-PRT-NP NW EA 10
WVEC CH.13 A 11%
M-F 10.00A 20T/C
REGIS&KELLY

	6	21	34	36	42	13	12	12	8	3	6	21	(000)	45	47	42	21	24	8	2	1		WGNT	JERRY SPRINGER
	4	13	24	24	29	11	7	6	7	3			V/CVH		105	93	47	53	12	4	1		WTVZ	PEOPLE'S COURT
																							WAVY	700 CLUB

ODESSA-MIDLAND CE 6
KWES+ CH.9 N %
M-F 3.00P 20T/C
MAURY POVICH

	6	19	25	23	27	8	2	5		3	6	19	(000)	9	10	8	4	4	2				KUPB	GORDO&-MF-UNI
	2	10	13	13	8	7	9	14		19			V/CVH		113	94	44	50	19				KOSA	FRNOS DRW CR
																							KPEJ	JUDGE J BROWN

OKLAHOMA CITY CE 11
KOCO CH.5 A 11%
M-F 3.00P 20T/C
GENRL HOSPITAL

	7	18	33	38	37	16	18	16	7	1	7	18	(000)	48	51	44	19	18	7	3	1		KFOR	INSD DT-HLLWD
	5	14	26	33	32	8	7	7		7			V/CVH		106	91	39	38	14	5	1		KWTV	MLLNR /PRMD
																							KOKH	JDG HTC/JDG HT

For explanation of symbols, see lead page.

518

FIG. 8.10. Sample page from NSI Report on Syndicated Programs. Reprinted by permission of Nielsen Media Research.

167

OPRAH WINFREY SHOW (AT)
(KINGWRLD MEDIA SALES)
WEEKS 12345 MINS 1380
MON-FRI DUR 60 CC

NSS NAD REPORT — NOVEMBER 2003
TABLE 6A – ADULT & GENERAL AUDIENCE
AUDIENCE BY MARKET SECTION
INDIVIDUAL PROGRAMS IN SYNDICATION (TOTAL DURATION)

RATINGS(%)	HOUSE-HOLDS	WOMEN WRK WOM 18+	WOMEN 18+	18-34	18-49	25-54	35-64	55+	MEN 18+	18-34	18-49	25-54	35-64	55+	TEENS 12-17	TOTAL FEMALE 12-17	CHILDREN 2-11	6-11
TOTAL U.S.	7.2	4.7	6.3	4.4	5.1	5.8	6.5	8.5	1.7	1.0	1.4	1.6	1.9	2.3	1.2	1.7	.9	.6
TERRITORY																		
NORTHEAST	6.8	4.0	5.8	4.6	4.8	5.4	5.7	7.7	1.8	.9	1.5	1.8	2.1	2.3	.8	1.0V	.6A	.5V
EAST CENTRAL	7.0	4.1	6.0	4.9	4.7	4.9	5.6	8.5	1.8	1.1	1.8	1.7A	1.7V	2.3A	.8V	IFR	.7A	.4V
WEST CENTRAL	7.7	5.0	6.8	5.3	6.1	6.6	6.6	9.0	1.5	.8	1.1A	1.4A	1.9	2.5A	1.4A	IFR	1.0A	.7V
SOUTHEAST	7.7	5.8	7.1	4.6	5.4	6.3	7.2	9.6	1.8	1.0A	1.3	1.5	1.9	2.7	1.3A	1.6A	1.3A	.9A
SOUTHWEST	7.5	5.3	6.7	3.8	5.9	7.1	8.3	7.7	1.9	1.5A	1.8	1.9A	1.9A	2.0A	2.1A	2.1A	.8A	.8V
PACIFIC	6.6	4.3	5.4	3.5	4.0	4.8	6.0	8.1	1.5	.7	1.1	1.6	1.9	2.1A	1.0A	1.6A	.8A	.5V
COUNTY SIZE																		
A	7.2	4.7	6.1	4.5	4.9	5.8	6.4	8.3	1.7	.9	1.3	1.6	1.9	2.6	1.3	1.9A	.7A	.6A
B	7.4	5.0	6.6	5.1	5.1	5.9	6.8	9.3	1.8	.8A	1.4	1.8	2.0	2.5	1.0	1.5A	1.0A	.4A
C & D	6.9	4.5	6.2	4.4	5.3	5.7	6.2	8.0	1.6	1.2A	1.5	1.6	1.7	1.9	1.3	1.7A	.9A	.6A
CABLE/DVD STATUS																		
CABLE PLUS ADS	7.0	4.7	6.1	4.2	4.9	5.6	6.2	8.1	1.6	.8	1.3	1.5	1.8	2.3	1.4	1.8	.7	.5A
CABLE PLUS WITH PAY	7.4	4.7	6.5	4.7	5.1	5.6	6.7	7.7	1.8	1.1	1.5	1.7	2.1	2.7	1.4	2.3	.7	.5A
BROADCAST ONLY	8.2	5.2	7.5	5.1	6.1	6.9	7.9	10.8	2.2	1.8A	1.9	2.2	2.3	2.7A	1.3A	1.3V	1.4A	1.3A
DBS	6.3	4.5	5.5	3.5	4.5	5.5	5.4	7.6	1.4	.4V	1.0	1.3	1.4	2.2A	1.4A	2.4A	.6	.2V
DVD OWNERSHIP	7.4	4.6	5.9	4.6	5.1	5.8	6.4	8.9	1.5	1.0	1.3	1.5	1.8	2.6	1.3	2.1	.8	.6A
HHLD SIZE																		
1	6.3	7.1	9.4	7.2	7.4	8.2	8.0	10.2	2.0	1.1V	1.9A	2.0	2.5	2.0A	IFR	IFR	IFR	IFR
2	7.6	5.0	6.7	5.0	5.8	6.0	6.8	9.0	2.3	1.3A	1.9	2.3	2.3	2.5	IFR	IFR	4.2A	IFR
3+	7.4	4.0	5.1	3.9	4.8	5.4	5.9	7.1	1.3	.8	1.2	1.3	1.4	2.1	1.1	1.7	.8	.5
4+	7.0	3.8	4.8	3.7	4.5	5.0	5.6	8.5	.9	.7A	.9	.9	1.0	1.4A	1.1	1.6	.6	.5A
PRESENCE OF NON-ADULTS																		
ANY UNDER 18	6.8	4.1	4.9	4.3	4.8	5.2	5.4	6.6	1.1	.8	1.0	1.2	1.3	1.6A	1.2	1.7	.8	.6
ANY UNDER 12	6.7	3.7	4.8	4.5	5.0	5.2	5.3	6.7A	1.1	.9A	1.1	1.2	1.3	IFR	1.2	1.8A	.8	.6
ANY UNDER 6	7.0	3.7	5.2	4.9	5.0	5.8	5.7	IFR	.9	1.0A	1.3	1.3	1.5A	IFR	1.6A	2.7A	.9	.5A
ANY 6-11	5.9	3.6	4.2	3.7	4.3	4.3	4.7	IFR	.9	.7	.9	.9	.9	IFR	1.2A	1.8A	.7	.6
ANY 12-17	6.7	4.3	4.5	2.8	4.5	5.0	5.2	IFR	1.0	.6V	1.0	1.1	1.1	IFR	1.2	1.7	.7	.5A
HOUSEHOLD INCOME																		
$40,000+	7.3	4.4	5.7	4.3	5.1	5.6	6.1	8.0	1.5	.9	1.3	1.4	1.7	2.4	1.3	2.1	.8	.4A
$60,000+	7.5	4.6	5.6	4.6	5.0	5.9	6.1	7.3	1.5	.9	1.5	1.5	1.9	1.9	1.3	2.0A	.8	.4A
$75,000+	7.5	4.3	5.3	4.1	4.8	5.6	5.8	6.7	1.1	.6A	.9	1.1	1.3	1.7	1.1	1.5A	.7A	.3V
$100,000+	6.9	4.0	4.9	3.9	4.3	5.2	5.3	6.1	1.1	.8	1.0	1.1	1.2	1.7A	1.2	1.6A	.7A	.3V
SELECTED UPPER DEMOS																		
$75,000+ WITH NON-ADULTS	7.3	4.3	5.1	5.0	5.1	5.7	5.2	IFR	.8A	.8V	.8A	.9A	.8A	IFR	1.1	1.5A	.7A	.3V
$75,000+ & HOH-POM	5.8	3.4	4.4	2.9	3.7	4.3	5.0	7.0	.7	.8	.7A	.8A	.7A	1.0V	1.0	1.1V	.6V	.3V
$75,000+ & HOH 1+ YRS. COLLEGE	7.1	4.7	5.6	4.8	5.2	6.0	6.8	6.8	1.1	.8A	.9	1.1	1.1	1.3A	1.1	1.6A	.6A	.3V
EDUCATION OF HEAD OF HOUSE																		
4+ YEARS OF COLLEGE	6.7	4.8	6.0	5.3	5.3	5.8	5.9	7.8	1.3	1.0A	1.1	1.3	1.3	1.6	1.4A	2.0A	.5A	.3V
RACE																		
BLACK	9.6	5.3	8.1	5.3	6.8	6.8	7.5	15.0	3.0	1.2A	2.3	2.7	3.5	5.3A	1.6	1.9V	1.3A	1.2A

FIG. 8.11. Sample page from NSS National Audience Demographics Report.

several new companies entered the business of generating audience research data for the Web, but the field is now dominated by Nielsen/Netratings and comScore/MediaMetrix. These organizations provide data to online subscribers based on panels of Internet users that are recruited in different ways. For the most part, the numbers convey very similar information to that which is available in television and radio ratings reports. Subscribers can find out information like the number of different visitors to a Web site, how long they spent on a particular page, and the demographic profile of audiences for specific types of content.

Although audience/user data affect the rates that advertisers pay for Internet availabilities, the determination is still somewhat qualitative in nature. This is because the standards for audience measurement and reporting are still under development within the industry. Differences in methodologies can lead to vastly different audience estimates from competing research firms, and it is difficult to predict which sampling and measurement methods will be universally adopted by Internet research providers.

CUSTOMIZED RATINGS REPORTS

The ratings products we have reviewed so far have been the standardized offerings of the major ratings companies. Whether in print or electronic form, they are reports designed to answer the most common of the research questions we developed in chapters 2 and 3. But, as we noted in the first section of this book, there are many questions that can be addressed by a creative analysis of ratings data. Often, these questions are so specialized that they simply do not justify the publication of a standardized report. Nevertheless, if there are paying customers who want something that cannot be found in a ratings book, ratings firms have ways to accommodate them. Clients can request any number of customized reports, from analyses of specific socioeconomic groups to reach and frequency estimates to complex studies of audience flow. These *custom reports* are priced individually and run to the client's specifications. Depending on the data requested, these studies can cost anywhere from a few hundred dollars to several thousand dollars.

Customized reports are created using one of three methods, distinguished by where the data in the report comes from. First, the ratings company can run special analyses based on individual client requests. Second, the ratings data collected in the usual way can be combined with data available from some other sources. Third, ratings companies can actually go out and gather more data than they would otherwise collect.

The first option for creating a customized analysis is the most common. Standardized reports only scratch the surface of the analytical possibilities offered by a ratings database. In the last section of the book, we discuss how such analyses can be conceptualized. Suppose you were a programmer interested in knowing whether the audience for a syndicated game show stays tuned and watches the local news that follows it. No ratings book published in the United States will give you the answer. Even if the game show and news have exactly the same rating, you cannot tell whether the same people watched both programs. Yet, if you could look at the diaries that the ratings company collected, you would be able to figure it out, because the diaries track individuals from one time period to the next. The ratings services vary in the degree to which they offer subscribers direct access to respondent level data. Arbitron sells this data as part of its subscription packages; Nielsen does not.

The array of customized services gets more confusing when new sources of data are introduced into the mix. Recall that advertisers are most often interested in what audience members are likely to buy. For this reason there is considerable pressure on the ratings companies to introduce some sort of product-usage data into the ratings database. Although the single-source technology we described earlier may be the most powerful tool for producing these data, those systems have never made it past the testing stage of development. More typically, product usage data, along with information on lifestyles, homeownership, and so forth are added to ratings data after the fact.

This is done by matching audience behavior in a very small geographic area, usually a zip code, to other information about that area. Zip codes tend to be relatively homogeneous in composition. For example, some areas are known to be affluent, others poor. Some neighborhoods have large owner-occupied homes, others have a lot of rental units. This information, along with product purchase information, is used by services like Claritas and Scarborough to identify certain "clusters" or categories based on their similarities. By assuming that a diary keeper living in a particular kind of area is like others in that area, it is possible to associate ratings data with other variables not in the original database.

The last kind of customized research available from the ratings services involves collecting additional data at the behest of the client. Of course, if the price is right, a ratings company might be persuaded to gather almost any kind of audience data, but two methods of new data collection are worth mentioning here. First, even though it is not their standard method of data collection, both Arbitron and Nielsen will conduct telephone coincidentals. This gives a client the option of getting a ratings report from a major supplier, especially when there is no ratings sweep in progress. Second, it is possible to arrange for diary keepers to be interviewed after their diaries have been collected. By asking questions of a diary keeper, and then matching those responses with the diary record, new insights into the behavior of the audience may be possible. In either case, because new data must be gathered for a single client, these services are not inexpensive.

Although customized ratings reports can provide analysts with many insights that would not otherwise be available, the users of these reports should exercise caution in the interpretation of the numbers they contain. Remember that the ratings companies are in business to make a profit, and that finding new ways to exploit or resell their existing databases represents a golden opportunity. Remember also that customized reports are, by their nature, not subject to the same, ongoing, scrutiny of a syndicated report. Ratings companies may very well give a buyer the kind of report asked for, even if it does not make good sense as a piece of research. We have seen, for example, customized market areas constructed from a hand-picked group of counties with too few diaries in-tab to offer reliable audience estimates. In evaluating any ratings report, but especially a customized product, the user must be sure he or she understands the research design upon which the data are based.

BUYING RATINGS DATA

The fees charged for syndicated research products vary greatly. A television station in a small market might spend as little as several thousand dollars a year to get basic ratings reports. An affiliate in a major market might spend closer to a million dollars on ratings and related services. A network will spend much more. There are a number of factors that affect the cost of ratings data, and prices may well be subject to negotiation—especially if a station is owned by a powerful group that accounts for a large share of a research firm's subscription revenues. In 2003, Nielsen and NBC/Universal announced agreement on the largest research contract in history—estimated between $400 million and $500 million. The contract covered the various types of media organizations owned by the company. Also in 2003, Viacom signed a $400-million contract on behalf of its own media properties.

Market size is an important determinant of price. All things being equal, stations in smaller markets can expect to pay less for ratings than stations in big markets. In part, this is a reflection of the cost of data collection. Within a given market, there may also be differences in the cost of ratings to different clients. Agencies typically pay less than stations. In fact, in local market research, broadcasters account for about 90% of ratings service revenues. Different stations may also pay different amounts depending on whether they are independents or affiliates, UHF stations or VHF stations. Although we have never seen any analysis of this, it is likely that the price stations pay for basic ratings data varies more or less in tandem with the advertising rates they charge based on those same audience estimates. The length of the contract a client signs can also affect prices. Those who sign long-term contracts should get a discount. A station's subscription to a ratings service will usually run from 3 to 5, or even 7 years. Stations making longer commitments lock in a lower yearly increase for the service. In metered markets, however, longer commitments may be required in advance to induce the ratings company to establish the service.

Academic users can also get special pricing consideration. Nielsen offers packages of both NTI and NSI data designed for educational institutions, and Arbitron provides miscellaneous reports to academics upon request. It has also established an archive of its ratings at the University of Georgia. Unfortunately, Nielsen has no public archive of its data, although individual Nielsen offices may maintain informal collections. Ratings services also make some data available online.

Generalizing about the cost of customized ratings reports is even more difficult. Despite the analytical possibilities offered by such research, these still account for only a modest portion of ratings service revenues. To learn more about them, or the specific cost of any ratings product, you must deal with the rating services directly.

Occasionally, a ratings company and one of its clients will have serious differences. A station might be suspected of inappropriate practices during a sweep, or a ratings company might be suspected of mishandling some aspect of the research process. Sometimes a good deal of money can ride in the balance. Although going to court is always a possibility, the parties may find it advisable to opt for a less costly solution. If normal channels of communication fail, the Media Rating Council (MRC) can invoke mediation procedures that involve representatives from the appropriate industries and trade associations.

RELATED READINGS

Arbitron. (annually). *A guide to understanding and using radio audience estimates*. New York: Author.

Beville, H. M. (1988). *Audience ratings: Radio, television, cable* (Rev. ed.). Hillsdale, NJ: Lawrence Erlbaum Associates.

Fletcher, A. D., & Bower, T. A. (1988). *Fundamentals of advertising research* (3rd ed.). Belmont, CA: Wadsworth.

Nielsen Station Index. (annually). *Your guide to reports & services*. New York: Nielsen Media Research.

Poltrack, D. F. (1983). *Television marketing: Network, local, cable*. New York: McGraw-Hill.

III

ANALYTICAL
TECHNIQUES

Chapter 9

Understanding Audience Behavior

Audience research comes in many different forms and has a wide variety of applications. This abundance can be a bit overwhelming. How does one make sense of all those numbers? What is a high rating, or what is a low one? What is an unusual or important feature of audience behavior, and what is routine? In this chapter we offer a framework for evaluating and analyzing the information contained in audience data. The emphasis here is on broad concepts and theories. This approach is intended to give readers a sense of perspective on the audience, to help them see the forest instead of an endless succession of trees.

Perhaps it is best to begin this exercise by reminding ourselves what commercial audience measurement is really about. The information collected by the research firms may be vast in size, and reported in a great many ways, but conceptually it is rather straightforward. At their core, most databases are simply a record of people's reported exposure to media. They don't say anything about the effects of that exposure, nor do they typically explain people's motivations for listening or viewing. Any useful framework for analyzing these data, then, requires that we develop an understanding of the complexities of how people use media. If we know what determines exposure to media, if we can predict the patterns of use that are likely to emerge under given circumstances, then we have a way of interpreting the numbers that confront us.

The chapter is divided into four sections. First we take a closer look at just what a ratings analyst is trying to assess—exposure to media. We categorize and discuss the principal measurements of audience behavior. This framework will organize the last two chapters in the book. Second, we review the most common theories for explaining people's choice of media offerings. These rely very heavily on individual preferences to explain what the audience is doing. Third, we introduce a number of other factors that seem critical in understanding audience formation. Finally, we present a model of audience behavior that reflects all of these considerations and offers a more complete way to understand exposure to media. This is the key to interpreting audience information.

EXPOSURE TO MEDIA

As noted previously, most commercial audience research is simply a record of what kinds of people are exposed to what kinds of media. The practice in the television and radio industries has been to define exposure as program choice, or tuning behavior, rather than as attention or involvement. By studying a properly drawn sample of individuals and accurately measuring each one, we can have considerable confidence in our ability to describe exposure to media. Of course, research firms encounter various problems in sampling, measurement, and data processing. All of these take a toll on the accuracy of those estimates. But even experienced users, who are aware of error in the data, tend to take the numbers at face value in their day-to-day work. For the most part, that is our approach. When substantial methodological problems or biases suggest a qualified interpretation of the data, it is noted, but otherwise we treat the audience ratings as valid measures of exposure.

We have already encountered many ways to measure or somehow quantify media audiences. Some of these are routinely reported by the ratings services, others are routinely calculated by ratings users. It is useful, at this point, to draw a rather broad distinction between these various audience measurements and indices. We call one type *gross measures* and the other *cumulative measures*. The distinction has to do with whether we track the behavior of individuals over time. If an audience statistic does not depend on tracking, it is a gross measure. If it does, it is cumulative. This temporal quality in the data defines a fundamental distinction that is carried through the rest of the book.

Gross Measures of the Audience

Gross measures of exposure include estimates of audience size and composition made at a single point in time. The best examples are audience ratings and market shares, although summaries like the circulation of print media or total sales (e.g., movie ticket or record sales) are also gross measures of the audience. Even the number of hits on a Web site would seem to qualify. In none of these instances do we have any clear sense of the number of "repeat customers" involved. In effect, these are snapshots of the population.

Electronic media can take these snapshots with great rapidity. Ratings services estimate how many people listen to a station in an average quarter hour, or watch a program in an average minute. Projections of total audience size, HUT and PUT levels, belong in this category as well. Gross measures of exposure can also include secondary calculations derived from other gross measurements. Gross rating points (GRPs) are such calculations. You will recall that GRPs are just a summation of individual ratings over a schedule. Simple cost calculations, like cost per point (CPP) and cost per thousand (CPM) can, similarly, be thought of as gross measures.

Gross measures are the most common summaries of audience, and most of the numbers reported in syndicated research reports are of this type. As a result, they are the best known and most widely used of audience measurements. Useful as they are, however, they fail to capture information about how individual audience members behave over time. That kind of behavior is expressed in cumulative measures.

Cumulative Measures of the Audience

The most familiar example of the second group of audience measurements is a station's cumulative audience, or *cume*. To report a weekly cume audience, a ratings company must sort through each person's media use for a week, and summarize the number who used the station at least once. Analogous audience summaries are reach and unduplicated audience. A closely related cumulative measure that has become increasingly familiar to advertisers is frequency. You will recall that this summarizes how often an individual sees a particular advertising message over some period of time. Studies of program audience duplication, likewise, depend on tracking individual media users over time.

With the exception of the various cume ratings, cumulative measures are less commonly reported by syndicated research services than are gross measurements. Customized studies of audience duplication, however, may be useful in a variety of applications. For example, programmers studying audience flow or advertisers tracking the reach and frequency of a media plan are concerned with how the audience is behaving over time. Indeed, as we suggested in chapter 5, this sort of tracking can be illuminating for social scientists interested in any number of questions. Table 9.1 lists the most common gross and cumulative measures of media exposure.

Comparing Gross and Cumulative Measurements

To get a clearer picture of the difference between gross and cumulative measures, and to begin to appreciate the analytical possibilities offered by such data, consider Fig. 9.1. The large box in the upper left-hand corner of the page represents a simplified ratings database. The data are from a hypothetical sample of 10 households. These are numbered 1

TABLE 9.1
Common Measures of Exposure to Media

Gross measures	Cumulative measures
Audience ratings	Cume ratings
Market shares	Reach
Circulation	Frequency
Web site hits	Audience duplication
Total sales	Inheritance effects
Attendance	Channel loyalty
Rentals	Repeat viewing

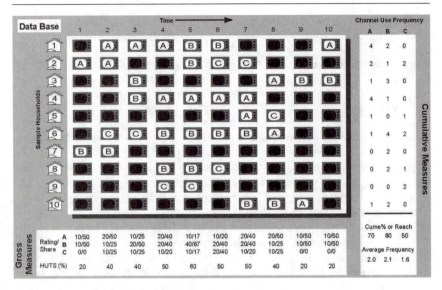

FIG. 9.1. Gross versus cumulative measures in rating data.

through 10, down the left-hand column. The media use of each household is measured at 10 points in time, running from Time 1 to Time 10 across the top of the page. Both types of measures can be generated for such a database.

In practice, of course, a ratings sample would be much larger, including hundreds or thousands of units of analysis. Those units could be individual people or households, as indicated in the figure. There would also be many more points in time. For example, a standard television diary divides each of 7 days into 80 quarter hours. That means that each person is measured across 560 (i.e., 7 × 80) points in time, rather than the 10 we have illustrated. Now try to imagine how many points in time we could identify in peoplemeter data that track viewing moment to moment over a period of years!

Figure 9.1 portrays television viewing in households, but radio listening or Web site visits could be conceptualized in much the same way. In our illustration, we have assumed a three-station market, which means that each household can be doing one of four things at each point in time. It can be tuned to Channel A, Channel B, Channel C, or nothing at all. These behaviors are indicated by the appropriate letters, or a blackened box, respectively.

The most commonly reported gross measures of exposure are shown in the box directly under the database. Each column of data is like Fig. 2.1, and is treated in the same way. Hence, Channel A has a rating of 20 and a share of 40 at Time 4. All one needs to do is look down the appropriate column. Unlike the calculation of a cume, whatever happened before or after that time period is irrelevant to the calculation of a rating.

The box on the right-hand side of the page includes common cumulative measures. To calculate these, we must first examine each household's viewing behavior across time. That means moving across each row in the database. The first household, for example, watched Channel A four times, and Channel B two times, but never watched Channel C. Moving down each channel's column of cumulative viewing, we can then determine its reach, or cume. Each channel's cumulative audience is expressed as a percentage of the total sample who viewed it at least once over the 10 points in time. Therefore, the first household would be included in the cume of A and B, but not C. Further, among those who did view a channel, if we compute the arithmetic average of the numbers in the column, we can report the mean frequency of viewing. This is essentially what an advertiser does when calculating reach and frequency, with the relevant points in time being determined by when a commercial message runs.

Studies of program audience duplication can also be executed from this database. For example, we might be interested in how well Station A retains an audience from one show to the next. We could determine that by seeing how many people who watched Station A at one point in time continued to watch the program that aired after it. For that matter, we could compare any pair of program audiences to assess repeat viewing, audience loyalty, and so on. In each case, however, we would have to track individual households across at least two points in time. Hence, we would be doing a cumulative analysis of exposure.

Depending on the kind of question they want to answer, ratings analysts would interpret gross measures, cumulative measures, or numbers that are derived from these two ways of defining exposure. As you will see, there are a large number of analytical techniques that can be organized in this way. In fact, these techniques are likely to maintain their usefulness even as the new technologies develop. Whether audiences are reached through the Internet, DBS, or traditional over-the-air broadcasting, the concepts of gross and cumulative measurements convey important information to programmers and advertisers. To exploit those analytical techniques to their fullest, however, we must develop a better understanding of the factors that shape audiences from moment to moment.

COMMON THEORIES OF MEDIA CHOICE

The question most often asked by students of audience behavior is, "Why do people choose specific media content?" The answer most commonly given is, "They choose what they like." This kind of reasoning is typical of industry practice, communications policy, and most academic theories of choice. It suggests equivalence between program preferences and program choices. This section reviews four of the most popular theories of media choice: the working theories used by industry practitioners; economic models of program choice; selective exposure theory; and uses and gratifications research. All rely very heavily, if not exclusively, on the idea of preferences. They provide a background against which our own framework can be better understood.

Working Theories of Program Choice

Working theories are the principles and assumptions used by media professionals in the conduct of their jobs. These "rules of thumb" may or may not have been subjected to systematic investigation. They may or may not correspond to the more academic theories of choice we review in the following sections. But they certainly deserve our attention. Programmers and media planners base these working theories on a day-to-day familiarity with the audience and how it responds to the media environment.

The people who craft media content are quite attentive to overall trends in popular culture as they try to anticipate what the audience will do next. Often, interest centers around the types of content people will like. We are all familiar with program "types." In television, we talk about soap operas, cop shows, game shows, and situation comedies. In radio, we describe station formats as contemporary hits, country, new age, or all–news. These are the familiar industry categories, but we can actually define program types in any number of ways. For example, content could be grouped as entertainment or information, adult or children's, and so on.

It is widely assumed that people will have consistent preferences for content of a type. We see anecdotal evidence of such reasoning in the operation of media industries. Popular movies are made into television series of the same sort. Hit TV programs are imitated the following years, all apparently on the assumption that there is an audience out there who likes that kind of material. As one pundit phrased it, in television nothing succeeds like excess. Marketing researchers have conducted more formal studies to identify the content characteristics that seem to polarize people's likes and dislikes. What they have generally discovered is that commonsense industry categories come as close to a viewer–defined typology as anything. That is to say, the people who like one soap opera do, in fact, tend to like other soap operas, and so on. Similar patterns of preference for rap music, country and western, opera, and most other types of music are also common (MacFarland, 1997).

An interesting facet of people's program preferences has emerged from this type of research. People's dislikes are more clearly related to program type than are their likes. In other words, what we like may be rather eclectic, but what we dislike is more readily categorized. You might test yourself on this point by writing down the five TV shows you like most and the five you like least. For some people, it is hard to express dislikes in anything other than program types. If program choice is as much a matter of avoidance as anything else, this could be an important insight.

Another significant feature of program type preferences is the linkage that is often found between certain types of content and the demographic characteristics of the audience. In television, for example, it is well established that news and information draws an older audience. Similarly, men tend to watch more sports than women do, children seem drawn to animation, and many of the most popular programs among African Americans feature Black characters. The same kinds of linkages exist in other forms of media. Women are the more usual readers of romance novels. Young men appear to have a preference for action adventure films. Video game use also seems to be related to age and gender. None of these associations is intended to suggest a lock-step connection between preferences and demographics, they are only tendencies. But working professionals should certainly be aware of their existence.

As important as preferences are in determining people's choice of media materials, programmers know full well that many other factors enter the picture. We noted in chapter 3 the importance of understanding audience flow. Radio and television programs are placed in a carefully crafted line-up. If a program is scheduled immediately after a popular show, it will enjoy a significant advantage in building an audience. Programming strategies such as lead-in effects and block programming all depend on this type of reasoning.

It is also important to consider when the audience is likely to be using the medium in question. The idea that things other than the programming determine the total audience is common to both the conventional wisdom of programmers and to at least some formal theories of audience behavior. In 1971, the late Paul Klein, then a researcher at NBC, offered a tongue-in-cheek description of the television audience. Struck by the amazing predictability of audience size, Klein suggested that people turn the set on out of habit, without much advance thought about what they will watch. After the set is on, they simply choose the *least objectionable program (LOP)* from available offerings.

In effect, what Klein suggested was that audience behavior is a two-stage process in which a decision to use the media precedes the selection of specific content. The tendency of people to turn on a set without regard to programming is often taken as evidence of a *passive audience*, though this seems a needlessly value-laden label. The conceptual alternative, a thoroughly *active audience*, appears to be unrealistic. Such an audience would turn on a set whenever favorite programs were aired, and turn off a set when they were not. We know, however, that daily routines (e.g., work, sleep, etc.) effectively constrain when we turn sets on. We also know that many people will watch or listen to programming they are not thrilled with, rather than turning off their sets.

Of course, this is a broad generalization about audience behavior. It is not intended to rule out the possibility that people can be persuaded to turn their sets on by media content. Major events, like the Super Bowl or dramatic news stories, undoubtedly attract people to the media who would not otherwise be there. Heavy promotion and advertising can sometimes get the attention of potential viewers who then remember to tune in. It is also likely that levels of activity vary by medium. Print and the Internet may be intrinsically more engaging even though they require more effort on the part of media consumers. Moreover, levels of activity can vary over time. The same person might be choosy at one time and a "couch potato" the next. Overall, though, a two-stage process, including the role of habit, appears to explain audience behavior rather well.

Economic Models of Program Choice

Economic theory presents a more formal model for explaining program choice. Though it is more abstract, it shares many of the elements embedded in the working theories we just reviewed. Peter Steiner (1952) is credited with groundbreaking work in this field. He, and those who have extended his work (e.g., Owen & Wildman, 1992), take the approach that a person's choice of programming is analogous to his or her choice of more conventional consumer products. Hence, older theories of product competition have served as the model for economic theories of program choice.

These theories make two rather important assumptions about the audience. First, it is assumed that there are program types that can be defined in terms of audience preferences. To stipulate that a program typology must be "defined in terms of audience preferences," as the economists do, forces us to consider exactly which categories of content are systematically related to audience likes and dislikes. In theory, such a typology must mean that people who like one program of a type will like all other programs of that type. Conversely, people who dislike a program must dislike all others of that type. As we have seen, there is some reason to believe that such program types exist.

Second, when considering advertiser-supported programming, it is assumed that programs are a "free good" to the audience member. This deserves further consideration. In the process of stating the assumption, those who invoke it often acknowledge, then ignore, both the opportunity cost of audience time and the potential increased costs of advertised products. Assuming that programs are like free products has an important implication. If programs have no price, it seems logical that the only thing left to explain audience choice is preference. The assumption that preference is a cause of choice is certainly in keeping with the other economic theories, and resembles a psychologist's expectation of attitude-behavior consistency.

Economic models of program choice differ in how they resolve the active-passive question that we discussed previously. Steiner (1952) assumed a thoroughly active audience in which audience size was determined by the presence of people's preferred program types. According to Steiner's model, when your favorite program type wasn't on, neither was your set. Subsequent models, however, have relaxed that rather stringent assumption, and incorporated a two-stage process that allows for second and third choices, much like that proposed by Klein.

With these assumptions in place, it is possible to predict the distribution of audiences across channels. For example, if it is assumed that there is a relatively large audience for some particular type of programming, then two or more competing channels or stations will split that audience by offering programming of that type. This will continue to occur until that program type audience has been divided into small enough pieces that it makes sense for the next competitor to counter-program with different types of shows. Consequently, when there are only a few competitors, similar programs tend to be offered across channels. According to this body of theory, as the number of competitors increases, program services become more differentiated. This leads to a phenomenon known as *audience fragmentation*, as the audience is divided up among all competing program providers.

Selective Exposure Theory

Selective exposure theory offers another way to explain people's use of media content. It has been developed by social psychologists who, among other things, are interested in understanding the media's effect on audience members. In its earliest form, selective exposure theory assumed that people had certain attitudes, beliefs, or convictions that they were loath to change. These predispositions led people to seek out communications that were consistent with their beliefs and avoid material that challenged them. Simply put, people were thought to "see what they wanted to see," and "hear what they wanted to hear."

This commonsense notion gained greater credibility in the 1950s and 1960s with the introduction and testing of formal psychological theories, like cognitive dissonance. Early studies seemed to indicate that people did select media materials in such a way as to support their existing belief systems, or cognitions. Hence, selective exposure to news and information appeared to be an important principle in understanding an individual's choice of programming.

By the 1970s, however, more exacting studies began to cast doubt on the lock-step nature of selective exposure to information. Although research in this area languished for a while, more recent, broader, variations of selective exposure theory have been introduced. For example, experimental studies have shown that people's choices of entertainment vary with their moods and emotions. Excited or overstimulated people are more inclined to select relaxing program fare, whereas people who are bored are likely to choose stimulating content. Emotional states, in addition to more dispassionate cognitions, all seem to influence our program preferences. This particular type of research in selective exposure is being pursued under the general heading of "mood management theory" (Zillmann, 2000).

Uses and Gratifications Theory

Gratificationist theory provides a closely related, if somewhat more comprehensive, perspective on audience behavior. Studies of "uses and gratifications," as they are often called, are also the work of social psychologists. This approach emerged in the early 1970s, partly as a reaction against the field's apparent obsession with media effects research. Gratificationists argued that we should ask not only "what media do to people," but also "what people do with the media." Katz, Blumler, and Gurevitch (1974) spelled out the research agenda of this approach. According to them, gratificationists "are concerned with (1) the social and psychological origins of (2) needs, which generate (3) expectations of (4) mass media or other sources, which lead to (5) differential patterns of media exposure (or engagement in other activities), resulting in (6) need gratifications and (7) other consequences, perhaps mostly unintended ones" (p. 20).

Since the early 1970s gratificationist research and theory has attracted considerable attention. Of central importance to our discussion is the gratificationist's approach to explaining patterns of media exposure. Under this perspective, those patterns are determined by each person's expectations of how well different media or program content will gratify their needs. Such needs might be short-lived, like those associated with mood states, or they may be relatively constant. In any event, it seems likely that the gratifications being sought translate rather directly into preferences for the media and their content.

Gratificationist theory, therefore, has much in common with economic models of program choice and theories of selective exposure. All of them cast individual preferences, however they have emerged, as the central mechanism for explaining exposure. Grandiose theories aside, this view of audience behavior also has a great intuitive appeal. Why does the audience for a hard rock radio station tend to be young men? Because that is the kind of music they like. Why do males watch more televised sports than females? Because they like it more.

However, the power of preferences to determine exposure to the media is not as absolute as many have assumed. Audience formation is ultimately determined by many factors that fall outside these bodies of theory. We have seen recognition of this in the working theories reviewed earlier. But some of this is as much industry lore as a systematic body of knowledge. Economic theory attempts to integrate industry structure and program choice, but gives very little understanding of nuances like audience flow. Selective exposure and gratificationist theory are primarily concerned with an individual's choices, but tell us very little of the larger forces shaping a media audience. To really understand how media audiences form and change over time, we need to consider a number of other factors.

TOWARD A COMPREHENSIVE UNDERSTANDING OF AUDIENCE BEHAVIOR

If we consider exposure to media to be the interface between the audience and media content, we can identify many things that affect how that interface takes shape. In this section we consider both sides of the equation: *audience factors* and *media factors*. Each has a substantial effect on patterns of exposure. Within each category, we have made a further distinction between structural and individual determinants. Although the latter distinction is sometimes hard to make, it is intended to highlight differences in the levels of analysis. It also reflects traditional divisions in research and theory on media exposure. By *structural determinants* we mean factors that are common to, or characteristic of, populations. These are "macro-level" variables typically conceptualized as common to markets or masses of people. *Individual determinants* are factors descriptive of a person or household. They are "micro-level" variables that vary from person to person. Taken together, these factors offer a more thorough analytical framework for identifying the causes of exposure to the media.

Audience Factors

Structural Features of the Audience. The first structural feature of the audience that shapes exposure to media is the size and location of *potential audiences*. Sometimes, potential audience is easy to determine, like the number of people living within reach of a broadcast signal. But the potential audience can also be more elusive. For example, with universal postal service, any newspaper can technically reach a national audience, yet as a practical matter most papers have a distinctly local character. Other forms of media, like films, CDs, and web pages may have a truly global potential. Obviously, no form of media can have an audience larger than the size of the relevant market population. The population, in effect, sets an upper bound on the audience potential for any program service. The larger the potential, the more media organizations are willing to invest to win a "piece of the pie."

In broadcasting, ratings services typically divide the country into well over 200 local market areas (see Appendix A). Clearly, the potential audience for a station in one market can be vastly larger than the audience in another. This does not, of course, guarantee that large market stations will have larger audiences, especially since large markets tend to have more media outlets. Nevertheless, it sets the stage for bigger audiences and bigger audience revenues.

Potential audiences, however, are not just a matter of the sheer number of people living within reach of a medium. The composition of the population can have an impact on long-term patterns of exposure as well. As the demographic makeup of potential audiences changes, it is reasonable to expect that patterns of media exposure will change as well. According to census data, for example, there have been shifts in the relative size of white-collar and blue-collar populations, the age of the population, and most notably in the level of education throughout the population. Occupation, age, and education are often associated with the choice of certain types of programming. A far-sighted media operator will take population shifts, most of which are quite predictable, into account when planning for the future.

The rise in Spanish-language programming can be viewed, at least in part, as a result of newly emerging potential audiences. For example, in 1970 Latinos or Hispanics accounted for 4.5% of the U.S. population, and by 1990 that figure had doubled. By some estimates, it will double again by 2025, with even higher concentrations in a number of U.S. markets. Rapid growth rates also characterize the U.S. Asian population. Such changes in ethnic or linguistic populations provide new markets for advertisers and the media, and may help explain corresponding changes in media use.

The second structural attribute of audiences, and one of the most powerful determinants of exposure to the electronic media, is *audience availability*. While potential audiences set an absolute physical limit on audience sizes, our daily routines set a practical limit on how many people are likely to be using either radio or television at any point in time. It is widely believed that the number of people using a medium has little, if anything, to do with programming and almost everything to do with who is available. Most practitioners take the size of the available audience as given, just as they would the size of the population itself. In practice, the available audience is most often defined as the number of people using a medium at any point in time.

The size of the available audience, like other forms of mass behavior, is quite predictable. Three patterns are apparent: seasonal, daily, and hourly. Seasonal patterns of media use are more evident in television than in radio. Nationwide, television use is heaviest in the winter months of January and February. Nielsen reports that the average household has a set in use for over 8.3 hours a day at this time of year. During the summer months, household usage drops to about 7.5 hours. This shift seems to occur because viewers have more daylight in the summer, and pursue outdoor activities that take them away from the set. These seasonal changes mean lower HUT levels in the summer and higher HUT levels in the winter. But household level data can mask important differences within demographic groups. For example, when school is out, daytime viewing among children and teenagers soars. The same vacation-time phenomenon appears to account for seasonal differences in movie theater attendance.

Audience size also varies by day of the week. Nationally, prime time television audiences are higher on weeknights and Sunday, and lower on Fridays and Saturdays. The late-night audience (e.g., midnight) on Friday and Saturday, however, is larger than it is during the rest of the week. This, too, seems to reflect a change in people's social activities on the weekends. Radio audiences also look different on weekdays than they do on weekends. The early morning audience is smaller on Saturday and Sunday, with a peak much later during midday.

The most dramatic shifts in audience availability, however, occur on an hourly basis. It is here that the patterns of each day's life are most evident. Figure 9.2, based on Arbitron data, depicts the size of the radio audience at various times during the day, Monday through Friday. It also indicates where listening occurs: at home or elsewhere. As you can see, the size of the total audience increases very rapidly from about 5 a.m. to 7:30 a.m. During the morning hours, much of that listening occurs in cars as people commute to work, hence the name "drive time." It is during this time period that a radio station can typically capture its largest audiences, so it may devote considerable resources to programming. Other stations, of course, are doing

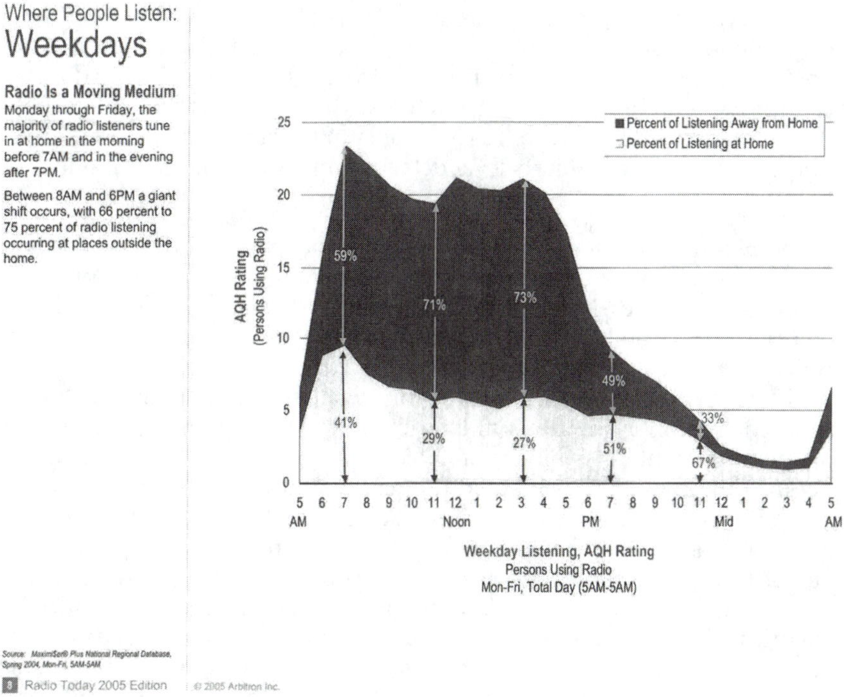

Where People Listen:
Weekdays

Radio Is a Moving Medium
Monday through Friday, the majority of radio listeners tune in at home in the morning before 7AM and in the evening after 7PM.

Between 8AM and 6PM a giant shift occurs, with 66 percent to 75 percent of radio listening occurring at places outside the home.

Weekday Listening, AQH Rating
Persons Using Radio
Mon–Fri, Total Day (5AM-5AM)

FIG. 9.2.   Where people listen. Reprinted by permission of Arbitron.

the same thing, and competition for the drive-time audience can be intense. Throughout the rest of the day the audience gradually shrinks in size, with much listening in the workplace. At about 2:30 p.m. the audience picks up again, creating what is called the afternoon drive time, which is longer than "morning drive" as listeners are often picking up children at school, shopping, and running errands. Thereafter, it trails off as people return home and television begins to command their attention.

Figure 9.3 represents the size of the television audience on an hourly basis. In some ways, it is the mirror image of the radio audience. Here, the early morning audience is relatively small. Throughout the day, however, it begins to grow. At about 5 p.m., when people arrive home from work, sets go on and HUT levels rise sharply. The total size of the audience peaks between 9 p.m. and 10 p.m., which marks the height of prime time—a peak that you can see is slightly depressed in summer. As we noted in the first chapter, it is during prime time that the broadcast networks are able to charge a premium for commercial time. It is also during this time period that networks air the most expensive programming. The competition is stiff, but the rewards for winning a healthy share of this large audience can be substantial.

Thus far, our approach to explaining exposure has had almost nothing to say about people's preferences, or the appeals of different kinds of programming. Remember, however, that we can characterize audience behavior as a two-stage process. Turning on a set may have little to do with specific content, but once a decision to use the media has been made, people's likes and dislikes, as well as a number of other factors, do play a role. These factors are the micro-level determinants of audience behavior.

Individual Audience Characteristics. The most important micro-level determinants of exposure to programming are, broadly speaking, people's preferences. Much of a programmer's skill in building an audience comes from an ability to judge what people will or will not like. As we noted in the previous section, this strategy for explaining audience behavior is also popular with academics from a variety of disciplines including marketing, economics, and social psychology. While program preferences are an important determinant of choice, we need to do a better job of understanding how they operate in the real world of media use.

Most research and theory on the relationship between preference and choice focuses on the individual, and assumes that personal preferences can be freely exercised in the selection of programming. Economic models of program choice, selective exposure theory, and gratificationist theories all rely on this assumption. It is often justified on the basis of research done in laboratory settings that evaluates how individuals choose media content when they are alone. However, much of our media use is done not in isolation, but in the company of others. This is especially true of television viewing.

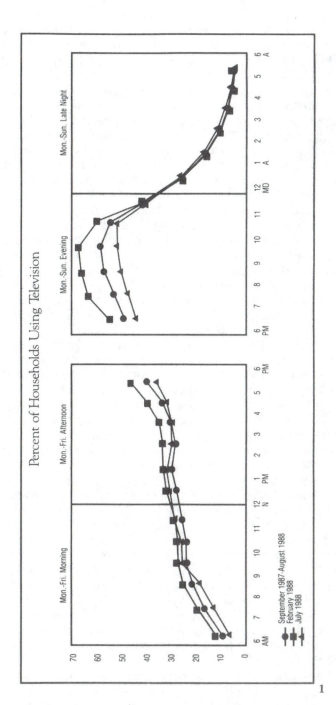

Percent of Households Using Television

FIG. 9.3.   Hourly variation.

189

The second individual-level audience factor, then, is *group viewing*. This is a rather common phenomenon, even today when most households have more than one set. The most typical group configuration is much of the family viewing together, followed by husband and wife together. What little research there is on the dynamics of group viewing suggests that negotiation among competing preferences is quite usual. Different members of the family seem to exercise more or less influence at different times of the day. For example, programmers take into account that children are often in control of the television set in the late afternoon when they return from school. Exposure to television programming, then, results not only from who is available and what they like, but who is actually making the program selections. People get their first choices some of the time but can be out-voted at other times. Even if they are overruled, however, they will often stay with the viewing group. Ask any parent of a young child whether they are watching more "Sesame Street" since the child's arrival. Ask children if they see more of the evening news than they would like. In effect, some of our exposure to media is enforced, in spite of our preferences. Group viewing, or for that matter group music listening or group movie attendance, can constrain the relationship between preference and choice. More solitary forms of media use (e.g., reading or Internet) may offer a cleaner linkage between these factors.

The last audience factor to complicate the relationship between preference and choice is *awareness*. By awareness we mean knowledge of the media content that is available to you. Much theorizing about the audience presupposes perfect awareness on the part of audience members. In other words, media selections are assumed to occur with a full knowledge of the content options. Although that assumption might be workable on a very abstract level, or in very simple media environments, it does not seem to work well in the media-rich environments that confront most audience members.

If, as is sometimes the case, people select programming without a full understanding of their options, the interpretation of choice as an expression of preference is an oversimplification. How often have you missed a show you might have enjoyed because you unthinkingly watched something else? Have you ever "discovered" a favorite program or station that had been on the air for some time? Even program guides, such as "TV Guide" and the television listings in a daily newspaper, cannot possibly report on all the options available to viewers. Instead, they list broadcast services and a selected number of cable channels. The same potential problems exist for the bewildering number of print media and Web sites. As more and more services compete for the attention of the audience, these sorts of breakdowns between preference and choice are likely to be increasingly common.

The role that audience preferences play in determining audience behavior is more complex than many researchers assume. For example, a small audience rating might indicate that people do not like a particular station or program. But it might also indicate that the desired audience was unavailable to tune in or that they simply did not know what was on. Any interpretation of media use should consider these factors, as summarized in Table 9.2. But audience factors are only half the picture. The structures of the media themselves have an impact on patterns of exposure.

Media Factors

As with audience factors, media factors can be grouped as structural or individual. The structural attributes of the media complement the structural features of the audience. They include market conditions and how available content is organized. Individual-level media factors vary in tandem with individual audience attributes, defining differences in the media environment from household to household.

Structural Features of the Media. The first structural characteristic of the electronic media is *coverage*, which is the extent to which people are physically able to receive a particular channel or medium of programming. In the United States, the universal availability of both radio and television is usually taken for granted. In other countries, especially in developing nations, universal coverage is not the rule. Even in the United States, newer forms of media are not available to all households. Table 9.3 summarizes the growth of various electronic media in this country.

Obviously, a medium's coverage of the population has a powerful impact on its ability to attract audiences. Early television audiences had to be small because few people had receivers. Similarly, cable television's audiences are shaped, in the first instance, by the fact that about two thirds of U.S. households subscribe to that medium. Even when you factor in Direct Broadcast Satellites and other "alternative delivery sys-

TABLE 9.2
Audience Factors Affecting Exposure

Structural	Individual
Potential audiences	Preferences
Local vs. national vs. global	Program type preferences
Demographic factors	Tastes
Ethnic or linguistic populations	Gratifications sought
Available audiences	Group vs. solitary media use
Seasonal variation	Awareness of options
Weekly variation	
Hourly variation	

TABLE 9.3

Growth of Electronic Media in the United States

Year	Total U.S. Households	Radio	Television	Cable	ADS	VCRs	DVDs	Computers	Internet online
						Percent of households with			
1930	30,000,000	46							
1940	35,000,000	81							
1950	43,000,000	95	9						
1960	53,000,000	96	87						
1970	61,000,000	98	95	6					
1980	78,000,000	98	98	19		1			
1990	94,000,000	99	98	55		67		23	2
1995	98,000,000	99	98	62		80		35	8
2000	103,000,000	99	98	66	18	87	12	51	42
2001	104,000,000	99	98	66	22	90	23	58	53
2002	106,000,000	99	98	66	23	91	34	62	57
2003	107,000,000	99	100	67	24	94	40	64	61
2004	108,000,000	99	100	65	25	93	49	66	62

Note. ADS includes all "alternative delivery systems" like direct broadcast satellites.

tems" it's unlikely that cable networks will ever achieve the coverage of the established broadcast networks. The same is true of audiences reached through the Internet. While the number of households with personal computers continues to climb, roughly a third of households still don't have access to the Internet. Coverage of this medium is likely to remain well below 100%, which limits its potential to reach large audiences. Moreover, the pricing of connect time may alter the "free good" character we have come to associate with electronic media.

Even when the media are able to offer "free" content to a truly national audience, local outlets may affect coverage by refusing to carry certain programs. For example, with the exception of a few TV stations that are actually owned and operated (O & Os) by the networks, affiliates are independent businesses that act in their own self-interest. This means that an affiliate may not carry (or "clear") all of a network's programming if it believes some other programming strategy will be more profitable. This could involve an entire series, or it could be a onetime preemption for a program of more interest to the local community, or one that is likely to generate higher revenues. These variations in *network clearance* mean that some programs don't reach the entire population. The same is true of syndicated program clearances. Once again, this puts a cap on the total possible audience size.

Within any given medium, a number of other structural factors operate to affect audience behavior. The first consideration is the sheer number of options that confronts the audience. For most forms of media, that number has increased dramatically in recent years. In the world of 1950s television, for example, the average TV household could receive roughly four channels. Today, with the inclusion of cable television, the average household receives over 100 channels. For those who have access to the Internet, the number of available Web sites seems almost limitless.

Presenting the audience an array of services, most of which are in competition for a limited amount of audience time and attention, has a number of important consequences for exposure to media messages. More competitive markets almost inevitably mean smaller ratings and shares for each of the competitors. You can get a sense of how different levels of competition affect audience size by looking at how prime time network shares have eroded over time. Figure 9.4 presents such a trend data.

The table summarizes information about audience shares and the level of competition across the last 18 years, beginning with the 1985-86 TV season. The dark bars represent the combined audience share of the big-three (i.e., ABC, CBS, NBC) networks. In '85-'86 they accounted for almost 70% of all the time people spent watching prime time television. As of the '02–'03 season, that had dropped to a combined share of less than 30%. This has happened because, over the same span of years, the number of new viewing options has increased dramatically. The light-colored bars show what percent of TVHHs had access to cable and, more recently, other delivery systems. Today, well

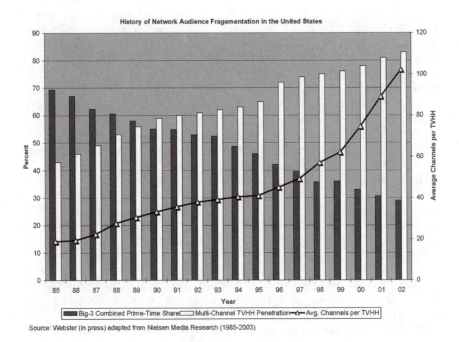

History of Network Audience Fragmentation in the United States

Source: Webster (in press) adapted from Nielsen Media Research (1985-2003)

FIG. 9.4. History of network audience fragmentation in the United States. Adapted from Nielsen Media Research (1985–2003).

over 80% of homes have some sort of multi-channel service. The line punctuated by the triangles shows the average number of channels available to households. It has grown at an increasingly rapid rate, and newer delivery systems (e.g., DBS and digital cable) have ratcheted up their channel capacities. Certainly, no one cable network is likely to match the audience of a broadcast network, but they do fragment the audience and in combination take a considerable toll, just as economic theory would predict.

The structural complexities of the media, however, go beyond the simple number of channels or programs that are available. In radio and television, programs are offered up as a series of forced choices. It is quite possible to encounter situations in which two desirable programs are aired opposite one another, and the viewer has to choose between them. Had they been scheduled at different times, the viewer could have watched both. *Program scheduling*, within and across channels, therefore, is widely believed to be an important factor in shaping the size, composition, and duplication of audiences.

As we have seen, programmers use their knowledge of audience flow to encourage people to watch their programs rather than those of the competition. Indeed, there are well-documented patterns of audience duplication, such as inheritance effects, channel loyalty, and repeat viewing, that all seem to derive from structural factors (Goodhardt, Ehrenberg, & Collins, 1987; Webster & Phalen, 1997). The ability to tape and replay programming can, in principle, break this rigid structure, but in practice relatively little taping has been done. Perhaps digital video recorders (DVRs) will someday lessen the power of programming structures, but at present their penetration in the marketplace is too limited to render any final judgments.

There appear to be structural biases built into the Internet as well. Search engines may have protocols favoring some Web sites over others. Certainly the growth of pay-for-placement keyword searches stacks the deck. Within web pages, there are various links, encouraging certain patterns of audience duplication and discouraging others. All these media structures are another reason why a person's preferences may not be the best guide to actual patterns of exposure.

But even these factors do not entirely exhaust explanations of variability among audience members. There are a few micro-level media factors that we should review to complete the picture.

Individual Media Environments.   Factors like network coverage and program scheduling are generally beyond the control of an audience member. But certain aspects of the media environment are within the individual's control. In fact, this is truer today than it has ever been. As new technologies and programming alternatives enter the marketplace, each of us has greater latitude in shaping a media environment to suit our purposes. These decisions can certainly affect our exposure to the media and are closely related to the micro-level audience factors we reviewed earlier.

One of the first considerations is the kind of *technologies owned* by individual audience members. While radio and television have been in virtually all U.S. households for decades, the characteristics of these receivers have changed over time. Color television, once a novelty, is now in all U.S. television households. Over three fourths of homes now have more than one television set. The location and capability of these receivers are all within the control of individual viewers and can affect the quality of the media environment within the home.

In the 1980s, for example, the widespread introduction of remote control devices (RCDs) seemed to signal major changes in patterns of exposure. Before remotes were available, viewers had to leave their chairs to change channels. Today 98% of homes have remote controls, especially on the main set where much viewing occurs. Because they made channel changing so easy, RCDs struck fear in the hearts of advertisers and programmers alike. From the advertiser's perspective, viewers might be more likely to change channels when an advertisement came on. This practice, called *zapping*, could obviously reduce exposure to commercial messages. From the programmer's perspective, audiences lost during commercial breaks or a lull in the program itself could be difficult to regain. The inclination of at least some viewers to change channels at the drop of a hat has been dubbed *grazing*. It now seems that many of the initial concerns regarding RCDs were overblown.

Videocassette recorders (VCRs) were another technology with great potential to alter the media environment of audience members. At the beginning of the 1980s, they were virtually nonexistent as a household appliance. Today, they have far surpassed cable penetration and are in over 90% of all households. Historically, VCR usage has fallen into two broad categories: *time shifting* and *library use*. As the labels suggest, time shifting involved taping a program for replay at a more convenient time, while library use involved recording or buying material for longer-term use. However, it now seems that two even newer technologies will gradually supplant VCRs.

Increasingly, time shifting will be accomplished by DVRs, sometimes called personal video recorders (PVRs). DVRs are easier to use than VCRs, and offer advanced search and record functions. TiVo is the brand most commonly associated with DVRs. Although the technology is in relatively few households, direct broadcast satellite services and digital cable systems may soon make similar DVR functionality widespread. If DVRs penetrate even a sizable minority of households, and if people use them aggressively to rearrange their personal programming options, it could mitigate the structural factors we discussed in the previous sections.

DVDs, a somewhat more mature technology, are likely to inherit the library building function of VCRs. DVD penetration in American households has risen dramatically. In fact, VCR penetration has recently dropped off as more and more homes opt for the superior clarity and resolution of DVDs.

Even newer technologies will help shape the media environment in individual homes. People with receivers capable of showing HDTV signals are likely to choose programs produced in that format. The introduction of digital television and sets capable of Internet access will create further differences among households. Indeed, the lines between radio, television, cable, and computers may gradually disappear. The speed at which these developments take shape remains to be seen. The rate of adoption will almost certainly vary with household characteristics, further complicating the media environment in which audience behavior should be understood.

Subscriptions are yet another type of decision that each person or household must make. For some time now, people have subscribed to different newspapers, magazines, and book clubs. More recently, people now subscribe to things like Internet providers, direct broadcast satellites (DBS), and video stores. This obviously encourages differential patterns of exposure. Perhaps the most widely studied form of subscription in the electronic media is cable television.

We have touched on cable often in the preceding discussions. Although much about cable's organization and availability is appropriately conceptualized as a structural variable beyond a person's control, the decision to subscribe is ultimately made by each individual household. Cable, in other words, is not just something that is done to us, it is also something we elect to do. This self-selection into the cable universe is one reason why comparisons of cable and noncable households must be made with caution.

Just why people subscribe to cable varies from home to home. We do know that cable subscribers have higher incomes than nonsubscribers. We also know that cable households tend to have more people living in them. This is especially true of families that buy a pay cable service. With more children, or more money to spend, subscription to cable probably makes sense. Gratificationists have pointed out that cable subscribers express a need for greater variety and control over their viewing environment. Others undoubtedly subscribe just to improve the quality of over-the-air reception.

Researchers have also observed that cable subscribers have a somewhat different style of viewing television. Confronted with a large number of channels from which to choose, cable subscribers apparently develop a *channel repertoire*, or set of frequently viewed channels. This repertoire is a subset of total number of channels available to the subscriber. The more channels there are, the larger is the repertoire. But there is not a one-to-one correspondence. As the number of available channels increases, the proportion that is actually used decreases. The net result is that each cable viewer constructs an array of channels from which to choose on a day-to-day basis. This effectively precludes viewing most channels, even if they can be received on the set. In fact, many TV remote control devices now allow users to set up their own "menu" of preferred choices. In radio the newest tuners even allow the listener to indicate a format preference which the tuner then seeks out. The same phenomenon is likely to develop with the Internet, as users create bookmarks, or other shortcuts to favorite Web sites. Table 9.4 summarizes the media factors we have discussed.

AN INTEGRATED MODEL OF AUDIENCE BEHAVIOR

Audience behavior is influenced by many factors. We have defined and discussed most of them in the preceding sections of the chapter, but have not yet put the pieces of the puzzle together. It may be useful at this point to step back, reflect briefly on what has been presented, and then try to forge an overall framework for examining media exposure. With a comprehensive model of audience behavior, the job of summarizing, evaluating, and anticipating the data contained in the ratings will be more manageable.

Audience researchers have devoted much time and effort to understanding people's use of the electronic media. Ad agencies and the media have done very pragmatic studies of audience formation, economists

TABLE 9.4
Media Factors Affecting Exposure

Structural	Individual
Coverage	Technologies owned
Household penetration	Radio & TV sets
Signal carriage	VCRs, DVDs, DVRs
Clearance	Computers
Content options	Subscriptions
Number of choices	Print media
Program schedules	Cable
Linked Web sites	DBS
	Internet service
	Repertoires
	Channel repertoires
	Bookmarking

have developed rather abstract theories of program choice, and social psychologists have performed a seemingly endless succession of experiments and surveys to reveal the origins of audience behavior. Despite progress in these, and many other fields, there has been an unfortunate tendency for each group to work in isolation from the others. Instances of collaborative work between theorists and practitioners or even across different academic disciplines are all too rare.

At the risk of greatly oversimplifying matters, two fairly distinct approaches to understanding the audience can be identified. The first emphasizes the importance of the individual factors we discussed earlier. This perspective is typical of work in psychology, communication studies, and to some extent, marketing and economics. It also has enormous intuitive appeal, and is likely to characterize most commonsense explanations of the audience. After all, audiences are simply collections of individuals. Surely, if we can understand behavior at the individual level, then our ability to explain larger patterns of mass behavior will follow. When we conceptualize audience behavior at the individual level, we tend to look for explanations by thinking of those things that distinguish us as individuals. Above all, we have invoked preferences as a way to explain behavior. With this focus, however, we often miss seeing things that crystallize different levels of analysis. For instance, it is doubtful that any one television viewer chooses to create an inheritance effect, yet night after night the total audience manifests this form of behavior.

The second perspective emphasizes structural factors as key determinants of mass behavior. This approach is more typical in sociology, human ecology, and at least some forms of marketing and advertising research. It downplays individual needs and wants, and concentrates on things like total audience size, coverage areas, and program schedules in an attempt to understand audience behavior. Although work in this area can be highly successful in creating statistical explanations of aggregate data, it often has a hollow ring to it. One is often tempted to ask, "What does this mean in human terms—what does it tell us about ourselves?" Such explanations are usually possible, but not always apparent.

It is important to recognize that neither approach is right or wrong. They are simply different ways to know the audience. It is also important to note that neither approach is fully complete without the other. Despite the fact that these models of audience behavior are sometimes advanced as mutually exclusive alternatives, we believe that there is much to be gained by trying to integrate them. Specifically, analyses of individual behavior might be enhanced by a more deliberate consideration of the structural factors suggested here. We know through observation that these variables are highly correlated with audience behavior, and weaving them into micro-level studies might increase the latter's power and generalizability. Conversely, research in mass behavior might be more explicit about its relationship to theoretical concepts central in the individual approach. This could improve its popular acceptance and utility. It is in this spirit that we propose the following model.

The Model

The model presented in Fig. 9.5 is intended to help organize our thinking about audience behavior as it is commonly defined in audience research. The model suggests a few very broad relationships, but it does not, in and of itself, provide hypotheses to be tested. It certainly falls short of being a mathematical model, although we use Fig. 9.5 as a springboard for discussing several such models in chapter 11. We should also point out that the model focuses primarily on short-term features of audience behavior.

The central component of the model, the thing we are trying to explain, is exposure to media. As we argued in chapter 1, audience analysts are interested in mass behavior. We saw earlier in this chapter that the most common measures of that behavior can be categorized as gross or cumulative. Two broad categories are shown as the causes of exposure: audience factors and media factors. The shape of the "boxes" indicates the direction of influence. For example, the model suggests that audience factors help determine ratings, not vice versa. There are also cause-and-effect relationships among the factors within each box. For instance, audience preferences probably contribute to patterns of avail-

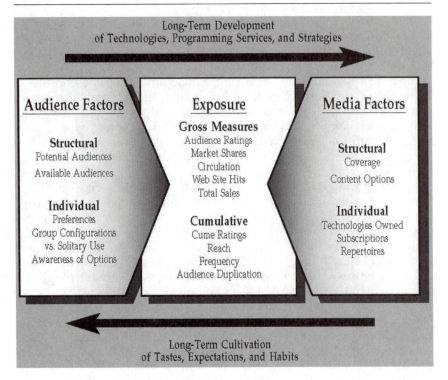

FIG. 9.5. A model of audience behavior.

ability, and cable subscription helps shape cable network coverage. We have opted to omit the arrows suggesting these interrelationships, to keep the model a bit cleaner.

To use the model, you should identify the sort of audience behavior you wish to analyze. Are you concerned with the size of an audience at a single point in time (i.e., a gross measure), or are you interested in how audience members are behaving across time (i.e., a cumulative measure)? To begin the process of evaluating, explaining, or predicting that behavior, consider the structural determinants first. There are three reasons why we recommend you look initially for structural explanations. First, like the measures of exposure you are analyzing, they are pitched at the macro-level of analysis. Second, they are more knowable. Information on program schedules, network coverage, and total audiences are typically in the research reports themselves. Individual factors, like audience awareness and the use of remote control devices, are a bit harder to pin down. Third, we know from experience that structural explanations work well with most forms of audience data. If they fail to provide a satisfying answer, however, begin the process of thinking through the individual-level factors on either side of the model.

Let us work our way through an example to get a better sense of the model. Keep in mind that the model is not designed to provide a quick answer to difficult audience research questions, but to guide the analyst in considering all the relevant factors. Consider, for instance, the ratings of a local television news program. Why do some stations have high ratings, and others have low ratings? What factors will shape a station's audience size in the future? Advertisers, as well as local station managers and programmers, would probably have an interest in this sort of analysis. Imagine that you work for a station and you want to assess its situation.

A rating, of course, is a gross measure of audience size. Local news ratings, in particular, have an important impact on station profitability. To explain the size of a station's news audience, we should first consider structural factors. If audience size is to be expressed as an absolute number, we would need to know the size of the potential audience defined by the population in the market. At the same time, we would want to consider the nature of the station's coverage area. Is it a VHF or a UHF station? If it is the latter, you're probably already at a disadvantage. Is there anything about the station's signal or local geography that would limit the station's ability to reach all of the potential audience? Next, we would want to know the size of the audience at the time when the news is broadcast. An analysis of share data, of course, might overlook this, but since we are interested in ratings, the bigger the available audience, the better are our chances of achieving a large rating. We might pay special attention to those segments of the audience that are more likely to be local news viewers. Experience tells us that these are probably going to be older adults. Next, we would consider a variety of program scheduling factors.

The first scheduling consideration would involve assessing the competition. Just how many competitors are there? As they increase in number, your ratings are likely to decrease. Do other stations enjoy any special advantages in covering the market? To what extent has cable television or DBS penetrated the market? What are your principal competitors likely to program opposite the news? Will you confront only news programs, or will the competition counterprogram with something different? The latter is much more likely if you are an affiliate facing other independent stations. If the available audience contains a large segment who are less likely to watch the news (e.g., children and young adults), that could damage your ratings. Consider the programming you have before and after your news. A highly rated lead-in is likely to help your ratings, especially if it attracts an audience of news viewers. If you are an affiliate, pay close attention to the strength of your network's news program. Research has shown that there is a very strong link between local and network news ratings.

More often than not, these structural factors explain most of the variations in local news ratings. A station can control some things, like lead-in programming. Other things, like the number of competitors it has, are beyond its control. Because a single ratings point might make a substantial difference in a station's profitability, however, consideration of individual factors may be warranted, especially if these are things a station can manipulate.

Among the most likely candidates for consideration are viewer preferences and awareness. Are there certain personalities or program formats that are going to be more or less appealing to viewers? Every year, consultants to stations—news doctors they are called—charge large fees to make such determinations. Are there certain news stories that will better suit the needs and interests of local viewers? In markets that are not measured continuously, stations often schedule sensationalist special reports to coincide with the ratings sweeps. A riveting investigative report is unlikely to boost a program's ratings, however, unless additional viewers are made aware of it. So stations must simultaneously engage in extraordinary promotional and advertising efforts. Of course, all the stations in a market are probably doing the same thing. Therefore, although catering to audience preferences is very important in principle, in practice it may not make a huge ratings difference. Even so, a small edge can be crucial to a program's profitability.

The analysis of radio audience behavior follows along the same lines as television, except we typically define exposure in terms of stations and dayparts rather than programs. Listeners do occasionally tune in to specific programs, but more often they will select a station without any notion of having chosen a discrete radio show. The key determinants of radio audience size and flow are still structural in nature, but individual factors may take on added salience. Radio stations usually operate in relatively competitive markets, and specialize in a particular kind of programming. The choice of station to listen to is more likely to be the decision of a single individual than a group. Radio listeners are also likely to select a station by searching through a very limited repertoire. They may leave the radio tuned to a favorite station all the time or they may select a station by pressing a pre-set button instead of consulting any sort of programming guide. For all of these reasons, people's preferences and their awareness of what particular stations have to offer weigh more heavily in the analysis of radio audience behavior.

We have much more to learn about the behavior of Internet and DVR users. In a media environment where there are fewer structural constraints, it seems reasonable to expect that notions of selective exposure and related theories may gain added weight. Web users are typically characterized as individuals actively seeking information, so a theory that posits an active audience seems to offer an appealing interpretation of behavior. Even the term "user" implies a more actively engaged individual than does the more passive term "viewer."

In closing, we might comment briefly on the long-term nature of exposure to media. One danger of characterizing audience behavior as the result of nicely drawn arrows and boxes is that things are made to seem simpler than they really are. For instance, the model defines exposure as the result, but not the cause, of other factors. Over a period of months, or even weeks, ratings can have a substantial effect on the structure of the media. Programs are cancelled, new shows developed, schedules altered, and clearances changed, often on the basis of audience behavior. Such relationships have been the subject of a number of interesting investigations. Similarly, the model, as we have presented it, suggests a high degree of independence between audience and media factors. In the short term, that seems to be a workable assumption. Over the long haul, however, it could promote a distorted picture of audience behavior.

To address these issues, we have specified some long-term relationships between audience and media factors. For example, the growth of potential audiences and patterns of availability clearly affect the development of media services and programming strategies. Conversely, the structure and content of the media undoubtedly cultivate certain tastes, expectations, and habits on the part of the audience. These are important relationships, but not central to our purpose. Bearing such limitations in mind, we hope the model can provide a useful framework for evaluating ratings data and exploiting the analytical techniques discussed in the remaining chapters. We also hope that it dispels the myth that preference translates easily into choice.

RELATED READINGS

Barwise, P., & Ehrenberg, A. (1988). *Television and its audience*. London: Sage.

Comstock, G., & Scharrer, E. (1999). *Television: What's on, who's watching, and what it means*. San Diego: Academic Press.

Heeter, C., & Greenberg, B. S. (1988). *Cable-viewing*. Norwood, NJ: Ablex.

MacFarland, D. T. (1997). *Future radio programming strategies: Cultivating listenership in the digital age*. Mahwah, NJ: Lawrence Erlbaum Associates.

McPhee, W. N. (1963). *Formal theories of mass behavior*. New York: The Free Press.

McQuail, D. (1997). *Audience analysis*. Thousand Oaks, CA: Sage.

Neumann, W. R. (1991). *The future of the mass audience*. Cambridge: Cambridge University Press.

Owen, B. M., & Wildman, S. W. (1992). *Television economics*. Cambridge: Harvard University Press.

Rosengren, K. E., Wenner, L. A., & Palmgreen, P. (Eds.). (1985). *Media gratifications research: Current perspectives*. Beverly Hills, CA: Sage.

Steiner, G. A. (1963). *The people look at television*. New York: Alfred A. Knopf.

Webster, J. G., & Phalen, P. F. (1997). *The mass audience: Rediscovering the dominant model*. Mahwah, NJ: Lawrence Erlbaum Associates.

Zillmann, D., & Bryant, J. (Eds.). (1985). *Selective exposure to communication*. Hillsdale, NJ: Lawrence Erlbaum Associates.

Zillmann, D., & Vorderer, P. (2000). *Media entertainment: The psychology of its appeal*. Mahwah, NJ: Lawrence Erlbaum Associates.

Audience Ratings:
Analysis of Gross Measures

In the preceding chapters, we outlined the many uses of audience research, described how audience data are collected and reported, and offered a general framework for understanding audience behavior. It should be clear that many questions can be asked and answered using audience research techniques. However, as we noted in the first chapter, for many people who deal with electronic media, "audience research" means nothing more than ratings research. While that view is certainly not held by everyone in the business, it is true that no other form of audience research so dominates the industry. For this reason, we have focused on the systems for generating audience ratings. In the last two chapters we discuss some specific analytical techniques that are used with ratings data.

While ratings are a fairly straightforward type of audience research, they can be analyzed in many ways. In fact, the practice of ratings analysis may be constrained more by the skill and imagination of analysts than by limitations inherent in the data. Describing common analytical techniques, as we do in chapters 10 and 11, runs the risk of discouraging creative ways of looking at the data. That is certainly not our intent. Anyone with an understanding of audiences and a basic knowledge of quantitative research methods has the tools to analyze ratings information.

There are, however, some advantages to becoming familiar with the most common techniques of ratings analysis. First, you do not have to reinvent the wheel. Techniques have been tested, and their strengths and limitations are better known. Second, standardization of analytical techniques has many benefits. Comparisons of one sort or another play an important part in ratings analysis. If everyone calculated the cost of reaching the audience differently, meaningful comparisons would be difficult or impossible to make, thus limiting the utility of the analysis. Standardization can help us build a systematic body of knowledge about audiences and their role in the operation of the electronic media. If one study can be directly related to the next, progress and/or dead ends can be more readily identified.

In chapter 9 we discussed gross and cumulative measurements. Following this distinction, we have organized analytical techniques into two chapters—those that deal with gross measures, and those dealing with cumulative measures. We recognize that this distinction is not always obvious. Analyses of one sort are often coupled with the other; and there can be strict mathematical relationships between the two. However, this scheme of organization can help the reader manage a potentially bewildering assortment of ways to manipulate the data.

Within each chapter, we go from the least complicated analytical techniques to the most complicated. Unfortunately, as we make this progression, our language becomes increasingly complex and arcane, but we try to keep the technical jargon to a minimum. The majority of analytical techniques described in each chapter require only an understanding of simple arithmetic. Some, however, involve the use of multivariate statistics.

GROSS MEASURES

Gross measures can be thought of as snapshots of the audience taken at a point in time. Included in this category are the measures themselves (e.g., ratings and shares), any subsequent manipulations of those measures (e.g., totaling GRPs), or analyses of the measures using additional data (e.g., calculating CPPs). Excluded from this category are audience measurements that require tracking individual audience members over time.

Throughout the book, we have made frequent use of terms like *ratings* and *share*. Although basic definitions of these terms were provided in chapter 2, they ignored a good many nuances that an analyst should know. In fact, it is important to recognize that these measures are themselves a kind of first-order data analysis. Ratings, shares, and gross audience projections are all the result of mathematical operations being applied to the database.

Projected audiences are the most basic gross measurements of the audience. In this context "projection" means going from the sample to an estimate of what is happening in the population. It should not be confused with predicting future audiences. These projections are estimates of absolute audience size, intended to answer the question, "How many people watched or listened ... ?" Audience projections can be made for specific programs, specific stations, or for all those using a medium at any point in time. Projections can be made for households, persons, or various subsets of the audience (e.g., how many men ages 18 to 49 watched the news). Most of the numbers reported in a ratings book are simply estimates of absolute audience size.

Projections are made from samples. The most straightforward method of projection is to determine the proportion of the sample using a program, station, or medium, and multiply that by the size of the population. For example, if we wanted to know how many households watched Program Z, we would look at the sample, note that 20% watched Z, and multiply that by the estimated number of TV households in the market, say 100,000. The projected number of TVHH watching Program Z would therefore be 20,000. That proportion is, of course, a rating. Hence, projected audiences can be derived by the following equation:

RATING (%) × POPULATION = PROJECTED AUDIENCE

For many years, this was the approach Nielsen used with its metered samples. It assumed that the in-tab sample, without further adjustments, adequately represented the population. Today, as Nielsen folds local peoplemeters (LPM) into its national sample to boost sample size, it weights respondents accordingly—a methodological fix that has been standard operating procedure in audience measurement for years. You will recall that in-tab diary samples tend to over-represent some groups and under-represent others. In such instances, it is common to weight the responses of under-represented groups more heavily than others. The specific variables used for purposes of weighting and the way these weights are combined varies from market to market. The end result is that the weighted responses of households or individuals, commonly expressed as households per diary value (HPDV) or persons per diary value (PPDV), are combined to project audience size. Unlike the simple procedure described previously, here projected audiences must be determined before ratings. In fact, if sample weighting or balancing is used, audience projections are actually used to calculate a rating, not vice versa.

We saw in chapter 8 that audience projections for radio tell you how many hundreds of people listened to a station in an average quarter hour. The total number of people listening to radio without regard to stations is called persons using radio (PUR). In television, audiences are typically associated with specific programs in specific quarter hours. Depending on the unit of analysis, the total size of the TV audience is called households using television (HUT) or persons using television (PUT). All of these numbers express the absolute size of the audience at a single or average point in time.

Audience projections, used in the context of advertising, will sometimes be added to produce a number called gross audience or *gross impressions*. This is a summation of program or station audiences across different points in time. Those points in time are usually defined by an advertiser's schedule of spots. Table 10.1 is a simple example of how gross impressions, for women ages 18 to 49, would be determined for a commercial message that aired at four different times.

Gross impressions are just like GRPs, except they are expressed as a whole number rather than percentage points. They provide a crude measure of the total audience exposure to a particular message or campaign. They do not take frequency of exposure or audience duplication into account. As a result, 10,000 gross impressions might mean that 10,000 people saw a message once, or 1,000 people saw it 10 times.

Ratings are the most familiar of all gross measures of the audience. Unlike projected audience, they express the size of the audience as a percent-

TABLE 10.1
Determining Gross Impressions

Spot availability	Audience of women ages 18–49
Monday, 10am	2,500
Wednesday, 11am	2,000
Thursday, 4pm	3,500
Friday, 9pm	1,500
Total (Gross Impressions)	9,500

age of the total population, rather than a whole number. The simplest calculation for a rating, therefore, is to divide a station or program audience by the total potential audience. In practice, the "%" is understood, so a program with 20% of the audience is said to have a rating of 20.

The potential audience on which a rating is based can vary. Household ratings for the broadcast networks are based on all U.S. households equipped with television (TVHH). But ratings can also be based on people, or different categories of people. Local market reports have station ratings for different market areas, like DMA and metro ratings. Some national cable networks will base their ratings not on all TVHH, or even all cable households, but only on those homes that can receive a network's programming. Although there is a rationale for doing that, such variation can affect our interpretation of the data. A ratings analyst should, therefore, be aware of the potential audience on which a rating is based.

In addition to these distinctions, there are several different kinds of ratings calculations. These are summarized in Table 10.2. To simplify the wording in the table, everything is described in terms of television, with TV households (TVHH) as the unit of analysis. Radio ratings, and TV ratings using persons as the unit of analysis, would be just the same, except they would use slightly different terminology (e.g., PUR vs. HUT).

The most narrowly defined audience rating is the average audience rating reported by NTI, Nielsen's national service. This rating expresses the size of the audience in an average minute, within a given quarter hour. To obtain that level of precision, metering devices must be used. As a result, this sort of rating cannot be reported for diary-based data.

Also summarized in Table 10.2 are calculations for GRPs and HUT levels. These are analogous to gross impressions and HUTs, respectively. They carry essentially the same information as those projections of audience size, but they are expressed as percentages instead of whole numbers. They are also subject to the same interpretive limitations as their counterparts. Reporting HUT or PUT as percentages means they are a kind of rating. To avoid confusion, we will refer to them as such. In

TABLE 10.2
Ratings Computations[a]

Basic rating (R)

$$R(\%) = \frac{\text{TVHH watching program or station}}{\text{Total TVHH}}$$

Quarter-hour rating (QH)

$$QH = \frac{\text{TVHH watching more than 5 minutes in a quarter hour}}{\text{Total TVHH}}$$

Average quarter-hour rating (AQH)

$$AQH = \frac{\text{Sum of quarter hour ratings}}{\text{Number of quarter hours}}$$

Average audience rating[b] (AA)

$$AA = \frac{\text{Total minutes all TVHH spend watching a program}}{\text{Program duration in minutes X total TVHH}}$$

Total Audience Rating (TA)

$$TA = \frac{\text{TVHH watching program for more than 5 minutes}}{\text{Total TVHH}}$$

HUT rating (HR)

$$HR = \frac{\text{Projected HUT level}}{\text{Total TVHH}}$$

Gross rating points (GRP)

$$GRP = R_1 + R_2 + R_3 + R_4 + R_5 \ldots + R_n$$

[a]The precise method for computing a rating depends on whether the responses of sample members are differentially weighted. When they are, program audiences must be projected and then divided by the total estimated population. When the responses of sample members are not weighted, or have equal weights, proportions within the sample itself determine the ratings and subsequent audience projections.

[b]In this computation, the number of minutes each TVHH spends watching a program is totaled across all TVHH. This is divided by the total possible number of minutes that could have been watched, as determined by multiplying program duration in minutes by total TVHH. AA can also be reported for specific quarter hours within the program, in which case the denominator is 15 × total TVHH.

practice, however, these percentages are usually called HUTs or PUTs, without appending the word "rating."

Shares, the third major measure, express audience size as a percentage of those using the medium at a point in time. The basic equation for determining audience share among TV households is:

$$\frac{\text{\# OF TVHH TUNED TO STATION OR PROGRAM}}{\text{HUT LEVEL}} = \text{SHARE}$$

The calculation of person shares is exactly the same, except persons and PUT levels are in the numerator and denominator, respectively. In either case, the rating and share of a given program or station have the same number in the numerator. The difference is in the denominator. HUT or PUT levels are always less than the total potential audience, so a program's share will always be larger than its rating.

Like ratings, audience shares can be determined for various subsets of the total audience. Unlike ratings, however, shares are of somewhat limited value in buying and selling audiences. Although shares indicate performance relative to the competition, they do not convey information about actual size of the audience, and that is what advertisers are most often interested in. The only way that a share can reveal information about total audience size is when it is related to its associated HUT level, as follows:

$$\text{PROGRAM SHARE} \times \text{HUT} = \text{PROJECTED PROGRAM AUDIENCE}$$

or

$$\text{PROGRAM SHARE} \times \text{HUT RATING} = \text{PROGRAM RATING}$$

Audience shares can also be calculated over periods of time longer than program lengths. In ratings books, for example, audience shares are often reported for entire dayparts. When long-term average share calculations are made, the preferred method is to derive the average quarter hour (AQH) share from the average quarter hour rating within the same daypart. The following equation summarizes how such a daypart share might be calculated with TV data:

$$\frac{\text{AQH Rating}}{\text{AQH HUT Rating}} = \text{AQH Share}$$

Unlike AQH ratings, it is not appropriate to calculate AQH shares by adding a station's audience share in each quarter hour, and dividing by the number of quarter hours. That is because each audience share has a different denominator, and it would distort the average to give them equal weight.

Defining audience size in these ways presents some interesting problems. Many of them occur when households are the unit of analysis. We noted in chapter 9 that most homes have more than one television set. Suppose that a household is watching two different programs on different sets. To which station should that home be attributed? Standard practice in the ratings business is to credit the household to the audiences of both stations. In other words, it counts in the calculation of each station's household rating and share. However, it will only be allowed to count once in the calculation of HUT levels. This means that the sum of all program ratings can exceed the HUT rating, and the sum of all program shares can exceed 100. This was an insignificant problem in the early days of TV because most homes had only one television set. But now over three fourths of all homes have multiple sets.

Because households are typically collections of two or more people, household ratings tend to be higher than person ratings. Imagine, for example, that some market has 100 homes, with four people living in each. Suppose that one person in each household was watching Station Z. That would mean that Station Z had a TVHH rating of 100 and a person rating of 25. Some programs, like "family shows," do better at attracting groups of viewers, whereas others garner more solitary viewing. It is, therefore, worth keeping an eye on discrepancies between household and person ratings, because differences between the two can be substantial.

Even when people are the unit of analysis, aberrations in audience size can occur. Most ratings services require that a person be in a program or quarter hour audience for at least 5 minutes in order to be counted. That means it is quite possible for a person to be in two programs in a quarter hour, or to show up in several program audiences of longer duration. This creates a problem analogous to multiple set use at the household level. In the olden days, when person ratings could only be made with diaries, and people had to get up to change the channel, it wasn't much of a problem. Today, with peoplemeters tracking a population that has remote control devices and dozens of channels from which to choose, the potential for viewers to show up in more than one program audience is considerably greater.

As if this were not complicated enough, technology is now drawing into question the very act of viewing itself. Nielsen has, for some time, credited people who taped a program with their VCR to the program audience, and simply noted the size of the VCR contribution. In effect, to tape a program was to watch it. Of course, many taped programs are never watched. But the total amount of taping was so limited that no one was particularly concerned. With DVR sales on the rise, however, the definition of viewing becomes problematic. DVR users can time-shift within a program on a near-live basis or stockpile content for later viewing. Nielsen will segregate all time-shifted viewing, even if a viewer pauses for a few seconds; any recorded material that is actually played within a 7-day period can be added back into the audience, producing a "live plus" rating. While syndicators have used ratings compiled from multiple airings for years, this type of system is new to networks. Obviously it has the potential to alter our understanding of "overnights" and even fundamental concepts like ratings, HUTs, and shares.

The most common way to extend the data reported in a typical ratings book is to introduce information on the cost of reaching the audience. Cost calculations are an important tool for those who must buy and sell media audiences. There are two such calculations in wide use, and both are based on manipulations of gross audience measurements.

Cost per thousand (CPM), as the name implies, tells you how much it costs to reach 1,000 members of a target audience. It is a yardstick that can be used to compare stations or networks with different audiences and different rate structures. The standard formula for computing CPMs is:

$$\frac{\text{COST OF SPOT (\$)} \times 1000}{\text{PROJECTED TARGET AUDIENCE}} = \text{CPM}$$

The projected target audience is expressed as a whole number. It could simply be the number of households delivered by the spot in question, or it could also be men ages 18 to 49, working women, teens ages 12 to 17, and so on. CPMs can be calculated for whatever audience is most relevant to the advertiser, as long as the ratings data can be calculated to project that audience. Occasionally, when a large number of spots are running, it is more convenient to compute the average CPM for the schedule in the following way:

$$\frac{\text{COST OF SCHEDULE (\$)} \times 1000}{\text{TARGET GROSS IMPRESSIONS}} = \text{AVERAGE CPM}$$

CPMs are the most widely used measure of the advertising media's cost efficiency. They can be calculated to gauge relative costs within a medium, or used to make comparisons across different media. In print, for example, the cost of a black-and-white page or a newspaper's line rate, is divided by its circulation or the number of readers it delivers. In chapter 4 we presented CPM trends across radio, television, and print media. Comparisons within a medium are generally easier to interpret than intermedia comparisons. As long as target audiences are defined in the same way, CPMs do a good job of revealing which spot is more cost efficient. There is less agreement on what is the magazine equivalent of a 30-second spot.

The electronic media have a unique form of cost calculation called cost per point (CPP). Like CPM, it is a yardstick for making cost efficiency comparisons, except here the unit of measurement is not thousands of audience members, but ratings points. CPP is computed as follows:

$$\frac{\text{COST OF SPOT (\$)}}{\text{TARGET AUDIENCE RATING}} = \text{CPP}$$

An alternative method for calculating CPP can be used when a large number of spots are being run and an average CPP is of more interest than the efficiency of any one commercial. This is sometimes called the cost per gross ratings point (CPGRP), and it is calculated as follows:

$$\frac{\text{COST OF SCHEDULE (\$)}}{\text{GROSS RATING POINTS}} \quad = \quad \text{CPGRP}$$

As you know by now, there are different kinds of ratings. In network television, average audience ratings (AA) are preferred for CPP computations because they more accurately express the size of the audience at the moment a spot is run. For ratings based on diary data, a quarter-hour rating is used. Television market reports also estimate station break ratings by averaging quarter hours before and after the break. This procedure gives buyers an estimate for the time closest to when a spot actually runs.

CPP measures are part of the everyday language of people who specialize in broadcast advertising. Stations' representatives, and the media buyers with whom they deal, often conduct their negotiations on a CPP basis. This measure of cost efficiency has the additional advantage of relating directly to GRPs, which are commonly used to define the size of an advertising campaign. CPPs, however, have two limiting characteristics that affect their use and interpretation.

First, they are simply less precise than CPMs. Ratings points are rarely carried beyond one decimal place. They must, therefore, be rounded. Rounding off network audiences in this way can add or subtract tens of thousands of people from the audience, causing an unnecessary reduction in the accuracy of cost calculations. Second, ratings are based on different potential audiences. We would expect the CPP in New York to be more than it is in Louisville because each point represents many more people. But how many more? CPMs are calculated on the same base—1,000 households or persons—so they can be used for inter-market comparisons. Even within a market, problems can crop up when using CPP. Radio stations whose signals may cover only part of a market should be especially alert to CPP buying criteria. It is quite possible, for example, that one station delivers most of its audience within the metropolitan area, whereas another has an audience of equal size located mostly outside the metropolis. If CPPs in the market are based on metropolitan ratings, the second station could be at an unfair and unnecessary disadvantage.

Comparisons

Comparing the gross measures we have just reviewed is the most common form of ratings analysis. There are an endless number of comparisons that can be made. Some might show the superiority of one station over another, the relative cost efficiency of different advertising media, or the success of one program format as opposed to another. There are certainly more of these than we can catalog in this chapter. We can, however, provide illustrative examples of comparisons that may be useful in buying or selling time and programs, or simply reaching a better understanding of the electronic media and their audiences.

One area of comparison deals with the size and composition of the available audience. You know from chapter 9 that the nature of the available audience is a powerful determinant of station or program audiences. Therefore, an analyst might want to begin by taking a closer look at who is watching or listening at different times. This kind of analysis could certainly be of interest to a programmer who must be cognizant of the ebb and flow of different audience segments when deciding what programs to run. It might also be of value to an advertiser or media buyer who wants to know when a certain kind of audience is most available. The most straightforward method of comparison is to graph the size of various audience segments at different hours throughout the day.

As we noted earlier, the single most important factor affecting the size of broadcast audiences is when people are available to listen. Work hours, school, commuting, and meal times, as well as seasons of the year, are the strongest influences on when people are available and potentially interested in using mass media. There are no regular surveys that provide detailed information on such availabilities, but several older studies can be reconstructed to give a rough idea of the availability of men, women, teens, and children throughout the day (see Fig. 10.1A).

Holidays, special events, and coverage of especially important news stories can certainly alter these patterns of availability, but as a rule they translate rather directly into the patterns of media use depicted in Fig. 10.1B. The instances when a single program, or big event, has influenced a rise in HUTs are relatively rare. The most famous such occasions were the assassination of President Kennedy, men landing on the moon, the verdict in the O. J. Simpson trial, and the events of 9/11.

With few exceptions, though, the best indicator of how many people will use media at any given time is existing reports of total audience size. Any new program or network that plans to find an audience among those who are not already listening or viewing is very unlikely to be successful. New programs, formats, and program services, for the most part, divide the existing potential and available audiences into smaller pieces of the pie rather than cause new viewers to tune in. The most obvious evidence of this is the recent decline in national network share due to the increasing number of cable and DBS competitors.

Thus, to plot when various audience segments are using a medium in a market is a valuable starting point for the audience analyst. Radio market reports have a section of daypart audience estimates with people using radio (PUR) levels, as well as different station audiences. Television

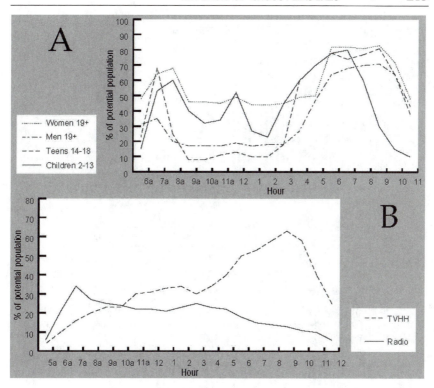

FIG. 10.1. Hypothetical audience availabilities and typical patterns of radio and television use.

reports typically estimate audiences by the quarter hour or the half hour. For illustration purposes, Fig. 10.2 shows radio listening—at home, at work, and in cars—for three different gender-age categories.

These data paint rather different pictures of radio and television use for each demographic group. Note especially the amount of radio use by working men on the job and in their vehicles. For teens, while school is in session there is very little daytime listening but a lot at night. Older people are heavy radio users who listen mostly at home. The distinct patterns of radio use clarify the parameters within which the programmer must operate.

Advertisers, of course, must eventually commit to buying time on specific stations or networks. To do so, they need to determine the most effective way to reach their target audience. This relatively simple requirement can trigger a torrent of ratings comparisons. From the time buyer's perspective, the comparisons should be responsive to the advertiser's need to reach a certain kind of audience in a cost efficient manner. From the seller's perspective, the comparisons should also show his or

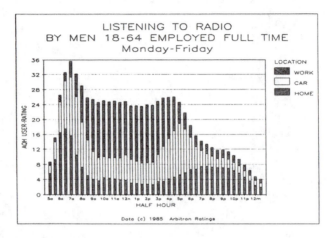

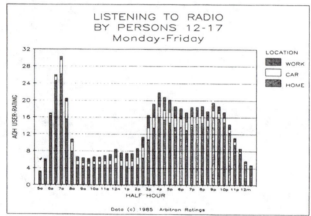

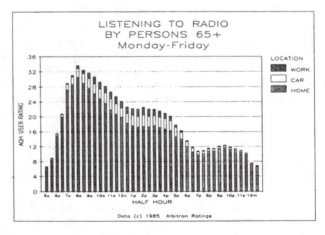

FIG. 10.2. Comparison of radio use by location.

216

her audiences in the best possible light. Although these two objectives are not mutually exclusive, they can cause audience analysts to look at ratings data in different ways.

The simplest form of ratings analysis is to compare station or program audiences in terms of their size. This can be determined by ranking each program, station, or network by its average rating and, in effect, declaring a winner. One need only glance at the trade press to get a sense of how important it is to be "Number 1" by some measure. Of course, not everyone can be Number 1. Further, buying time on the top-rated station may not be the most effective way to spend an advertising budget. Comparisons of audience size are typically qualified by some consideration of audience composition.

The relevant definition of audience composition is usually determined by an advertiser. An avail request, for instance, will usually specify the target audience in demographics. If the advertiser has a primary audience of women ages 18 to 24, it would make sense for the analyst to rank programs by ratings among women 18 to 24 rather than by total audience size. In all probability, this would produce a different rank ordering of programs, and perhaps even a different Number 1 program. For radio stations, which often specialize in a certain demographic, ranking within audience subsets can allow several stations to claim they are Number 1.

At this point, we should emphasize a problem in ratings analysis about which researchers are quite sensitive. Analysis or comparison of audience subsets reduces the actual sample size on which those comparisons are based. Casual users can easily ignore or forget this because published ratings seem so authoritative once the ink on the page has dried or the numbers have been downloaded to a desktop computer. But remember that ratings estimates are subject to sampling error, and the amount of error increases as the sample size decreases. That means, for instance, that the difference between being Number 1 and Number 2 among men ages 18 to 24 might be a chance occurrence rather than a real difference. A researcher in this case would say the difference was not statistically significant. The same phenomenon produces what people in the industry call *bounce*, which is defined as a change in station ratings from one book to the next that is a result of a sampling error rather than any real change in the station's audience size. An analyst should never be impressed by small differences, especially those based on small samples.

Having so cautioned, we must also point out that comparisons are sometimes made using statistics other than sheer audience size. Ratings data can be adjusted in a way that highlights audience composition, and then ranked. This may produce very different rank orderings. There are two common techniques used to make these adjustments.

Indexing is a common way to make comparisons across scores. An index number simply expresses an individual score, like a rating or CPM, relative to some standard or base value. The basic formula for creating index numbers is as follows:

$$\frac{\text{Score} \times 100}{\text{Base Value}} = \text{Index Number}$$

Usually the base value is fixed at a point in time to give the analyst an indication of how some variable is changing. Current CPMs, for instance, are often indexed to their levels in an earlier year. Base values have been determined in other ways as well. Suppose a program had a high rating among women ages 18 to 24, but a low rating overall. An index number could be created by using the overall rating as a base value. That would make the target audience rating look strong by comparison. CPM indices are also created by comparing individual market CPMs to an average CPM across markets (see Poltrack, 1983).

Thus far, we have defined target audiences only in terms of two demographic variables: age and gender. These are the segmentation variables most commonly used to specify an advertiser's audience objectives. Age and gender, of course, may not be the most relevant descriptors of an advertiser's target market. Income, buying habits, lifestyle, and a host of other variables might be of critical importance to someone buying advertising time. Target audiences defined in those terms make effective sales tools. Unfortunately, this kind of specialized information is not reported in ratings books.

We noted in chapter 8 that ratings services are capable of producing customized ratings reports. The widespread use of personal computers and Internet access to databases has made this sort of customization increasingly common. As a consequence, it is now possible to describe audiences in ways that are not reported on the printed page of a ratings book.

For example, ratings services keep track of the zip code in which each member of the sample lives. Zip code information is valued because knowing where a person lives can reveal a great deal about that individual. Inferences can be made about household incomes, occupations, ethnicity, education levels, lifestyles, and so on. As long as sample sizes are sufficiently large, these inferences will be reasonably accurate on average. In fact, some companies, like Claritas, specialize in analyzing zip code areas and grouping those with similar characteristics. The use of this *geodemography* means that audiences can be defined and compared in a virtually unlimited number of ways.

Of course, these audience comparisons alone will not necessarily convince an advertiser to buy time. As with any product for sale, no matter how useful or nicely packaged, the question usually comes down to how much it costs. In this context, CPM and CPP comparisons are critical. Such comparisons might be designed to illuminate the efficiency of buying one program, station, or daypart as opposed to another. Table 10.3 compares CPMs for network and spot television across several

TABLE 10.3

Cost-per-Thousand Homes Reached Trends for Network and Spot TV 30-Second Units (1975–2004)

	1975	1980	1985	1990	1995a	2000b	2001	2002	2003	2004
Network TV										
Daytime	$0.94	$1.81	$2.69	$2.46	$3.32	$4.35	$4.30	$3.70	$4.04	$4.59
Early news	1.27	2.23	3.94	5.41	5.72	5.89	5.91	5.06	5.06	5.85
Prime evening	2.39	3.79	6.52	9.74	8.79	13.42	15.07	16.79	15.31	19.85
Late evening	1.16	2.70	3.45	6.97	6.43	9.15	9.38	9.40	10.83	10.87
Spot TVc										
Daytime	NA	NA	3.32	4.07	4.16	6.34	6.80	5.82	5.61	5.54
Early news	NA	NA	4.81	5.73	6.75	11.35	10.49	9.36	9.61	10.35
Prime Access	NA	NA	NA	NA	NA	14.77	12.94	11.92	12.36	14.14
Prime time	NA	NA	10.01	11.56	13.36	24.55	26.79	26.79	24.38	27.27
Late news	NA	NA	7.83	8.12	10.40	15.49	17.52	15.79	16.15	16.91
Late fringe	NA	NA	5.24	6.27	6.76	11.53	11.65	9.86	10.00	10.00

Note. Data are from the Television Bureau of Advertising. Reprinted by permission of Magna Global USA.

aIncludes FOX.

bIncludes WB, UPN, & Pax.

cTop 100 markets.

dayparts, and indicates how these costs have changed over time. Note that gaining access to 1,000 homes during daytime is relatively cheap, while the same unit costs several times more during prime time. CPM levels for cable networks are generally lower.

Programmers use rating and share comparisons as well. Consider, for example, how they might use zip codes to segment and compare audiences. A radio station might compare its ratings across zip code areas within a market to determine whether ratings are highest in areas with the highest concentration of likely listeners. If a station places a strong signal over an area with the kind of population that should like its format, but has few listeners, special promotions might be called for. One station that used this kind of analysis placed outdoor advertising and conducted a series of remote broadcasts in the areas where it was underperforming.

Radio programmers may also find it useful to represent the audience for each station in the market on a special *demographic map*. This can be done by creating a two-dimensional grid, with the vertical axis expressing, for example, the percent of males in each station's audience, and the horizontal axis expressing the median age of the audience. Once these values are known, each station can be located on the grid. The station audiences could also be averaged in order to map formats rather than individual stations. Local radio market reports contain the information needed to determine these values, although a few preliminary calculations are necessary.

The most difficult calculation is determining the median age of each station's audience. The median is a descriptive statistic, much like an arithmetic average. Technically, it is the point at which half the cases in a distribution are higher and half are lower. If, for example, 50% of a station's audience is younger than 36, and 50% are older, then 36 is the median age.

To determine the median age of a station's audience, you must know the audience size of individual age categories reported by the ratings service. Table 10.4 contains this data for a single station in a single daypart as well as the estimated numbers of men and women who are listening. The station has 43,200 listeners in an AQH. Because radio books report audiences in hundreds, it is more convenient to record that as 432 in the table. The number of listeners 65+ must be inferred from the difference between the total audience 12+, and the sum of all other categories (i.e., 432 – 408 = 24).

The median can now be located in the following way. First, figure out the cumulative frequency. This is shown in the column on the far right-hand side of the table. Second, divide the total size of the audience in half. In this case, it is 216 (i.e., 432/2 = 216). Third, look at the cumulative distribution and find the age category in which the 216th case falls. We know that 206 people are 34.5 or younger, and that there are 103 people in the next oldest group. Therefore, the 216th case must be between 34.5 and 44.5. Fourth, locate the 216th case by interpolating

ge group. To do that, assume that the ages of the 103 peo-
roup are evenly distributed. To locate the median, we must
es deep into the next age group. Stated differently, we need
3 of the way into a 10-year span. That translates into .97
0/103 × 10 = .97). Add that to the lower limit of the cate-
ingo, the median age is 35.47 (i.e., 34.5 + .97 = 35.47).
cedure sounds more burdensome than it really is. Once you
ng of it, it can be done with relative ease. It is simply a way to
reat deal of information about the age of the station's audi-
a single number. Similarly, the gender of the audience is re-
a single number by using the male/female breakdowns in each
In the example just given, 48% of the audience was male.
o numbers could become coordinates that allow us to plot a
a two-dimensional grid. Figure 10.3 shows how stations with
formats would look on a demographic map of radio stations.

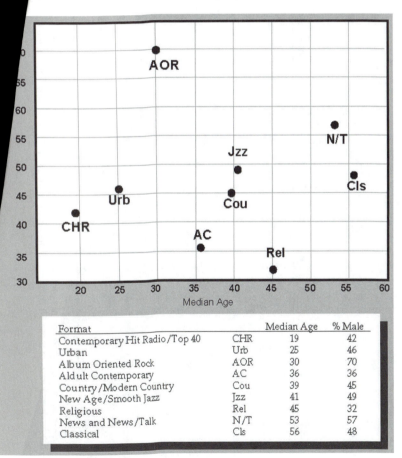

Format		Median Age	% Male
Contemporary Hit Radio/Top 40	CHR	19	42
Urban	Urb	25	46
Album Oriented Rock	AOR	30	70
Aldult Contemporary	AC	36	36
Country/Modern Country	Cou	39	45
New Age/Smooth Jazz	Jzz	41	49
Religious	Rel	45	32
News and News/Talk	N/T	53	57
Classical	Cls	56	48

FIG. 10.3.   Demographic map of radio stations.

TABLE 10.4

Calculating Median Age and Gender of Station Audience

Age Group	Male (in 00s)	Female (in 00s)	Group frequency (in 00s)	Cumulative frequency (in 00s)
12–17	?	?	23	23
18–24	29	50	79	102
25–34	63	41	104	206
35–44	43	60	103	309
45–54	35	27	62	
55–64	20	17	37	
65+	8	16	?	
Total 12+	?	?		
Total 18+	198	211		
Percent M–F[a]	48%			

[a]Because radio market repor
determined on the

Figure 10.3 is a fairly typical array of formats and the audiences associated with each one. As you can see, formats can vary widely in terms of the type of listener they attract. Both an album rock station and a contemporary hits station will tend to have young listeners, but they typically appeal differently to young men and women. A classical station tends to attract older listeners. Music syndicators often package radio formats designed to appeal to very specific demographics, and the pronounced differences in audience composition explain how different stations can be Number 1 with different categories of listeners.

This kind of demographic mapping can be used by programmers in a number of ways. For example, it can help identify "holes" in the market by drawing attention to underserved segments of the population. It can also offer a different way to look at the positioning of stations in a market, and how they do or do not compete for the same type of listeners. By creating maps for different dayparts, the programmer can look for shifts in audience composition.

A number of cautions in the interpretation of the map should, however, be kept in mind. First, it tells the analyst nothing about the size of the potential audiences involved. There may be a hole in the market because there are relatively few people of a particular type. Some markets, for example, have very old populations, others do not. Similarly, the map reports no information on the size of the station's actual audience, only its composition. Second, the analyst should remember that different types of listeners may be more valuable to advertisers, and hence constitute a more desirable audience. This could be attributable to their demographic composition, or the fact that many listen exclusively to their favorite station. Third, just because two or more stations occupy the same space on the map, it does not mean that they will share an audience. A country/western station and a public radio station will often fall side-by-side on a map, but typically they have very little crossover audience. The tendency of listeners to move back and forth between stations can be more accurately studied by using the audience duplication section of the ratings book. We discuss such cumulative measurements later. Finally, remember that age and gender are not the only factors that might be related to station preferences. The map could look quite different if ethnicity or education were among the dimensions. Just such a map can be constructed when other demographic variables, such as education and income, are available.

Median age can also be a useful way to differentiate among television program sources. Table 10.5 shows a comparison of six broadcast networks on the median age of their audiences. Newer networks have programmed aggressively to younger demographics. The WB's prime time audience has a median age of only 33 years, and UPN and Fox have successfully appealed to audiences with an average age in the mid-30s. The more established networks, particularly CBS, are attracting older viewers. Cable networks show an even wider range of median ages. Nickelodeon's prime time audience is 11.2, MTV's is 22.2. As you might

TABLE 10.5

Prime Time Median Age by Network

	ABC	CBS	NBC	FOX	UPN	WB
1999/00	43.4	52.4	45.2	35.2	32.8	28.7
2000/01	46.6	51.2	45.1	36.0	34.1	29.1
2001/02	46.0	51.7	45.9	36.0	34.2	31.2
2002/03	43.6	52.2	46.2	35.0	33.1	31.0
2003/04	45.3	52.6	45.9	36.4	34.2	33.4

Note. Data are from Steve Sternberg (2004), *Median Age Report,* MAGNA Global USA. Reprinted by permission. Analysis of copyrighted Nielsen Media Research Data.

expect, news networks occupy the other end of the spectrum. The FOX News prime time audience is 61.2, and CNN's is over 65. Similarly, median ages are also calculated for specific TV programs.

Ratings comparisons are also made longitudinally, over several points in time. In fact, most local market ratings reports will include data from previous sweeps under the heading of ratings trends. There could be any number of reasons for looking at audience trends. A radio programmer might want to determine how a format change had altered the composition of the station's audience, perhaps producing a series of maps like Fig. 10.3. A financial analyst might want to examine the ratings history of a particular media property. A policymaker or economist might want to study patterns of audience diversion to assess the competitive positions of old and new media.

Modern metering devices also permit what might be called a "micro-longitudinal" study of audiences. Instead of comparing gross measures over a period of weeks or months, the analyst can assess audience behavior on a second-by-second basis. We noted in chapter 7 that DVRs, like those sold by TiVo Inc., could become the functional equivalent of household meters—capturing what a group of television sets are looking at moment to moment. Figure 10.4 is a report of how TiVo users watched Super Bowl XXXVIII on an aggregate, anonymous basis. The horizontal axis is the time dimension, showing each second of the telecast. The vertical axis, labeled "Percent of Audience In Play Speed," is the number of times that each second was played divided by the number of subscribers tuned in. Because many TiVo users watched the game on a delayed basis, skipping over what they found uninteresting, the typical reading hovers just under 100%. The line spikes during amusing commercials or big plays as viewers replay the seconds in question. During halftime, Janet Jackson had her infamous "wardrobe malfunction." As you can see, it was replayed repeatedly. This is, perhaps in more ways

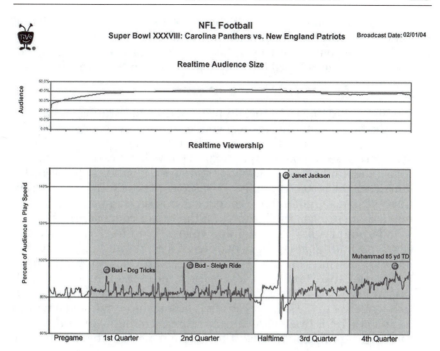

FIG. 10.4.   NFL Realtime Audience Size. Courtesy of TiVo Inc.

than one, a true "gross" measure of the audience because the spike could have been produced by many viewers or, in theory, just one fan re-watching the event thousands of times.

Aside from offering a footnote to popular culture, such micro-longitudinal studies of program audiences can be of value to advertisers and programmers alike. The former can assess the attention-grabbing power of their commercials or, conversely, the rate at which DVR users are skipping the ads altogether. The latter can look at the same information the way they use "program analyzer" data—identifying those parts of the show that people want to skip or see again and again.

As you can surely tell by now, there are any number of ways to manipulate and compare estimates of audience size and composition. In fact, because the major ratings services now produce electronic ratings books that are read by a computer, the time involved in sorting and ranking ratings data can be drastically reduced. As we noted in chapter 8, both Arbitron and Nielsen now sell software packages that will manipulate their data in a variety of ways. Some private vendors have also produced software that can turn ratings data into bar graphs, pie charts, and so on.

Although most of these developments are a boon to ratings analysts, a number of cautions should be exercised in either producing or consuming all the comparative statistics. Do not let the computational power or colorful graphics of these programs blind you to what you are actually dealing with. Remember that all gross measures of the audience are simply estimates based on sample information. Keep the following points in mind:

- Be alert to the size of the sample used to create a rating or make an audience projection. One consequence of zeroing in on a narrowly defined target audience is that the actual number of people on which estimates are based becomes quite small. That will increase the sampling error surrounding the audience estimates. A national peoplemeter sample might be big enough to break out the audience into narrow subsets. It does not follow that local market samples, which are smaller, can provide similar target estimates of equal accuracy.
- Techniques like indexing and calculating target efficiency can have you taking percentages of percentages, which tend to obscure the original values on which they are based. For example, comparing a 1.4 rating to a .7 rating produces the same index number (i.e., 200) as comparing a 14.0 to a 7.0. Sampling error, however, will be much larger relative to the smaller ratings. This means you should have less confidence in the first index value because even slight variations in its component parts could cause it to fluctuate wildly. The fact that the second index number is more reliable is not readily apparent with this sort of data reduction.
- Keep it simple. The ability to manipulate numbers in a multitude of ways does not necessarily mean that it is a good idea. This is true for two reasons. First, the more twists and turns there are in the analysis, the more likely you are to lose sight of what you are actually doing to the data. In other words, you are more likely to make a conceptual or computational error. Second, even if your work is flawless, more complex manipulations are harder to explain to the consumers of your research. You may understand how some special index was created, but that does not mean that a media buyer will have the time or inclination to sit through the explanation.

Prediction and Explanation

Most people schooled in quantitative research and theory are familiar with the concepts of prediction and explanation. In fact, the major reason for developing social scientific theory is to allow us to explain and/or predict the events we observe in the social world around us. In the context of ratings research, we can use the theories of audience behavior we developed in chapter 9 to help explain and predict gross measures of audience size and composition. Although prediction and explanation are certainly of interest to social theorists, they are not mere academic exercises. Indeed, predicting audience ratings is one of the principal activities of industry users.

It is important to remember that all ratings data are historical. They describe something that has already happened. It is equally important to remember that the buying and selling of audiences is always conducted in anticipation of future events. Although it is certainly useful to know which program had the largest audience last week, what really determines the allocation of advertising dollars is an expectation of who will have the largest audience next week or next season. Hence, ratings analysts who are involved in sales and advertising often spend a considerable portion of their time trying to predict ratings.

In the parlance of the industry, the job of predicting ratings is sometimes called pre-buy analysis (not to be confused with the pre-buy analyses done by financial planners and programmers when they evaluate a program acquisition). The buyer and seller of advertising time must each estimate the audience that will be delivered by a specific media schedule. The standard method of prediction is a two-stage process.

In the first stage, the analyst estimates the size of the total audience, as reflected in HUT or PUT levels, at the time a spot is to air. This is largely a matter of understanding audience availability. You will recall from our discussion in chapter 9 that total audience size is generally quite predictable. It varies by hour of the day, day of the week, and week of the year. It can also be affected by extremes in the weather (e.g., snow storms, heat waves, etc.), although these are obviously harder to know far in advance.

The simplest way to predict the total audience level for a future point in time is to assume it will be the same as it was exactly 1 year ago. This takes hourly, daily, and seasonal variations into account. A somewhat more involved procedure is to look at HUT/PUT over a period of months or years. By doing so, the analyst may identify long-term trends, or aberrations, in audience levels that would affect his or her judgment about future HUT levels. For instance, a 4-year average of HUT levels for a given hour, day, or month, might produce a more stable estimate of future HUTs than looking only at last year, which could have been atypical. In fact, to determine audience levels during months that are not measured, HUT levels should be interpolated by averaging data from sweeps before and after the month in question.

In the second stage, the analyst must project the share of audience that the station or program will achieve. Here, the simplest approach is to assume that an audience share will be the same as it was during the last measurement period. Of course, a number of factors can affect audience shares, and an analyst must take these into account. Programming changes can have a dramatic effect on audience shares. In radio, rival stations may have changed formats, making them more or less appealing to some segment of the market. In television, a competing station might be counter-programming more effectively than in the past. Less dramatic, long-term trends might also be at work. Perhaps cable penetration has caused a gradual erosion in audience shares that is likely to continue in the near future. Just as in estimating HUT levels, making comparisons across several measurement periods might reveal subtle shifts that would otherwise go unnoticed.

Once total audience levels and specific audience shares have been estimated, predicting an audience rating is simple. Multiply the HUT level you expect by the projected audience share, and you have a predicted rating. This formula is summarized as follows:

ESTIMATED HUT × PROJECTED SHARE (%) = PREDICTED RATING

In effect, it simply codifies the conventional wisdom expressed in Paul Klein's (1971) theory of the "least objectionable program." That is, exposure is best thought of as a two-stage process in which an already available audience decides which station or program to watch. The procedure to predict ratings for specific demographic subsets of the audience is the same, except that you must estimate the appropriate PUT level (e.g., men ages18 to 49) and determine the program's likely share among that audience subset. In either case, there are now a number of computer programs marketed by the ratings companies and independent vendors that perform such pre-buy analyses.

Although these formulas and computer programs are useful, remember that predicting audience ratings is not an exact science. It involves experience, intuition, and an understanding of the factors that affect audience size. Unfortunately, we can only offer help in the last category. Our advice would be to consider the model of audience behavior in chapter 9. Systematically work your way through the structural- and individual-level factors that are likely to affect audience size, and begin to test them against your own experience. Sometimes that will lead you to make modifications that just seem to work.

For instance, one of the most difficult and high-stakes occasions for predicting ratings occurs during the upfront market in network television. Major advertising agencies and network sales executives must try to anticipate how the fall line-ups will perform. This is especially tricky because new programs have no track record to depend on. At least one major agency has found, through experience, that it can predict network ratings more accurately if it bases those predictions not on total HUT levels, but on network-only HUT levels. In other words, the first stage in the process is to estimate the total number of viewers who will watch broadcast network television. Why this results in better predictions is not entirely clear.

Armed with share projections and predicted ratings for various segments of the audience, buyers and sellers negotiate a contract. Sellers are inclined to be optimistic about their ratings prospects, whereas buyers tend to be more conservative. In fact, the ratings projections that each brings to the table may be colored by the need to stake out a negotiating position. Eventually a deal is struck. Because most spot buys involve a schedule of several spots, the sum total of audience to be delivered is usually expressed in GRPs.

After a schedule of spots has run, both buyers and sellers want to know how well they did. Just as programmers and financial managers evaluate program buys, salespeople and buyers evaluate ratings predictions through a *post-buy analysis*. In markets that are continuously measured, it is possible to know exactly how well programs performed when a spot aired. Most local markets, however, are only surveyed during certain months. Consequently, precise data on ratings performance may not be available. Table 10.6 identifies the sweeps that are traditionally used for post-buy analysis in different months. The point is to use the best available data for evaluative purposes.

With the schedule of spots in one hand and the actual ratings in the other, the schedule is "re-rated." For example, it may be that the original contract anticipated 200 GRPs, but the actual audience delivered totaled 210 GRPs. If that is true, the media buyer did better than expected. Of course, the opposite could have occurred, resulting in an audience deficiency. In upfront deals, networks have traditionally made up such deficiencies by running extra spots. More often, however, it is simply the media buyer's bad luck.

Questions are often raised about how accurate ratings predictions are, or should be. The standard practice in the industry has been to view delivered audience levels within plus or minus 10% of the predicted levels as acceptable. There are three sources of error that can cause such discrepancies—forecasting error, strategic error, and sampling error. *Forecasting errors* are usually the first that come to mind. Included are errors of judgment and prediction. For example, the analyst might not have properly gauged a trend in HUT levels or foreseen the success of some programming strategy. *Strategic errors* are those errors deliberately introduced into the process at the time of contractual negotiations. A researcher might, for instance, honestly believe that a particular program will deliver a 10 rating while the person selling the program believes that it could be sold at 12 if a projection justified that number. To make a more profitable deal, the projection is knowingly distorted.

TABLE 10.6
Sweeps Used for Post-Buy Analysis[a]

February	January-February-March
May	April-May-June
July	July-August-September
November	October-November-December

[a]This schedule for post-buy analysis assumes the market is measured four times a year. Additional sweeps in January, March, and October would, if available, be used for post-buy analysis in January, March-April, and September-October, respectively.

Sampling error can also affect the accuracy of ratings predictions, and should serve to remind us once again that these numbers are simply estimates based on sample information. As we saw in chapter 7, any rating is associated with a certain amount of sampling error. The larger the sample on which the rating is based, the lower the associated error. In addition, the error surrounding small ratings tends to be rather large relative to the size of the rating itself. The same logic can be applied to a schedule of spots as expressed in GRPs. In the mid-1980s, Arbitron did an extensive study of the error (Jaffe, 1985) in GRP estimates. The principal conclusions were as follows:

•GRPs based on larger effective sample bases (ESB) had smaller standard errors. In effect, this means that GRPs based on large audience segments (e.g., men ages 18+) are more stable than those based on smaller segments (e.g., men ages 18 to 34). It also means that larger markets, which tend to have larger samples, will generally have less error than small markets.

•The higher the pairwise correlation between programs in the schedule, the higher the standard error. In other words, when there is a high level of audience duplication between spots in the schedule, there is a higher probability of error. This happens because high duplication implies that the same people tend to be represented in each program rating, thereby reducing the scope of the sample on which GRPs are based.

•For a given GRP level, a schedule with relatively few highly rated spots was less prone to error than a schedule with many low-rated spots.

•All things being equal, the larger the schedule in terms of GRPs, the larger the size of absolute standard error, but the smaller the size of relative standard error.

As a practical matter, all this means that a post-buy analysis is more likely to find results within the plus-or-minus 10% criterion if GRPs are based on relatively large segments of the market and programs or stations with relatively high ratings. A match of pre-buy predictions to post-buy ratings is less likely if GRPs are based on small ratings among small audience segments, even if forecasting and strategic error are nonexistent. As increased competition fragments radio and television audiences, and as advertisers try to target increasingly precise market segments, this problem of sampling error is likely to cause more post-buy results to fall outside the 10% range. For a thoughtful discussion of buying and selling predicted audiences, see Napoli (2003).

The method for predicting ratings we have described thus far is fairly straightforward, requires relatively little in the way of statistical manipulations, and depends heavily on intuition and expert judgment. There have, however, been a number of efforts to model program ratings in the form of mathematical equations. With either approach, the underlying theory of audience behavior is much the same. In attempts to model the ratings, however, many expert judgments are replaced by empirically determined, quantitative relationships.

Gensch and Shaman (1980) and Barnett, Chang, Fink, and Richards (1991) developed various models that accurately estimate the number of viewers of network television at any point in time. Consistent with our earlier discussions, they discovered that total audience size was not dependent on available program content but rather was a function of time of day and seasonality. Once the size of the available audience was predicted, the second stage in the process, determining each program's share of audience, was modeled independently. This is analogous to the standard method of prediction in the industry.

A number of writers have developed integrated models of viewer choice, considering factors such as lead-in effects, counter-programming, a program's rating history, program type, even the demographic characteristics of cast members (e.g., Cooper, 1993; Rust, Kamakura & Alpert, 1992; Shachar & Emerson, 2000; Weber, 2003; Webster & Phalen, 1997). In addition to these general predictive models, more specialized studies have also been done. Researchers have used correlational studies of gross audience measurements to assess the success of different programming strategies (e.g., Lin, 1995; McDowell & Dick, 2003; Tiedge & Ksobiech, 1986, 1987), to determine the cancellation threshold of network programs (Adams, 1993; Atkin & Litman, 1986), to assess the impact of media ownership on ratings performance (Parkman, 1982), and to examine the role of ratings in the evolution of television program content (McDonald & Schechter, 1988). In our judgment, these sorts of analyses represent a fertile area for further study.

RELATED READINGS

Balen, R. E. (1995). *The new rules of the ratings game*. Washington, DC: National Association of Broadcasters.

Katz, H. E. (2003). *The media handbook: A complete guide to advertising media selection, planning, research and buying* (2nd ed.). Mahwah, NJ: Lawrence Erlbaum Associates.

Napoli, P. M. (2003). *Audience economics: Media institutions and the audience marketplace*. New York: Columbia University Press.

Rust, R. T. (1986). *Advertising media models: A practical guide*. Lexington, MA: Lexington Books.

Sissors, J. Z., & Baron, R. B. (2002). *Advertising media planning* (6th ed.). Chicago: McGraw-Hill.

Surmanek, J. (2003). *Advertising media A to Z*. New York: McGraw Hill

Webster, J. G., & Phalen, P. F. (1997). *The mass audience: Rediscovering the dominant model*. Mahwah, NJ: Lawrence Erlbaum Associates.

Chapter 11

Audience Ratings:
Analysis of Cumulative Measures

Cumulative measures are the second kind of audience summary that a ratings analyst has to deal with. These measures of exposure are distinguished from gross measures because they depend on tracking individual audience members over some period of time. Although some cumulative measures are routinely reported by the ratings services, they are less common than the gross measurements we have just reviewed. Nevertheless, we believe that thoughtful analyses of cumulative measures can provide an analyst with considerable insights into the nature of audience behavior and its possible effects.

CUMULATIVE MEASURES

We begin our discussion with a review of common cumulative measurements of the audience. A few of these appear on the printed pages of ratings books. Several more are easily, and routinely, calculated from material contained in the books. Many other cumulative measurements are possible, but they require access to the appropriate database.

The most common cumulative measure of the audience is called a *cume*. A cume is the total number of different people or households who have tuned in to a station at least once over some period of time—usually a daypart, day, week, or even a month. The term *cume* is often used interchangeably with "reach" and "unduplicated audience." When a cume is expressed as a percentage of the total possible audience, it is called a *cume rating*. When it is expressed as the actual number of people, it is called *cume persons*. These audience summaries are analogous to the ratings and projected audiences we discussed in the previous section.

Like ordinary ratings and audience projections, variations on the basic definition are common. Cumes are routinely reported for different subsets of the audience, defined both demographically and geographically. For example, Arbitron reports a station's metropolitan cume ratings for men and women of different age categories. Cume persons can also be estimated within different areas of the market, like the Metro and DMA. Regardless of how the audience subset is defined, these numbers express the total, unduplicated audience for a station. Each person or household in the audience can only count once in figuring the cume. It does not matter whether they listened for 8 minutes or 8 hours.

In addition to reporting cumes across various audience subsets, the ratings services also report station cumes within different dayparts. Radio ratings books estimate a station's cume audience during so-called morning drive time (i.e., Monday through Friday, 6 a.m.–10 a.m.), afternoon drive time (i.e., Monday through Friday, 3 p.m.–7 p.m.), and other standard dayparts. Cume audiences can also be calculated for a station's combined drive-time audience (i.e., how many people listened to a station in a.m. and/or p.m. drive time).

The period of time over which a cume audience can be determined is constrained by the measurement technique that the ratings service employs. Radio cumes cannot exceed 1 week, because the diaries used to measure radio listening are only kept for 1 week. The same is true for television cumes in diary-only markets. Barring repeated call-backs, telephone recall techniques face similar limitations. Meter measurements, on the other hand, allow the ratings services to track cume audiences over longer periods of time.

In principle, household meters could produce household cumes, and peoplemeters could produce person cumes over any period of continuous operation (e.g., years). As a practical matter, cume audiences are rarely tracked for more than 1 month. These 4-week cumes are commonly reported with meter-based data, and they are particularly useful for television programs that air only once per week.

Two other variations on cumes are reported in radio. The first is called an *exclusive cume*. This is an estimate of the number of people who listen to only one particular station during a given daypart. All other things being equal, a large exclusive audience may be more saleable than one that can be reached over several stations. Arbitron also reports *cume duplication*. This is the opposite of an exclusive audience. For every pair of stations in a market, the rating services estimate the number of listeners who are in both stations' cume audiences. It is possible, therefore, to see which stations tend to have an audience in common.

The various cume estimates can be used in subsequent manipulations, sometimes combining them with gross measures of the audience, to produce different ways of looking at audience activity. One of the most common is a measure of *time spent listening* (TSL). The formula for computing TSL is as follows:

$$\frac{(\text{AQH PERSONS FOR DAYPART} \times \text{NUMBER OF QUARTER HRS IN THE DAYPART})}{\text{CUME PERSONS FOR DAYPART}} = \text{TSL}$$

The first step is to determine the average quarter hour (AQH) audience for the station, within any given daypart, for any given segment of the audience. This will be a projected audience reported in hundreds. Multiply that by the total number of quarter hours in the daypart. For a.m. or p.m. drive time, that is 80 quarter hours. For the largest daypart (Monday through Sunday, 6 a.m.–Midnight), it is 504 quarter hours. This product gives you a gross measure of the total number of person quarter hours people spent listening to the station. Dividing it by the number of people who actually listened to the station (i.e., the cume persons) tells you the average amount of time each person in the cume spent listening to the station. At this point, the average TSL is expressed as quarter hours per week, but it is easy enough to translate this into hours per day, in order to make it more interpretable. Table 11.1 shows how this exercise could be done to compare several stations.

As you will note, the average amount of time listeners spend tuned in varies from station to station. All things being equal, a station would rather see larger TSL estimates than smaller TSL estimates. Of course, it is possible that a high TSL is based on only a few heavy users, whereas a station with low TSLs has very large audiences. For example, compare the first two stations on the list in Table 11.1. In a world of advertiser support, gross audience size will ultimately be more important. Nonetheless, TSL comparisons can help change aggregated audience data into numbers that describe a typical listener, and so make them more comprehensible. Although TSLs are usually calculated for radio stations, analogous *time spent viewing* estimates could be derived by applying the same procedure to the AQH and cume estimates in the daypart summary of a television ratings report.

With direct access to the audience database it's possible to simply count the number of quarter hours a person spends watching TV or listening to a particular station. Further, if the data are based on meters rather than diaries, you can count the actual minutes spent watching or listening. Since many large consumers of ratings information now pay

TABLE 11.1
Calculating TSL Estimates Across Stations[a]

Station	AQH Persons	×	504 Qtr Hrs	Cume / Persons	=	TSL QH per week	/ 28 days =	TSL HR per day
WAAA	500		252,000	3,500		72.0		2.57
WXXX	1,500		756,000	20,000		37.8		1.35
WBBB	6,500		3,276,000	40,000		81.9		2.93
WZZZ	1,000		504,000	12,000		42.0		1.5

[a]This sample calculation of TSL is based on estimated audiences Monday–Sunday from 6 a.m. to midnight. That daypart has 504 quarter hours.

for direct access to the data, a new kind of *cumulative share* calculation has become increasingly common, especially in studies of television audiences. Essentially what the analyst does is count the number of minutes that a given audience spends viewing a particular source (e.g., a network, station, or program) over some period of time and divides that by the total time they spend watching all television over the same time period. Recall Table 9.4, which depicted the way in which big-three prime time audience shares had declined over the years. That pictured a succession of cumulative shares in each of the last 18 TV seasons. Analogous share values could conceivably be computed for individuals by counting the number of minutes each person spent watching a channel and dividing by the total time they spent watching all TV. The equation below shows the basic recipe for calculating cumulative shares. Be aware that the unit of analysis could be anything the analyst chooses (e.g., households, adults ages 18+, etc.), as could the programming source (e.g., channel, station, program, etc.).

$$\frac{\text{TIME SPENT VIEWING CHANNEL}}{\text{TIME SPENT VIEWING TV}} = \text{CUMULATIVE SHARE}$$

Another combination of cume and gross measurements that can be derived from summaries published in ratings books is called audience turnover. The formula of audience turnover is:

$$\frac{\text{CUME PERSONS IN A DAYPART}}{\text{AQH PERSONS IN A DAYPART}} = \text{TURNOVER}$$

Estimates of audience turnover are intended to give the ratings user a sense of how rapidly different listeners cycle through the station's audience. A turnover ratio of 1 would mean that the same people were in the audience quarter hour after quarter hour. Although that kind of slavish devotion does not occur in the "real world," relatively low turnover ratios do indicate relatively high levels of station loyalty. Because listeners are constantly tuning into a station as others are tuning out, turnover can also be thought of as the number of new listeners a station must attract in a time period in order to replace those who are tuning out. As was the case with TSL estimates, however, the rate of audience turnover does not tell you anything definitive about audience size. A station with low cume and low AQH audiences could look just the same as a station with large audiences in a comparison of audience turnover. For a discussion of other inventive ways to use published data to measure radio station loyalty, see Dick and McDowell (2004).

Another fairly common way to manipulate the cume estimates that appear in radio ratings books is to calculate what is called *recycling*. This manipulation of the data takes advantage of the fact that there are cumes reported for both morning and afternoon drive time, as well as the combination of those two dayparts. It is, therefore, possible to answer the question, "Of the people who listened to a station in a.m. drive time, how many also listened in p.m. drive time?" This kind of information could be valuable to a programmer in scheduling programs or promotion. Estimating the recycled audience is a two-step process.

First, you must determine how many people listened to the station during both dayparts. Suppose, for instance, that a station's cume audience in morning drive time was 5,000 persons. Let's further assume that the afternoon drive time audience was also reported to be 5,000. If it was exactly the same 5,000 people in both dayparts, then the combined cume would be 5,000 people as well (remember each person can only count once). If they were entirely different groups, the combined cume would be 10,000. That would mean no one listened in both dayparts. If the combined cume fell somewhere in between those extremes, say 8,000, then the number of people who listened in both the morning and the afternoon would be 2,000. This is determined by adding the cume for each individual daypart, and subtracting the combined cume (i.e., a.m. Cume + p.m. Cume – Combined a.m. & p.m. Cume = Persons who listen in both dayparts).

Second, the number of persons who listen in both dayparts is divided by the cume persons for either the a.m. or p.m. daypart. The following formula defines this simple operation:

$$\frac{\text{CUME PERSONS IN BOTH DAYPARTS}}{\text{CUME PERSONS IN ONE DAYPART}} = \text{RECYCLING}$$

Essentially, this expresses the number of persons listening at both times as a percentage of those in either the morning or afternoon audience. Using the hypothetical numbers in the preceding paragraph we can see that 40% of the morning audience recycled to afternoon drive time (i.e., 2,000 / 5,000 = 40%).

Nearly all radio stations get their largest audiences during the morning hours when people are first waking up, so programmers like to compare that figure with the number who listen at any other time of the day. It may also be useful to compare whether these same listeners tune in during the weekend, for example. In both television and radio, the promotion department can use data detailing when the most people are listening to schedule announcements about other programs and features on the station. Thus, stations hope to "recycle" their listeners into other dayparts—this builds a larger AQH rating for the station.

An alternative way to express cumulative measures of the audience is in terms of reach and frequency. These concepts are widely used among advertisers and media planners. The term *reach* means essentially the same thing as cume—that is, how many different people were reached. Just as a broadcaster might want to know the weekly cume of his or her station, an advertiser wants to know the reach of an advertising campaign. Quite often that means counting exposures across different stations or networks. As is the case with cumes, reach can be expressed as the actual number of people or households exposed to a message, or it can be expressed as a percent of some population.

Unlike station cumes, which are usually based on 1 week's worth of data, reach estimates are generally made over a 4-week period. This makes it somewhat easier for a media buyer to make comparisons between the reach of a network schedule and monthly magazines.

Although reach expresses the total number of audience members who have seen or heard an ad at least once, it does not tell anything about the number of times any one individual has been exposed to the message. *Frequency* expresses how often a person is exposed, and is usually reported as the average number of exposures among those who were reached. For example, a media planner might say that a campaign reached 80% of the population, and it did so with a frequency of 2.5.

Reach and frequency, which are both cumulative measures of the audience, bear a strict mathematical relationship to gross rating points (GRPs). That relationship is as follows:

$$\text{REACH} \times \text{FREQUENCY} = \text{GRPS}$$

A campaign with a reach of 80% and a frequency of 2.5 would, therefore, generate 200 GRPs. Knowing the GRPs of a particular advertising schedule, however, does not give you precise information on the reach and frequency of a campaign. This is because many combinations of reach and frequency can add up to the same number of ratings points. Nonetheless, the three terms are related, and some inferences about reach and frequency can be made on the basis of GRPs.

Figure 11.1 depicts the usual nature of the relationship. The left-hand column shows the reach of an advertising schedule. Along the bottom are frequency and GRPs. Generally speaking, ad schedules with low GRPs are associated with relatively high reach and low frequency. This can be seen in the fairly steep slope of the left-hand side of the curve. As the GRPs of a schedule increase, gains in reach occur at a reduced rate, while frequency of exposure begins to increase.

The diminishing contribution of GRPs to reach occurs because of differences in the amount of media people consume. People who watch a lot of TV are quickly reached with just a few commercials. The reach of a media schedule, therefore, increases rapidly in its early stages. Those who watch very little TV, however, are much harder to reach. In fact, reaching 100% of the audience is virtually impossible. Instead, as more and more GRPs are committed to an ad campaign (i.e., as more and more commercials are run), they simply increase the frequency of exposure for relatively heavy viewers. That drives up the average frequency. Across mass audiences, these patterns of reach and frequency can be predicted with a good deal of accuracy. Later in the chapter, we discuss mathematical models that are designed to do just that.

As the preceding discussion suggests, reporting the average frequency of exposure masks a lot of variation across individuals. An average frequency of 2.5 could mean that some viewers have seen an ad 15 times and others have only seen it once. It is useful to consider the actual distribution on which the average is based. These distributions are usually lopsided, or skewed. The majority of households could be exposed to far fewer advertising messages than the arithmetic average, and a relatively small number of "heavy viewing" households might see a great many ads. In light of these distributions, advertisers often ask, "How many times must a commercial be seen or heard before it is effective?" Is one exposure enough for a commercial to have its intended effect, or even to be noticed? Conversely, at what point do repeated exposures become wasteful, or even counterproductive? Unfortunately, there are no simple answers to these questions. For many years the consensus was that an ad had to be seen or heard at

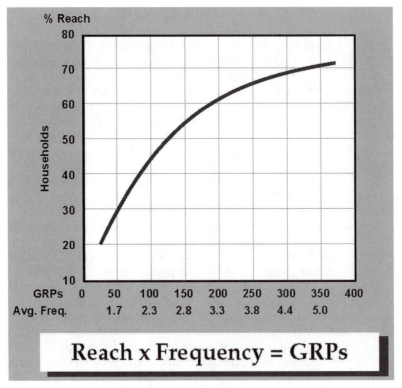

FIG. 11.1. Reach and frequency as a function of increasing GRPs.

least three times before it could be effective. More recent research and theory suggests that one exposure, particularly if it occurs when a consumer is ready to buy, is sufficient to trigger the desired effect. Whatever the number, the fewest exposures needed to have an effect is referred to as the *effective frequency*.

If one exposure, timed to hit the consumer when they were ready to buy, constitutes effective communication, then achieving reach becomes the primary concern of the media planner. This idea, sometimes called "recency theory," along with increasing concern about audience fragmentation and the cost of TV time, caused advertisers to push for new ways to optimize reach. The solution came in the form of *optimizers*. These are computer programs that take respondent-level data from Nielsen and cost estimates for various kinds of spots and identify the most cost-effective way to build reach. For example, instead of simply buying expensive prime time spots to achieve reach, an optimizer might find a way to cobble together many smaller, less expensive audiences to accomplish the same result. Today, optimizers, which tend to be expensive to run, are used by most big advertisers and media services companies to plan their advertising schedules.

Yet another way to conceptualize cumulative audience behavior is in terms of *audience duplication*. Simply stated, analyses of audience duplication ask, "Of the people who were watching or listening at one point in time, how many were also watching or listening at another point in time?" Time periods might be broadly defined dayparts, as is the case with recycling, or they might be selected minutes within different programs. In fact, audience duplication across several points in time produces the kind of reach and frequency data just described.

Studying patterns of audience duplication is one of the most powerful and potentially illuminating techniques of analysis available to audience researchers. Studies of television audience behavior have identified such well-established patterns of duplication as inheritance effects, channel loyalty, and repeat viewing (e.g., Goodhardt et al., 1987; Webster & Phalen, 1997).

Unfortunately, most questions of audience duplication cannot be answered by looking at the numbers published in a typical ratings report. To observe that one TV program has the same rating as its lead-in is no assurance that the same audience watched both. Nevertheless, if one has access to the respondent-level data on which the ratings are based, a variety of analytical possibilities are open.

Studies of audience duplication begin with a straightforward statistical technique called *cross-tabulation*. Cross-tabulation is described in detail in most books on research methods, and is a common procedure in statistical software packages. Cross-tabs, as they are sometimes called, allow an analyst to look at the relationship between two variables. If, for instance, we conducted a survey about magazine readership, we might want to identify the relationship between reader demographics and subscription (e.g., are women more or less likely than men to buy

Cosmopolitan?). Each person's response to a question about magazine subscription could be paired with information on their gender, resulting in a cross-tabulation of those variables.

When cross-tabulation is used to study audience duplication, the analyst pairs one media-use variable with another. Suppose, for example, we had diary data on a sample of 100 people. We would then be in a position to answer questions like, "Of the people who watched one situation comedy (e.g., SC1), how many also watched a second situation comedy (e.g., SC2)?" These are two behavioral variables, among a great many, contained in the data. A cross-tabulation of the two would produce a table like Table 11.2.

The numbers along the bottom of Table 11.2a show that 20 people wrote "yes," they watched SC1, whereas the remaining 80 did not watch the program. The numbers in these two response categories should always add up to the total sample size. Along the far right-hand side of the table are the comparable numbers for SC2. We have again assumed that 20 people reported watching, and 80 did not. All the numbers reported along the edges, or margins, of the table are referred to as *marginals*. We should point out that when the number of people viewing a program is reported as a percentage of the total sample, that marginal is analogous to a program rating (e.g., both SC1 and SC2 have person ratings of 20).

A study of audience duplication asks whether the same 20 people viewed both SC1 and SC2. The cross-tabulation reveals the answer in the four cells of the table. The upper left-hand cell indicates the number of

TABLE 11.2

Cross-Tabulation of Program Audiences

(a)		Viewed SC1		
		yes	no	total
	yes	5	15	20
Viewed SC2				
	no	15	65	80
	total	20	80	100
(b)		Viewed SC1		
		yes	no	total
	yes	O = 5	O = 15	20
Viewed SC2		E = 4	E = 16	
	no	O = 15	O = 65	80
		E = 16	E = 64	
	total	20	80	100

people who watched both SC1 and SC2. Of the 100 people in the sample, only 5 saw both programs. That is what is referred to as the *duplicated audience*. Conversely, 65 people saw neither program. When the number in any one cell is known, all numbers can be determined because the sum of each row or column must equal the appropriate marginal.

Once the size of the duplicated audience has been determined, the next problem is one of interpretation. Is what we have observed a high or low level of duplication? Could this result have happened by chance, or is there a strong relationship between the audiences for the two programs in question? To evaluate the data at hand, we need to judge our results against certain expectations. Those expectations could be either statistical or theoretical/intuitive in nature.

The statistical expectation for this sort of cross-tabulation is easy to determine. It is the level of duplication that would be observed if there were no relationship between two program audiences. In other words, because 20 people watched SC1 and 20 watched SC2, we would expect that a few people would see both, just by chance. Statisticians call this chance level of duplication the *expected frequency*. The expected frequency for any cell in the table is determined by multiplying the row marginal for that cell (R) times the column marginal (C) and dividing by the total sample (N). The formula for determining the expected frequency, is:

$$R \times C / N = E$$

So, for example, the expected frequency in the upper left-hand cell is 4 (i.e., $20 \times 20 / 100 = 4$). Table 11.2b shows both the observed frequency (O) and the expected frequency (E) for the two sitcom audiences. By comparing the two, we can see that the duplicated audience we have observed is slightly larger than the laws of probability would predict (i.e., $5 > 4$). Most computer programs will also run a statistical test, like *chi-square*, to tell you whether the difference between observed and expected frequencies is "statistically significant."

From one time period to another, audiences will overlap. For example, if 50% of the audience is watching television at one time, and 50% is watching later in the day, a certain percentage of the audience will be watching at both times. The statistical expectation of overlap is determined exactly as in the example just given, except now we are dealing with percentages. If there is no correlation between the time period audiences, then 25% will be watching at both times, just by chance (i.e., $50 \times 50 / 100 = 25$). We routinely observe a level of total audience overlap, or duplication, that exceeds chance. It is in this sort of circumstance that the second kind of expectation comes into play. An experienced analyst knows enough about audience behavior to have certain theoretical or intuitive expectations about the levels of audience duplication he or she will encounter. Consider the two sitcoms again. Suppose we knew that they were scheduled on a single channel, one after the other, at a time when other stations were broadcasting longer programs. Our understanding of inheritance effects would lead us to expect a large duplicated audience. If each show were watched by 20% of our sample, we might be surprised to find anything less than 10% of the total sample watching both. That is well above the statistical expectation of 4%. On the other hand, if the two shows were scheduled on different channels at the same time, we would expect virtually no duplication at all. In either case, we have good reason to expect a strong relationship between watching SC1 and SC2.

The research and theory we reviewed in chapter 9 should give you some idea of the patterns of duplication that are known to occur in actual audience behavior. You should be alert, however, to the different ways in which information on audience duplication is reported. The number of people watching any two programs, or listening to a station at two different times, is often expressed as a percentage or a proportion. That makes it easier to compare across samples or populations of different sizes. Unfortunately, percentages can be calculated on different bases. For each cell in a simple cross-tab, each frequency could be reported as a percent of the row, the column, or the total sample.

Table 11.3 is much like the 2 × 2 matrix in Table 11.2. We have decreased the size of the SC1 audience however, to make things a bit more complicated. First, you should note that changing the marginals has an

TABLE 11.3

Cross-Tabulation of Program Audiences With Expected Frequencies and Cell Percentages

		Viewed SC1		
		yes	no	total
Viewed SC2	yes	E = 2	E = 18	20
		T = 2%	T = 18%	
		R = 10%	R = 90%	
		C = 20%	C = 20%	
	no	E = 8	E = 72	80
		T = 8%	T = 72%	
		R = 10%	R = 90%	
		C = 80%	C = 80%	
		10	90	100

impact on the expected frequencies (E) within each cell. When SC1 is viewed by 10, and SC2 by 20, E equals 2 (10 × 20 / 100 = 2). That change, of course, affects all the other expected frequencies. For convenience, let us also assume that we actually observe these frequencies in each box. We can express each as one of three percentages or proportions. Because our total sample size is 100, the duplicated audience is 2% of the total sample (T). Stated differently, the proportion of the audience seeing both programs is .02. We could also say that 20% (C) of the people who saw SC1 also saw SC2. Alternatively, we could say that 10% (R) of the people who saw SC2 also saw SC1.

Different expressions of audience duplication are used in different contexts. The convention is to express levels of repeat viewing as an average of row or column percentages. These are usually quite similar because the ratings of different episodes of a program tend to be stable. This practice results in statements like, "The average level of repeat viewing was 55%." Channel loyalty is usually indexed by studying the proportion of the total sample that sees any pair of programs broadcast on the same channel. We will have more to say about this later on when we discuss the "duplication of viewing law." Inheritance effects are studied and reported both ways. Proportions of total audience have been used to model this kind of audience flow; row and column percentages are often used to report typical levels of duplication between adjacent programs.

Computer programs, like Nielsen's NPower, estimate the duplicated audience for as many pairs of programs as the analyst identifies. The output is a rather dense spreadsheet of numbers that reports the various percentages you would find in each cell of the cross-tab. That sort of presentation is difficult for a non-researcher to digest, so research analysts often translate those data into more user-friendly representations like the one depicted in Fig. 11.2.

As we noted previously, audience duplication can be used to study inheritance effects or audience flow within a given evening. Figure 11.2 is a depiction of how the television audience flowed from one half hour to the next over a 2-hour period on a Tuesday evening. Each row of boxes is the lineup for each of the six largest broadcast networks. The first row shows the programs on WB. *Gilmore Girls*, an hour-long drama, had a rating among adults ages 18 to 34 of 2.5 for each of its half hours. It retained 92% of its audience from the first half hour to the second, so obviously a few viewers dropped out and an equal number tuned in. At 9:00 p.m., when *Smallville* came on, and all the other networks were beginning new programs, WB retained only 44% of the lead-in audience. However, *Smallville* obviously attracted other viewers, since its ratings actually inched upward. The data for each of the other networks tells its own story about how well audience flow was managed on the night in question.

We can tell from Fig. 11.2 that viewers were moving in and out of the WB audience during the evening, but we cannot see where they are coming from or where they are going. Drilling deeper into the Nielsen data allows the analyst to make that determination. Figure 11.3 shows

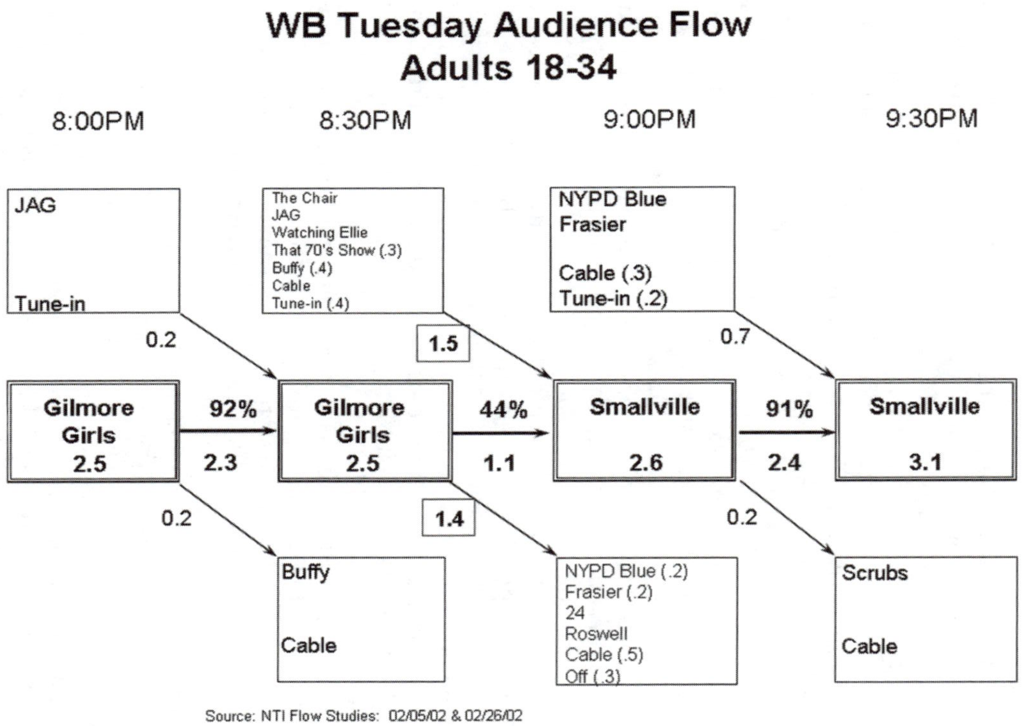

WB Tuesday Audience Flow
Adults 18-34

| 8:00PM | 8:30PM | 9:00PM | 9:30PM |

8:00PM

JAG

Tune-in

8:30PM

The Chair
JAG
Watching Ellie
That 70's Show (.3)
Buffy (.4)
Cable
Tune-in (.4)

9:00PM

NYPD Blue
Frasier

Cable (.3)
Tune-in (.2)

9:30PM

Smallville 3.1

Gilmore Girls 2.5 → 92% 2.3 → Gilmore Girls 2.5

0.2

1.5 → 44% 1.1 → Smallville 2.6

0.7

91% 2.4 → Smallville 3.1

1.4 →

Buffy
Cable

0.2

NYPD Blue (.2)
Frasier (.2)
24
Roswell
Cable (.5)
Off (.3)

Scrubs
Cable

0.2

Source: NTI Flow Studies: 02/05/02 & 02/26/02

FIG. 11.2.   WB Tuesday audience flow (adults 18–34). Data are from NTI Flow Studies, 02/05/02 and 02/26/02. From Barwise & Ehrenberg (1998). Reprinted by permission.

that the viewers who defected after the *Gilmore Girls* went primarily to cable networks or simply turned the TV off. The *Smallville* audience that was not already watching WB came from *Buffy, That '70s Show,* and people just tuning in. This kind of information can be particularly valuable to a programmer who is trying to understand the effects of various programming strategies.

Of course, many ratings users do not have access to the respondent-level data necessary to do bona fide studies of audience duplication, so they make inferences about the existence of audience duplication without the benefit of direct observation. For example, programs with small ratings may be aired more than once a day. Under such circumstances, it is not unusual for the rating from each airing to be totaled and sold as if it were a single program rating. It is assumed that no one watches the same program twice in a day, so no audience duplication occurs across programs. It seems likely that as cable networks—which often repeat programming—continue to fragment the audience, this practice may increase. Furthermore, as DVR penetration increases, the media will seek audience estimates that account for viewer control of timing. A rating that aggregates viewing over a day, or even over a week, will become standard in the industry. Whether these

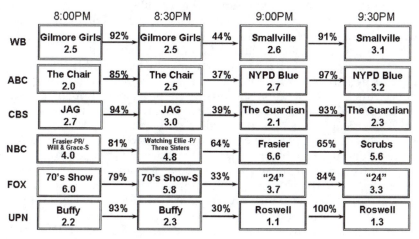

FIG. 11.3. Tuesday audience flow (adults 18–34). Data are from NTI Flow Studies, 02/05/02 and 02/26/02.

changes are based on a sound understanding of audience behavior could and should be examined.

Similarly, some ratings analysts have inferred levels of audience duplication by looking at correlations between program ratings or shares. Under this approach, it is assumed that pairs of programs with highly correlated ratings have relatively high levels of duplication, and program pairs with low correlations have low levels of duplication. For instance, researchers have examined the correlations among adjacent program audience shares, arguing that conditions that produce high correlations indicate relatively pronounced inheritance effects (e.g., Davis & Walker, 1990; McDowell & Dick, 2003; Tiedge & Ksobiech, 1986). No direct observation of audience duplication is made, so such correlational data give only "circumstantial evidence" of audience flow. Although this approach is clearly less desirable than studying actual levels of duplication it can, nonetheless, produce useful insights into audience behavior.

Comparisons

As is the case with gross measures of the audience, it is common practice to make comparisons among cumulative measures. Comparisons, after all, can provide a useful context within which to interpret the numbers. However, with cumulative measures, part of the impetus for comparing every conceivable audience subset, indexed in every imaginable way, is absent. As a practical matter, gross measures are used more extensively in buying and selling audiences than are cumulative measures, so there is less pressure to demonstrate some comparative advantage, no matter how obscure. Although some cume estimates, like reach, frequency, and exclusive cumes, can certainly be useful in buying and planning media, much of the comparative work with cumulative measures is done to realize some deeper understanding of audience behavior.

Interesting analyses have been performed by looking at the reach and time spent viewing of television stations. Barwise and Ehrenberg (1988) have argued that television stations rarely have small-but-loyal audiences. Instead, it is almost always the case that a station that reaches a small segment of the audience is viewed by that audience only sparingly. This is sometimes labeled a *double jeopardy* effect because a station suffers not only from having relatively few viewers, but also from having relatively disloyal or irregular viewers. To demonstrate the double jeopardy effect, they constructed a graph based on television ratings data in both the United States and the United Kingdom (see Fig. 11.4).

Along the horizontal axis is the weekly reach achieved by various types of stations, expressed as a percent of the total audience. Along the vertical axis is the average number of hours each station's audience spent viewing the station in a week. This can be determined in the same way that TSL estimates are made in radio. As you can see, the slope of the curve is rather flat to begin with, but rises sharply as the reach of the

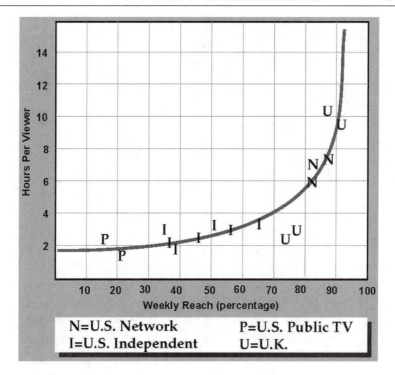

FIG. 11.4. Channel reach and time spent viewing television (adapted from Barwise & Ehrenberg, 1988, with permission).

station increases. This means that, as a rule, low levels of station reach are associated with small amounts of time viewing, but as reach moves beyond 50% or so, increased reach is associated with dramatic increases in weekly time spent viewing (TSV).

A more recent study (Webster, 2005) has extended this kind of analysis to 62 of the most prominent broadcast and cable television networks in the United States. These are listed down the left-hand side of Table 11.4. For each network, the table reports percent of all TVHHs capable of receiving the signal, its cumulative share among adults ages 18+ (i.e., the percent of all the week's viewing devoted to that network), its cumulative rating (i.e., the percent of A 18+ who watched for at least one minute during the week), and the average TSV—in minutes—among those who did watch.

As with Barwise and Ehrenberg (1988), the double jeopardy effect can be seen by assessing the relationship between the weekly cume rating (or reach) and TSV. The networks are rank ordered by their TSV. Within the broadcast group, the double jeopardy effect holds true. Those with bigger weekly cume ratings claimed higher TSV. Within the cable group, how-

TABLE 11.4
Network Shares, Cumes and Time Spent Viewing
February 2003

Network	TVHH Universe	Cumulative share of viewing A 18+	Cumulative rating A 18+	Average weekly minutes TSV A 18+
Broadcast networks				
CBS	95%	6.3	65.0	189
NBC	95%	5.9	67.0	173
ABC	97%	5.1	66.0	152
PBS	99%	2.0	45.0	89
FOX	93%	1.9	47.0	78
WB	90%	0.8	25.0	59
PAX	85%	0.4	15.0	55
UPN	86%	0.4	18.0	46
Cable networks				
HBO	33%	2.0	20.0	196
FOX News Channel	77%	2.7	27.0	193
Lifetime Movie	34%	0.6	7.0	167
Cinemax	20%	0.7	9.0	159
SHOWTIME	21%	0.6	9.0	146
Turner Network Television (TNT)	81%	2.3	34.0	134
Lifetime	81%	1.9	28.0	130
Game Show Network	47%	0.4	6.0	128
TV Land	73%	1.1	16.0	127
CNN	81%	2.1	35.0	118
Nickelodeon	81%	1.5	25.0	117
TBS Superstation	82%	2.3	39.0	116
SOAP Network	27%	0.1	2.0	115
Hallmark Channel	47%	0.5	9.0	110
Court TV	71%	0.8	16.0	103
Home & Garden TV	75%	1.0	20.0	97
USA Network	81%	1.6	34.0	95
Cartoon Network	77%	0.7	15.0	95
SCI-FI Channel	75%	0.8	17.0	87
The Movie Channel	19%	0.2	5.0	86
ESPN	81%	1.1	25.0	85
History Channel	77%	1.0	23.0	85
A&E	81%	1.1	26.0	85

MSNBC	73%	0.9	23.0	76
Food Network	73%	0.7	17.0	75
Black Entertainment TV (BET)	70%	0.5	14.0	75
Toon Disney	35%	0.1	3.0	72
The Learning Channel	79%	1.1	30.0	71
American Movie Classics	79%	0.9	25.0	71
Disney Channel	76%	0.6	18.0	70
FX	75%	0.9	26.0	66
WGN Superstation	53%	0.6	17.0	64
Animal Planet	76%	0.7	21.0	63
Discovery	81%	0.9	29.0	59
MTV	80%	0.7	26.0	55
Comedy Central	77%	0.6	22.0	53
CNN Headline News	78%	0.7	25.0	51
Spike TV (TNN)	81%	0.7	26.0	51
CNBC	79%	0.4	14.0	51
Weather Channel	80%	0.6	24.0	50
Speed Channel	52%	0.1	6.0	48
Discovery Health	39%	0.1	5.0	45
Country Music Television (CMT)	62%	0.3	12.0	43
ESPN2	79%	0.4	21.0	41
ABC Family	80%	0.5	23.0	40
Woman's Entertainment (WE)	47%	0.2	8.0	38
Bravo	65%	0.3	14.0	36
Entertainment TV (E!)	75%	0.5	25.0	36
Travel Channel	66%	0.3	16.0	36
VH1	78%	0.4	23.0	34
TV Guide Channel	53%	0.3	19.0	32
National Geographic	39%	0.1	5.0	31
Outdoor Life	47%	0.1	5.0	28
FUSE	28%	0.0	2.0	16
All Other Sources		35.0		
TOTAL		100.0		

Note. Data are adapted from J. G. Webster (2005), "Beneath the Veneer of Fragmentation: Television Audience Polarization in a Multi-Channel World," *Journal of Communication,* 55(2), 366–382.

ever, the picture is more complicated. Some networks, like HBO or FOX News Channel, had modest cume ratings and very high TSV. Others, like The Learning Channel, MTV, and E!, had respectable ratings but relatively low TSV. Across all 62 networks the correlation between cume ratings and TSV was .38. However, when the big-three broadcast networks (i.e., ABC, CBS, NBC) were dropped from that calculation, the correlation became statistically insignificant. It seems that in the world of cable networks, there are both small-but-loyal and small-but-disloyal audiences.

Prediction and Explanation

The audience behavior revealed in cumulative measurements can be quite predictable—at least in the statistical sense. We are dealing with mass behavior occurring in a relatively stable environment over a period of days or weeks, so that behavior can be approximated with mathematical models—often with great accuracy. This is certainly a boon to media planners attempting to orchestrate effective campaigns, especially because actual data on audience duplication is always after the fact and often hard to come by. As a result, much attention has been paid to developing techniques for predicting reach, duplication, and frequency of exposure.

The simplest model for estimating the reach of a media vehicle is given by the following equation:

$$\text{REACH} = 1 - (1 - r)^n$$

where r is the rating of the media vehicle, and n is the number of ads, or insertions, that are run in the campaign. When applying this equation, it is necessary to express the rating as a proportion (e.g., a rating of 20 = .20). Although straightforward, this model of reach is rather limited. In the early 1960s, more sophisticated models were developed based either on binomial or beta binomial distributions (e.g., Agostini, 1961; Metheringham, 1964). These and other models of reach are described in detail by Rust (1986).

Although models of reach embody some assumptions about audience duplication, to predict duplication between specific pairs of programs, it is best to employ models designed for that purpose. One of the most often-cited models, called the "duplication of viewing law," was developed by Goodhardt et al. (1987). It is expressed in the following equation:

$$r_{st} = kr_s r_t$$

where r_{st} is the proportion of the audience that sees both Programs s and t, r_s is the proportion seeing program s, r_t is the proportion seeing program t (i.e., their ratings expressed as proportions), and k is a constant whose value must be empirically determined. When the ratings are expressed as percentages, the equation changes slightly to:

$$r_{st} = kr_s r_t / 100$$

The logic behind the duplication of viewing law is not as complicated as it might appear. In fact, it is almost exactly the same as determining an expected frequency in cross-tabulation. If we were trying to predict the percent of the entire population that saw any two programs, we could begin by estimating the expected frequency. Remember, that is determined by $E = R \times C / N$. If we are dealing with program ratings, that is the same as multiplying the rating of one program (s) by the rating of another (t), and dividing by 100 (the total N as a percentage). In other words, the general equation for expected frequency becomes $r_{st} = r_s r_t /100$, when it is specifically applied to predicting audience duplication. That is exactly the same as the duplication of viewing equation, with the exception of the k coefficient.

Goodhardt and his colleagues compared the expected level of duplication with the actual, or observed, level of duplication across hundreds of program pairings. They discovered that under certain well-defined circumstances, actual levels of duplication were either greater or less than chance by a predictable amount. For example, for any pair of programs broadcast on ABC, on different days, it was the case that audience duplication exceeded chance by about 60%. In other words, people who watched one ABC program were 60% more likely than the general population to show up in the audience for another ABC program on a different day. To adapt the equation so that it accurately predicted duplication, it was necessary to introduce a new term, the k *coefficient*. If duplication exceeded chance by 60%, then the value of k would have to be 1.6.

The values of k were determined for channels in both the United States and the United Kingdom. American networks have a duplication constant of approximately 1.5 to 1.6, whereas English channels have a constant on the order of 1.7 to 1.9. These constants serve as an index of *channel loyalty*; the higher the value of k, the greater the tendency toward duplication or loyalty.

Noting deviations from levels of duplication predicted by the duplication of viewing law also serves as a way to identify unusual features in audience behavior. In effect, the law gives us an empirically grounded theoretical expectation against which to judge specific observations. One important deviation from the law is inheritance effects. That is, when the pair of programs in question is scheduled back-to-back on the same channel, the level of duplication routinely exceeds that predicted by ordinary channel loyalty. Henriksen (1985) has suggested that a more flexible model of duplication, predicting both channel loyalty and inheritance effects, could be derived from models in human ecology. His model is in the form of a linear equation:

$$\log r_{st} = \log k + (b)\log r_s + (c)\log r_t$$

The duplication of viewing law has also been criticized for treating the k coefficient as a constant. In fact, there is evidence that k varies considerably across individual program pairings (e.g., Chandon, 1976; Headen, Klompmaker, & Rust, 1979; Henriksen, 1985). The duplication of viewing law is also incapable of explicitly incorporating other factors that may affect the level of duplication between program pairs.

To address these limitations, Headen et al. (1979) proposed using a more conventional regression equation to model audience duplication across program pairs. The equation takes the general form:

$$r_{st} = b_0(b_1^{X1})(b_2^{X2})(b_3^{X3})(b_4^{X4})(r_s r_t)(e^u)$$

where r_{st} is the proportion of the population seeing programs s and t, $r_s r_t$ is the product of the programs' ratings expressed as proportions, and X_1 through X_4 are dummy variables indicating whether the programs in a pair were on the same channel, of the same type, and so forth. As the duplication of viewing law would suggest, $r_s r_t$ is the single best predictor of audience duplication, although other factors, including similarities in program type, add significantly to explained variation in r_{st}. It might also be noted that when using linear regressions on data such as these, it is typically necessary to perform logarithmic transformations of the audience proportions to avoid violating the assumptions that underlie the linear model.

Webster and Phalen (1997) used a similar method of modeling to explain audience duplication between adjacent program pairs. However, they allowed each program rating (i.e., r_s and r_t) to enter the equation independently in order to assess the relative strength of lead-in versus lead-out effects. By doing so, they established that the ratings of the earlier program in an adjacent pair explained considerably more variation than the second program rating. Overall, a model with four predictor variables explained 85% of the variation in inheritance effects.

Frequency of exposure can also be modeled. If it is possible to predict reach on the basis of GRPs, average frequency at a certain GRP level can be determined, because the three are directly related. However, as we noted in our discussion of those concepts, it is often useful to know the entire distribution on which an average frequency is based. In that way, judgments about effective exposure can be made. Consequently, models predicting an entire distribution of exposures have been developed. There are, in fact, a great many such models. Some are based on binomial distributions, some on multivariate extensions of beta binomial distributions. Some require information on pairwise duplication as input, some do not. (For a full discussion of these alternatives, the reader is referred to Rust, 1986.)

Goodhardt et al. (1987) employed one such model, based on a beta binomial distribution (BBD), to predict what percent of the population will see a certain number of episodes in a series. Table 11.5 compares the predictions of the BBD model with actual observations for 11 episodes of the series "Brideshead Revisited." The table indicates that 40% of the population did not watch any broadcast of the series. Seventeen percent saw just 1 episode in 11, 11% saw two episodes, and so forth. These data are exactly like those reported by Nielsen in its *Program Cumulative Audience* reports, except they extend beyond the usual 4-week time frame. The line of numbers just below the observed frequency distribution is the prediction of the BBD model. Although there are some discrepancies, the model provides a good fit to actual patterns of audience behavior.

It should be apparent by now that cumes, reach, frequency, and audience duplication are just different ways of expressing the same underlying audience behavior. In fact, information on pairwise duplication can be used to predict frequency distributions, and frequency distributions can be translated into analogous statements about audience duplication (e.g., Barwise, 1986).

It should also be apparent that ratings data, when properly analyzed, have the potential to answer an enormous number of questions. These include the pragmatic concerns that prompted the creation of ratings in the first place. But, as we noted in chapters 4 and 5, the data are flexible enough to address problems in public policy, economics, cultural studies, and media effects. The successful application of ratings analysis to these problems, of course, requires access to the appropriate data, and an understanding of its limitations. Perhaps most importantly, it requires an appreciation of the audience behavior expressed in the ratings and the factors that shape it. Only then can we exploit the data for all the insights they might offer.

TABLE 11.5

**Observed Versus Theoretical Frequency Distribution for Episodes
of *Brideshead Revisited*[a]**

	Number of episodes seen											
	0	1	2	3	4	5	6	7	8	9	10	11
Observed												
frequency	40%	17%	11%	8%	4%	3%	3%	4%	2%	4%	2%	2%
Theoretical												
frequency	43	14	9	7	5	5	4	4	3	2	2	2

[a]Adapted with permission from G. J. Goodhardt, A. S. C. Ehrenberg, and M. A. Collins, 1987, *The Television Audience: Patterns of Viewing* (2nd ed.), Westmead, UK: Gower.

RELATED READINGS

Barwise, P., & Ehrenberg, A. (1988). *Television and its audience*. London: Sage.

Goodhardt, G. J., Ehrenberg, A. S. C., & Collins, M. A. (1987). *The television audience: Patterns of viewing*. Aldershot, UK: Gower.

Rust, R. T. (1986). *Advertising media models: A practical guide*. Lexington: Lexington Books.

Sissors, J. Z., & Baron, R. B. (2002). *Advertising media planning* (6th ed.). Chicago: McGraw-Hill.

Webster, J. G., & Phalen, P. F. (1997). *The mass audience: Rediscovering the dominant model*. Mahwah, NJ: Lawrence Erlbaum Associates.

Appendix A:
DMA Market Rankings

NIELSEN MEDIA RESEARCH LOCAL MARKET UNIVERSE ESTIMATES
FOR 2004–2005 SEASON

RANK	Designated Market Area (DMA)	TV Homes	% of US
1	New York	7,355,710	6.712
2	Los Angeles	5,431,140	4.956
3	Chicago	3,417,330	3.118
4	Philadelphia	2,919,410	2.664
5	Boston (Manchester)	2,391,840	2.183
6	San Francisco-Oak-San Jose	2,359,870	2.153
7	Dallas-Ft. Worth	2,292,760	2.092
8	Washington, DC (Hagrstwn)	2,241,610	2.045
9	Atlanta	2,059,450	1.879
10	Detroit	1,943,930	1.774
11	Houston	1,902,810	1.736
12	Seattle-Tacoma	1,690,640	1.543
13	Tampa-St. Pete (Sarasota)	1,671,040	1.525
14	Minneapolis-St. Paul	1,665,540	1.520
15	Phoenix (Prescott), AZ	1,596,280	1.457
16	Cleveland-Akron (Canton)	1,556,670	1.420
17	Miami-Ft. Lauderdale	1,496,810	1.366
18	Denver	1,401,760	1.279
19	Sacramnto-Stktn-Modesto	1,315,030	1.200
20	Orlando-Daytona Bch-Melbrn	1,303,150	1.189
21	St. Louis	1,216,700	1.110
22	Pittsburgh	1,186,010	1.082
23	Baltimore	1,087,730	0.993
24	Portland, OR	1,086,900	0.992
25	Indianapolis	1,053,020	0.961
26	San Diego	1,025,730	0.936

27	Hartford & New Haven	1,017,530	0.928
28	Charlotte	1,004,440	0.917
29	Raleigh-Durham (Fayetvlle)	966,720	0.882
30	Nashville	916,170	0.836
31	Kansas City	894,580	0.816
32	Milwaukee	886,770	0.809
33	Cincinnati	883,230	0.806
34	Columbus, OH	867,490	0.792
35	Greenvll-Spart-Ashevll-And	813,210	0.742
36	Salt Lake City	800,000	0.730
37	San Antonio	748,950	0.683
38	Grand Rapids-Kalmzoo-B.Crk	732,600	0.668
39	West Palm Beach-Ft. Pierce	729,010	0.665
40	Birmingham (Ann and Tusc)	717,300	0.655
41	Norfolk-Portsmth-Newpt Nws	707,750	0.646
42	Harrisburg-Lncstr-Leb-York	702,590	0.641
43	New Orleans	675,760	0.617
44	Memphis	658,250	0.601
45	Oklahoma City	655,250	0.598
46	Buffalo	651,970	0.595
47	Albuquerque-Santa Fe	650,350	0.593
48	Greensboro-H.Point-W.Salem	648,860	0.592
49	Providence-New Bedford	644,980	0.589
50	Louisville	637,680	0.582
51	Las Vegas	614,150	0.560
52	Jacksonville, Brunswick	613,000	0.559
53	Wilkes Barre-Scranton	592,560	0.541
54	Austin	567,870	0.518
55	Albany-Schenectady-Troy	555,640	0.507
56	Dayton	537,710	0.491
57	Little Rock-Pine Bluff	531,770	0.485
58	Fresno-Visalia	527,770	0.482
59	Knoxville	513,630	0.469
60	Tulsa	510,960	0.466
61	Richmond-Petersburg	509,860	0.465
62	Charleston-Huntington	508,750	0.464

63	Mobile-Pensacola (Ft Walt)	492,070	0.449
64	Lexington	481,120	0.439
65	Flint-Saginaw-Bay City	479,520	0.438
66	Wichita-Hutchinson Plus	445,690	0.407
67	Roanoke-Lynchburg	445,670	0.407
68	Ft. Myers-Naples	444,130	0.405
69	Green Bay-Appleton	433,640	0.396
70	Toledo	432,430	0.395
51	Honolulu	417,120	0.381
72	Tucson (Sierra Vista)	417,070	0.381
73	Des Moines-Ames	412,230	0.376
74	Portland-Auburn	409,060	0.373
75	Rochester, NY	396,880	0.362
76	Omaha	396,460	0.362
77	Syracuse	395,400	0.361
78	Springfield, MO	388,530	0.355
79	Paducah-Cape Girard-Harsbg	384,860	0.351
80	Spokane	384,060	0.350
81	Shreveport	382,700	0.349
82	Champaign&Sprngfld-Decatur	382,460	0.349
83	Columbia, SC	374,680	0.342
84	Huntsville-Decatur (Flor)	370,160	0.338
85	Madison	364,000	0.332
86	Chattanooga	353,210	0.322
87	South Bend-Elkhart	332,860	0.304
88	Cedar Rapids-Wtrlo-IWC&Dub	331,610	0.303
89	Tri-Cities, TN-VA	329,910	0.301
90	Burlington-Plattsburgh	329,200	0.300
91	Jackson, MS	327,670	0.299
92	Colorado Springs-Pueblo	313,170	0.286
93	Harlingen-Wslco-Brnsvl-McA	312,300	0.285
94	Davenport-R.Island-Moline	309,900	0.283
95	Waco-Temple-Bryan	308,970	0.282
96	Baton Rouge	306,910	0.280
97	Johnstown-Altoona	300,850	0.274
98	Savannah	293,170	0.267

99	Evansville	289,840	0.264
100	El Paso (Las Cruces)	288,440	0.263
101	Charleston, SC	282,740	0.258
102	Youngstown	281,340	0.257
103	Lincoln & Hstngs-Krny Plus	275,230	0.251
104	Ft. Wayne	271,890	0.248
105	Greenville-N.Bern-Washngtn	270,200	0.247
106	Springfield-Holyoke	267,500	0.244
107	Ft. Smith-Fay-Sprngdl-Rgrs	267,030	0.244
108	Myrtle Beach-Florence	265,370	0.242
109	Tallahassee-Thomasville	259,720	0.237
110	Lansing	259,240	0.237
111	Tyler-Longview(Lfkn&Ncgd)	254,170	0.232
112	Traverse City-Cadillac	249,450	0.228
113	Montgomery-Selma	247,800	0.226
114	Reno	246,700	0.225
115	Augusta	246,620	0.225
116	Sioux Falls(Mitchell)	242,930	0.222
117	Peoria-Bloomington	242,020	0.221
118	Fargo-Valley City	235,490	0.215
119	Macon	230,000	0.210
120	Eugene	229,360	0.209
121	SantaBarbra-SanMar-SanLuOb	224,710	0.205
122	Boise	223,890	0.204
123	Lafayette, LA	220,740	0.201
124	Monterey-Salinas	218,450	0.199
125	Columbus, GA	208,860	0.191
126	Yakima-Pasco-Rchlnd-Knnwck	207,180	0.189
127	La Crosse-Eau Claire	206,490	0.188
128	Bakersfield	194,180	0.177
129	Corpus Christi	193,290	0.176
130	Amarillo	190,120	0.173
131	Chico-Redding	189,310	0.173
132	Columbus-Tupelo-West Point	187,650	0.171
133	Wausau-Rhinelander	181,780	0.166
134	Rockford	181,180	0.165

135	Monroe-El Dorado	176,380	0.161
136	Duluth-Superior	175,030	0.160
137	Topeka	171,470	0.156
138	Beaumont-Port Arthur	168,740	0.154
139	Columbia-Jefferson City	167,390	0.153
140	Wilmington	163,560	0.149
141	Medford-Klamath Falls	162,260	0.148
142	Erie	158,910	0.145
143	Sioux City	157,340	0.144
144	Wichita Falls & Lawton	156,300	0.143
145	Lubbock	152,620	0.139
146	Joplin-Pittsburg	152,310	0.139
147	Albany, GA	151,970	0.139
148	Bluefield-Beckley-Oak Hill	148,760	0.136
149	Terre Haute	146,860	0.134
150	Salisbury	146,510	0.134
151	Bangor	144,740	0.132
152	Wheeling-Steubenville	144,330	0.132
153	Rochestr-Mason City-Austin	142,570	0.130
154	Binghamton	141,350	0.129
155	Anchorage	139,960	0.128
156	Biloxi-Gulfport	137,590	0.126
157	Minot-Bismarck-Dickinson	135,760	0.124
158	Odessa-Midland	135,450	0.124
159	Palm Springs	135,190	0.123
160	Panama City	134,770	0.123
161	Sherman, TX-Ada, OK	123,540	0.113
162	Gainesville	116,670	0.106
163	Abilene-Sweetwater	112,950	0.103
164	Idaho Falls-Pocatello	112,700	0.103
165	Clarksburg-Weston	109,480	0.100
166	Utica	106,690	0.097
167	Quincy-Hannibal-Keokuk	105,070	0.096
168	Hattiesburg-Laurel	104,800	0.096
169	Missoula	103,810	0.095
170	Billings	102,370	0.093

171	Yuma-El Centro	99,490	0.091
172	Dothan	98,850	0.090
173	Elmira (Corning)	98,270	0.090
174	Jackson, TN	94,770	0.086
175	Watertown	94,390	0.086
176	Alexandria, LA	94,350	0.086
177	Lake Charles	94,240	0.086
178	Rapid City	93,220	0.085
179	Jonesboro	93,100	0.085
180	Marquette	91,100	0.083
181	Harrisonburg	85,550	0.078
182	Bowling Green	81,470	0.074
183	Greenwood-Greenville	78,160	0.071
184	Meridian	72,280	0.066
185	Charlottesville	69,930	0.064
186	Lafayette, IN	65,060	0.059
187	Parkersburg	64,790	0.059
188	Great Falls	64,650	0.059
189	Grand Junction-Montrose	63,650	0.058
190	Laredo	62,720	0.057
191	Twin Falls	59,940	0.055
192	Eureka	58,380	0.053
193	Butte-Bozeman, MT	57,680	0.053
194	Lima	54,200	0.049
195	Cheyenne, WY-Scottsbluff,	53,920	0.049
196	San Angelo	53,530	0.049
197	Bend, OR	52,550	0.048
198	Casper-Riverton	51,850	0.047
199	Mankato	51,390	0.047
200	Ottumwa-Kirksville	51,190	0.047
201	St. Joseph	48,740	0.044
202	Zanesville	33,240	0.030
203	Presque Isle	31,840	0.029
204	Fairbanks	31,640	0.029
205	Victoria	30,180	0.028
206	Helena	25,360	0.023

207	Juneau, AK	25,070	0.023
208	Alpena	17,930	0.016
209	North Platte	15,590	0.014
210	Glendive	5,150	0.005
Total		109,590,170	100.000

Appendix B: Glossary

AAAA (American Association of Advertising Agencies): a trade association of U.S. advertising agencies.

Active Audience: a term given to viewers who are highly selective about the programming they choose to watch. Active audiences are sometimes defined as those who turn a set on only to watch favored programs, and turn the set off when those programs are unavailable. Activity can also mean being goal-directed in media selections, or cognitively engaged with the media. See LOP, and passive audience.

Adjacency: an advertising opportunity immediately before or after a specific program.

ADI (Area of Dominant Influence): the term once used by Arbitron to describe a specific market area. Every county in the United States was assigned to one, and only one, ADI. See DMA.

Advertising Agency: a company that prepares and places advertising for its clients. Agencies typically have media departments that specialize in planning, buying, and evaluating advertising time.

Adware: a program secretly placed on a user's computer that redirects the browser to selected sites and/or launches pop-up ads.

Affiliate: a broadcast station that has a contractual agreement to air network programming.

AMOL (Automated Measurement of Lineups): a system that electronically determines the broadcast network programs actually aired in a local market.

ANA (Association of National Advertisers): a trade organization of major national advertisers responsible for creating the first broadcast ratings service. See CAB.

A/P Meter (Active/Passive Meter): a type of meter developed by Nielsen that has the ability to pick up a code emitted by a television signal, thus identifying the programming on the set.

AQH (Average Quarter Hour): the standard unit of time for reporting average audience estimates (e.g., AQH rating, AQH share) within specified dayparts.

ARB (Audience Research Bureau): a ratings company established in 1949 that was the predecessor of the Arbitron Company.

Arbitron: a major supplier of local market and national network radio ratings.

Area Probability Sample: a type of random sample in which geographic areas are considered for selection in some stage of the sampling process. See probability sample, cluster sample.

ARF (Advertising Research Foundation): trade organization of advertising and marketing research professionals advancing the practice and validity of advertising research.

Arianna: software program that handles television ratings; joint venture between Nielsen and AGB.

Ascription: a procedure for resolving confused or inaccurate diary entries, such as reports of listening to nonexistent stations.

Audience Duplication: a cumulative measure of the audience that describes the extent to which audience members for one program or station are also in the audience of another program or station. See audience flow, channel loyalty, inheritance effect, repeat viewing, recycling.

Audience Flow: the extent to which audiences persist from one program or time period to the next. See audience duplication, inheritance effects.

Audience Deficiency (AD): a failure to deliver the numbers and kinds of audiences agreed to in a contract between time sellers and buyers. Sellers will often remedy audience deficiencies by running extra commercials, called "make-goods."

Audience Fragmentation: a phenomenon in which the total audience for a medium is widely distributed across a large number of program services. Cable is said to fragment the television audience, resulting in a decreased average audience share for each channel.

Audience Polarization: a phenomenon associated with audience fragmentation, in which the audiences for channels or stations use them more intensively than an average audience member. See channel loyalty, channel repertoire

Audience Turnover: a phenomenon of audience behavior usually expressed as the ratio of a station's cumulative audience to its average quarter hour audience.

Audimeter: Nielsen's name for several generations of its metering device used to record set tuning. See SIA.

Available Audience: the total number of people who are, realistically, in a position to use a medium at any point in time. It is often operationally defined as those actually using the medium (i.e., PUT or PUR levels).

Availabilities: advertising time slots that are unsold, and therefore available for sale. Sometimes called *avails*.

Average: a measure of central tendency that expresses what is typical about a particular variable. An arithmetic average is usually called a *mean*. See mean, median.

Average Audience Rating: the rating of a station or program during an average time interval over a specified period of time. Metered data, for example, allow reports of audience size during an average minute of a television program.

Average Time Per Page: a measure of the average time spent with a page of computer information (e.g., a web page) across however many pages are examined in a single visit.

Away-from-Home Listening: estimates of radio listening that occurs outside the home. Such listening usually takes place in a car or place of work. Also called Out-of-Home.

Banner advertising: a form of advertising on the Internet, in which a box containing the advertiser's message appears on a portion of the page being viewed. Banner advertising often allows users to be linked to the advertiser's Web site.

Barter: a type of program syndication in which the cash expenditure for programming is reduced, sometimes to zero, because it contains national or regional advertising that is sold by the syndicator.

Basic Cable: the programming services provided by a cable system for the lowest of its monthly charges. These services typically include local television signals, advertiser-supported cable networks, and local access.

Birch: a research company that once provided syndicated radio rating reports in competition with Arbitron.

Block Programming: the practice of scheduling similar programs in sequence in order to promote audience flow. See inheritance effect.

Bounce: the tendency of a station's ratings to fluctuate from one market report to the next due to sampling error, rather than real changes in audience behavior. Bounce is most noticeable for stations with low ratings.

Broadband: a term describing the channel capacity of a distribution system. A common label for multichannel cable service, it is also applied to digital networks capable of delivering full motion video. See cable system.

Browser: a computer program that allows users to gain access to pages on the World Wide Web.

Buffer Sample: a supplemental sample used by a rating company in the event that the originally designated sample is insufficient due to unexpectedly low cooperation rates.

Cable Advertising Bureau (CAB): a trade organization formed to promote advertising on cable television.

Cable Penetration: the extent to which households in a given market subscribe to cable service. Typically expressed as the percent of all TV households that subscribe to basic cable.

Cable System: a video distribution system that uses coaxial cable and optical fiber to deliver multichannel service to households within a geographically defined franchise area.

Call-Back: the practice of attempting to interview someone in a survey sample who was not contacted or interviewed on an earlier try. The number of call-back attempts is an important determinant of response rates and nonresponse error. See nonresponse error.

Cash-plus-Barter: a type of barter syndication in which the station pays the syndicator cash, even though the program contains some advertising. See barter.

CATV (Community Antenna Television): an acronym for cable television, used in many early FCC proceedings.

Census: a study in which every member of a population is interviewed or measured. Every 10 years, the federal government conducts a census of the U.S. population.

Channel Loyalty: a common phenomenon of aggregate audience behavior in which the audience for one program tends to be disproportionately represented in the audience for other programs on the same channel. See audience duplication, inheritance effects.

Channel repertoire: a set of channels from which a viewer chooses—typically much fewer than the total number of channels available.

Cinema Advertising Council (CAC): a trade organization to promote the sale of commercial time in theaters.

Circulation: the total number of unduplicated audience members exposed to a media vehicle (e.g., newspaper, station) over some specified period of time. See cume, reach.

Clearance: (1) the assurance given by a station that it will air a program feed by its affiliated network; (2) the sale of syndicated programs to individual markets.

Click: when the user of a web page interacts with (i.e., clicks on) a message.

Click fraud: any method of artificially inflating the number of hits on a Web site.

Click rate: the percentage of advertising responses as a function of the number of clicks.

Clickstream: the record of all http requests made from a browser.

Click-through: a measure of Web ad effectiveness that tracks how many web users actually click on the ad they see.

Cluster Sample: a type of probability sample in which aggregations of sampling units, called *clusters*, are sampled at some stage in the process. See probability sample.

CODE (Cable On-line Data Exchange): a service of Nielsen Media Research that maintains information on the stations and networks carried on all U.S. cable systems. See cable system.

Codes: (in survey research) the numbers or letters used to represent responses in a survey instrument like a diary. Coding the responses allows computers to manipulate the data.

Coincidental: a type of telephone survey in which interviewers ask respondents what they are watching or listening to at the time of the call. Coincidentals, based on probability samples, often set the standard against which other ratings methods are judged.

COLRAM (Committee on Local Radio Audience Measurement): a committee of the NAB concerned with a range of local radio measurement issues.

COLTAM (Committee on Local Television Audience Measurement): a committee of the NAB concerned with a range of local television measurement issues.

COLTRAM (Committee on Local Television and Radio Audience Measurement): a committee of the NAB which, in 1985, was divided into COLRAM and COLTAM.

comScore Media Metrix: Internet audience research firm, competes with Nielsen/NetRatings.

Confidence Interval: in probability sampling, it is the range of values around an estimated population value (e.g., a rating) with a given probability (i.e., confidence level) of encompassing the true population value.

Confidence Level: in probability sampling, it is a statement of the likelihood that a range of values (i.e., confidence interval) will include the true population value.

Cooperative Analysis of Broadcasting: the first ratings company. Formed in 1930 by Archibald Crossley, it ended operations in 1946.

CMSA (Consolidated Metropolitan Statistical Area): a type of metropolitan area, designated by the U.S. Office of Management and Budget, often used by ratings companies to define a media market's metropolitan area.

Convenience Sample: a nonprobability sample, sometimes called an accidental sample, that is used because respondents are readily available or convenient.

Correlation: a statistic that measures the strength and direction of the relationship between two variables. It may range in value from +1.0 to –1.0, with 0 indicating no relationship.

CPP (Cost Per Point): a measure of how much it costs to buy the audience represented by one rating point. The size of that audience, and therefore its cost, varies with the size of the market population on which the rating is based.

CPM (Cost Per Thousand): a measure of how much it costs to buy 1,000 audience members delivered by an ad. CPMs are commonly used to compare the cost efficiency of different advertising vehicles.

Cohort: a type of longitudinal survey design in which several independent samples are drawn from a population whose membership does not change over time. See longitudinal.

Cookies: unique electronic signatures placed on an Internet user's hard drive to track access to a given Web site.

Counter-programming: a programming strategy in which a station or network schedules material appealing to an audience other than the competition. Independents often counter-program local news with entertainment.

Coverage: the potential audience for a given station or network, defined by the size of the population that is reached, or covered, by the signal.

Cross-sectional: a type of survey design in which one sample is drawn from the population at a single point in time. See longitudinal.

Cross-tabs: a technique of data analysis in which the responses to one item are paired with those of another item. Cross-tabs are useful in determining the audience duplication between two programs. See audience duplication.

Cume: short for *cumulative audience*, it is the size of the total unduplicated audience for a station over some specified period of time. When the cume is expressed as percent of the market population it is referred to as *cume rating*. See circulation, reach.

Cume Duplication: the percentage of a station's cume audience that also listened to another station, within some specified period of time. See exclusive cume.

Daypart: a specified period of time, usually defined by certain hours of the day and days of the week (e.g., weekdays vs. weekends), used to estimate audience size for the purpose of buying and selling advertising time. Dayparts can also be defined by program content (e.g., news, sports).

Demographics: a category of variables often used to describe the composition of audiences. Common demographics include age, gender, education, occupation, and income.

Direct Broadcast Satellite (DBS): mode of television distribution that uses signals transmitted via satellite to provide programming directly to subscriber households.

Domain name level: the consolidation of multiple URLs associated with the same domain name.

Domain consolidation level: the consolidation of multiple domain names and/or URLs associated with a main site.

DMA (Designated Market Area): the term used by Nielsen to describe specific market areas. Every county belongs to one, and only one, DMA.

Diary: a paper booklet, distributed by ratings companies, in which audience members are asked to record their television or radio use, usually for one week. The diary can be for an entire household (television) or for an individual (radio).

DST (Differential Survey Treatment): special procedures used by a ratings company to improve response from segments of the population known to have unusually low response rates. These may include additional interviews and incentives to cooperate.

DVR (Digital Video Recorder): an electronic device that records video programming on a hard drive. Sometimes called a personal video recorder (PVR), it empowers viewers with the ability to easily record, fast forward, replay programming, and skip commercials. TiVo is the best known DVR system.

Early Fringe: in television, a daypart in late afternoon immediately prior to the airing of local news programs.

Editing: the procedures used by a ratings company to check the accuracy and completeness of the data it collects. Editing may include techniques for clarifying or eliminating questionable data. See ascription.

Effective Exposure: a concept in media planning stipulating that a certain amount of exposure to an advertising message is necessary before it is effective. Often used interchangeably with the term *effective frequency*. See frequency.

ESF (Expanded Sample Frame): a procedure used by Arbitron to include in its sample frame households whose telephone numbers are unlisted. See sample frame.

ESS (Effective Sample Size): the size of a simple random sample needed to produce the same result as the sample actually used by the rating company. ESS is a convenience used for calculating confidence intervals. Also called Effective Sample Base, or ESB.

Ethnography: a term that describes any one of several qualitative research techniques. Audience ethnographies include in-depth interviews or group discussions, studying what people post on the Internet, and a variety of observer and participant observer techniques.

Exclusive Cume Audience: the total size of the unduplicated audience that listens exclusively to one station within some specified period of time.

FCC (Federal Communications Commission): The independent regulatory agency, created in 1934, that has primary responsibility for the oversight of broadcasting and cable.

Flow texts: the succession of images actually experienced by the viewer, sometimes called viewing strips.

Format: the style of programming offered by a radio station. Common formats include MOR (middle of the road), news/talk, and adult contemporary.

Frequency: in advertising, the average number of times that an individual is exposed to a particular advertising message.

Frequency Distribution: a way of representing the number of times different values of a variable occur within a sample or population.

Fringe: in television, dayparts just before prime time (early fringe) and after the late news (late fringe).

Geodemographics: a type of variable that categorizes audiences by combining geographic and demographic factors. For example, organizing audiences by zip codes with similar population age and income.

Grazing: the term describing the tendency of viewers to frequently change channels, a behavior that is presumably facilitated by remote control.

Gross Impressions: the total number of times an advertising schedule is seen over a period of time. The number of gross impressions may exceed the size of the population, since audience members may be duplicated. See GRP.

GRP (Gross Rating Point): the gross impressions of an advertising schedule expressed as a percentage of the population. GRPs are commonly used to describe the overall size or media weight of an advertising campaign. GRP's = Reach × Frequency.

Group Quarters: dormitories, barracks, nursing homes, prisons, and other living arrangements that do not qualify as households, and are, therefore, not measured by ratings companies.

Hammocking: a television programming strategy in which an unproven or weak show is scheduled between two popular programs in hopes that viewers will stay tuned, thereby enhancing the rating of the middle program. See audience flow, inheritance effect.

Headend: the part of a cable system that receives TV signals from outside sources (e.g., off-the-air, satellite) and sends them through the wired distribution system. See cable system.

Home County: the county in which a station's city of license is located.

Home Market: the market area in which a station is located.

Home Station: any station licensed in a city within a given market area.

Household: an identifiable housing unit, such as an apartment or house, occupied by one or more persons. See group quarters.

HPDV (Households Per Diary Value): the number of households in the population represented by a single diary kept by a sample household. Used to make audience projections. See projected audience.

HUT (Households Using Television): a term describing the total size of the audience, in households, at any point in time. Expressed either as the projected audience size, or as a percent of the total number of households.

Hypoing: any one of several illegal practices in which a station, or its agent, engages in an attempt to artificially inflate the station's rating during a measurement period. Also called *hyping*.

IAB (Interactive Advertising Bureau): a trade association promoting the Internet and other interactive technologies as advertising media.

IP address: a bit of computer code specified under an "Internet Protocol" identifying your computer to servers on the Internet. IP addresses can be static, meaning they never change, or dynamic, meaning they are assigned each time you log on.

Independent: a commercial television station that does not maintain an affiliation with a broadcast network.

Inertia: a description of audience behavior that implies viewers are unlikely to change channels unless provoked by very unappealing programming.

Inheritance Effect: a common phenomenon of television audience behavior, in which the audience for one program is disproportionately represented in the audience of the following program. Sometimes called *lead-in effects*, audience inheritance can be thought of as a special case of channel loyalty. See audience duplication, audience flow, channel loyalty.

In-Tab: a term describing the sample of households or persons actually used in tabulating or processing results.

Internet: a network of computer networks around the world that makes possible services like e-mail and the World Wide Web.

Interview: a method of collecting data through oral questioning of a respondent, either in person, or over the telephone.

Interviewer Bias: the problem of introducing systematic error or distortions in data collected in an interview, attributable to the appearance, manner, or reactions of the interviewer. See response error.

Keyword Search: a kind of advertising on the Web in which advertisers bid to have their site appear in response to a user's search request. Also called pay-for-placement.

Late Fringe: in television, a daypart just after the late local news (11 p.m. EST).

Lead-In: the program that immediately precedes another on the same channel. The size and composition of a lead-in audience is an important determinant of a program's rating. See inheritance effect.

Lead-In Effect: See inheritance effect.

Longitudinal: a type of survey designed to collect data over several points in time. See cross-sectional.

LOP (Least Objectionable Program): a popular theory of television audience behavior, attributed to Paul Klein, that argues that people primarily watch TV for reasons unrelated to content, and they choose the least objectionable programs. See passive audience.

LPM (Local Peoplemeter): simply a peoplemeter installed to provide local market audience measurement.

Market Segmentation: the practice of dividing populations into smaller groups having similar characteristics or interests in order to market goods and services more precisely. See demographics.

Maximi$er: Arbitron's computer software leased to radio stations.

Mean: a measure of central tendency determined by adding across cases, and dividing that total by the number of cases. See average, median, mode.

Measure: a procedure or device for quantifying objects (e.g., households, people) on variables of interest to the researcher.

Measurement: the process of assigning numbers to objects according to some rule of assignment.

Measurement Error: systematic bias or inaccuracy attributable to measurement procedures.

Median: a measure of central tendency defined as that point in a distribution where half the cases have higher values, and half have lower values. See average, mean, mode.

Meter: a measuring device used to record the on-off and channel tuning condition of a TV set. See SIA, peoplemeter.

Metro Area: the core metropolitan counties of a market area as defined by a ratings service. Metros generally correspond to MSAs.

Metro Rating: a program or station rating based on the behavior of those who live in the metropolitan area of the market. See rating.

Metro Share: a program or station share based on the behavior of those who live in the metropolitan area of the market. See share.

Mode: a measure of central tendency defined as the value in a distribution that occurs most frequently. See average, mean, median.

Mortality: a problem of losing sample members over time, typically in longitudinal survey research.

MRC (Media Rating Council): an industry organization responsible for accrediting the procedures used by ratings companies and monitoring the improvement of ratings methodologies.

Minimum Reporting Standard: the number of listening or viewing mentions necessary for a station or program to be included in a ratings report.

MSA (Metropolitan Statistical Area): an urban area designated by the Office of Management and Budget, often used by ratings companies to define their metro areas.

MSO (Multiple System Operator): a company owning more than one cable system.

Multi-Set Household: a television household with more than one working television set.

Multi-Stage Sample: a type of probability sample requiring more than one round of sampling. See cluster sample, probability sample.

NAB (National Association of Broadcasters): an industry organization representing the interests of commercial broadcasters.

NATPE (National Association of Television Program Executives) an industry organization of media professionals responsible for television programming.

Narrowcasting: a programming strategy in which a station or network schedules content of the same type or appealing to the same subset of the audience. See block programming.

NCTA (National Cable Television Association): an industry organization representing the interests of cable systems.

Net Audience: See cume or reach.

Net Weekly Circulation: the cume or unduplicated audience using a station or network in a week. See cume.

Network: an organization that acquires or produces programming and distributes that programming, usually with national or regional advertising, to affiliated stations or cable systems.

Nielsen Agency, Broadcast and Syndicator Service (NABSS): division of Nielsen Media Research that handles audience measurement for network television and national syndication (combines NTI and NSS).

Nielsen Media Research: a major supplier of national and local market television ratings and other forms of audience measurement.

Nielsen Monitor Plus: commercial monitoring service that matches ratings with commercials and estimated costs in local markets.

Nielsen Net/Ratings: division of Nielsen Media Research that measures Internet audiences, competes with comScore Media Metrix.

Nonprobability Sample: a kind of sample in which every member of the population does not have a known probability of selection into the sample. See convenience sample, purposive sample, quota sample.

Nonresponse: the problem of failing to obtain information from each person originally drawn into the sample.

Nonresponse Error: biases or inaccuracies in survey data that result from nonresponse. See nonresponse.

Normal Distribution: a kind of frequency distribution that, when graphed, forms a symmetrical, bell-shaped curve. Many statistical procedures are premised on the assumption that variables are normally distributed. See skew.

NPower: a package of computer programs offered by Nielsen Media Research that affords clients access to its national peoplemeter database. It performs a wide range of customized analyses of gross and cumulative audience behavior.

NSI (Nielsen Station Index): a division within Nielsen Media Research that issues a series of local television market ratings reports.

NTI (Nielsen Television Index): division of Nielsen Media Research responsible for national television network ratings (now part of NABSS).

Off-Network Programs: programs originally produced to air on a major broadcast network, now being sold in syndication.

Opportunistic Market: the buying and selling of network advertising time on short notice, as unforeseen developments (e.g., cancellation, schedule changes) create opportunities. See scatter market, upfront market.

Optimizers: any one of several computer programs used by large advertisers or ad agencies that take respondent-level peoplemeter data as input to create advertising schedules that optimize campaign reach while minimizing costs.

O & O (Owned & Operated): a broadcast station that is owned and operated by a major broadcast network.

Overnights: the label given to ratings, based on meters, that are available to clients the day after broadcast.

Oversample: deliberately drawing a sample larger than needed in-tab to compensate for nonresponse, or to intensively study some subset of the sample.

Page Views: number of Web pages viewed by users in a given time period.

Panel: a type of longitudinal survey design in which the same sample of individuals is studied over some period of time. For example, meters are placed in a panel of television households. See cross-sectional, longitudinal, trend analysis.

Passive Audience: a term given to viewers who are unselective about the content they watch. Passive audiences are thought to watch TV out of habit, tuning to almost anything if a preferred show is unavailable. See active audience, LOP.

Pay Cable: the programming services provided by a cable system for a monthly fee above and beyond that required for basic cable. Pay cable may include any one of several "premium" services like HBO, Showtime, or The Disney Channel.

Pay-for-Placement: see keyword search.

PC Meter™: software, developed by Media Metrix, that renders a desktop computer capable of monitoring Internet use for purposes of audience measurement.

Peoplemeter: a device that electronically records the on-off and channel tuning condition of a TV set, and is capable of identifying viewers. If viewers must enter that information by button pressing, the meter is called *active*; if the meter requires no effort from viewers, it is called *passive*.

Periodicity: a problem encountered in systematic sampling in which the sampling interval corresponds to some cyclical arrangement in the list.

Placement Interview: an initial interview to secure the willingness of the respondent to keep a diary or receive a meter.

PMSA (Primary Metropolitan Statistical Area): an urban area designated by the Office of Management and Budget that is often used in defining ratings areas.

Pocketpiece: the common name given to Nielsen's weekly national TV ratings report.

Pod: a group of commercials, often numbering six to eight, that are aired one after the other. An ad's position in the pod is sometimes negotiated.

Population (or "universe"): the total number of persons or households from which a sample is drawn. Membership in a population must be clearly defined, often by the geographic area in which a person lives.

Portable Peoplemeter (PPM): a metering system in which respondents wear a pager-like device that detects an inaudible code embedded in a broadcast signal. When the meter "hears" the code it ascribes the respondent to the audience.

Post-Buy Analysis: The analysis conducted after a program runs. It could refer to: (1) a financial analysis to determine whether the price paid for the program was appropriate, or (2) the analysis of ratings performance to determine whether the predicted rating was correct.

Power Ratio: a statistic that expresses the relationship between share of revenue and share of audience. Also called the conversion ratio, or home market share ratio.

PPDV (Persons Per Diary Value): the number of persons in a population represented by a single diary kept by a member of a ratings sample. PPDV is used to project an audience. See projected audience.

Preempt: an action, taken by an affiliate, in which programming fed by a network is replaced with programming scheduled by the station. Certain types of commercial time can also be "preempted" by advertisers willing to pay a premium for the spot.

Prime Access (in local television): the first hour of prime time, prior to network programming. Local stations generally schedule syndicated programs or local productions during prime access.

Prime Time: a television daypart from 7 p.m. to 11 p.m. EST. Due to FCC regulations, broadcast networks typically provide prime time programming to affiliated stations from 8 p.m. to 11 p.m. EST.

Probability Sample: a kind of sample in which every member of the population has an equal or known chance of being selected into the sample. Sometimes called *random samples*, probability samples allow statistical inferences about the accuracy of sample estimates. See confidence interval, confidence level, sampling error.

Processing Error: a source of inaccuracies in ratings reports attributable to problems inherent in the mechanics of gathering and producing the data. See ascription, editing.

Program Type: a category of programming usually based on similarities in program content. Nielsen identifies over 35 program types, used in summarizing program audiences.

Projectable: a quality describing a sample designed in such a way that audience projections may be made. See projected audience, probability sample.

Projected Audience: the total size of an audience estimated to exist in the population, based on sample information. See HPDV, PPDV, probability sample.

Psychographics: a category of variable that draws distinctions among people on the basis of their psychological characteristics, including opinions, interests, and attitudes.

PTAR (Prime Time Access Rule): an FCC regulation, effective from the 1970s through the early 1990s, limiting the amount of network programming that affiliates could carry during prime time, and preventing affiliates in the top 50 markets from airing off-network reruns during prime access.

PUR (Persons Using Radio): a term describing the total size of the radio audience at any point in time. See HUT, PUT.

Purposive Sample: a type of nonprobability sample, sometimes called a *judgment sample*, in which the researcher uses his or her knowledge of the population to "handpick" areas or groups of respondents for research.

PUT (Persons Using Television): a term describing the total size of the television audience, in persons, at any point in time. See HUT, PUR.

PVR (Personal Video Recorder): another name for digital video recorders.

Qualitative Ratings: numerical summaries of the audience that not only describe how many watched or listened, but their reactions including enjoyment, interest, attentiveness, and information gained.

Qualitative Research: any systematic investigation of the audience that does not depend on measurement and quantification. Examples include focus groups and participant observation. Sometimes used to describe any nonratings research, even if quantification is involved, as in "qualitative ratings."

Quota Sample: a type of nonprobability sample in which categories of respondents called *quotas* (e.g., males), are filled by interviewing respondents who are convenient. See nonprobability sample, probability sample.

RAB (Radio Advertising Bureau): an industry organization formed to promote advertising on radio.

RADAR (Radio's All Dimension Audience Research): Arbitron's syndicated ratings service for radio network audiences.

Random Digit Dialing (RDD): in telephone surveys, a technique for creating a probability sample by randomly generating telephone numbers. By using this method, all numbers including unlisted have an equal chance of being called.

Random Sample: See probability sample.

Rate of Response: the percentage of those originally drawn into the sample who provide useable information. See in-tab.

Rate Card: a list of how much a station will charge for its commercial spots. Rate cards are sometimes incorporated with ratings data in computer programs that manage station inventories.

Rating: in its simplest form, the percentage of persons or households tuned to a station, program, or daypart out of the total market population.

Ratings Distortion: activity on the part of a broadcaster designed to alter the way audience members report their use of stations. See hypoing.

Reach: the total number of unduplicated persons or households included in the audience of a station or a commercial campaign over some specified period of time. Sometimes expressed as a percentage of the total market population. See cume, frequency.

Recency theory: the idea that an ad is most effective if it hits consumers when they are ready to buy. This places a premium on reach and timing, rather than frequency of exposure.

Recycling: the extent to which listeners in one daypart also listen in another daypart. See audience duplication.

Relative Standard Error: a means of comparing the amount of sampling error in ratings data to the size of different ratings. It is the ratio of the standard error to the rating itself. See sampling error.

Relative Standard Error Thresholds: the size of a rating needed to have a relative standard error of either 25% or 50%. Often published in market reports as a means of judging ratings accuracy. See relative standard error.

Reliability: the extent to which a method of measurement yields consistent results over time.

Repeat viewing: the extent to which the audience for one program is represented in the audience of other episodes of the series. See audience duplication.

Replication: a study repeating the procedures of an early study to assess the stability of results. In audience measurement, replications involve drawing subsamples from a parent sample to assess sampling error.

Respondent: a sample member who provides information in response to questions.

Response Error: inaccuracies in survey data attributable to the quality of responses, including lying, forgetting, or misinterpreting questions. See interviewer bias.

RFID (Radio Frequency Identification): a tiny chip or tag, often embedded in products, that emits a signal that can be picked up by a scanner. RFIDs might offer a way to measure exposure to print media.

Rich Media: a type of Web ad that features more dynamic, eye-catching, content. Such ads often require web connections with greater bandwidth to be effective.

Rolling Average: a ratings level based on the average of several successive samples. As new sample data become available, the oldest sample is dropped from the average. A rolling average is less susceptible to sampling error. See bounce.

ROS (Run of Schedule): a method of buying and scheduling ads in which the advertiser allows the station or network to run commercials at the best time that happens to be available.

Sample: a subset of some population. See probability sample.

Sample Balancing: see sample weighting.

Sample Frame: a list of some population from which a probability sample is actually drawn.

Sample Weighting: the practice of assigning different mathematical weights to various subsets of the in-tab sample in an effort to correct for different response rates among those subsets. Each weight is the ratio of the subset's size in the population to its size in the sample.

Sampling Distribution: the hypothetical frequency distribution of sample statistics that would result from repeated samplings of some population.

Sampling Error: inaccuracies in survey data attributable to "the luck of the draw" in creating a probability sample.

Sampling Rate: the ratio of sample size to population size.

Sampling Unit: the survey element (e.g., person or household), or aggregation of elements, considered for selection at some stage in the process of probability sampling.

Satellite Radio: mode of radio signal transmission that uses satellites to send digital quality programming to individual subscriber receivers.

Scatter Market: a period of time, just in advance of a given quarter of the year, during which advertisers buy network time. See opportunistic market, upfront market.

Search Engine: a Web site specifically designed to help Internet users find specific pieces of information on the World Wide Web.

Segmentation: the practice of dividing the total market into subsets, often related to the needs of a marketing plan or the programming preferences of the population. See target audience.

Sets-in-Use: the total number of sets turned on at a given point in time. As a measure of total audience size, it has become outdated since most households now have multiple sets. See HUT.

Share: in its simplest form, the percentage of persons or households tuned to a station or program out of all those using the medium at that time.

SIA (Storage Instantaneous Audimeter): a later version of Nielsen's original audimeter that allowed the company to retrieve electronically stored information over telephone lines.

Simple Random Sample: a one-stage probability sample in which every member of the population has an equal chance of selection. See probability sample.

Skew: a measure of the extent to which a frequency distribution departs from a normal, symmetrical shape. In common use, the extent to which some subset of population is disproportionately represented in the audience (e.g., "the audience skews old").

Spill: the extent to which nonmarket stations are viewed by local audiences, or local stations are viewed by audiences outside the market.

Spin-Off: a programming strategy in which the characters or locations of a popular program are used to create another television series.

Spyware: a program secretly placed on a user's computer that sends data on surfing activities back to an advertiser or other business.

SMSA (Standard Metropolitan Statistical Area): the former governmental designation of an urban area, once used by ratings companies to define local market areas. See MSA.

SRDS (Standard Rate and Data Service): a service that publishes the station rate cards and other information useful in buying commercial time. See rate card.

Standard Deviation: a measure of the variability in a frequency distribution.

Standard Error: the standard deviation of a sampling distribution. It is the statistic used to make statements about the accuracy of estimates based on sample information. See confidence interval, confidence level, relative standard error.

Station Rep: an organization that represents local stations to national and regional advertisers, selling the station's time and sometimes providing research information useful in programming.

Station Total Area: a Nielsen term meaning the total geographic area upon which total station audience estimates are based. The total area may include counties outside the NSI area.

Statistical Significance: the point at which results from a sample deviate so far from what could happen by chance that they are thought to reflect real differences or phenomena in the population. By convention, significance levels are usually set at .05 or lower, meaning a result could happen by chance only 5 times in 100. See confidence level.

Stratified Sample: a type of probability sample in which the population is organized into homogeneous subsets or strata, after which a predetermined number of respondents is randomly selected for each strata. Stratified sampling can reduce the sampling error associated with simple random samples.

Stripped Programming: a programming practice in which television shows are scheduled at the same time on 5 consecutive weekdays. Stations often strip syndicated programs.

Superstation: an independent television station whose programming is widely carried on cable systems around the country.

Sweep: in television, a 4-week period of time during which ratings companies are collecting the audience information necessary to produce local market reports. November, February, May, and July.

Syndicated Network Television Association (SNTA): trade association that supports syndicators' efforts to sell commercial time.

Syndication: selling a standardized product to many clients. A syndicated program is available to stations in many different markets. A syndicated ratings report is also sold to many users.

Systematic Sample: a kind of probability sample in which a set interval is applied to a list of the population to identify elements included into the sample (e.g., picking every 10th name).

Target Audience: any well-defined subset of the total audience that an advertiser wants to reach with a commercial campaign, or that a station wants to reach with a particular kind of programming.

Telephone Recall: a type of survey in which a telephone interviewer asks the respondent what they listened to or watched in the recent past, often the preceding day. See coincidental.

Television Household (TVHH): a common unit of analysis in ratings research, it is any household equipped with a working television set, excluding group quarters.

Theory: a tentative explanation of how some phenomenon of interest works. Theories identify causes and effects, which make them amenable to testing and falsification.

Tiering: the practice of marketing cable services to subscribers in groups or bundles of channels called *tiers*.

Time Buyers: anyone who buys time from the electronic media for purposes of running commercial announcements.

Time Period Averages: the size of a broadcast audience at an average point in time, within some specified period of time.

TiVo: a company that led the way in introducing DVRs to consumers. TiVo is, essentially, a software company that licenses its technology to different electronics manufacturers.

Total Audience: all those who tune to a program for at least 5 minutes. Essentially, it is the cumulative audience for a long program or miniseries.

Trend Analysis: a type of longitudinal survey design in which results from repeated independent samplings are compared over time.

TSL (Time Spent Listening): a cumulative measure of the average amount of time an audience spends listening to a station within a daypart.

Turnover: the ratio of a station's cumulative audience to its average quarter hour audience within a daypart.

TvB (Television Bureau of Advertising): an industry organization formed to promote advertising on broadcast television.

TVQ: a ratings system that assesses the familiarity and likability of personalities and programs.

UHF (Ultra High Frequency): a class of television stations assigned to broadcast on channels 14 through 80.

Unduplicated Audience: the number of different persons or households in an audience over some specified period of time.

Unique visitors: unique Web users that visited a site over the course of the reporting period. See cume and unduplicated audience.

Unit of Analysis: the element or entity about which a researcher collects information. In ratings, the unit of analysis is usually a person or household.

Universe: see Population.

Unweighted In-Tab: the actual number of individuals in different demographic groups who have returned usable information to the ratings company.

Unwired Networks: organizations that acquire commercial time (usually in similar types of programming) from stations around the country and package that time for sale to advertisers.

Upfront Market: a period of time several months in advance of the new fall television season during which networks, barter syndicators, and major advertisers agree to the sale of large blocks of commercial time for the broadcast year.

Validity: the extent to which a method of measurement accurately quantifies the attribute it is supposed to measure.

Variable: any well-defined attribute or characteristic that varies from person to person, or thing to thing. See demographic.

VCR (Video-Cassette Recorder): an appliance used for recording and playing videocassette tapes, now in a majority of U.S. households.

VHF (Very High Frequency): a class of television stations assigned to broadcast on channels 2 through 13.

View-through: a measure of Web ad effectiveness that tracks how many Web users take action within some period of time (e.g., 30 days) after having seen an ad. See click-through.

VPVH (Viewers Per Viewing Household): the estimated number of people, usually by demographic category, in each household tuned to a particular source.

Web site: a specific location on the World Wide Web offering information, entertainment, and/or advertising.

Weighted In-Tab: the number of individuals in different demographic groups who would have provided usable information if response rates were equivalent. See sample weighting.

Weighting: the process of assigning mathematical weights in an attempt to correct over- or under-representation of some groups in the unweighted in-tab sample. See sample weighting.

WWW (World Wide Web): a system of protocols and programs that enables Internet users to access pages of information on computer servers around the world.

Zapping: the practice of using a remote control device to avoid commercials or program content by rapidly changing channels. Often used interchangeably with zipping.

Zipping: the practice of using the fast-forward function on a VCR or DVR to speed through unwanted commercials or program content. Often used interchangeably with zapping.

Bibliography
and Additional Sources

Advertising Research Foundation. (1954). *Recommended standards for radio and television audience size measurements*. New York: Author.

Adams, W. J. (1993). TV program scheduling strategies and their relationship to new program renewal rates and rating changes. *Journal of Broadcasting and Electronic Media, 37*, 465–474.

Adams, W. J., Eastman, S. T., Horney, L. J., & Popovich, M. N. (1983). The cancellation and manipulation of network television prime-time programs. *Journal of Communication, 33*(1), 10–27.

Agostini, J. M. (1961). How to estimate unduplicated audiences. *Journal of Advertising Research, 1*, 11–14.

Agostino, D. (1980). Cable television's impact on the audience of public television. *Journal of Broadcasting, 24*, 347–363.

Albarran, A. (2001). *Management of electronic media* (2nd ed.). Belmont, CA: Wadsworth.

Albarran, A., & Arrese, A. (Eds.). (2003). *Time and media markets*. Mahwah, NJ: Lawrence Erlbaum Associates.

Albarran, A., & Chan-Olmsted, S. (Eds.). (1998). *Global media economics: Commercialization, concentration and integration of world media markets*. Ames, IA: Iowa State Press.

Allen, C. (1965). Photographing the TV audience. *Journal of Advertising Research, 5*, 2–8.

Allen, R. (1981). The reliability and stability of television exposure. *Communication Research, 8*, 233–256.

Alexander, A., Owers, J., Carveth, R., Hollifiend, C. A., & Greco, A. (Eds.). (2004). *Media economics: Theory and practice* (3rd ed.). Mahwah, NJ: Lawrence Erlbaum Associates.

American Research Bureau. (1947, May). *Washington DC market report*. Beltsville, MD: Author.

Anderson, J. A. (1987). *Communication research: Methods and issues*. New York: McGraw-Hill.

Ang, I. (1991). *Desperately seeking the audience*. London: Routledge.

Arbitron. (annually). *A guide to understanding and using radio audience estimates*. New York: Author.

Atkin, D., & Litman, B. (1986). Network TV programming: Economics, audiences, and the ratings game, 1971–1986. *Journal of Communication, 36*(3), 32–51.

Austin, B. A. (1989). *Immediate seating: A look at movie audiences*. Belmont, CA: Wadsworth.

Babbie, E. (2003). *The practice of social research* (10th ed.). Belmont, CA: Wadsworth.

Babrow, A. S., & Swanson, D. L. (1988). Disentangling antecedents of audience exposure levels: Extending expectancy-value analyses of gratifications sought from television news. *Communication Monographs, 55*, 1–21.

Baker, C. E. (2002). *Media, markets, and democracy*. Cambridge: Cambridge University Press.

Balen, R. E. (1995). *The new rules of the ratings game*. Washington, DC: National Association of Broadcasters.

Banks, M. (1981). *A history of broadcast audience research in the United States, 1920–1980 with an emphasis on the rating services*. Unpublished doctoral dissertation, University of Tennessee, Knoxville.

Banks, S. (1980). Children's television viewing behavior. *Journal of Marketing, 44,* 48–55.

Barnes, B. E., & Thompson, L. M. (1988). The impact of audience information sources on media evolution. *Journal of Advertising Research, 28,* RC9–RC14.

Barnett, G. A., Chang, H., Fink, E. L., & Richards, W.D. (1991). Seasonality in television viewing: A mathematical model of cultural processes. *Communication Research, 18*(6), 755–772.

Baron, R. (1988). If it's on computer paper, it must be right. *Journal of Media Planning, 2,* 32–34.

Bart, P. (1999). *The gross: The hits, the flops—the summer that ate Hollywood*. New York: St. Martin's.

Barwise, T. P. (1986). Repeat-viewing of prime-time television series. *Journal of Advertising Research, 26,* 9–14.

Barwise, T. P., & Ehrenberg, A. S. C. (1984). The reach of TV channels. *International Journal of Research in Marketing, 1,* 34–49.

Barwise, T. P, & Ehrenberg, A. S. C. (1988). *Television and its audience*. London: Sage.

Barwise, T. P., Ehrenberg, A. S. C., & Goodhardt, G. J. (1979). Audience appreciation and audience size. *Journal of Market Research Society, 21,* 269–289.

Barwise, T. P., Ehrenberg, A. S. C., & Goodhart, G. J. (1982). Glued to the box?: Patterns of TV repeat-viewing. *Journal of Communication, 32*(4), 22–29.

Bechtel, R. K., Achelpohl, C., & Akers, R. (1972). Correlation between observed behavior and questionnaire responses on television viewing. In E. A. Rubinstein, G. A. Comstock, & J. P. Murray (Eds.), *Television and social behavior: Vol. 4. Television in day-to-day life: Patterns of use* (pp. 274–344). Washington, DC: U.S. Government Printing Office.

Becknell, J. C. (1961). The influence of newspaper tune-in advertising on the size of a TV show's audience. *Journal of Advertising Research, 1,* 23–26.

Beebe, J. H. (1977). The institutional structure and program choices in television markets. *Quarterly Journal of Economics, 91,* 15–37.

Becker, L. B., & Schoenback, K. (Eds.). (1989). *Audience responses to media diversification: Coping with plenty*. Hillsdale, NJ: Lawrence Erlbaum Associates.

Besen, S. M. (1976). The value of television time. *Southern Economic Journal, 42,* 435–441.

Besen, S. M., Krattenmaker, T. G., Metzger, A. R., & Woodbury, J. R. (1984). *Misregulating television: Network dominance and the FCC*. Chicago: University of Chicago Press.

Beville, H. M., Jr. (1988). *Audience ratings: Radio, television, cable* (Rev. ed.). Hillsdale, NJ: Lawrence Erlbaum Associates.

Blumler, J. G. (1979). The role of theory in uses and gratifications studies. *Communication Research, 6,* 9–36.

Blumler, J. G., Gurevitch, M., & Katz, E. (1985). Reaching out: A future for gratifications research. In K. Rosengren, L. Wenner, & P. Palmgreen (Eds.), *Media gratifications research: Current perspectives* (pp. 255–273). Beverly Hills, CA: Sage.

Boemer, M. L. (1987). Correlating lead-in show ratings with local television news ratings. *Journal of Broadcasting & Electronic Media, 31,* 89–94.

Bogart, L. (1972). *The age of television*. New York: Frederick Ungar.

Bogart, L. (1988). Research as an instrument of power. *Gannett Center Journal, 2*(3), 1–16.

Bogart, L. (1996). *Strategy in advertising: Matching media and messages to markets and motivations* (3rd ed.). Lincolnwood, IL: NTC Business Books.

Bower, R. T. (1973). *Television and the public*. New York: Holt, Rinehart & Winston.

Bower, R. T. (1985). *The changing television audience in America*. New York: Columbia University Press.

Bowman, G. W., & Farley, J. (1972). TV viewing: Application of a formal choice model. *Applied Economics, 4*, 245–259.

Brotman, S. N. (1988). *Broadcasters can negotiate anything*. Washington, DC: National Association of Broadcasters.

Bruno, A. V. (1973). The network factor in TV viewing. *Journal of Advertising Research, 13*, 33–39.

Bryant, J., & Zillmann, D. (1984). Using television to alleviate boredom and stress: Selective exposure as a function of induced excitational states. *Journal of Broadcasting, 28*, 1–20.

Bryant, J., & Zillmann, D. (Eds.). (2002). *Media effects: Advances in theory and research* (2nd ed.). Mahwah, NJ: Lawrence Erlbaum Associates.

Byrne, B. (1988). Barter syndicators. *Gannett Center Journal, 2*(3), 75–78.

Buzzard, K. S. (1990). *Chains of gold: Marketing the ratings and rating the markets*. Metuchen, NJ: Scarecrow Press.

Cabletelevision Advertising Bureau. (2004). *Cable TV facts*. New York: Author.

Cannon, H. M. (1983). Reach and frequency estimates for specialized target markets. *Journal of Advertising Research, 23*, 45–50.

Cannon, H., & Merz, G. R. (1980). A new role for psychographics in media selection. *Journal of Advertising, 9*(2), 33–36.

Cantril, H., & Allport, G.W. (1935). *The psychology of radio*. New York: Harper & Brothers.

Carroll, R. L., & Davis, D. M. (1993). *Electronic media programming: Strategies and decision making*. New York: McGraw-Hill.

CBS. (1937). *Radio in 1937*. New York: Author.

Chaffee, S. (1980). Mass media effects: New research perspectives. In D. C. Wilhoit & H. DeBock (Eds.), *Mass communication review yearbook* (pp. 77–108). Beverly Hills, CA: Sage.

Chandon, J. L. (1976). *A comparative study of media exposure models*. Unpublished doctoral dissertation, Northwestern University, Evanston, IL.

Chappell, M. N., & Hooper, C. E. (1944). *Radio audience measurement*. New York: Stephen Daye.

Christ, W., & Medoff, N. (1984). Affective state and selective exposure to and use of television. *Journal of Broadcasting, 28*, 51–63.

Churchill, G. A., & Iachobucci, D. (2004). *Marketing research: Methodological foundations* (9th ed.). Belmont, CA: South-Western College Pub.

Cohen, E. E. (1989). *A model of radio listener choice*. Unpublished doctoral dissertation, Michigan State University, East Lansing.

Collins, J., Reagan, J., & Abel, J. (1983). Predicting cable subscribership: Local factors. *Journal of Broadcasting, 27*, 177–183.

Comstock, G. (1989). *The evolution of American television*. Newbury Park, CA: Sage.

Comstock, G., Chaffee, S., Katzman, N., McCombs, M., & Roberts, D. (1978). *Television and human behavior*. New York: Columbia University Press.

Comstock, G., & Scharrer, E. (1999). *Television: What's on who's watching, and what it means*. San Diego: Academic Press.

Converse, T. (Speaker). (1974, May 2). *Magazine* [Television documentary]. New York: CBS, Inc.

Cook, F. (1988, January). Peoplemeters in the USA: An historical and methodological perspective. *Admap*, 32–35.

Cooper, R. (1993). An expanded, integrated model for determing audience exposure to television. *Journal of Broadcasting & Electronic Media, 37*(4), 401–418.

Cooper, R. (1996). The status and future of audience duplication research: An assessment of ratings-based theories of audience behavior. *Journal of Broadcasting & Electronic Media 40*(1), 96–111.

Corporation for Public Broadcasting. (1980). *Proceedings of the 1980 technical conference on qualitative television ratings: Final report*. Washington, DC: Author.

Danaher, P. J., & Lawrie, J. M. (1998). Behavioral measures of television audience appreciation. *Journal of Advertising Research, 38*, 54–65.

Darmon, R. (1976). Determinants of TV viewing. *Journal of Advertising Research, 16*, 17–20.

Davis, D. M., & Walker, J. R. (1990). Countering the new media: The resurgence of share maintenance in primetime network television. *Journal of Broadcasting & Electronic Media, 34*, 487–493.

Dick, S. J., & McDowell, W. (2004). Estimating relative audience loyalty among radio stations using standard Arbitron ratings. *Journal of Radio Studies, 11*, 26–39.

Dimling, J. (1988). A. C. Nielsen: The "gold standard." *Gannett Center Journal, 2*(3), 63–69.

Dominick, J. R., & Fletcher, J. E. (1985). *Broadcasting research methods*. Boston: Allyn & Bacon.

Ducey, R., Krugman, D., & Eckrich, D. (1983). Predicting market segments in the cable industry: The basic and pay subscribers. *Journal of Broadcasting, 27*, 155–161.

Eastman, S. T. (1998). Programming theory under stress: The active industry and the active audience. In M. Roloff (Ed), *Communication Yearbook, 21*, 323–377.

Eastman, S. T., & Ferguson, D. (2005). *Media programming: Strategies and practice* (7th ed.). Belmont, CA: Wadsworth.

Eastman, S. T., Newton, G. D., Riggs, K. E., & Neal-Lunsford, J. (1997). Accelerating the flow: A transition effect in programming theory? *Journal of Broadcasting & Electronic Media 41*(2), 265–283.

Ehrenberg, A. S. C. (1968). The factor analytic search for program types. *Journal of Advertising Research, 8*, 55–63.

Ehrenberg, A. S. C. (1982). *A primer in data reduction*. London & New York: Wiley.

Ehrenberg, A. S. C., & Wakshlag, J. (1987). Repeat-viewing with people meters. *Journal of Advertising Research, 27*, 9–13.

Ettema, J. S., & Whitney, C. D. (Eds.). (1982). *Individuals in mass media organizations: Creativity and constraint*. Beverly Hills, CA: Sage.

Ettema, J. S, & Whitney, C. D. (Eds.). (1994). *Audiencemaking: How the media create the audience*. Thousand Oaks, CA: Sage.

Everett, S. E. (1998, July). *The "UHF Penalty" demonstrated*. www.nab.org/research/webbriefs/uhfdis.html.

Federal Communications Commission. (1979). *Inquiry into the economic relationship between television broadcasting and cable television* (51 F.C.C. 2d 241). Washington, DC: U.S. Government Printing Office.

Ferguson, D. A. , & Eastman, S. T. (2001). *Broadcast/cable programming: Strategies and practices* (6th ed.). Belmont, CA: Wadsworth.

Fisher, F. M., McGowan, J. J., & Evans, D. S. (1980). The audience–revenue relationship for local television stations. *Bell Journal of Economics, 11*, 694–708.

Fletcher, A. D., & Bower, T. A. (1988). *Fundamentals of advertising research* (3rd ed.). Belmont, CA: Wadsworth.

Fletcher, J. E. (Ed.). (1981). *Handbook of radio and TV broadcasting: Research procedures in audience, program and revenues.* New York: Van Nostrand Reinhold.

Fletcher, J. E. (1985). *Squeezing profits out of ratings: A manual for radio managers, sales managers and programmers.* Washington, DC: National Association of Broadcasters.

Fletcher, J. E. (1987). *Music and program research.* Washington, DC: National Association of Broadcasters.

Fournier, G. M., & Martin, D. L. (1983). Does government-restricted entry produce market power? New evidence from the market for television advertising. *Bell Journal of Economics, 14*, 44–56.

Fowler, M. S., & Brenner, D. L. (1982). A marketplace approach to broadcast regulation. *Texas Law Review, 60*, 207–257.

Frank, R. E., Becknell, J., & Clokey, J. (1971). Television program types. *Journal of Marketing Research, 11*, 204–211.

Frank, R. E., & Greenberg, M. G. (1980). *The public's use of television.* Beverly Hills, CA: Sage.

Fratrik, M. R. (1989, April). *The television audience–revenue relationship revisited.* Paper presented at the meeting of the Broadcast Education Association, Las Vegas, NV.

Gantz, W., & Razazahoori, A. (1982). The impact of television schedule changes on audience viewing behaviors. *Journalism Quarterly, 59*, 265–272.

Gantz, W., & Eastman, S. T. (1983). Viewer uses of promotional media to find out about television programs. *Journal of Broadcasting, 27*, 269–277.

Gans, H. (1980). The audience for television and in television research. In S. B. Witney & R. P. Abeles (Eds.), *Television and social behavior: Beyond violence and children* (pp. 55–81). Hillsdale, NJ: Lawrence Erlbaum Associates.

Garrison, G. (1939). Wayne University. In J. P. Porter (Ed.), *Journal of Applied Psychology, 23*, 204–205.

Gensch, D. H. (1969, May). A computer simulation model for selecting advertising schedules. *Journal of Marketing Research, 6*, 203–214.

Gensch, D. H., & Ranganathan, B. (1974). Evaluation of television program content for the purpose of promotional segmentation. *Journal of Marketing Research, 11*, 390–398.

Gensch, D. H., & Shaman, P. (1980). Models of competitive ratings. *Journal of Marketing Research, 17*, 307–315.

Gerbner, G., Gross, L., Morgan, M., Signorielli, N., & Shanahan, J. (2002). Growing up with television: Cultivation processes. In J. Bryant & D. Zillmann (Eds.), *Media effects: Advances in theory and research* (2nd ed., pp. 43–67). Mahwah, NJ: Lawrence Erlbaum Associates.

Gitlin, T. (1983). *Inside prime time.* New York: Pantheon.

Goodhardt, G. J. (1966). The constant in duplicated television viewing between and within channels. *Nature, 212*, 1616.

Goodhardt, G. J., & Ehrenberg, A. S. C. (1969). Duplication of viewing between and within channels. *Journal of Marketing Research, 6*, 169–178.

Goodhardt, G. J., Ehrenberg, A. S. C., & Collins, M. A. (1987). *The television audience: Patterns of viewing* (2nd ed). Westmead, UK: Gower.

Glasser, G. J., & Metzger, G. D. (1989, December). *SRI/CONTAM review of the Nielsen people meter: The process and the results*. Paper presented at the eighth annual Advertising Research Foundation Electronic Media Workshop, New York.

Grant, A. E. (1989). *Exploring patterns of television viewing: A media system dependency perspective*. Unpublished doctoral dissertation, University of Southern California, Los Angeles.

Greenberg, E., & Barnett, H. J. (1971). TV program diversity—New evidence and old theories. *American Economic Review, 61,* 89–93.

Greenberg, B., Dervin, B., & Dominick, J. (1968). Do people watch "television" or "programs"?: A measurement problem. *Journal of Broadcasting, 12,* 367–376.

Gunter, B. (2000). *Media research methods: Measuring audiences, reactions and impact*. London: Sage.

Hall, R. W. (1988). *Media math: Basic techniques of media evaluation*. Lincoln, IL: NTC Business Books.

Hayes, D., & Bing, J. (2004). *Open wide: How Hollywood box office became a national obsession*. New York: Miramax Books Hyperion.

Headen, R., Klompmaker, J., & Rust, R. (1979). The duplication of viewing law and television media schedule evaluation. *Journal of Marketing Research, 16,* 333–340.

Headen, R. S., Klompmaker, J. E., & Teel, J. E. (1977). Predicting audience exposure to spot TV advertising schedules. *Journal of Marketing Research, 14,* 1–9.

Headen, R. S., Klompmaker, J. E., & Teel, J. E. (1979). Predicting network TV viewing patterns. *Journal of Advertising Research, 19,* 49–54.

Heeter, C., & Greenberg, B. (1985). Cable and program choice. In D. Zillmann & J. Bryant (Eds.), *Selective exposure to communication* (pp. 203–224). Hillsdale, NJ: Lawrence Erlbaum Associates.

Heeter, C., & Greenberg, B. S. (1985). Profiling the zappers. *Journal of Advertising Research, 25*(2), 15–19.

Heeter, C., & Greenberg, B. S. (1988). *Cable-viewing*. Norwood, NJ: Ablex.

Henriksen, F. (1985). A new model of the duplication of television viewing: A behaviorist approach. *Journal of Broadcasting & Electronic Media, 29,* 135–145.

Herzog, H. (1944). What do we really know about daytime serial listeners? In P. J. Lazarsfeld & F. N. Stanton (Eds.), *Radio research 1942–1943* (pp. 23–36). New York: Duell, Sloan & Pearce.

Hiber, J. (1987). *Winning radio research: Turning research into ratings and revenues*. Washington, DC: National Association of Broadcasters.

Hill, D., & Dyer, J. (1981). Extent of diversion to newscasts from distant stations by cable viewers. *Journalism Quarterly, 58,* 552–555.

Hirsch, P. (1980). An organizational perspective on television (aided and abetted by models from economics, marketing, and the humanities). In S. B. Withey & R. P Abeles (Eds.), *Television and social behavior* (pp. 83–102). Hillsdale, NJ: Lawrence Erlbaum Associates.

Horen, J. H. (1980). Scheduling of network television programs. *Management Science, 26,* 354–370.

Hotelling, H. (1929). Stability in competition. *Economic Journal, 34,* 41–57.

Hwang, H. (1998). *Audience and the TV networks rating games*. Unpublished manuscript.

Initiative Futures Worldwide. (2004, January). Spheres of influence 2004: Global advertising trends report.

Israel, H., & Robinson, J. (1972). Demographic characteristics of viewers of television violence and news programs. In E. A. Rubinstein, G. A. Comstock, & J. P.

Murray (Eds.), *Television and social behavior: Vol. 4. Television in day-to-day life: Patterns of use* (pp. 87–128). Washington, DC: U.S. Government Printing Office.

Jaffe, M. (1985, January 25). Towards better standards for post-analysis of spot television GRP delivery. *Television/Radio Age*, pp. 23–25.

Jeffres, L. W. (1997). *Mass media effects* (2nd ed.). Prospect Heights, IL: Waveland.

Jhally, S., & Livant, B. (1986). Watching as working: The valorization of audience consciousness. *Journal of Communication, 36*(3), 124–143.

Kaplan, S. J. (1978). The impact of cable television services on the use of competing media. *Journal of Broadcasting, 22,* 155–165.

Katz, E., Blumler, J. G., & Gurevitch, M. (1974). Utilization of mass communication by the individual. In J. G. Blumler & E. Katz (Eds.) *The uses of mass communications: Current perspectives on gratifications research* (pp. 19–32). Beverly Hills, CA: Sage.

Katz, E., Gurvitch, M., & Haas, H. (1973). On the use of mass media for important things. *American Sociological Review, 38*(2), 164–181.

Katz, E., Petters, J. D., Liebes, T., & Orloff, A. (2003). *Cononic texts in media research: Are there any? Should there be? How about these?* Cambridge: Polity Press.

Katz, H. E. (2003). *The media handbook: A complete guide to advertising media selection, planning, research and buying* (2nd ed.). Mahwah, NJ: Lawrence Erlbaum Associates.

Killion, K. C. (1987). Using peoplemeter information. *Journal of Media Planning, 2*(2), 47–52.

Kirsch, A. D., & Banks, S. (1962). Program types defined by factor analysis. *Journal of Advertising Research, 2,* 29–31.

Klapper, J. (1960). *The effects of mass communication.* Glencoe, IL: The Free Press.

Klein, P. (1971, January). The men who run TV aren't stupid.... *New York,* pp. 20–29.

Krueger, R. A., & Casey, M. A. (2000). *Focus groups: A practical guide for applied research* (3rd ed.). Thousand Oaks, CA: Sage.

Krugman, D. M. (1985). Evaluating the audiences of the new media. *Journal of Advertising, 14*(4), 21–27.

Krugman, D. M., & Rust, R. T. (1993). The impact of cable and VCR penetration on network viewing: Assessing the decade. *Journal of Advertising Research, 33*(1), 67–73.

Krugman, D. M., Cameron, G. T., & White, C. M. (1995). Visual attention to programming and commercials: The use of in-home observations. *Journal of Advertising, 24*(1), 1–12.

Krugman, H. E. (1972). Why three exposures may be enough. *Journal of Advertising Research, 12,* 11–14.

Kubey, R., & Csikszentmihalyi, M. (1990). *Television and the quality of life: How viewing shapes everyday experience.* Hillsdale, NJ: Lawrence Erlbaum Associates.

LaRose, R., & Atkin, D. (1988). Satisfaction, demographic, and media environment predictors of cable subscription. *Journal of Broadcasting & Electronic Media, 32,* 403–413.

Larson, E. (1992). *The naked consumer: How our private lives become public commodities.* New York: Henry Holt and Company.

Lavine, J. M., & Wackman, D. B. (1988). *Managing media organizations: Effective leadership of the media.* New York: Longman.

Lazarsfeld, P. F., & Stanton, F. N. (Eds.). (1941). *Radio research.* New York: Duell, Sloan & Pearce.

Leckenby, J. D., & Rice, M. D. (1985). A beta binomial network TV exposure model using limited data. *Journal of Advertising, 3,* 25–31.

LeDuc, D. R. (1987). *Beyond broadcasting: Patterns in policy and law*. New York: Longman.

Lehmann, D. R. (1971). Television show preference: Application of a choice model. *Journal of Marketing Research, 8*, 47–55.

Levin, H. G. (1980). *Fact and fancy in television regulation: An economic study of policy alternatives*. New York: Russell Sage.

Levy, M. R. (Ed.). (1989). *The VCR age: Home video and mass communication*. Newbury Park, CA: Sage.

Levy, M. R., & Fink, E. L. (1984). Home video recorders and the transience of television broadcasts. *Journal of Communication, 34*(2), 56–51.

Levy, M. R., & Windahl, S. (1984). Audience activity and gratifications: A conceptual clarification and exploration. *Communication Research, 11*, 51–78.

Lichty, L., & Topping, M. (Eds.). (1975). *American broadcasting: A sourcebook on the history of radio and television*. New York: Hastings House.

Lin, C. A. (1994). Audience fragmentation in a competitive video marketplace. *Journal of Advertising Research, 34*, 30–38.

Lin, C. A. (1995). Network prime-time programming strategies in the 1980's. *Journal of Broadcasting & Electronic Media, 39*, 482–495.

Lin, C. A., Atkin, D. J., & Abelman, R. (2002). The influence of network branding on audience affinity for network television. *Journal of Advertising Research, 42*, 19–32.

Lindlof, T. R. (Ed.). (1987). *Natural audiences: Qualitative research on media uses and effects*. Norwood, NJ: Ablex.

Lindlof, T. R., & Taylor, B. C. (2002). *Qualitative communication research methods* (2nd ed). Thousand Oaks, CA: Sage.

Litman, B. R., & Kohl, L. S. (1992). Network rerun viewing in the age on new programming services. *Journalism Quarterly, 69*, 383–391.

Little, J. D. C., & Lodish, L. M. (1969). A media planning calculus. *Operations Research, 1*, 1–35.

LoSciuto, L. A. (1972). A national inventory of television viewing behavior. In E. A. Rubinstein, G. A. Comstock, & J. P. Murray (Eds.), *Television and social behavior: Vol. 4. Television in day-to-day life: Patterns of use* (pp. 33–86). Washington, DC: U.S. Government Printing Office.

Lowery, S., & DeFleur, M. L. (1994). *Milestones in mass communication research: Media effects* (3rd ed.). New York: Addison-Wesley.

Lull, J. (1980). The social uses of television. *Human Communication Research, 6*, 197–209.

Lull, J. (1982). How families select televisions programs: A mass observational study. *Journal of Broadcasting, 26*, 801–812.

Lull, J. (Ed.). (1988). *World families watch television*. Newbury Park, CA: Sage.

Lumley, F. H. (1934). *Measurement in radio*. Columbus, OH: The Ohio State University.

MacFarland, D. T. (1990). *Contemporary radio programming strategies*. Hillsdale, NJ: Lawrence Erlbaum Associates.

MacFarland, D. T. (1997). *Future radio programming strategies: Cultivating listenership in the digital age* (2nd ed.). Mahwah, NJ: Lawrence Erlbaum Associates.

McCombs, M. E., & Shaw, D. L. (1972). The agenda-setting function of the mass media. *Public Opinion Quarterly, 36*, 176–187.

McDonald, D. G., & Reese, S. D. (1987). Television news and audience selectivity. *Journalism Quarterly, 64*, 763–768.

McDonald, D. G., & Schechter, R. (1988). Audience role in the evolution of fictional television content. *Journal of Broadcasting & Electronic Media, 32*, 61–51.

McDowell, W. S., & Dick, S. J. (2003). Has lead-in lost its punch? An analysis of prime time inheritance effects: Comparing 1992 and 2002. *International Journal of Media Management, 5*, 285–293.

McKnight, L. W., & Bailey, J. P. (Eds.). (1997). *Internet economics*. Boston: MIT Press.

McLeod, J. M., & McDonald, D. G. (1985). Beyond simple exposure: Media orientations and their impact on political processes. *Communication Research, 12*, 3–33.

McPhee, W. N. (1963). *Formal theories of mass behavior*. New York: The Free Press.

McQuail, D. (1994). *Mass communication theory: An introduction* (3rd ed.). Thousand Oaks, CA: Sage.

McQuail, D. (1997). *Audience analysis*. Thousand Oaks, CA: Sage.

McQuail, D., & Gurevitch, M. (1974). Explaining audience behavior: Three approaches considered. In J. G. Blumler & E. Katz (Eds.), *The uses of mass communications: Current perspectives on gratifications research* (pp. 287–302). Beverly Hills, CA: Sage.

Media Dynamics, Inc. (2004). *TV Dimensions 2004*. New York: Author.

Meehan, E. R. (1984). Ratings and the institutional approach: A third answer to the commodity question. *Critical Studies in Mass Communication, 1*, 216–225.

Metheringham, R. A. (1964). Measuring the net cumulative coverage of a print campaign. *Journal of Advertising Research, 4*, 23–28.

Miller, P. V. (1987, May). *Measuring TV viewing in studies of television effects*. Paper presented at the meeting of the International Communication Association, Montreal.

Miller, P. V. (1994). Made-to-order and standardized audiences: Forms of reality in audience measurement. In J. Ettema & C. Whitney (Eds.), *Audiencemaking: How the media create the audience*. Thousand Oaks, CA: Sage.

Moores, S. (1993). *Interpreting audiences: The ethnography of media consumption*. London: Sage.

Morley, D. (1986). *Family television: Cultural power and domestic leisure*. London: Comedia.

Naples, M. J. (1979). *The effective frequency: The relationship between frequency and advertising effectiveness*. New York: Association of National Advertisers.

Napoli, P. M. (2001). *Foundations of communications policy: Principles and process in the regulation of electronic media*. Cresskill, NJ: Hampton Press.

Napoli, P. M. (2003). *Audience economics: Media institutions and the audience marketplace*. New York: Columbia University Press.

Neuendorf, K. A., Atkin, D. J., & Jeffres, L. W. (2001). Reconceptualizing channel repertoire in the urban cable environment. *Journal of Broadcasting & Electronic Media, 45*(3), 464–482.

Neuman, W. R. (1991). *The future of the mass audience*. Cambridge: Cambridge University Press.

Newcomb, H. M., & Alley, R. S. (1983). *The producer's medium*. New York: Oxford University Press.

Newcomb, H. M., & Hirsch, P. M. (1984). Television as a cultural forum: Implications for research. In W. Rowland & B. Watkins (Eds.), *Interpreting television* (pp. 58–73). Beverly Hills, CA: Sage.

Nielsen, A. C. (1988). Television ratings and the public interest. In J. Powell & W. Gair (Eds.), *Public interest and the business of broadcasting: The broadcast industry looks at itself* (pp. 61–63). New York: Quorum Books.

Nielsen Media Research. (1985–2004). *Television audience report*. New York: Author.

Nielsen Station Index. (annually). *Your guide to reports & services*. New York: Nielsen Media Research.

Niven, H. (1960). Who in the family selects the TV program? *Journalism Quarterly, 37,* 110–111.

Noam, E. (Ed.). (1985). *Video media competition: Regulation, economics, and technology.* New York: Columbia University Press.

Noll, R. G., Peck, M. G., & McGowan, J. J. (1973). *Economic aspects of television regulation.* Washington, DC: Brookings Institution Press.

Noll, R. G., & Price, M. E. (Eds.). (1998). *A communications cornucopia: Markle Foundation essays on information policy.* Washington, DC: Brookings Institution Press.

Ogburn, W. F. (1933). The influence of invention and discovery. In W. F. Ogburn (Ed.), *Recent social trends* (pp. 153–156). New York: McGraw-Hill.

Owen, B. M. (1975). *Economics and freedom of expression: Media structure and the first amendment.* Cambridge, MA: Ballinger.

Owen, B. M., Beebe, J., & Manning, W. (1974). *Television economics.* Lexington, MA: D.C. Heath.

Owen, B. M., & Wildman, S. S. (1992). *Video economics.* Cambridge, MA: Harvard University Press.

Palmgreen, P., Wenner, L. A., & Rayburn, J. D. (1981). Gratification discrepancies and news program choice. *Communication Research, 8,* 451–478.

Park, R. E. (1970). *Potential impact of cable growth on television broadcasting* (R-587–FF). Santa Monica, CA: Rand Corporation.

Park, R. E. (1979). *Audience diversion due to cable television: Statistical analysis of new data.* R-2403-FCC. Santa Monica, CA: Rand Corporation.

Parkman, A. M. (1982). The effect of television station ownership on local news ratings. *Review of Economics and Statistics, 64,* 289–295.

Perse, E. M. (1986). Soap opera viewing patterns of college students and cultivation. *Journal of Broadcasting and Electronic Media, 30,* 175–193.

Peterson, R. (1972). Psychographics and media exposure. *Journal of Advertising Research, 12,* 17–20.

Phalen, P. F. (1996). *Information and markets and the market for information: An analysis of the market for television audiences.* Unpublished doctoral dissertation, Northwestern University, Evanston, IL.

Phalen, P. F. (1998). The market for information systems and personalized exchange: Business practices in the market for television audiences. *Journal of Media Economics, 11*(4), 17–34.

Phalen, P. F. (1999). *Buying Internet audiences: The more things change.* Paper presented at the Broadcast Education Association annual conference, Las Vegas, NV, April 16–19, 1999.

Phalen, P. F. (2003). Trading time and money for information in the television advertising market: Strategies and consequences. In A. Albarran & A. Arrese (Eds.), *Time and markets* (pp. 145–159). Mahwah, NJ: Lawrence Erlbaum Associates.

Phalen, P. F. (in press-a). Audience research and analysis. In A. Albarran, T. Wirth, & S. Chan-Olmsted (Eds.), *Handbook of media management and economics* (pp. 621–634). Lawrence Erlbaum Associates.

Phalen, P. F. (in press-b). Market research in the U.S. In D. Gomery & L. Hockley (Eds.), *The television industry book.* London: British Film Institute.

Philport, J. (1980). The psychology of viewer program evaluation. In *Proceedings of the 1980 technical conference on qualitative ratings.* Washington, DC: Corporation for Public Broadcasting.

Poltrack, D. (1983). *Television marketing: Network, local, and cable.* New York: McGraw-Hill.

Poltrack, D. (1988). The "big 3" networks. *Gannett Center Journal, 2*(3), 53–62.

Potter, W. J. (1996). *An analysis of thinking and research about qualitative methods*. Mahwah, NJ: Lawrence Erlbaum Associates.

Rao, V. R. (1975). Taxonomy of television programs based on viewing behavior. *Journal of Marketing Research, 12*, 335–358.

Reagan, J. (1984). Effects of cable television on news use. *Journalism Quarterly, 61*, 317–324.

Robinson, J. P. (1977). *How Americans used their time in 1965*. New York: Praeger.

Robinson, J. P., & Levy, M. R. (1986). *The main source: Learning from television news*. Beverly Hills, CA: Sage.

Rogers, E. M. (1994). *A history of communication study: A biographical approach*. New York: The Free Press.

Rosengren, K. E., Wenner, L. A., & Palmgreen, P. (Eds.). (1985). *Media gratifications research: Current perspectives*. Beverly Hills, CA: Sage.

Rosenstein, A. W., & Grant, A. E. (1997). Reconceptualizing the role of habit: A new model of television audience activity. *Journal of Broadcasting & Electronic Media, 41*(3), 324–344.

Rothenberg, J. (1962). Consumer sovereignty and the economics of TV programming. *Studies in Public Communication, 4*, 23–36.

Rowland, W. (1983). *The politics of TV violence: Policy uses of communication research*. Beverly Hills, CA: Sage.

Rubens, W. S. (1978). A guide to TV ratings. *Journal of Advertising Research, 18*, 11–18.

Rubens, W. S. (1984). High-tech audience measurement for new-tech audiences. *Critical Studies in Mass Communication, 1*, 195–205.

Rubin, A. M. (1984). Ritualized and instrumental television viewing. *Journal of Communication, 34*(3), 67–77.

Rubin, A. M. (1993). Audience activity and media use. *Communication Monographs, 60*, 98–115.

Rubin, A. M., & Perse, E. M. (1987). Audience activity and soap opera involvement. *Human Communication Research, 14*, 246–268.

Rubin, A. M., & Perse, E. M. (1987). Audience activity and television news gratifications. *Communication Research, 14*, 58–84.

Rust, R. T. (1986). *Advertising media models: A practical guide*. Lexington, MA: Lexington Books.

Rust, R. T., & Alpert, M. I. (1984). An audience flow model of television viewing choice. *Marketing Science, 3*(2), 113–124.

Rust, R. T., & Donthu, N. (1988). A programming and positioning strategy for cable television networks. *Journal of Advertising, 17*, 6–13.

Rust, R. T., Kamakura, W. A., & Alpert, M. I. (1992). Viewer preference segmentation and viewing choice models of network television. *Journal of Advertising, 21*(1), 1–18.

Rust, R. T., & Klompmaker, J. E. (1981). Improving the estimation procedure for the beta binomial TV exposure model. *Journal of Marketing Research, 18*, 442–448.

Rust, R. T., Klompmaker, J. E., & Headen, R. S. (1981). A comparative study of television duplication models. *Journal of Advertising, 21*, 42–46.

Sabavala, D. J., & Morrison, D. G. (1977). A model of TV show loyalty. *Journal of Advertising Research, 17*, 35–43.

Sabavala, D. J., & Morrison, D. G. (1981). A nonstationary model of binary choice applied to media exposure. *Management Science, 27*, 637–657.

Salomon, G., & Cohen, A. (1978). On the meaning and validity of television viewing. *Human Communication Research, 4*, 265–270.

Salvaggio, J. L., & Bryant, J. (Eds.). (1989). *Media use in the information age: Emerging patterns of adoption and consumer use.* Hillsdale, NJ: Lawrence Erlbaum Associates.

Schramm, W., Lyle, J., & Parker, E. B. (1961). *Television in the lives of our children.* Stanford, CA: Stanford University Press.

Schudson, M. (1984). *Advertising, the uneasy persuasion: Its dubious impact on American society.* New York: Basic Books.

Sears, D. O., & Freedman, J. L. (1972). Selective exposure to information: A critical review. In W. Schramm & D. Roberts (Eds.), *The process and effects of mass communication* (pp. 209–234). Urbana, IL: University of Illinois Press.

Schroder, K. (1987). Convergence of antagonistic traditions? The case of audience research. *European Journal of Communication, 2,* 7–31.

Shachar, R., & Emerson, J. W. (2000). Cast demographics, unobserved segments, and heterogeneous switching costs in a television viewing choice model. *Journal of Marketing Research, 37,* 173–186.

Sherman, B. L. (1995). *Telecommunications management: Broadcasting/cable and the new technologies* (2nd ed.). New York: McGraw-Hill.

Sims, J. (1988). AGB: The ratings innovator. *Gannett Center Journal, 2*(3), 85–89.

Singer, J. L., Singer, D. G., & Rapaczynski, W. S. (1984). Family patterns and television viewing as predictors of children's belief's and aggression. *Journal of Communication, 34*(3), 73–89.

Sissors, J. Z., & Baron, R. B. (2002). *Advertising media planning* (6th ed.). Chicago: McGraw-Hill.

Sizing up the Market. (2004, January 12). *Broadcast and Cable, 21.*

Smythe, D. (1981). *Dependency road: Communications, capitalism, consciousness, and Canada.* Norwood, NJ: Ablex.

Soong, R. (1988). The statistical reliability of people meter ratings. *Journal of Advertising Research, 28,* 50–56.

Sparkes, V. (1983). Public perception of and reaction to multi-channel cable television service. *Journal of Broadcasting, 27,* 163–175.

Spaulding, J. W. (1963). 1928: Radio becomes a mass advertising medium. *Journal of Broadcasting, 7,* 31–44.

Stanford, S. W. (1984). Predicting favorite TV program gratifications from general orientations. *Communication Research, 11,* 419–436.

Stanton, F. N. (1935). *Critique of present methods and a new plan for studying listening behavior.* Unpublished doctoral dissertation, The Ohio State University, Columbus, OH.

Statistical Research, Inc. (1975). *How good is the television diary technique?* (Report prepared for the National Association of Broadcasters). Washington, DC: Author.

Steiner, G. A. (1963). *The people look at television.* New York: Alfred A. Knopf.

Steiner, G. A. (1966). The people look at commercials: A study of audience behavior. *Journal of Business, 39,* 272–304.

Steiner, P. O. (1952). Program patterns and preferences, and the workability of competition in radio broadcasting. *Quarterly Journal of Economics, 66,* 194–223.

Swanson, C. I. (1967). The frequency structure of television and magazines. *Journal of Advertising Research, 7,* 3–7.

Sterling, C. H., & Kittross, J. M. (1990). *Stay tuned: A concise history of American broadcasting* (2nd ed.). Belmont, CA: Wadsworth.

Sterling, C. H., & Kittross, J. M. (2001). *Stay tuned: A History of American broadcasting* (3rd ed.). Mahwah, NJ: LEA.

Sudman, S., & Bradburn, N. (1982). *Asking questions: A practical guide to questionnaire design.* San Francisco: Jossey-Bass.

Sunstein, C. (2001). *Republic.com.* Princeton, NJ: Princeton University Press.

Surmanek, J. (2003). *Advertising media A to Z.* New York: McGraw Hill.

Takada, H., & Henry, W. (1993, Fall). Analysis of network TV commercial time pricing for top-rated prime time programs. *Journal of Current Issues and Research in Advertising, 15*(2) 59–70.

Television Audience Assessment. (1983a). *The audience rates television.* Boston, MA: Author.

Television Audience Assessment. (1983b). *The multichannel environment.* Boston, MA: Author.

Tiedge, J. T., & Ksobiech, K. J. (1986). The "lead-in" strategy for prime-time: Does it increase the audience? *Journal of Communication, 36*(3), 64–76.

Tiedge, J. T., & Ksobiech, K. J. (1987). Counterprogramming primetime network television. *Journal of Broadcasting & Electronic Media, 31*, 41–55.

Turow, J. (1997). *Breaking up America: Advertisers and the new media world.* Chicago: University of Chicago Press.

Turow, J. (1997). *Media systems in society: Understanding industries, strategies and power* (2nd ed.). New York: Longman.

Urban, C. D. (1984). Factors influencing media consumption: A survey of the literature. In B. M. Compaine (Ed.), *Understanding new media: Trends and issues in electronic distribution of information* (pp. 213–282). Cambridge, MA: Ballinger.

Veronis Suhler Stevenson. (2004). *Communications industry forecast & report* (18th ed.). New York: Author.

Vogel, H. L. (1986). *Entertainment industry economics: A guide for financial analysis.* Cambridge: Cambridge University Press.

Vogel, H. L. (2004). *Entertainment industry economics: A guide for financial analysis* (6th ed.). Cambridge: Cambridge University Press.

Wakshlag, J., Agostino, D., Terry, H., Driscoll, P., & Ramsey, B. (1983). Television news viewing and network affiliation change. *Journal of Broadcasting, 27*, 53–68.

Wakshlag, J., Day, K., & Zillmann, D. (1981). Selective exposure to educational television programs as a function of differently paced humorous inserts. *Journal of Educational Psychology, 73*, 27–32.

Wakshlag, J., & Greenberg, B. (1979). Programming strategies and the popularity of television programs for children. *Human Communication Research, 6*, 58–68.

Wakshlag, J., Reitz, R., & Zillmann, D. (1982). Selective exposure to and acquisition of information from educational television programs as a function of appeal and tempo of background music. *Journal of Educational Psychology, 74*, 666–677.

Wakshlag, J., Vial, V. K., & Tamborini, R. (1983). Selecting crime drama and apprehension about crime. *Human Communication Research, 10*, 227–242.

Walker, J. R. (1988). Inheritance effects in the new media environment. *Journal of Broadcasting & Electronic Media, 32*, 391–401.

Walker, J., & Ferguson, D. (1998). *The broadcast television industry.* Boston: Allyn and Bacon.

Wand, B. (1968). Television viewing and family choice differences. *Public Opinion Quarterly, 32*, 84–94.

Warner, C. (2003). *Selling media: Broadcast, cable, print and interactive* (3rd ed.). Ames, IA: Iowa State Press.

Waterman, D. (1986). The failure of cultural programming on cable TV: An economic interpretation. *Journal of Communication, 36*(3), 92–107.

Waterman, D. (1992). "Narrowcasting" and "broadcasting" on nonbroadcast media: A program choice model. *Communication Research, 19*(1), 3–28.

Weber, R. (2003). Methods to forecast television viewing patterns for target audiences. In A. Schorr, B. Campbell, & M. Schenk (Eds.), *Communication research in Europe and abroad: Challenges for the first decade* (pp. 271–285). Berlin: DeGruyter.

Webster, J. G. (1982). *The impact of cable and pay cable on local station audiences.* Washington, DC: National Association of Broadcasters.

Webster, J. G. (1983a). *Audience research.* Washington, DC: National Association of Broadcasters.

Webster, J. G. (1983b). The impact of cable and pay cable television on local station audiences. *Journal of Broadcasting, 27,* 119–126.

Webster, J. G. (1984a). Cable television's impact on audience for local news. *Journalism Quarterly, 61,* 419–422.

Webster, J. G. (1984b, April). Peoplemeters. In *Research & Planning: Information for management.* Washington, DC: National Association of Broadcasters.

Webster, J. G. (1985). Program audience duplication: A study of television inheritance effects. *Journal of Broadcasting & Electronic Media, 29,* 121–133.

Webster, J. G. (1986). Audience behavior in the new media environment. *Journal of Communication, 36*(3), 77–91.

Webster, J. G. (1989a). Assessing exposure to the new media. In J. Salvaggio & J. Bryant (Eds.), *Media use in the information age: Emerging patterns of adoption and consumer use* (pp. 3–19). Hillsdale, NJ: Lawrence Erlbaum Associates.

Webster, J. G. (1989b). Television audience behavior: Patterns of exposure in the new media environment. In J. Salvaggio & J. Bryant (Eds.), *Media use in the information age: Emerging patterns of adoption and consumer use* (pp. 197–216). Hillsdale, NJ: Lawrence Erlbaum Associates.

Webster, J. G. (1990). The role of audience ratings in communications policy. *Communications and the Law, 12*(2), 59–72.

Webster, J. G. (1998). The audience. *Journal of Broadcasting & Electronic Media, 42*(2), 190–207.

Webster, J. G. (2005). Beneath the veneer of fragmentation: Television audience polarization in a multi-channel world. *Journal of Communication, 55*(2), 366–382.

Webster, J. G., & Coscarelli, W. (1979). The relative appeal to children of adult versus children's television programming. *Journal of Broadcasting, 23,* 437–451.

Webster, J. G., & Lin, S. F. (2002). The Internet audience: Web use as mass behavior. *Journal of Broadcasting & Electronic Media, 46*(1), 1–12.

Webster, J. G., & Newton, G. D. (1988). Structural determinants of the television news audience. *Journal of Broadcasting & Electronic Media, 32,* 381–389.

Webster, J. G., & Phalen, P. F. (1997). *The mass audience: Rediscovering the dominant model.* Mahwah, NJ: Lawrence Erlbaum Associates.

Webster, J. G., & Wakshlag, J. (1982). The impact of group viewing on patterns of television program choice. *Journal of Broadcasting, 26,* 445–455.

Webster, J. G., & Wakshlag, J. (1983). A theory of television program choice. *Communication Research, 10,* 430–446.

Webster, J. G., & Wakshlag, J. (1985). Measuring exposure to television. In D. Zillmann & J. Bryant (Eds.), *Selective exposure to communication* (pp. 35–62). Hillsdale, NJ: Lawrence Erlbaum Associates.

Webster, J. G., & Wang, T. (1992). Structural determinants of exposure to television: The case of repeat viewing. *Journal of Broadcasting & Electronic Media, 36*(4), 125–136.

Weibull, L. (1985). Structural factors in gratifications research. In K. E. Rosengren, L. A. Wenner, & P. Palmgreen (Eds.), *Media gratifications research: Current perspectives* (pp. 123–148). Beverly Hills, CA: Sage.

Wells, W. D. (1969). The rise and fall of television program types. *Journal of Advertising Research, 9*, 21–27.

Wells, W. D. (1975). Psychographics: A critical review. *Journal of Marketing Research, 12*, 196–213.

White, K. J. (1977). Television market shares, station characteristics and viewer choice. *Communication Research, 4*, 415–434.

White, B. C., & Satterthwaite, N. D. (1989). *But first these messages … The selling of broadcast advertising.* Boston: Allyn and Bacon.

Why's and wherefores of syndex II. (1988, May 23). *Broadcasting,* 58–59.

Wildman, S. S., & Owen, B. M. (1985). Program competition, diversity, and multichannel bundling in the new video industry. In E. Noam (Ed.), *Video media competition: Regulation, economics, and technology* (pp. 244–273). New York: Columbia University Press.

Wildman, S. S., & Siwek, S. E. (1988). *International trade in films and television programs.* Cambridge: Ballinger.

Wimmer, R., & Dominick, J. (2002). *Mass media research: An introduction* (7th ed.) Belmont, CA: Wadsworth.

Wirth, M. O., & Bloch, H. (1985). The broadcasters: The future role of local stations and the three networks. In E. Noam (Ed.), *Video media competition: Regulation, economics, and technology* (pp. 121–137). New York: Columbia University Press.

Wirth, M. O., & Wollert, J. A. (1984). The effects of market structure on local television news pricing. *Journal of Broadcasting, 28*, 215–224.

Wober, J. M. (1988). *The use and abuse of television: A social psychological analysis of the changing screen.* Hillsdale, NJ: Lawrence Erlbaum Associates.

Wober, J. M., & Gunter, B. (1986). Television audience research at Britain's Independent Broadcasting Authority, 1974–1984. *Journal of Broadcasting and Electronic Media, 30*, 15–31.

Wulfemeyer, K. T. (1983). The interests and preferences of audiences for local television news. *Journalism Quarterly, 60*, 323–328.

Zeigler, S. K., & Howard, H. (1991). *Broadcast advertising: A comprehensive working textbook* (3rd ed.). Ames, IA: Iowa State University Press.

Zenaty, J. (1988). The advertising agency. *Gannett Center Journal, 2*(3), 79–84.

Zillmann, D. (2000). Mood management in the context of selective exposure theory. *Communication Yearbook, 23*, pp. 103–122.

Zillmann, D., & Bryant, J. (Eds.). (1985). *Selective exposure to communication.* Hillsdale, NJ: Lawrence Erlbaum Associates.

Zillmann, D., Hezel, R. T., & Medoff, N. J. (1980). The effect of affective states on selective exposure to televised entertainment fare. *Journal of Applied Social Psychology, 10*, 323–339.

Zillmann, D., & Vorderer, P. (2000). *Media entertainment: The psychology of its appeal.* Mahwah, NJ: Lawrence Erlbaum Associates.

Author Index

303

Subject Index

Note: Page numbers ending in *f* refer to figures. Page numbers ending in *t* refer to tables.